FARM BROADCASTING
The First Sixty Years

JOHN C. BAKER

The Iowa State University Press, Ames

1940

1980

JOHN C. BAKER has worked with or known most of the men and women who have worked in farm broadcasting since the twenties.

He was born in Indiana in the year that Admiral Peary reached the North Pole (1909), grew up in apple orchard, and received an undergraduate degree in agriculture from Purdue University in 1930.

He made his first broadcast to farmers over the Purdue radio station, WBAA, when he was assistant extension editor, 1930–1931, and continued for four years as radio extension editor in Massachusetts. Then followed two periods each on WLS, Chicago, and in the radio service of the U.S. Department of Agriculture, where he took part in the "National Farm and Home Hour" on NBC and "The American Farmer" on ABC. In the fifties and sixties he was an information officer in the U.S. Department of Agriculture and the Bureau of the Census.

He has been a member of the farm broadcasters' organization, under its several names, since its first national convention in 1945.

He and his wife, Mary, live in Arlington, Virginia, "close enough but not too close" to their daughter, son, and five grandchildren.

First edition, 1981

Library of Congress Cataloging in Publication Data

Baker, John Chester, 1909–
    Farm broadcasting.

    Bibliography: p.
    Includes index.
    1. Radio in agriculture—United States—History. 2. Television in agriculture—United States—History. I. Title.
S494.5.C6B34   070.4'4963'0973   80–24623
ISBN 0–8138–1485–5

To my wife Mary

CONTENTS

PREFACE

THERE is an interesting parallel between the increase of farm productivity and the increase in farm broadcasting during the six decades covered in this chronicle. In 1923, when the first full-time farm broadcaster started to work, the average U.S. farmer fed about 8 people; in 1945 there were about 85 farm broadcasters and the average farmer fed 15 people. In the seventies there are about 500 farm broadcasters and the average farmer feeds more than 55 people.

It is tempting to try to show a cause and effect relationship, but I'll resist it.

Farmers have increased their production dramatically, especially since the end of World War II, because they have adopted the new technology that has become available in the form of increasingly bigger and better machines, better breeding of plants and animals, new fertilizers and chemicals, and better conservation measures.

Farm broadcasters did not develop the new machine or fertilizer; they did not set market prices or forecast the weather, but in most instances they brought the word to farmers first and brought it most often. This is not to belittle the many other sources of information which farmers use: farm magazines with their articles and advertisements, county agents, dealers, salesmen, neighbors, and others. Farmers consult them frequently. But most farmers hear or see a farm broadcaster almost every day, usually several times each day, and receive the latest market reports, weather forecasts, and news—information that contributes to more efficient production, wiser marketing, and better living.

Every farm broadcaster knows that to attract listeners and hold them he or she must know the subject, be sincere, and be friendly. Those are the characteristics of the people you will meet in this book, and of the other farm broadcasters whose stories I was unable to obtain. I admire them and I like them. I hope you will too.

Chapter One

Before the Beginning

BEFORE there could be a farm broadcast, a good many things had to happen off the farm, over a period of twenty-six centuries.

A Greek named Thales, around 600 B.C., wrote that amber, if you rubbed it, would attract feathers. The Greek word for amber is *elektron*.

In the early eighteenth century, the mayor of Magdeburg, Germany, invented a machine for generating electricity: a rod with a ball of sulfur at one end and a crank at the other. Turn the crank, hold your hand against the ball of sulfur, and it would shoot sparks. A few years later, Professor van Musschenbreck at the University of Leyden found he could capture electricity in a glass jar containing water. It came to be called the Leyden jar.

In the 1740s Benjamin Franklin conducted many kinds of experiments with electricity and other forms of "natural philosophy." Franklin was the first to use the words *armature, battery, charge, positive,* and *negative.* And he introduced the idea that electric current, lightning, and magnetism are all the same "fluid."

William Sturdevant, an Englishman, developed the first electromagnet in the early 1800s, and an American artist, Samuel F. B. Morse, put it to work in an instrument he called a telegraph that he patented in 1837 and demonstrated to Congress in 1843 with his well-publicized query, "What hath God wrought?"

Morse thought it would be even better if his telegraph instrument could send messages without wires. He proved it could send signals through water, from one side of the Potomac to the other, but he couldn't make it work through the air.

In Civil War days a Washington, D.C., dentist named Mahlon Loomis was conducting experiments with magnets, coils, telegraph instruments, and the like, and somehow he found a way to do what Morse had been unable to do. In 1866 he led a party of friends into the mountains northwest of Washington. They divided into two groups, each equipped with electrical gadgets and a kite. One group went to Catoctin Mountain, near what is now Camp David, hideaway of the presidents; the other party went to the top of Bear's Den Mountain, eighteen miles away. Both groups flew their kites with slender wire in place of string. Dr. Loomis attached a telegraph key to his kite wire; on the other mountain the kite wire was attached to a magnetic compass. Dr. Loomis jiggled his telegraph key and eighteen miles away the compass needle swung like crazy. An electric signal through the air!

3

In 1872 Dr. Loomis was granted a patent on his wireless telegraph and the next year Congress issued a charter to the Loomis Aerial Telegraph Company. That's as far as it went. Nobody was willing to invest in the company. Dr. Loomis died in 1886, age sixty; his aerial telegraph, age twenty, died with him.

At the Centennial Exposition in Philadelphia, in 1876, Thomas Edison displayed his electric light and Alexander Graham Bell demonstrated his telephone, both of which were to change lives around the world.

In Murray, Kentucky, a local farm boy named Nathan Stubblefield became the town's first electrician, installing lights in several homes and businesses. In his spare time he found what makes a telephone work, and in 1887 he installed two telephones for a Murray storekeeper named Charles Hamlin, one in his store and another in his home. It was different enough from Mr. Bell's telephone that in 1888 Nathan Stubblefield was granted a patent for his phone. Once he made his telephone work with wires he set out to make it work without wires. He probably succeeded as early as 1892, according to Stubblefield's biographer, Professor L. J. Hortin of Murray State University. The Federal Communicative System says the first words spoken over a wireless telephone probably were, "Hello, Rainey," when Nathan Stubblefield spoke to his friend Rainey Wells. That may have been in 1892 or it may have been ten years later when Stubblefield staged a public demonstration on New Year's Day, 1902, for his fellow citizens of Murray. They sent him to Washington, D.C., where he put his transmitter on the steamer Bartholdi and set up his receiver on the Virginia shore of the Potomac. He invited members of Congress, other government officials, and the press to see and hear. Part of the demonstration was a senator's son playing his harmonica. This demonstration on March 20, 1902, was a success in every way. Nathan Stubblefield became a celebrity. On May 30 he staged a land-based demonstration in Philadelphia and again scored big. Investors were interested. Stubblefield was offered $40,000 for a part interest in his invention, but he seemed to be afraid that investors, or somebody, would steal it, and he refused all offers. In 1908 he obtained a U.S. patent on his radio telephone and published a brochure that invited investments. But again his fear of investors overcame him and he refused all offers. He seemed to turn sour on the world, and he stayed sour. In time he separated from his family, refused to see his friends, and holed up in a shack on a friend's farm near Murray. In March of 1928 they found his body. The coroner estimated he had been dead two days. The cause, "malnutrition."

By that time others had unraveled the mysteries Nathan Stubblefield had solved but held secret. About 700 broadcasting stations and two networks were on the air, and radio receivers were in about 8 million homes.

Murray State University has an exhibit of Nathan Stubblefield's inventions, and the Murray, Kentucky, radio station WNBS has memorialized the initials of the man who developed the first radio transmitter and receiver.

When he was 21, Guglielmo Marconi, son of an Irish mother and Italian father, developed the equipment to send a telegraph signal without wires in 1895. He couldn't get financial backing in his native Italy, so he went to England. He proved he was a whiz in public relations by reporting ship to shore on the progress and results of a big yacht race in which he knew Queen Victoria was interested. When the Queen was interested, money followed, and the Marconi Company was formed, destined to become worldwide. More and more ships installed wireless telegraph equipment; some rescues at sea were made possible by wireless. Congress passed the Wireless Ship Act in 1910, requiring all U.S. ships carrying passengers to have wireless equipment and operators.

The U.S. Department of Agriculture stuck one toe into the water of wireless telegraphy around 1900 when the Weather Bureau (then part of USDA) hired Richard Fessenden away from Thomas Edison's laboratory and gave him $3,000 to set up two wireless telegraph stations on the coast of North Carolina. The transmitters and receivers worked, but evidently the Weather Bureau decided to let the army and navy provide facilities for reporting the weather. Fessenden went to the University of Pittsburgh and later set up his own wireless telegraph company that was ultimately bought by Marconi. But before those things happened, he made broadcasting history on Christmas Eve, 1906, at Brant Rock, Massachusetts. He turned on his wireless telephone and played his violin. Several ships' wireless operators out on the Atlantic beeped messages telling him they heard his music. This happened four years after Nathan Stubblefield's demonstration.

Thomas Edison reported that there seemed to be electric particles of some kind shooting back and forth in the vacuum between the filaments of his light bulbs. An English physicist, J. A. Fleming, followed up on this information and in 1904 developed a vacuum bulb with two filaments that produced a constant stream of electrons. He called it a "valve."

In New York, Dr. Lee De Forest improved on Fleming's valve by placing a "grid" between the two filaments. He used his "audion" tube to broadcast phonograph records from the top of the Eiffel Tower, a live opera from the Met, and the wrong results of the 1916 presidential contest between the winning candidate, Woodrow Wilson, and Charles Evans Hughs.

The next big contribution, according to the experts, was a "regenerative circuit" developed by Edwin H. Armstrong in 1914. A generation later he also developed the frequency modulation system of broadcasting, commonly called FM.

In its early years the fledgling gadget was usually called "wireless telephone," and putting out a signal was called "radiating." Then two new words came into the electronic language: *radio* and *broadcasting*.

The U.S. Bureau of Standards says *radio* was coined in 1911 by one of its young physicists, J. Howard Dellinger, who realized there was a similarity between X rays and wireless communication.

The new word got official status when Congress passed the "Radio Act of 1912" authorizing the Secretary of Commerce and Labor to issue experimental licenses for radio stations; within a short time, more than a thousand applications were received.

As to the word *broadcasting,* farmers had been broadcasting seed for centuries, but the navy began to apply it to wireless about 1912 to indicate messages intended for all ships or for anyone listening, as opposed to messages intended for only one ship. *Radiate* hung around for a few years but eventually dropped out of usage.

When the United States entered World War I in April 1917, virtually all experimental work with radio telephones came to a halt unless it contributed directly to the war effort. At the University of Wisconsin, Earle M. Terry and his assistants got permission to work with the Great Lakes naval radio station about 100 miles away during the war and made further improvements in their station, 9XM. When the wartime ban was lifted, they were ready with a regular schedule of test broadcasts beginning January 1, 1919. Two years later 9XM started daily weather reports, the first in the nation. Farm market reports came that fall and then talks to farmers on a regular schedule.

At the Westinghouse laboratories in Pittsburgh, further developments came about in 1915 when the assistant chief engineer, Dr. Frank Conrad, bought a $12 watch, made a $5 bet as to its accuracy, and built a radio receiver so he could get the navy time signals broadcast each day at noon. The next step was a transmitter, 8XK, so he could talk to other amateur broadcasters from his home. During World War I he developed an improved radio tube, and Westinghouse made radio equipment for the American and British armies.

After the war, radio became a favorite hobby; and Frank Conrad put his amateur station on a regular schedule of musical programs by putting his phonograph in front of the telephone that he used as a microphone.

One day in the summer of 1920, Conrad's boss, H. P. Davis, saw an ad by a department store featuring radio receivers, and he got an idea. "Let's start making radio receivers. Then, let's build a broadcasting station to give people something to listen to, with programs publicized in advance." Some years later Dr. Davis was called "the father of broadcasting," and he smiled and bowed.

It fell to Frank Conrad to design and build the transmitter. It was to be a giant—fifty watts!! Most of the amateur and experimental stations were only five or ten watts. The target date for completion was the first Tuesday in November, Election Day. Dr. Davis wasn't happy about the experimental call, 8ZZ, issued to the upcoming station; he appealed for a commercial license and it was granted on October 27, 1920 with the call letters KDKA.

On the evening of election day, the *Pittsburgh Post* provided a steady flow of election returns by telephone and they were broadcast immediately over KDKA. In contrast to 1916, there was no last minute surprise, and KDKA correctly announced that Warren G. Harding had won the 1920 election over James Cox.

Of course, as noted, these broadcast results of a presidential election were not the first. And prior to this, in August 1920 the *Detroit News'* experimental station had broadcast results of the primary election in Michigan; it also reported the national results at the same time as KDKA.

But KDKA broke new ground by going on the air every day and publicizing its schedules in advance. Later it would have the first daily program of farm market reports, and still later the first full-time farm director.

Another kind of beginning sprang up during World War I that was to have significance to the development of farm broadcasting. The three leading electrical and electronics companies, General Electric, Westinghouse, and ATT, plus the United Fruit Company, joined hands to form the Radio Corporation of America, to engage in manufacturing, research, and communications. A government representative sat on the board of directors. The newly formed company bought the Marconi Company's U.S. interests, patents, equipment, and transmitting stations, and hired one of its bright young men as RCA's general manager. His name was David Sarnoff. He had been the Marconi operator who first picked up the SOS from the Titanic when the ship hit an iceberg and sank in 1912. Gleason Archer in his book *History of Radio to 1926* quotes a memo that David Sarnoff wrote in 1916 to the Marconi general manager, Edward J. Nally:

> I have in mind a plan of development which would make radio a household utility. The idea is to bring music into the home by wireless. The receiver can be designed in the form of a simple radio music box and arranged for several different wave-lengths, which should be changeable with the throwing of a single switch or the pressing of a single button. Baseball scores can be transmitted in the air. *This proposition would be especially interesting to farmers and others living in outlying districts.* (Italics mine)

It was in 1926 that RCA created the National Broadcasting Company which in 1928 started the "National Farm and Home Hour." David's proposition indeed proved to be especially "interesting to farmers and others living in outlying districts."

Chapter Two

Some Beginnings in Farm Broadcasting

ONCE the physicists and engineers at the land-grant colleges and in the private laboratories had learned how to make a radio telephone reproduce the human voice more naturally, first weather forecasters and then other agricultural people began to use the radio to talk to farmers. Weather was considered an ''agricultural property'' because the Weather Bureau was part of the U.S. Department of Agriculture. Moreover, farmers, more than any other group, could gain or lose by changes in the weather.

The Weather Bureau said in *A Century of Weather Service, 1870–1970,* the first regularly scheduled weather report on voice radio was on 9XM at the University of Wisconsin beginning January 3, 1921. Malcolm Hanson, physicist and the station's most frequent announcer, probably provided the voice. In the early fall of 1921, 9XM began to broadcast market reports, and on July 10, 1922, after the call letters changed to WHA, W.A. Sumner of the agricultural journalism department broadcast the first talk to farmers. This was the beginning of the station's ''Farm Hour.'' The support behind this program was a dynamic editor and evangelist, Andrew W. Hopkins, who saw radio as a means for the university to teach everyone in the state. Not long afterward Dr. Frank Morrison, assistant director of the experiment station, gave a series of talks on ''The Vitamin Family.''

In March 1921 James L. Bush, a grain dealer in Tuscola, Illinois, put his radio station, WDZ, on the air for the sole purpose of reporting grain prices to elevator operators, without having to spend money on telephone calls.

On May 19, 1921, KDKA, Pittsburgh, began carrying ''Market Reports'' by J. K. Boyd, USDA's market reporter in Pittsburgh. About one year later, the staff of the *National Stockman and Farmer* began to broadcast news and advice to farmers. Mason Gilpin made the first broadcast and was a frequent spokesman until 1923 when the magazine created the new job of ''radio editor,''someone who would devote full time to radio.

Two days after KDKA began its market news broadcasts, H. E. Green, an accountant in Greeley, Colorado, put his station KFKA on the air and began making three-a-week train trips between Greeley and Denver so he could report Denver livestock prices to ranchers who were his principal accounting clients. The station has reported prices and other farm information daily ever since.

Westinghouse put its second radio station, WBZ, Springfield,

8

USDA employees assembled to listen to one of the early market news broadcasts, in 1920, over the Bureau of Standards' experimental radio station. The receiver was hitched to a phonograph to amplify the sound. W. A. Wheeler, who arranged for the broadcasts, is seated third from the right.

Massachusetts, on the air in September 1921. The inaugural program had an agricultural flavor, since it originated from the Eastern States Exposition in Springfield. This was a one time shot, however, and there was little if any agriculture on WBZ until 1924 when the Massachusetts Agricultural College extension service put on a thirteen-week "Poultry School of the Air." About twelve hundred people paid a dollar each for the literature that accompanied the course.

Some time in 1921 George F. E. Story, county agricultural agent in Worcester, Massachusetts, began broadcasting over the experimental station assigned to Clark University. That program grew into a daily presentation over WTAG, Worcester, beginning in 1924.

WOI at Iowa State College began to broadcast market reports in the spring of 1922. Andy Woolfries, a freshman engineer who had helped build the transmitter a few months earlier, usually was the person who copied the reports in code from Great Lakes Naval Training Station and then talked them into the

Earle M. Terry, professor of physics at the
University of Wisconsin, put station 9XM on the
air in 1917.

WOI microphone. In September the director of extension services began
assigning extension specialists to make occasional talks about farming.

At Kansas State, extension editor Sam Pickard arranged for staff members
to travel once a week to Kansas City, Missouri, to broadcast over WDAF; next
year they broadcast from the campus over station KFKB at Coffeyville until the
college's own station, KSAC, went on the air near the end of 1924.

At Michigan State, WKAR went on the air in 1922 and extension editor
James B. Hasselman started regular talks by agricultural specialists. He also
became the station's football announcer.

At Texas A&M, WTAW also began broadcasting in 1922 and soon had a
daily agricultural program, the "Texas Farm and Home Hour," guided by Dr.
E. P. Humbert, head of the genetics department.

In Tennessee it was the county agent in Memphis, W. M. Landess, who
first began to talk to farmers by radio over WREC in 1922. Landess and his successor, Leonard Kerr, broadcast regularly on WREC for thirty years, until Kerr
retired from his job as county agent and immediately became farm director of
the station.

The Missouri Department of Agriculture in 1922 baptized its radio sta-

In 1920 an ordinary telephone served as microphone for the first USDA broadcasts of market news over government-owned stations.

tion, WOS in Jefferson City, with daily market reports while the extension service joined in with a daily message and later with live speakers.

The Chicago stockyards put WAAF on the air to report livestock prices. The first reports may have been made by Jim Poole who worked for the Livestock Exchange or by Charles Whalen, the USDA reporter. Whalen, in 1923, told his bosses he was broadcasting daily over three Chicago stations.

Westinghouse built its third station, KYW, in Chicago in 1922 and soon scheduled a program for farmers each evening at 6:30 with speakers provided by the American Farm Bureau Federation, the Illinois Agricultural Association, and the National Grain Growers Association.

Early in 1922 the USDA reported that of the thirty-six stations licensed by the Department of Commerce, thirty-five of them had been approved to broadcast market reports and twenty to broadcast weather forecasts.

All stations were licensed to broadcast on just two frequencies, equivalent to about 833 and 620 on a modern dial; a station was supposed to use one for markets and weather, the other for entertainment and other programs. By 1924 there would be approximately 500 stations crowded into those two wavelengths, and to most listeners it became an impossible mess. For a time all the two dozen or so stations in the Chicago area shut down each Monday night so listeners could tune in distant stations.

Stations went on the air when they pleased and shut off when they pleased. No station broadcast for more than a few hours at a time; sometimes it would be only five minutes for a market report, and then silence. Some stations publicized their schedules; some did not.

The Association of Agricultural College Editors (AACE) first took notice of radio at its annual meeting in 1922 by inviting Professor H. E. Dudley of the University of Wisconsin to discuss the twin-topic, "Movies and Radio." Next year, radio was upgraded to a spot all its own; a speaker from the National

Around 1923 some of the crystal receivers and
some of the listeners looked like this.

Radio Chamber of Commerce brought the latest word. In 1924 two spots on
the program were devoted to radio: a panel of several editors talking about
their own experiences in using radio to reach farmers, and George C. Biggar,
director of agriculture and markets for WLS, a station which had been on the
air for about four months. The following year the editors created a committee
on radio, a sign that as a group they were beginning to take radio seriously.

In 1923, county agents conducted a nationwide survey for USDA that indicated there were about 145 thousand radios on the nation's 6.4 million
farms.

It was in March 1923, that the nation's first full-time farm broadcaster
went on the air, over KDKA, Pittsburgh. His name was Frank E. Mullen, a
native of Kansas, raised in South Dakota, and a recent graduate of Iowa State
College. He was on the payroll of the *Stockman and Farmer* magazine, with the
title of radio editor. He had the responsibility for market reports, provided by
the USDA, and farm news, gathered by the *Stockman and Farmer* staff. Soon
he had more time on the air and established a schedule of talks by county
agents and extension specialists from Pennsylvania, Ohio, and West Virginia.

In Oregon, beginning in 1922, the assistant county agent leader, Wallace
Kadderly, arranged for extension workers to talk over KGW Portland until in
1924, the State College at Corvallis put KOAC on the air, and Kadderly was
named program director and agricultural director.

Alabama Polytechnic Institute, at Auburn, put its radio telephone station,
WMAV, on the air in February 1923 with an antenna supported by a forty-foot

pole cut from the tallest pine tree the students could find. Extension editor
P. O. Davis was in charge of programs, and at the start it principally was a
weather, markets, and farming improvement station.

In Chicago, the Board of Trade decided if the stockyard could have a radio
station, the Board should have one also for grain prices. The Board then bought
a station already on the air, WDAP.

The following year, 1924, brought several milestones. In Shenandoah,
Iowa, Henry Field built a radio station to sell his seeds, nursery stock, and particularly his opinions.

In Chicago, the Sears Roebuck Agricultural Foundation put WLS on the
air in April. KYW, already on the air with a daily program for farmers, made a
strong bid to hold its farm audience by staging an all-evening broadcast with
speeches by the secretary of agriculture, the president of the Farm Bureau, and
many other agricultural leaders, just before WLS was to make its debut.

In Philadelphia, WCAU hired a magazine writer, Charles Shoffner, to
start a farm service program in 1924. Possibly he was the first man to rack up
twenty-two years as farm director of one station, 1924–1946.

At Kansas State College, station KSAC went on the air in December 1924.
The station made a modest ripple among farmers in Kansas, but the side effects
were to be felt nationwide. The college president, William M. Jardine, was
about to become secretary of agriculture and start a migration of Kansas State
people who would put the United States Department of Agriculture into
broadcasting more deeply than ever before.

The 1924 USDA survey of farm families with radios produced a figure of
about 370 thousand, more than twice the number of the year before. A
Westinghouse official calculated there were more than three thousand factories
making radio sets and parts, about 250 thousand people were employed in
making and selling them, and thirty radio magazines had sprung up.

The USDA's extension service called a National Agricultural Radio Conference in Chicago near the end of 1924. Several hundred people were there
representing radio stations, agricultural colleges and extension services, farm
organizations, and several branches of government. After a couple of days of
speech-making and committee meetings, the conference adopted some resolu-
tions.
  • Broadcasters should use only accurate and dependable information.
  • Programs for farmers should be timely.
  • Weather forecasts, especially storm warnings, are important.
  • Federal and state extension people should coordinate their material.
  • Consumer interests should be recognized.
  • Public agencies should release material to radio in the same manner as to
    the press.
  • The secretary of agriculture should call similar conferences in the future.

About the middle of 1925 the USDA's new director of information,
Nelson A. Crawford from Kansas State, started his press staff to rewriting
newspaper releases into talk style and mailing them to radio stations.

In Shenandoah, Iowa, Henry Field's rival in the seed and nursery business,

Earl May, also became his rival in broadcasting by putting KMA on the air. The May family is still broadcasting in the early eighties.

The Sears Roebuck Agricultural Foundation moved George Biggar from WLS to Dallas, Texas, to start a daily farm program on WFAA. The Foundation paid for the staff and talent; the station provided the time. No payment from one to the other. On WLS Fred Petty became agricultural director in Biggar's old job.

A survey of land grant schools in 1925, conducted by the AACE, showed twenty-four schools had radio stations, fourteen of them with 500 watts power or more; a dozen were broadcasting regularly on commercial stations.

One of those using a commercial station was Colorado State, where extension editor Glenn Kinghorn started a weekly program on KOA in the spring of 1925. This program continued for eleven years.

In November 1925 an announcer on WGY, Schenectady, persuaded his bosses to let him start a program for farmers using information and speakers from extension services, USDA, and farm organizations. He called the program "Farm Paper of the Air." Instead of using his real name, George Emerson Markham, he posed as "County Agent Robbins" for several years. The program was to be around for many years.

In any chronology of farm broadcasting, 1926 has to be designated as a vintage year, for several reasons.

• The Radio Corporation spawned the National Broadcasting Company which created the first radio network, starting with stations owned by RCA and its member corporations, Westinghouse and General Electric.

• Later in the same year came a second network, formed by the Columbia Phonograph Broadcasting Company.

• In Washington the year started with the creation of a Radio Service in USDA, headed by Sam Pickard from Kansas State. He hired a small crew of writers, gave a name "Noontime Flashes" to the script service, and started the "Farm School of the Air" with schoolmasters on more than twenty stations before its two school years were concluded.

• Westinghouse put a powerful station, KFKX, on the air in Hastings, Nebraska, primarily to provide farmers with market reports off the USDA telegraph wire and transferred the pioneer farm director, Frank Mullen, to take charge in Hastings. His place at KDKA was taken by an actor and entertainer, Ralph Griffith, who called himself "Stockman Sam." After about a year the KFKX call letters were moved to Chicago and the USDA market reports were moved to KMMJ, Clay Center, Nebraska, under the care of George Kister, who had become acquainted with market reports at KFKX. Frank Mullen moved to Chicago where he helped open NBC's new headquarters and began dreaming up a farm program for the network.

• About that same time, Everett Mitchell, singer-announcer on WENR, Chicago, started a daily program that he called "Farmers Exchange." A few years later, after Frank Mullen's dream of a network farm program became a reality, Everett Mitchell became the announcer on the "National Farm and Home Hour," and stayed with it to the end, almost thirty years.

Frank E. Mullen, the nation's first full-time farm broadcaster, went on the air over KDKA in March 1923. He was on the payroll of the *Stockman-Farmer* magazine for the first year he was on the air. Five years later he started the "National Farm and Home Hour."

• The University of Nebraska started KFAB in 1926 with market reports and talks on farming. Later, extension editor Elton Lux began to perk up the programs with dramatic programs which he wrote and performed in.

• George Biggar started his third program for the Sears Foundation on WSB, Atlanta. The University of Georgia asked for separate time on WSB. The Sears program ended two years later but the University of Georgia program, with a couple of brief interruptions, has been on WSB since 1926.

• In 1926 about 500 stations were on the air on several frequencies, and the USDA estimated nearly one million farm families had receivers. The new receivers in 1926 came equipped with loudspeakers, and if you had electricity in your house you could plug a modern set right into it. But about nineteen out of twenty farm families had to continue to use batteries because "the lights" (REA) hadn't reached out to them.

The Department of Commerce, charged with issuing broadcast licenses, had held conferences with broadcasters and other concerned people in 1923, 1924, and 1925, to try to straighten out the tangle of too many stations broadcasting on too few frequencies. It managed to make some improvements, but many broadcasters chose their own frequencies and used as much power as their equipment would put out. In 1927 Congress created the Federal Radio Commission that assigned stations to certain frequencies and to certain power, put a stop to on-again, off-again broadcasting; a station must broadcast continuously, either dawn to dusk, or at least twelve hours a day if it had a full-time license. These requirements were going to cost money for engineers, power, announcers, talent, and program production. About 150 stations gave up their licenses, cutting the number back to around 600. Most of those that remained had only one course: they had to sell advertising. Agricultural programs usually were not sold, principally because the USDA would not allow its information or people to be used for the benefit of an advertiser.

Early in 1928, Morse Salisbury succeeded Sam Pickard as chief of the USDA's Radio Service. He looked with favor on the "Noonday Flashes," but decided the "Farm School of the Air" was much too expensive to continue.

The USDA's market news people joined with state departments of agriculture and extension services in New England and with WBZ to finance the New England Radio News Service that began a daily program of farm news and talks on WBZ. The USDA put up most of the money and provided the first director, Frank Scruggs. The project would continue for twenty-two years.

The USDA opened market news offices at stockyards in Buffalo, New York; Cleveland, Ohio; Indianapolis, Indiana; and St. Joseph, Missouri; and market reporters began broadcasting over local stations, often several times a day.

The Sears Roebuck Agricultural Foundation was one license holder who decided it wanted to get out of the radio business. It wiped out the programs it had started on WFAA, WSB, and WMC; let the Sears company worry about a new program started by George Biggar on KMBC, Kansas City; and sold WLS to Burridge D. Butler, publisher of *Prairie Farmer* magazine.

Those were all important in their place, but they shrink in comparison to the start of the "National Farm and Home Hour" on the NBC network the first week of October, 1928. This was the creation of Frank Mullen of NBC and RCA, and that story is told later in Chapter 5. So now we're at the end of 1928. In most farming areas, farmers with radios can hear market reports, weather forecasts, and the latest in how-to-do-it. Two-thirds of the state extension services and a substantial number of county agents are broadcasting regularly. The "National Farm and Home Hour" is heard six days a week from the Atlantic to the Rockies on thirteen stations affiliated with NBC. A few stations plus NBC have full-time farm directors. Stations are broadcasting full time, and they are selling time to advertisers, called "sponsors."

The number of farms held fairly steady all through the 1920s at just under 6.5 million; farm population slipped just a little to about 30 million; one farmer or farm worker fed about ten people; the number of farm workers

George C. Biggar was the first agricultural director of WLS, Chicago, in 1924.

dropped from 11.4 million in 1920 to 10.3 million in 1928, and the number of horses and mules dropped from 25 to 21 million. The million workers and 4 million horses were replaced by 500 thousand tractors, bringing the total to nearly 800 thousand in 1928. With the tractors came three-bottom plows, ten-foot discs, four-row cultivators; combine harvesters. corn pickers, cotton strippers and milking machines. Also, rubber tires appeared for tractors and other farm machinery. Threshing machines and threshing rings were being used in most wheat areas. Hybrid corn and soybeans were catching on in the Midwest. Farmers spread a lot of fertilizer during World War I, were forced to cut back in the twenties, but gradually increased its use again.

On most farms there was a cream separator and the cream was collected several times a week by a truck from the creamery and made into sour cream butter; the skim milk went to the hogs. Some families sold their milk or cream and bought pasteurized milk, but many of their neighbors thought this was just putting on airs.

Most families produced their own milk, eggs, poultry, vegetables, fruits, and berries. Winter was butchering time. Summer and fall were canning seasons. ''We eat what we can. What we can't we can.''

About one-half the farm families had cars by 1928, almost one-third had telephones, about one-tenth had electricity, a similar share had running water, about one-eighth had radios.

A general depression occurred in the twenties; the rest of the country grew out of it; and factories boomed. But farm prices stayed low. Total farm income dropped from about $16 billion in 1920 to $10 billion the next year and had gradually edged upward to the $13 billion range. Out of their total earnings, farmers had spent $6 to $8 billion per year for hired workers, feed, fertilizer, seed, and equipment; about 60 percent of what they took in.

This then, was the situation in farm broadcasting, broadcasting in general, and agriculture at the end of 1928.

Chapter Three

USDA Weather

WHEN it came to using wireless, first telegraph and then telephone, weather forecasters were far ahead of other groups in the USDA. In 1900, twenty years before any other branch of the USDA tried the ether waves, the Weather Bureau hired a young Canadian physicist, Richard Fessenden, away from Thomas Edison and allotted him $3,000 to build several wireless telegraph stations on the coast of North Carolina. The stations worked but President Theodore Roosevelt ordered the Weather Bureau to get out of the communications business, leaving it to the Coast Guard, the navy, and the army. The Coast Guard began Weather Bureau reports as early as 1902 to ships on the Atlantic and on the Great Lakes, and the ships beeped back local conditions.

On land the Weather Bureau cooperated with the University of North Dakota in 1914 to broadcast weather forecasts over the university's wireless telegraph station. Nine amateur operators over the state copied the forecasts and distributed them in their communities. Later several other universities did the same.

Weather forecasts moved regularly across the country by telegraph lines, and in many communities they were broadcast locally by party line telephone. The Weather Bureau records show that as early as 1904, sixty thousand farm families in Ohio alone got weather forecasts by telephone. By 1926 more than 5 million families across the nation received weather information by telephone.

At the University of Wisconsin, station 9XM had carried occasional weather reports by radio telephone as part of its testing program, and on January 3, 1921, the station began to broadcast daily weather reports on schedule. That was a ''first,'' according to the Weather Bureau; weather broadcasts have been continuous since that date.

When radiophone stations were licensed by the Department of Commerce, they had to apply to the USDA for permission to broadcast market or weather reports. Of the 36 licensed radio stations in June, 1922, 35 were approved for market reports, but only 20 applied to carry weather reports. By January, 1923, 140 radio stations were licensed and all were authorized to broadcast both weather and market reports.

In 1935 KFI, Los Angeles, and the chief of the local Weather Bureau started a special frost warning service in winter and spring for the benefit of citrus growers in southern California. They divided the area into several zones, mostly valleys, and each evening the Weather Bureau predicted how cold it was likely to be that night in each zone and advised growers in some areas to ''Light your heaters tonight''; in others ''Relax, no danger tonight.''

In Massachusetts and Wisconsin, beginning in the forties, a local station or two broadcast frost warnings for the benefit of cranberry growers.

In the fifties, George Haefner of WHAM, Rochester, New York, began a daily conference telephone call between the Weather Bureau and several county agents. The weather forecaster predicted what the weather would be and the county agents advised orchard owners whether today would be a good day for spraying.

A heavy blizzard in Nebraska in 1949 led to building a radio station owned by a farmers' cooperative and within a year KRVN, Lexington, Nebraska, was on the air devoting plenty of attention to weather forecasts, especially to storm warnings. The station is still owned cooperatively by about 3,500 farmers.

In 1959 Congress appropriated some money for a pilot project in agricultural weather forecasting and research and set up an agricultural experiment station at Stoneville, Mississippi, that would be concerned only with cotton in the Delta area. Meteorologist Jack Riley was put in charge. Twice a day special agricultural forecasts and "advisories" were put on the Weather Bureau's teletype system to broadcasting stations and newspapers.

The special weather service, as an example, reported area-by-area soil temperatures and told cotton growers when the soil had warmed enough to safely plant their crops; it notified them when boll worms and boll weevils were about to appear and if the day would be good for spraying; it warned about days when dew was likely to be heavy in early morning so picking should be delayed. If rain was in the forecast, there was also a warning that newly picked cotton should be put under shelter.

Jack Riley reported to his superiors that every dollar spent on the agricultural weather project at Stoneville during the first year had returned forty dollars in increased yields, higher quality, reduced damage from weather, insects, and diseases. The project at Stoneville has been continued and similar projects were established at agricultural experiment stations at Auburn, Alabama; West Lafayette, Indiana, (Purdue); and Texas A&M. These are called Environmental Studies Service Centers, and they carry on research as well as issue day-to-day agricultural weather forecasts and advisories. They do things like develop computer models of how corn crops grow during the season and how their growth can be affected by hot weather, cool spells, drought, or heavy rain. Similar models were developed for cotton, peanuts, soybeans, and other crops.

Sometimes weather research gets very complicated. Back in the sixties, D. A. Davis found that leaf fleck in shade-grown tobacco is caused by too much ozone in the air, and excessive ozone appears right after a thunderstorm. But if the tobacco is slightly wilted when the thunderstorm hits, almost no damage occurs. So the weather advisories would warn farmers not to irrigate their shade-grown tobacco until after the thunderstorms had passed. Leaf fleck used to cost growers about $2 million a year; after the agricultural weather service started, the losses dropped to just a few thousand dollars a year.

In Indiana, the weather team, working with crop and insect specialists, found that cumulative temperatures controlled the period when alfalfa weevils became active. If alfalfa growers sprayed at precisely the right time and kept the weevils under control, yields could be increased three- or four-fold. On one May 30, for example, the agricultural advisory using the weather teletype circuit fed out of Purdue read like this: "In North Central Indiana, brisk winds will be unfavorable for spraying alfalfa on Saturday and Sunday, but Monday should be a good day to spray."

Dr. Ray Jensen, director of the Environmental Studies Service Center at College Station, Texas, divided Texas and Oklahoma into seven zones, based on climate and agricultural production, and in the late seventies his staff cranked out a weather advisory for each zone every working day. Jensen said, "Several hundred broadcasting stations subscribe to the weather teletype service, which is the quickest and surest way to disseminate the agricultural advisories to farmers. I look forward to the time when we have maybe two dozen centers like this in the U.S., and even more broadcasters using our agricultural advisories. Then we'd be getting close to our objective of getting the right information to the right farm at the right time."

After experimenting for almost twenty years with its own radio stations and broadcasting nothing but forecasts, the National Weather Service in the U.S. Department of Commerce unveiled a plan for 340 weather broadcasting stations located nationwide to reach about 90 percent of the U.S. population. Each station would cover a radius of about forty miles and broadcast weather forecasts continuously for its particular area. Several state and local governments provided money or manpower to help establish stations, and by 1979 more than 300 of the stations were on the air. Special receivers were required to pick up the weather broadcasts, in the high FM band, above 162 MHz. As more stations began to broadcast, farmers, school officials, vacationers, and others bought receivers. Manufacturers were then able to lower the price to the ten to fifteen dollar range. In 1978 one manufacturer alone reported he had sold 1.4 million receivers, and many retailers reported that weather receivers had replaced CB as their "hot item" in 1979.

In the early seventies, the Weather Service began a project to enlist farmers as weather reporters. The Weather Service provided about 120 farmers on Maryland's eastern shore with thermometers, rain gauges, and special telephone transmitters. Twice each day the weather reporter read his thermometer and checked his rain gauge and punched the information into a card; the card fitted into the telephone that fed the information into a computer at the University of Maryland. Then the summarized data were fed to the Weather Service and used in making the next forecast.

From the Maryland project the farmer reporter system was extended nationwide in 1977. By using computers, information from all part of all states can be brought to forecasting headquarters near Washington and built into localized forecasts for the areas where it originated.

Those things are with us now. For a glimpse of the kinds of weather service farmers may be getting some day, look into the crystal ball of Dr. Bill Marlett, of the Department of Environmental Science at Colorado State University. Backed by the National Aeronautics and Space Administration funds, Dr.

Marlett and his associates have developed what they call "Nowcasting." On television an agricultural weather forecaster can use satellite views plus data provided by a world-wide reporting system to show what weather is coming, and when. Part of the TV presentation is a local map on a scale large enough so farmers can locate their own places and figure out whether rain is coming, when it will arrive, and how long it will last.

Bill Marlett proposes a ten-minute agricultural weather program each morning, followed by five minute shorts every hour until mid-afternoon, combining weather information with suggestions about plowing, planting, spraying, harvesting, curing, and other farm operations in their proper season. He's done his planning-dreaming with the agricultural weather project at Stoneville, which stands as the foundation and is linked by microwave to the educational TV station, WMAA, in Jackson, Mississippi where the station officials are willing and able. Marlett said, "Several farmers told us they'd put a TV set in their pickup truck and take it to the field so they could keep up with the weather."

He added that the pilot project would cost about $3 million to set up and operate for three years, but other projects that might come later would cost much less.

Another phase of weather forecasting is aimed at predicting weather for the next month or the next ninety days, and these medium-range forecasts seem to be getting more accurate. The winter of 1976–1977 in the eastern half of the U.S. was bitterly cold. After it was over the Weather Service modestly asserted, "Our 90-day forecast at the end of November was right on the button."

A University of California agriculturist figures that bad weather costs farmers about twelve percent of their production and that half of this loss could be prevented if farmers had the right kind of information in ample time. This figures out to be a possible saving of maybe $5 billion per year.

Chapter Four

Market News Broadcasting

THE market news people in the USDA were the first to employ wireless telegraph and then wireless telephone aggressively, but market news has been kept separate from the USDA's other broadcasting activities.

In 1920 W.A. Wheeler, a Minnesotan, was put in charge of reporting market news from the USDA's twenty market news offices. The offices were connected by telegraph wire, and each office mimeographed USDA reports on livestock, grain, or other commodities and mailed them to farmers, dealers, and others who were interested.

Wheeler had a teenage son, Harold, who was an amateur wireless operator. Later, Harold invented some wondrous electronic devices—a volume control now used on millions of radio and TV sets; mine detecting devices used during World War II; and an antenna system used in landing men on the moon. In 1920 his antenna system consisted of his bedsprings, but he sent messages to other ham operators over a radius of 200 miles.

It occurred to Harold's father that his son's amateur wireless friends represented a great network for spreading market reports. Wheeler enlisted the cooperation of the U.S. Bureau of Standard's broadcasting station, WWV, and the first wireless market report beeped out at 5:00 P.M., December 15, 1920. Dozens of amateur operators copied the messages in code, translated them to English, and made them available to farmers, dealers, and others, within a 200 mile radius of Washington, D.C.

The next step was to create a network of wireless stations. The Post Office had a series of wireless stations at intervals, east-to-west, across the nation, at Washington; Bellefonte, Pennsylvania; St. Louis; and Omaha to provide weather and navigation information to pilots flying the mail. On April 15, 1921, four wireless stations began moving reports on grain, livestock, fruits, and vegetables each day at noon and again at 5:00 P.M.

About a year later, the navy transmitters at Arlington, Virginia; Great Lakes, Illinois; and San Francisco were brought into the act and soon replaced the Post Office stations.

About twenty-five hundred amateur operators were provided with the market news telegraph code so they could convert "SR 1 R 75-2 R 00" to "New Jersey Irish Cobbler potatoes in 100 pound bags sold at $1.75 to $2.00."

Many reports indicated that amateur operators were tuning in on the market news broadcasts, copying the reports, and posting them at grain elevators, feed mills, post offices and banks. A local telephone company in Il-

W. A. Wheeler, of the USDA Bureau of Markets, put market reports on the air beginning in 1920, first on wireless telegraph, a few months later on wireless telephone.

linois tuned in on the broadcast from St. Louis, copied the market reports, and then had an operator broadcast them by party line telephone.

The *Nebraska Farmer* of May 28, 1921, editorialized, "The plan . . . has great possibilities for county farm bureaus. Why not have one of the receiving instruments in every farm bureau office and have the county agent and his clerk learn how to take the messages? Then interested farmers can get up to the minute reports by telephoning the county agent's office."

Successful Farming, published in Des Moines, said similar things the same month, singing the praises of coded market reports by wireless telegraph.

In May 1921 Wheeler arranged for voice reports over KDKA Pittsburgh, and both voiced and coded market reports were transmitted over 9XM at the University of Wisconsin. But a meeting with radio manufacturers convinced him that the many legal tangles involving patents would inhibit production, and it would be along time before many radiophones would be on the air to transmit or receive. In a memo to his USDA bosses in June 1921, he wrote, "The immediate handling of crop, weather, and market reports by radio telegraph will probably be performed by operators engaged by county agricultural agencies or others who are in a position to make a special effort to receive such a report."

In October 1921 Westinghouse, General Electric, and Western Electric agreed among themselves to let each other use any patents held by any of the three companies. That opened the way for more stations, and Wheeler's *Radio Information Circular* issued in April 1922 listed thirty-six radio (telephone) stations on the air, thirty-five of them authorized to broadcast market news, twenty authorized for weather reports, twenty-seven of them broadcasting news and entertainment. Geographically they ranged from Boston to San Francisco and Los Angeles; and Minneapolis to Atlanta. The Missouri Department of Markets had its own station, WOS; so did the Chicago stockyards and the Wichita Board of Trade; the state universities in Wisconsin, Nebraska, Ohio, Iowa and Minnesota, plus Nebraska Wesleyan and Saint Louis University were authorized to broadcast market reports. Stations owned by newspapers in Atlanta; Rochester; Detroit; and Richmond, Indiana; and the Westinghouse stations in Pittsburgh, Springfield, and Chicago carried market reports.

All stations were licensed to broadcast market news and weather on a wavelength of 485 meters (about 620 kHz), news and entertainment on 360 meters (about 830 kHz).

The "National Farm and Home Hour" started in the fall of 1928 on a network of thirteen stations. More stations were being added each month and each daily program included a summary of the day's principal trends in farm markets. About 115 other stations also carried market reports each day, a number that remained fairly constant for several years. The reports were unsponsored and presented as a public service.

World War II, with the government seeking time on sponsored broadcasts, put an end to the USDA's ban on its information being used in programs sponsored by advertisers, and when stations could provide market reports with sponsors paying for the time, more and more stations carried them. By 1955, 1,311 radio and 82 TV stations were carrying market reports, most of them paid for by sponsors.

The USDA had no more up-to-date figures because Congress had criticized government agencies for too many surveys, putting an undue burden on business people required to fill out government forms.

The chance to make an honest dollar from the market reports brought at least one controversy. In 1963 the Ritter publications, which controlled the *Journal of Commerce* and the Commodity News Service, brought suit against the USDA, contending that its distribution of market news was interfering with private enterprise. The Federal District Court in Washington ruled that the USDA might continue to report markets as it had been doing but should not do anything to promote more extensive use of its reports by broadcasters, such as encouraging them to tap into USDA circuits. The message to broadcasters was, "If you want market news quickly and often, subscribe to a commercial news service."

From 1963 to 1975 the USDA directory of market news services merely listed the location of market news offices. Intentionally omitted was a map of the 23,000 miles of teletype circuits showing where the circuits might be tapped by a broadcasting station.

The court order was withdrawn in 1975 when the Knight newspaper interests bought control of CNS, and sweetness and light came to rest on relations between the USDA and CNS. By that time, CNS had demonstrated its ability to deliver market news to a broadcaster more promptly than the USDA. But early in 1977, the USDA hitched to a computer its market news service in twenty eastern and midwestern cities. This system spewed out data at the rate of twelve-hundred words a minute, ten or twelve times as fast as a teletype. Almost immediately the Dow Jones news service, UPI, and AP linked up to the USDA computer for the benefit of their broadcaster clients.

Now, a few words about futures trading. For a long time the USDA faithfully reported cash prices for grains, eggs, butter, and other commodities but barely mentioned the sinful futures prices.

But in the seventies it became a different story. Farmers and ranchers asked increasingly for reports on futures prices as well as cash prices, and the

USDA began reporting them; many stations went to schedules of a market report every hour, even every half hour, during trading hours with emphasis on futures. Are farmers hedging? Or are they speculating? Broadcasters believe most farmers are interested in futures as a hedging operation. For example, at planting time a farmer might sell corn for delivery in October. When October arrives, if the cash price is better, he will sell for cash and buy up his futures contract. But an Illinois broadcaster told me, "One guy said he might sell a corn crop next year without even planting one."

It is evident that many farmers in the seventies think of futures trading not as sin but as part of the marketing system. Our fathers and grandfathers made great strides in their ability to produce food; today's farmer is sharpening his skill in marketing it.

Chapter Five

USDA Mainstream

WHEN William M. Jardine moved from the presidency of the Kansas State Agriculture College to become secretary of agriculture in March 1925, he already knew the value of radio. He brought with him Nelson Antrim Crawford, head of the college's English department, as director of information in the USDA. Crawford had his press service employees choose at least one story to rewrite each day for use by individual radio stations. Early in 1926 he imported extension editor Sam Pickard from Kansas State and made him head of the USDA's newly created Radio Service. Pickard started three daily script services: "Noontime Flashes," for farmers; "Housekeepers' Chats"; and his favorite program, the "Radio Farm School." The "School" scripts were broadcast by station announcers designated as "schoolmasters" presenting the daily lecture on animal husbandry, poultry raising, and other farm related topics. Each student who signed up was sent the USDA bulletins appropriate to the subject he was interested in, and by the end of two school years, 500,000 students were enrolled. This was a more costly job of duplicating and mailing than the Radio Service budget could stand, and the program ended because it was too successful. By early 1928, Pickard had moved to the position of secretary of the Federal Radio Commission, and the end of "Radio Farm School" was decreed by Pickard's successor Morse Salisbury, another Kansas Stater, who had taught journalism and had done some broadcasting at Kansas State.

Salisbury inherited a three person staff of writers. The staff included a Kentuckian named "Colonel" Charles A. Herndon; Solon Barber, who, like Herndon, had been a reporter in Washington; and Josephine Hemphill from Kansas State.

The two daily series of scripts, "Housekeepers' Chats" and "Noontime Flashes," were now used on about 150 stations. Soon afterward the names were changed to "Homemakers' Chats" and "Farm Flashes."

Salisbury had hardly settled into his new job before his first challenge was thrown at him: a campaign to stop the corn borer in the eastern corn belt. County agents, the press, and USDA resources would be used. The Radio Service arranged for a special script service to go to forty-six radio stations that broadcast nine scripts, once a week for nine weeks. The Radio Service's efforts considerably enhanced its and Salisbury's prestige within the USDA.

The "Noontime Flashes" had followed the lines on which the USDA was organized at that time, and each script generally had been devoted to one

Morse H. Salisbury

broad subject—livestock, dairying, poultry, economics, crops, and so on. When the name was changed to "Farm Flashes," the pattern also changed so one day's script might include several shorts on different subjects.

Around 1929 Salisbury considered distributing the USDA's agricultural wisdom on platters with the experts themselves talking, but he found the cost was more than his budget would allow; and the stations refused to pay for the privilege of carrying a noncommerical program. Salisbury decided he could live with scripts.

In 1930 Salisbury and Emerson Markham of WGY conducted an experiment in how to present information. The USDA's writers would turn out scripts written in several different ways: talks, interviews, roundtable discussions, comedy routines, anecdotes, and jokes. Markham lined up several dozen families among WGY listeners to report on how they liked each program, how well it presented its information, how much they remembered. Forty-odd years later, Dana Reynolds, a USDA writer at the time of the experiment, recalled that the WGY audience heard the story about the farmer who got a washing machine but didn't like it. Why not? "I tried three times to wash my feet and the durn thing kept throwing me out." In another program the listeners heard,

> I mix my peas with honey
> I've done it all my life
> I know it may sound funny
> But it keeps them on my knife.

At the end of the experiment the listeners reported they would rather have their information straight, without jokes or dramatics. The "Farm Flashes" continued on their way without nonsense.

Another policy decision began to take shape about that same time. In the 1930 Office of Information annual report, Salisbury wrote:

> The present task of the Department of Agriculture is to bring the local stations into closer relation, not with Washington, but with the state agricultural college and its extension field force. When the agricultural colleges are equipped with the editorial personnel to work with the Department radio writers, the Department Radio Service should turn over contacts with individual stations to the colleges and become a service agency to them (the colleges) rather than direct to the stations.

To put the words into action, he created the job of extension radio specialist and switched Alan Dailey from writing "Farm Flashes" to the new position. Dailey was a bachelor, and for several years he lived out of a suitcase as he made the rounds of the agricultural colleges.

The Massachusetts extension service was one of the first to hire an editor to localize the "Farm Flashes," and I was appointed, in 1931. Dailey visited me in 1932. A year later he reported forty of the forty-eight state extension services were localizing and distributing "Farm Flashes," to 217 stations, all in public service time.

When the New Deal farm programs came into existence in 1933, farmers learned about federal programs that would improve prices, put money in their pockets, and bring electric lights to their homes. Often they heard about a program first through the "Farm Flashes," delivered by a station announcer or by a county agent.

For the most part, the production of daily "Farm Flashes" was a separate section of the USDA's Radio Service, managed by Herndon. He usually had

Wallace L. Kadderly (R), head of the USDA Radio Service, 1938–1945, receiving the NAFB's 1964 Award for Meritorious Service from Wally Erickson of KFRE.

Layne Beaty, Chief of USDA Radio-TV 1955 to 1980 with his staff at the time he took over. L-R: Gordon Webb, Alice Skelsey, Jules Renaud, Beaty, Charles A. Herndon, Jack Towers.

two or three assistants and at different times they included Francis Perkins, Dana Reynolds, Frank Teuton, Forney Rankin, and C. R. Briggs. During World War II, Besty Pitt, Marguerite Gilstrap, and Virginia Watkins did much of the writing and editing.

The USDA's script services, begun in 1925, continued under several Radio Service chiefs, Sam Pickard, Morse Salisbury, Wallace Kadderly, John Baker, and Kenneth Gapen. In 1955 Layne Beaty moved into the job and decided the future lay with tape recording. "Farm Flashes" and "Homemakers' Chats" were discontinued, and "Colonel" Charles A. Herndon retired. Name any change in agriculture that had occurred over the past thirty years during depression, war, peace, and prosperity and the Colonel had handled a "Farm Flash" about it for radio listeners. But to my knowledge he never talked into a microphone.

Now we back up to the plateau of 1928 and pick up the "National Farm and Home Hour." It was the brainchild of Frank Mullen, of NBC, but it was made to order for the USDA, and the USDA's participation was essential in NBC's view. No other branch of government was ever approached by a network with an invitation to, "Come on the air every day and tell people what you're doing and how it will help them."

Thirteen stations would be in the network at first, mostly in the eastern half of the U.S., but NBC planned to add more stations coast to coast. Music and entertainment would be provided by NBC; information by the USDA. Montgomery Ward would sponsor the daily sixty-minute program.

The prospect of a daily network program was mouth-watering to USDA officials. But a sponsor? What would Sears Roebuck say, perhaps to appropriations committees in Congress? No, the USDA could not, would not, take part in a totally sponsored program. So Mullen, Salisbury, and Milton Eisenhower, the USDA director of information, worked out a compromise: Montgomery Ward would sponsor just three-fourths of the daily program, and there would be a quarter hour in which USDA people would appear with no sponsor.

But USDA people took part in the dress rehearsal of the inaugural program for the benefit of Montgomery Ward officials, and about six months later the new secretary of agriculture, Arthur M. Hyde, wrote a "thank you" letter to George B. Everitt, a vice-president of Montgomery Ward.

The "National Farm and Home Hour" went on the air October 2, 1928. It was heard six days each week, with USDA people participating five days. Saturday programs were divided among the national farmer organizations, 4-H, and vocational agriculture.

Secretary Hyde seldom broadcast on the "National Farm and Home Hour," but one of his few appearances was the high point in a comedy of errors. It started when the Bureau of Commerical Fisheries in the Department of the Interior published a bulletin on how to raise frogs for market. A senator who didn't read very carefully ridiculed the USDA for wasting taxpayers' money studying "the love life of the bullfrog." The speech was widely publicized, and the USDA within a few days received several thousand requests for the bulletin. Thinking he would stop the flow of requests, Secretary Hyde preempted several minutes of time on the "National Farm and Home Hour" to rebut the senator and to explain that the USDA never had had a bulletin on the love life of the bullfrog. The secretary's speech was a great success. It brought in ten thousand more requests for the bulletin.

NBC's Frank Mullen had studied forestry at Iowa State University before he joined the army in World War I, and there was a soft spot in his heart for trees and foresters. He proposed a dramatic series built around a forest ranger. If the USDA would provide the scripts for a once-a-week program, NBC would hire actors and handle the actual production.

The job of writing these scripts fell to C. E. Randall of the Forest Service Information staff. "Uncle Sam's Forest Rangers" ran on the "National Farm and Home Hour" from 1932 until 1943, and millions of people believed in Ranger Jim Robbins and his loyal, understanding wife, and in Jim's assistant, Jerry Quick, who kept courting and courting and courting his girl friend, but never got her to say "yes." Harvey Hay, the Chicago actor who played Ranger Jim, got a citation from the forester organization.

The quarter hour allocated to the USDA was fairly evenly divided among the agencies in the department. From October 1928 to the end of June 1929, 198 USDA speakers took part. Some of the talks had a direct bearing on health, because one of the USDA's agencies was the Food and Drug Administration; another was the Bureau of Biological Survey, which had its name changed to Fish and Wildlife Service when it was moved to the Department of the Interior. After a year or two, the Bureau of Home Economics was given a spot every week, and the regular speaker was Ruth Van Deman, who rivaled Everett Mitchell, master of ceremonies, as the best-known personality on the program. A two-minute summary of markets was a daily feature spotted just before the end of the Washington portion of the program. The report soon fell into a standard pattern; prices on cattle, hogs, sheep, wheat, corn, oats, soybeans, potatoes, apples, and so on, always in the same order. Mitchell recalls, "The boys in the orchestra in Chicago would go out of the studio for a smoke during the USDA portion of the program. They knew it was time to get back on the job when I'd open the studio door and yell—'They're into the potatoes.' "

All the speakers were live, for NBC policy in those days forbade recordings, and every speaker had to use a script; a few managed to talk naturally. About a year later, NBC provided them with a microphone control panel and amplifier speakers and the USDA set up a rehearsal studio, which helped some of the speakers to improve their oral reading. Along the way some people learned to write for radio.

The main job of the USDA's chief of the Radio Service was the daily "Farm and Home Hour" program, which required scheduling speakers, seeing that scripts were written, approving for policy and style, rehearsing the speakers, and then acting as subhost on the program. Salisbury had this role from 1928 to 1938, and Kadderly presided over the USDA portions of the programs until the daily series ended in 1944, after sixteen years and some 4,700 programs.

The second Saturday of each month was 4-H Club day, with music provided by the United States Marine Band, and the talk portion of the program as well as the music usually originated at the auditorium of the marine barracks in Washington, D.C.

Ken Gapen remembered his greatest embarrassment in a long career of broadcasting as the time he introduced a musical number "Played by the United States Army Band" and was promptly corrected by Captain Taylor Branson, "This is the band of the United States Marine Corps." Yes Sir!

For several years, beginning in the late thirties, one program a month originated on the campus of a land grant college with the college band, chorus, president, dean of agriculture, and director of extension. The USDA arranged the schedule, and over several years, most of the schools were included.

THE NEW DEAL. When Henry A. Wallace became secretary of agriculture in 1933 and sparked new government programs over the next few years to forestall farm mortgage foreclosures, support farm prices, conserve the soil, help farm tenants become owners, and extend electric lines to farms, there was a system of farm broadcasting ready and waiting. When the first price support programs for cotton, corn, and hogs were announced, the USDA asked for additional network time in the Southeast and the Midwest and received it from NBC and CBS. Part of this extra time was given during evening hours. For several weeks in 1933, the USDA's share of the "National Farm and Home Hour" was doubled to thirty minutes each day. A quick USDA survey in Arkansas indicated that most of the farmers who came to county offices to sign up for the cotton program had learned about it by radio.

For several years, whatever the new government programs, or changes in established programs might be, the officials responsible for them used radio to spread the word. Secretary Wallace was a frequent speaker on the "National Farm and Home Hour," and so were the heads of the new "action agencies" created by the USDA, the Agricultural Adjustment Administration, the Soil

Conservation Service, the Farm Security Administration, the Rural Electrification Administration, and others.

For the most part, the new farm programs worked fairly well. Farm prices and farm income worked their way upward. With more money to spend, farmers added about 100,000 tractors a year, used more fertilizer, installed lights and running water when REA lines came to the community, and bought more things from stores. All the encouraging signs were reported by speakers on the "National Farm and Home Hour" and in the "Farm Flash" scripts out of the USDA and the state extension services.

When the bombing of Pearl Harbor got the U.S. actively involved in the shooting phase of World War II, the USDA's job became one of informing farmers where, when, and how to get the materials they needed to produce food and fiber. Secretary of Agriculture Claude Wickard coined the phrase, "Food Will Win the War and Write the Peace," a rallying cry to farmers and a message to brass hats in Washington who controlled manpower, steel, chemicals, and other things needed for both war and agriculture. Secretary Wickard was a frequent speaker on the "National Farm and Home Hour" and so was Chester Davis, head of the War Food Administration.

But sad to say, the "National Farm and Home Hour" no longer had the strong, far-reaching voice it once possessed.

As early as 1935, when NBC Blue Network stations were given the option of carrying the program or not, some stations dropped it immediately and others followed. In 1942 the Blue Network became independent of NBC and Frank Mullen, executive vice-president of NBC, no longer could protect the program he had founded fourteen years earlier. The new management of the Blue Network saw the "Farm and Home Hour" as a money-losing program, occupying valuable midday time and unpopular with many listeners and stations. On September 2, 1942 Edgar Kobak, president of the Blue, wrote to the USDA, "Frankly, if we can't improve it and get more stations to carry it and get more coverage, we ought to move it or find another way of handling the situation."

So far as the USDA was concerned, the principal effort to improve the program was to divide its daily ten minutes of agricultural information into three segments.

In many ways, relations between the USDA and the Blue Network became a battle between farm and city, between service and show business. In January 1944 Blue Network officials told the USDA to "Kill the market reports." The USDA retorted, "We will be the judge of what kinds of agricultural information are needed by farmers." The market reports stayed in the show, but bad news was on its way.

In May the network announced that effective June 19, 1944, the "National Farm and Home Hour" would become a weekly program, presented only on Saturday. The USDA proposed that the name be changed to "Home and Garden," since there would be nothing in the new program that had to do with farming. "Home and Garden," hosted by ex-movie star Billie Burke and Wallace Kadderly from the USDA, lasted until the end of 1944.

If there had been a formal eulogy over the "Farm and Home Hour," it would have noted that the program had had a longer run than any other daily program on any radio network, some forty-seven hundred broadcasts, from October 1928 to June 1944; it had presented virtually every agricultural leader and organization in the nation; it had helped unite farmers through good years and bad, through depression and war; and it had served to tell agriculture's story to consumers.

The "National Farm and Home Hour" would be resurrected, but this is a good moment to back up and consider its western offspring.

The "National Farm and Home Hour" in its first two years had no station west of Denver, but in January 1931 NBC and the USDA joined resources to launch the "Western Farm and Home Hour," an hour at noon, on eight NBC western stations. Later the program was cut to forty-five minutes and then to thirty minutes. USDA mobilized speakers from the western agricultural colleges, its western regional offices of the Food and Drug Administration, the various research bureaus, and, beginning in 1933, the AAA, SCS, FSA, and others. The market reporters stationed in San Francisco, where the program originated, made their reports each day. The Washington office provided copies of scripts used on the network program out of Washington and Chicago, so there was a western version of "Uncle Sam's Forest Rangers" and a western "Aunt Sammy" with the voice provided by Jean Stewart, a nutritionist from the staff of Stanford University Hospital in San Francisco. For a couple of years, a dramatic feature was built around "John and Mollie Farmer," a couple who operated an imaginary farm somewhere in irrigation country. The California Dairy Council paid for the actors in this skit.

Jennings Pierce was the producer and announcer for NBC, while Kadderly coordinated the USDA and agricultural college speakers. Each testified that the other was a great guy to work with. When Kadderly was moved to Washington, D.C., in 1937, and soon afterward became chief of the Radio Service, his place was taken by C. R. "Cy" Briggs, who earlier had succeeded him at Oregon State College.

In 1938 the "National Farm and Home Hour," originating in Chicago and Washington, was extended to the west coast stations of NBC, and the "Western Farm and Home Hour" was ended. However, NBC gave the USDA a quarter hour at noon called "Western Agriculture," roughly the same amount of time that had been assigned to the USDA in the "Western Farm and Home Hour." Seemingly everybody was happy. In the summer of 1940, Cy Briggs transferred to the Radio Service in Washington and was succeeded by Kenneth Gapen, a Soil Conservation Service employee with many years of broadcast experience. He arrived just in time for a change of schedule. "Western Agriculture" was moved from noon on the Blue Network to 7:00 A.M. on the western Red Network—not as good an hour, but more high-power stations. In November 1941 the program was shifted back to the Blue Network, and scheduled to follow the "National Farm and Home Hour" at 10:00 A.M., a poor hour for farm listeners.

The NBC Blue Network and its stations were unhappy because the daily

One program each month on the daily "National
Farm and Home Hour" was devoted to 4-H
Clubs. This broadcast in 1939 featured
Oklahoma 4-H members and leaders and was
fed to the network by KVOO, Tulsa. John Baker
is on the left. (USDA)

combination of farm programs represented money going out and none coming in. In 1943, with permission from Washington, Gapen told Blue Network officials that "Western Agriculture" could be offered for sale to sponsors. The Blue Network sales manager didn't know of a prospective sponsor and had no interest in finding one. The program was offered to NBC, with the same result. One by one, local stations dropped "Western Agriculture." In January 1944 "Western Agriculture" was given a quiet burial alongside the "Western Farm and Home Hour." The daily "National Farm and Home Hour" was to follow in June of that year.

THE PLATEAU 1945-1946. The Big Event of the period, of course, was the end of World War II and the homecoming of millions of men. Kadderly was sending a weekly newsletter to about ninety farm broadcasters, at least two-thirds of them conducting commercial programs.

"Farm Flashes" were adapted and distributed by state extension editors in forty states and used on 522 stations.

CBS "Country Journal" had moved its headquarters to Washington early in the war and the Radio Service had helped its director, Chuck Worcester, with seventy-one interviews during the period 1943-1944; supplied Press Associations (Associated Press service to radio stations) with thirty-one stories, and lent a hand almost every day to Lee Hannify of United Press for his feature "On the Farm Front."

At NBC, Mullen and Drips watched the end of the "National Farm and Home Hour" on the Blue Network and planed to resurrect it on NBC. Things probably were made easier when the Blue was bought by the makers of Lifesavers candy, and Mark Woods became president of the new company, called the American Broadcasting Company.

But three bits of magic had to be performed to bring off the resurrection. First, get control of the name; second, find a sponsor; third, persuade the USDA to participate in a sponsored program.

Kadderly negotiated for, and received, a telegram from Mark Woods giving USDA legal title to the name "The National Farm and Home Hour" with assurance that ABC would not object to its use on another network. Score One!

As to sponsors, no company was interested in footing the bill for a daily program, but the Allis Chalmers Company was interested in a once-a-week version of the "National Farm and Home Hour" if the USDA would take part.

The people who originally had established the USDA's policy of no commercial broadcasting had reluctantly relaxed it during World War II and had now left the USDA. The key man was the new secretary of agriculture, Clinton P. Anderson, a former congressman. When asked if the USDA would take part in the weekly "National Farm and Home Hour" sponsored by Allis Chalmers, his only question was, "When do we start?"

The weekly "National Farm and Home Hour" went on the air the first Saturday in September 1945. The USDA climbed into bed with Allis Chalmers while NBC played madam, providing the entertainment and collecting the money.

Everett Mitchell greeted the audience with his familiar "It's a Beeeyoutiful day in Chicago"; the Homesteaders orchestra, fattened to twenty-four pieces, played familiar music; the USDA provided a summary of the week's markets; Ruth Van Deman and later Lucille Holmes Cohan talked to homemakers; and news highlights and a talk were given by a USDA official. Ken Gapen was the USDA's host for the first nine years except for a few months when I played the role.

Milton Eisenhower, who had been USDA director of information from 1927 to 1942 and had shaped the USDA early policy of "no participation in commercial broadcasts," said in 1975 about sponsorship, that he would have advised the secretary of agriculture to refuse to participate in the "National Farm and Home Hour" in 1945, sponsored by a farm machinery company.

At the beginning of its sponsorship, Allis Chalmers paid for time on only 44 stations, but another 58 stations carried the program, using public service announcements written by the USDA in place of the commercials. Later the company sponsored the program on the entire network, and by 1953 it was carried by 199 stations.

In its commercial announcements, Allis Chalmers never hinted that the USDA thought A-C tractors or balers were better than any other. In fact there was hardly a suggestion that even Allis Chalmers thought so. The message was always one of "better farming, better living, conservation, abundance." As the program drew to a close in 1960, an Allis Chalmers man said, "We can't prove that the "Farm and Home Hour" ever sold one tractor or any other piece of equipment."

Near the end, NBC invited Frank Mullen from his TV scenery business in Hollywood to try to revitalize the "Farm and Home Hour" and find another sponsor. But it was too late. The final program went on the air in July 1960.

"AMERICAN FARMER." The weekly "National Farm and Home Hour" was only a few weeks old, and I was even younger as the USDA radio service chief, when Bob White of ABC asked the USDA to take part in the "American Farmer," in head-to-head competition with the NBC program each Saturday at noon. I proposed a package based on the USDA's economic and statistical information and named it "The Business Side of Farming." Dana Reynolds, who had written thousands of scripts but seldom had faced a microphone for the USDA before the war, had just returned from the navy. He took on the task of assembling, writing, and broadcasting the weekly feature beginning the first Saturday of 1946.

Gapen continued the feature when he became chief of the Radio Service in 1946, and assigned Jack Towers, then a script writer, the responsibility of producing the program beginning about 1952. In 1955 ABC announced it no longer would produce the "American Farmer." However, if the USDA wanted to take responsibility for producing, ABC would feed the program to its stations. Jack Towers rolled his sleeves a little higher and produced twenty-nine minutes of network programming each week instead of the customary ten or twelve minutes, scheduling the speakers, recording them, and writing the continuity which was read by the ABC announcer assigned as host. The ABC host at first was Chuck Bill and then Hugh Casey, who spoke from Chicago. When the USDA took over production, members of ABC's Washington staff introduced the speakers: at first Jackson Weaver, then Felix Grant, and in the final years, Charlie Hughes. The "American Farmer" continued until 1969, nine years after the rival "Farm and Home Hour" had expired. Jack Towers said ABC never was able to tell just which stations were carrying the program, but it brought enough mail to indicate that some people were listening.

OTHER USDA BROADCASTS. Gapen reported in July 1950 that the number of TV stations on the air had increased in one year from 50 to 105, that several of the eastern states were completely blanketed by television signals and the TV audience had leaped from 8 million to 28 million persons. On the other hand, for the first time in history, the number of radio stations had declined from the year before, with 2,137 AM stations operating, a decrease of 42; and 698 FM stations on the air, a decrease of 167.

Helping extension workers use radio more effectively has been an important task of USDA broadcasters. Kenneth Gapen presided over this training session in Oregon in 1946. (USDA)

The RFD letter summarizing USDA news was mailed weekly to 388 radio farm directors; 400 stations used "Farm Flashes," localized by extension editors in thirty-eight states, and the USDA originated 231 different stories during the year in this service, written by C. A. Herndon, Robert Crom, and Milton Bliss.

In 1952, Gapen calculated the value of radio time devoted to USDA information at approximately $2 million, if the stations charged their published commercial rates. He arrived at his total this way: the USDA news, moved by wire services and broadcast by 544 farm broadcasters—$900,000; special recordings for farm broadcasters—$100,000; 400 stations carrying three weekly network programs—$750,000; "Farm Flashes" used on 800 stations—$250,000.

Gapen transferred to the Soil Conservation Service in 1954, and Layne Beaty became chief of the USDA's Radio and TV Service. Beaty was an Oklahoman who had worked briefly for the Farm Security Administration and then for the Oklahoma Department of Agriculture. He started radio and TV farm programs on WBAP, Fort Worth, and was president of the National Association of Farm Broadcasters before he went to Athens and then to Paris to help foster farm broadcasts in postwar Europe.

For more than a quarter century, under six Secretaries of Agriculture, both Republican and Democrat, he kept his superiors and associates happy by getting out the information they thought should be broadcast. At the same time he provided farm broadcasters and news directors with the information they wanted from the USDA. Beaty was the only government employee given special classification as a voting member of the National Association of Farm Broadcasters. He retired in February 1980.

For twenty-two years the good right arm on the radio side of the Radio and

Television Service was Jack Towers. He wrote many scripts for "Farm Flashes" and network programs, but when Beaty decided about 1955 to cancel the "Farm Flashes" and get into recording, Towers came into his favorite element. In the thirties as radio editor at South Dakota State College he had lugged a Presto disc recorder and portable generator over the state by plane, train, and car to record interviews with farmers, ranchers, county agents, and incidentally a Duke Ellington dance program that has become a classic. He joined the USDA in Washington in 1942.

When the USDA acquired a tape recorder, Towers was off and running. Around 1957 he and a young assistant from Kansas State named George Loesing (who for professional reasons became George Logan when he moved to WLW) hitched together five Magnecorders to make five dubbings at a time. They decided to experiment: "We offered a series of two- and three-minute interviews on tape to just twenty-five farm broadcasters five a week for thirteen weeks, and asked them to let us know if they'd like more." They would. Agritape customers kept increasing until there were not enough hours in the week to dub all the copies, five at a time, at regular recording speeds. Somewhere Layne Beaty found a few hundred dollars and bought a high speed duplicator, which Towers installed, which could make five dubbings of a quarter hour program in two minutes. Later, Towers added other high-speed units so he and his assistants could make fifteen copies at a time. In the seventies, Agritape went out each week to between 400 and 500 stations.

The clear channel stations in the fifties wanted to make a showing that they were serving agriculture, and Towers started a special series for them called "Agriculture USA," providing an in-depth interview on one subject 13½ minutes long, in contrast to Agritape's pattern of several short interviews. At first the Clear Channel Broadcasters Association distributed them to their member stations, but after a time the USDA decided such gems should be made available to any station that wanted them. The number of takers climbed to about 300 in the sixties and then settled back to about 250 that received a quarter hour tape each week in the seventies.

Towers had a succession of associates who shared the duties of interviewing and recording speakers on the programs that went out by mail and on "The American Farmer": Bob Marburger, John Weidert, Jim Palmer, Janet Christiansen, Arnold Hartigan, and in the mid-seventies Gary Crawford.

In the late sixties the USDA's Radio Service installed a Spotmaster telephone playback system to benefit the farm broadcasters. Broadcasters anywhere in the U.S. can dial the USDA number, hear the titles, and decide if they want any of the stories. If they want one or more, they record it for broadcast on their own program. Many of the calls are made late at night and broadcast on early morning farm shows.

The NAFB gave Towers its Meritorious Service Award in 1971 in recognition of the thousands of programs he had provided over the years. At his retirement party in the summer of 1974, Hollis Seavey, of the National Association of Broadcasters, recited this limerick:

There was a young fellow named Jack
Who recorded ag tapes by the stack
But now he is leaving
With all hands bereaving
Is there no way we can get him back?

There was no way to get Jack Towers back, but his place was taken by Jim
Johnson, who had been a radio specialist and an extension editor in the states of
Washington and Idaho. Of course the USDA's recorded services to farm broad-
casters continued to go out on schedule.

TELEVISION. It was Kenneth Gapen who reluctantly put the USDA into
television. He had all he could do keeping up with three weekly network radio
programs, daily scripts, in the "Farm Flashes" and "Homemakers' Chats"
series, plus increasing requests from newly appointed farm broadcasters over
the country. This all was accomplished with fewer people in the Radio Service
as a result of budget cuts two years in succession. As Gapen recalled many years
later, it was early in 1948 that Bill Drips of NBC came to town with a message
from Frank Mullen. "Television is here; it's going to get more important; the
USDA ought to get into it."

Congress had provided the USDA with money for "research in
marketing." Gapen proposed a five year research project in how to develop
television programs dealing with agriculture. His proposal was approved and
RMA Project 255 was born, allocating $20,000 a year for agricultural marketing
research in television. Gapen hired Maynard Speece and Corinne Murphy to be
television research specialists; they were succeeded during the five years by Bob
Crom, Tom Noone, Alice Skelsey, and Jules Renaud.

At the end of five years, Gapen reported that the TV researchers had produced 370 live programs, from two to ninety minutes in length testing different techniques and visual aids; twenty short subjects were put on film to test
the production of low-cost films; USDA people held sixty-nine conferences
with people in other organizations, most of them in land grant colleges; the
Radio and TV Service issued a catalog of USDA films suitable for use on television (which meant principally that the music was not under copyright). A how-
to-do-it handbook on films for TV, visual aids to be used on live TV, and program methods for TV were created. A similar handbook was created for state
and county extension workers, which included several case studies of how well
people learned to do things by watching a series of TV programs and a
bibliography of publications dealing with TV.

By the end of the five year research period, the USDA was sending TV
package programs, one each week, to about 100 television stations. The stations
were notified of the subjects in advance, and each station chose those it wanted.

By that time, January 1, 1954, there were 356 TV stations on the air and
200 more authorized. Viewers had bought about 28 million black and white

receivers. Color was just ahead, but a conflict existed between the CBS and NBC systems of color transmission. The CBS system involved a many colored disc but its color pictures could not be picked up on a black and white receiver; the NBC system projected color electronically and its color pictures could be picked up on a black and white receiver. In 1953 NBC had broadcast the "Colgate Comedy Hour" in color. Meanwhile NBC wanted to experiment further with its color equipment on its Washington station, WRC-TV; so it asked the USDA to provide some live programs for local broadcast. Jules Renaud taxied each week to the WRC studios with one of his program packages and put it on the air. It was broadcast in color although at that time about the only receivers that could pick it up in color were in the control room.

These experimental programs might be considered the ancestor of "Across the Fence," started in July 1961. The program was much like the USDA portion of the "Farm and Home Hour" radio program converted to television, with Layne Beaty, Jules Renaud, and Edith Swing of the Radio and TV Service as regulars, with assorted guests, drawn from all agencies of USDA. The USDA people planned the programs and NBC provided the technical production. The program was videotaped each Thursday evening and was broadcast on WRC-TV Saturday morning and again on Sunday. NBC offered a duplicate of the videotape to the USDA with permission for other stations to use it if the USDA could find any takers. Beaty recalls the first taker was WESH-TV in Daytona Beach, then KRON-TV San Francisco, then the Nebraska Network. Others followed until about 120 stations were getting the program each week, with 20 copies of each tape circulating among them. In the seventies the number of users slipped down to about 100.

Beaty and Renaud decided the USDA had enough good television stories to support a daily series, and in 1962 they started "Down to Earth," intended for inclusion in farm TV programs. Each segment was 4½ minutes in length, and Renaud and his guests taped five programs in one recording session with the duplicated tapes going to stations once a week. Ted Hutchcroft, Gordon Webb, Leo Geier, and John Wagner, at different times helped produce the series. The duplicating was done at no charge by the Army Signal Corps, until Signal Corps people decided after several years that national defense did not include duplicating videotapes for USDA. Since then the tapes have been duplicated commercially.

In 1959 Renaud summarized U.S. farm TV programs in a talk at an international television workshop held in England. There were 516 commercial and 37 educational TV stations on the air; almost 44 million homes, 86 percent of all homes and 70 percent of farm homes, had TV receivers. About ninety people were producing a daily or weekly farm TV program of whom sixty were members of the National Association of Television and Radio Farm Directors. A survey indicated a total of nearly 115 hours of TV farm programs each week, about two percent of total broadcast time. The USDA package service went to 140 persons who used them on 169 stations. He also reported that "Farm Newsreel" (produced by a free lance producer, Martin Andrews, and sponsored by the American Cyanamid Company)—a weekly, quarter hour program—ran for twenty-six weeks on 52 stations in 1958 at a total cost of about $500,000 for time and production. A couple of other efforts to produce similar programs never got off the ground. Television networks sold only $51,000 worth of time to agricultural advertisers but $88 million to food advertisers in the first ten months of 1958.

Four years later Renaud summarized the farm television situation in his master's degree thesis in 1964. He found that of the 654 U.S. TV stations operating during December 1963, about 500 produced a farm program of some kind, about half of the programs daily, varying from five minutes to an hour, with thirty and fifteen minutes most common. About 100 stations had a professional farm broadcaster. In 1963 TV stations used 2,969 USDA films for a total of 1,163 broadcast hours, mostly on Saturday and Sunday. County extension workers participated in 28,841 TV programs during 1962. Of the 159 series on which he got detailed information, roughly two-thirds were available for sponsorship, including seventy of seventy-five programs conducted by members of NATRFD and nineteen of fifty-one programs by extension workers. Ten percent were broadcast in color.

Renaud propounded that the central farm problem in the United States "in our generation, is the excess productive capacity of the American farmer which is reflected in price-depressing surpluses." He noted that advisory committees to the secretary of agriculture credited the USDA with getting information to farmers but had been critical of a lack of effort to tell agriculture's story to city people. "The gap of understanding is widening between the people who produce the nation's food and fiber and those who use it. Television can be a factor in strengthening rural-urban understanding."

He reviewed the gradual relaxing of USDA rules about its people appearing on sponsored broadcasts; first a flat prohibition; then permission to appear if the broadcaster stated that appearance of a government worker was not an endorsement of a product or service. In 1963, "no such disclaimer is now required because of a history of good judgment and discretion exercised by broadcasters, advertisers and government officials." It was still that way in 1979.

Renaud left the Radio and TV Service in 1965, and was succeeded by O. Pat Morgan from the Louisiana extension service. During his nine years in the job, Morgan had help from Margaret Desatnik, Glenn Sheffer, Bill Pemble, and Don Elder. Desatnik and Elder were still staff members when Larry Quinn moved from the Texas extension service to head the TV section in 1974.

The USDA's two major TV program series "Across the Fence" and "Down to Earth" continued into the late seventies, but 1975 brought a change in each: new management at WRC-TV decided fourteen years of producing "Down to Earth" without charge was long enough; so Layne Beaty negotiated a contract with another station to do the program for a fee.

"Across the Fence" became "A Better Way" with a new concept: what the future may hold in food production and homemaking. The WRC people saluted this by providing a new set: brighter, more modern. Thus, the USDA's TV programs marched through the late seventies and into the eighties.

The Radio and TV Service budget got above $40,000 per year in the wartime years; immediately after the war it was cut back to about $34,000. The addition of "research" in television added $20,000 from 1948–1953.

In his thesis, Renaud reported the Radio-TV Service staff in 1963 included ten people. Two years later four technical and clerical workers were added to duplicate and mail radio tapes, and from that time through 1979 the number of workers remained at about the same level, including eight professional writers and broadcasters and six or seven technical and clerical people. The annual budget climbed from its 1946 level of $40,000 to $188,000 in 1963, and $545,000 in 1979, more an indication of the inflated economy than of an expansion of activity.

Although it has been equipped to produce movies since the twenties and radio tapes since the fifties, the USDA never has invested in broadcast quality television cameras, studios, or videotape equipment. "TV cameras and videotape equipment are much more expensive than comparable equipment for radio, so it's cheaper to have our work done under contract than to invest in equipment and hire a crew which we could keep busy only part of the time."

Most of the new USDA agencies created in the thirties hired radio specialists who wrote scripts for their bosses and often served as speakers for their agencies on the "National Farm and Home Hour." In the thirties M. L. DuMars of AAA, Forney Rankin of SCS, and Marvin Beers of Farm Security Administration were an important part of the "National Farm and Home Hour" as writers and speakers. The biggest mail puller of them all was Ruth Van Deman, information chief of the Bureau of Home Economics in the thirties and forties, who had the knack of making almost any subject sound interesting. She could be, on occasion, something of a con artist though. She arrived at the Baker home one Sunday morning with a duck and supervised me while I made the stuffing and roasted the duck for dinner. Then guess who wrote the script around the theme, "It's so easy even I managed to do it." In the mid-forties, she discovered she had cancer, but she insisted on coming to the NBC studios Saturday at noon to do a spot on the "National Farm and Home Hour." I've never felt more regretful than I did in the spring of 1946 when I told this gallant woman she was to stay home on Saturdays and take care of herself. Lucille Holmes Cohan took over the homemakers spot on the show, capably, but a lot of listeners wrote that they missed Ruth Van Deman.

E. J. "Mike" Rowell moved from the New England Radio News Service to the USDA's Marketing Service and saw to it that market news summaries were available for the "National Farm and Home Hour" when it was a daily and then a weekly program. He was followed by Lance Hooks during the fifties, by Pete Keay in the sixties, and by John Nicholas, Eleanor Ferris, and Dale May in the seventies. Rowell also presided over production of a weekly "Consumer Time" program on NBC in the forties. The best scripts of this program as I remember them were written by a member of Rowell's staff named Christine Kempton, and the voices were those of a couple of professionals, Evelyn Freyman and Johnny Batchelder.

One of the most effective radio spokesmtn for the USDA's agricultural research service in the forties and fifties was Ernest Moore. He not only reported on results of research, but drew on his hobby of gardening to be the answer man in the garden program, which followed the "Farm and Home Hour" on the Blue Network in 1944. Duke DuMars was the curious, novice gardener and Moore had all the answers.

Howard Hass was the first radio specialist hired for the research agency, and he was followed over a period of twenty years by Vince Marclay, Bert Hutchison, Bill Ewin, Jim Anderson, and Glenn Sheffer.

Several of us had held the title of radio extension specialist before the end of World War II: Dailey, Kadderly, Baker, DuMars, and Bond. Our salaries were paid by the Radio Service, with the Extension Service paying traveling expenses. Joe Tonkin started on the same basis, but in 1946 went on the Extension Service payroll. He was followed in the sixties by Foster Mullinax, and in the seventies by Gary Nugent, Bill Pemble, and Doug Wakefield.

Kent Miller became radio-TV specialist for agricultural economics and statistical agencies services in the sixties and seventies.

Several experienced radio and TV people who had an urge to see the world gravitated to the Foreign Agricultural Service, including J. K. McClarren, Don Looper, Jules Renaud, and Wally Dunphy. In the seventies with sales of U.S. farm products overseas increasing, Wally Dunphy made the reports more timely by interviewing U.S. agricultural attachés in Moscow, Tokyo, Bucharest, and other capitals by overseas phone. Some of the long distance interviews went into the USDA's "Agritape" or "Spotmaster" series, and some became "actualities" in the Associated Press audio reports.

REGIONAL OFFICES. Market news and consumer information got a boost during World War II that continued long afterward when the USDA War Food Administration set up regional information offices in New York, Atlanta, Chicago, Dallas, and San Francisco.

These regional information offices put out reams of propaganda urging people to save fats or to buy foods that were most plentiful and were not rationed. So far as farmers were concerned, the principal thing the offices did was to assemble market news from USDA offices in their respective regions and feed it several times a day to the wire services which in turn supplied it by teletype to radio stations. This type of assistance gave farmers more market information than they had had before, and when the number of radio stations began to increase following the war, the number that were broadcasting market reports went up also, from approximately 300 in 1947 to 1,400 in 1956.

A thirty-year summary of only regional office chiefs makes a longish list. In the New York City office Stanley Flower, Harry Carr, Phil Fleming, and Bryan Killikelly held the top spot. In Atlanta, Arthur Susott occupied the job for about a quarter century, followed by Stan Prochaska, and then by Connie Crankleton. In Chicago, Judd Wyatt was the first appointee, followed by Walter John, John Baker, Paul Ostendorf, and in the seventies by Herb Jackson. In Dallas, Meno Schoenbach started the service and was followed in the fifties by Harold Bryson who was still on the job in 1979. In San Francisco,

USDA, Office of Governmental and Public
Affairs, Broadcasting and Film, L–R: (seated)
Brenda J. Curtis-Heiken; DeBoria Janifer;
(standing) Jim L. Johnson; Larry A. Quinn; Doug
Wakefield; Gary Crawford; Don L. Elder; Kent
Miller. (March 1980)

Don Walsh opened the office, followed by J. Stanley Livingstone for more than twenty-five years, succeeded in the late sixties by Ralph Cless and then by Ben Darling. I don't imagine 100 farmers could have named any of these people or their even more anonymous helpers, but they were important members of the bucket brigade which passed along market news to farmers.

Chapter Six

New England Radio News Service

THE New England Radio News Service was a one-of-a-kind venture, started in 1928 by J. Clyde Marquis, information chief of the USDA's Bureau of Agricultural Economics. It was to be a daily radio service of market news, drawing on the USDA's nationwide market news reporting system with other information for farmers, provided by the New England state departments of agriculture and extension services, which were linked together in the New England Research Council. Marquis sold the idea to the council and to WBZ, the Westinghouse station, which recently had moved from Springfield to Boston.

The USDA put up most of the $6,000 per year needed for the project by providing an experienced market news man, Frank Scruggs, to report the markets and act as the program's host during the early months. WBZ agreed to carry three programs each day: 10:30 A.M.; noon, following the "National Farm and Home Hour"; and 6:30 P.M., in the noncommercial time provided by WBZ. The first programs went on the air November 20, 1928.

During the first year talks were given about "Functions of the Boston Fruit and Produce Exchange," "Progress of the New England Milk Producers Association," "Economic Research in Dairying," "The Vermont Rural Life Survey," "How to Operate the Incubator," and "Outlook for Dairying in New England."

By the end of June 1929, end of the government's fiscal year, the morning market report had been dropped, and the noon program expanded to a half hour to allow for more talks in addition to the market reports.

Scruggs was assigned to other duties as a USDA market reporter and Elwyn J. "Mike" Rowell became director of the program.

Rowell had grown up in Amherst, Massachusetts, within walking distance of Massachusetts Agricultural College. After graduating from there in 1927, he became the principal broadcaster for the county agent's staff in Worcester, Massachusetts, which had been using radio to talk to Worcester County farmers since 1921.

The WBZ announcers introduced the program as "New England Agriculture," but by the time I became involved in it, in 1932, it was known off the air as "Mike Rowell's Show."

In the early thirties the evening program was canceled, leaving a half hour

E. J. "Mike" Rowell,
1929–1937, was director of
the New England Radio
News Service. He later
supervised USDA market
news and consumer in-
formation broadcasts in
Washington.

at noon for Rowell to report the USDA market reports and to introduce such speakers as a USDA statistician or persons from a state department of agriculture or a farm organization.

The Massachusetts extension service was assigned three programs per week, one each on agriculture, homemaking, and 4-H Club work. The Middlesex County extension staff was assigned one program per week. Extension services in Vermont, New Hampshire, and Maine figured few of their people listened to WBZ; so they provided less money and fewer speakers.

Most of the programs were straight talks or interviews, but around 1934 the Massachusetts extension service began supplying "drama." On the weekly homemakers' feature, my wife and I became Vance and Sally Hubbard, who lived on a farm and had several children. Once each week the Hubbard family encountered a home economics specialist with whom we discussed canning, gardening, sewing, raising children, and other related topics. Although it was magnificently written and acted, for some reason the program was never given an award.

When I left Massachusetts in 1935, G. O. "Oley" Oleson took over the extension service radio programs, including the features on "New England Agriculture."

The daily programs rocked along in rather routine fashion until 1937, and then three changes occurred. Rowell moved to a job in the USDA Agricultural Marketing Service in Washington, D.C., and his job was taken over by John Myers, who had been his assistant for several years. WBZ withdrew its contribution of money, which amounted to about one-sixth of the budget; canceled the noontime program but agreed to continue a program at 6:30 in the morning. John Myers moved the noon program to the Colonial Network with WAAB, Boston, as the key station and outlets in Waterbury, Bridgeport, and Hartford, Connecticut; New Bedford, Lowell, and Springfield, Massachusetts; Bangor and Augusta, Maine; and Laconia, New Hampshire. No high-power stations were included, but if a farmer wanted to hear the program, he could find it on the dial.

Myers also acquired an assistant, Charles Eshbach, who had been a student assistant to Oleson and me two years earlier at Massachusetts State College.

The next year, Myers and Eshbach started a daily script service, which they mailed to any New England station that would use it. Starting with about twelve stations, the script service built up over several years to about eighty stations.

In 1939 Myers resigned and was succeeded as director by Eshbach; Phil Fleming then came aboard as assistant, and Helen Stubbs joined as secretary and stayed throughout the war. Also the first FM station, W 1'XOJ, Boston, joined the Colonial Network, carrying the noontime program with its market reports and talks. This is the earliest record I could find of a farm program on FM radio.

The year 1941 was notable for attacks and the FCC hit before the Japanese. It ordered companies that owned two networks to dispose of one. John Shepard operated both the Colonial and Yankee Networks covering New England, and he decided to dissolve the Colonial Network. But he liked Colonial's "New England Agriculture" program and put it on his Yankee Network, fed by WNAC, Boston, at 6 A.M.

The same ruling had the effect of removing the "National Farm and Home Hour" from the WBZ schedule, and that station decided to start its own program, the "New England Farm Hour," 6:00 to 7:00 A.M. daily, with Malcolm McCormick in charge. He was a longtime WBZ announcer, lived on a farm and smoked a corncob pipe. This program represented an important outlet, and Eshbach and Fleming of the New England Radio News Service became regular participants, in addition to their early morning program on the Yankee Network. Unlike other farm programs in New England that preceded it, WBZ's "Farm Hour" would be available to sponsors.

Charles Eshbach was director of NERNS 1939–1948.

Having jumped off to an early start, with two live broadcasts each morning, they settled down to writing a daily fifteen-minute script, sent to twenty-one stations in 1942; a three-minute script especially for WTIC, Hartford; a weekly script for five Vermont stations; another for thirteen Massachusetts stations; and one for WTIC. Each day they fed market reports to four wire news services, UP, PA, INS, and Transradio. And lest life grew dull, they broadcast a quarter hour for food shoppers each Thursday afternoon over WHDH, Boston. All this was accomplished by two men and a woman on a budget of $7,100 per year.

Moreover, a war was on, and men were being called to serve. Stanley Flower joined the NERNS staff as a trainee in November 1942; Fleming went into the army on December 11; and Eshbach left for the air corps on December 30. Sidney Vaughn, of the Worcester County extension staff filled in for three months, and on April 1, 1943, Flower was named director and Dorothy Crandall, who had been on the Worcester County extension staff, was named his assistant. For two years Flower, Crandall, and Stubbs kept market reports and speakers going on WBZ and the Yankee Network, wrote daily scripts for other stations over New England, and broadcast the weekly shoppers program on WHDH. About the end of 1944, Flower put on a uniform, and Lloyd Williams moved from the Connecticut Department of Agriculture to become director.

By 1946 Eshbach was a civilian and back in his old job, but the job was not going to be the same. Rowell came from Washington in May to deliver the bad news: the USDA was no longer going to give any money to NERNS. About 100 stations across the country by this time had hired their own farm directors and the USDA decided WBZ and the Yankee Network should do the same. The New England departments of agriculture and extension services that had been making token contributions to NERNS through the years decided to give more money to keep it going as a two person operation.

Eshbach and Stubbs would have three major duties: first, provide a daily script service from all New England agencies offered to all New England stations; second, act as a scheduling agency for speakers from the public organizations to appear on the farm programs, run by McCormick on WBZ, Joe Kelly on WHDH, and Jesse Buffum on WEEI, all in Boston; and by Frank Atwood on WTIC, Hartford; third, assemble market reports and feed them to the wire services, fifteen per day, plus a similar number of weekly summaries. They supplied no live broadcasting.

On occasion Eshbach could write enough scripts in advance to let him travel over New England visiting stations and cooperating organizations, while Stubbs handled the daily flow of market news. But Eshbach was a broadcaster who was not on the air. In 1949, when the six New England extension services decided to establish a marketing education program and asked Eshbach to head it, he saw it as a chance to become a broadcaster once more and resigned from NERNS. Clem Lewis, son of a New Jersey fruit grower, took over as the new director of NERNS, but the operation had been living on borrowed time, and in 1951 it died, at twenty-two years of age.

Chapter Seven

National Networks and Wire News Services

OVER the years, the United States has had almost as many kinds of network farm programs as Heinz has pickles.

Some of the programs move by wire, some by rebroadcasting programs from one station to another; some are recorded on tape or film and distributed by mail or parcel delivery service. Some of the farm programs keep company with news and entertainment; some stand alone.

The farm network programs that serve only one state or one agricultural region are described in the chapters devoted to the states. This section is concerned with network farm programs on radio and television, covering the nation or large regions, beginning in 1928.

NBC NATIONAL FARM AND HOME HOUR. "It's a beeeyoutiful day in Chicago."

Millions of people, many of whom may not have known corn from alfalfa, listened regularly for that greeting by Everett Mitchell as he introduced the "National Farm and Home Hour" on NBC radio during most of its life, from 1928 to 1960. The fact that Wallace Butterworth was announcer on the program for the first two years has been forgotten by most, as has Montgomery Ward's sponsorship during the first year, 1928–1929. The participation of the USDA in the program is described in Chapter 5.

The program was on the air at midday, sixty or forty-five minutes, six days each week for sixteen years, 1928 to 1944; Saturday at midday for another fifteen years, 1945 to 1960. It had music, comedy, drama, and information about agriculture and homemaking, some of it intended for farm families, some of it about farming, intended for consumers. Especially during the period when it was a daily program, the "National Farm and Home Hour" was government's voice to farmers and agriculture's voice to the nation.

The "National Farm and Home Hour," the first network farm broadcast, was the brainchild of Frank E. Mullen, who had been the nation's first full-time farm director, on KDKA, from 1923 to 1926 before he joined the newly formed NBC and helped to open studios in Chicago. As the network's first agricultural director, given the title in 1928, he was seldom heard on the air, but he determined who would be heard. He was succeeded in 1934 by William

Everett Mitchell (L) made "Beautiful day in Chicago" famous during his nearly thirty years as announcer on the "National Farm and Home Hour." **Kenneth Gapen** (R) was USDA's principal spokesman 1946–1954.

E. Drips, who like Mullen had been raised in South Dakota and graduated from the University of Wisconsin. He had also been a farmer, farm magazine writer, county agent, and journalism teacher.

Music was an important part of the program, with an orchestra named "The Homesteaders" which started with eight pieces and gradually grew to twenty-four. A male quartet, "The Four Cadets," was a fixture for many years. Marches, hymns, and "standard classics" set the musical tone. Two women comics provided laughs with their homespun humor, "Mirandy of Persimmon Holler," who never was identified, and "Aunt Fanny," a character created by Fran Allison who became even better known on other radio and television programs. More humor was provided in the weekly reading of news items and editorials from a fictitious newspaper, "The Bugle," whose slogan was, "It Serves the Farmer Right."

The entertainment portion of the program usually originated in NBC's Chicago studios with USDA speakers and newsman H. R. Baukhage talking from Washington.

As major agricultural events were held, the "National Farm and Home Hour" was there: the International Livestock Exposition and the 4-H Club Congress in Chicago; the American Royal and the FFA convention in Kansas City; national conventions of the Farm Bureau, Grange, and Farmers' Union.

In the fifties Everett Mitchell made several overseas trips to Western Europe, South America, Asia, Australia, and Russia. He also made several "Farm and Home Hour" broadcasts during each trip.

From 1928 to 1934, the NBC network was growing, and increasing numbers of stations received the program and broadcast it because the program was scheduled in time controlled by NBC. Beginning in 1935, after the newly created Federal Communications Commission had told Congress that the broadcasting industry was serving the public interest well, NBC rewrote its contracts with affiliated stations. Among the changes, the "Farm and Home Hour" was moved from time controlled by the network and placed in time periods controlled by the individual stations. From that time on, NBC and USDA officials struggled to keep the program on enough stations so it could be heard everywhere in the nation.

In 1936 the Goodyear Company came to NBC waving money: the company wanted to sponsor a quarter hour of farm news to be chopped out of the "National Farm and Home Hour," but it was not interested in the Southeast or the Far West. Goodyear hired farm reporters in New York, Washington, and Chicago; NBC added reporters in the other two regions. The "Farm and Home Hour" was cut to forty-five minutes and remained at that length even after the Goodyear farm-news programs were discontinued in 1937.

When the Blue Network and the "Farm and Home Hour" were separated from NBC in 1942 (see Chapter 5), the most obvious change in the farm program was that Curly Bradley replaced Everett Mitchell as announcer. Behind the scenes Bob White succeeded Bill Drips as planner of the programs and agricultural director of the Blue Network. But affiliated stations and network officials became increasingly unhappy with a farm program which produced no revenue, and the daily version of the "National Farm and Home Hour" came to an end in June 1944.

In 1945, when the Blue Network had become the American Broadcasting Company, NBC and the USDA collaborated in getting the title "National Farm and Home Hour" assigned to the USDA, and the program was broadcast on the NBC radio network as a Saturday noon program, thirty minutes, sponsored by Allis Chalmers with Everett Mitchell's "Beeeyoutiful day" greeting, the Homesteaders orchestra, farm talks, and markets from the USDA. Bill Drips once again planned the programs, with the strong backing of the program's founder, Frank Mullen, who had been executive vice-president of NBC since 1940.

Drips's health forced his retirement in 1950, and he was succeeded by Paul Visser. Milton Bliss took over in 1952 and continued planning the weekly "Farm and Home Hour" until Allis Chalmers withdrew its sponsorship and the series ended in July 1960.

NBC did not completely turn its back on agriculture after the burial of the "National Farm and Home Hour." It hired John Lewis, a Maryland native who had worked as assistant to Secretary of Agriculture Ezra Benson to present each

Frank E. Mullen (L) inaugurated the "National Farm and Home Hour" in 1928, and **William E. Drips** (R) became director of the program in 1934. Photo taken in 1960, shortly after the program ended.

Saturday a weekly quarter hour program called "Farm Review." Lewis reported on highlights of agricultural news in Washington, actions of Congress, progress of legislation, and the latest from the USDA. At its peak, about seventy-five NBC stations carried the program, but the number had dwindled to around forty-five when the program ended in 1969.

"COLUMBIA'S COUNTRY JOURNAL." CBS entered network farm programming in 1939 with "Columbia's Country Journal," conducted by Charley Stookey, farm director of KMOX, Saint Louis. The first program, on Sunday afternoon, July 30, 1939, originated at the World's Poultry Congress in Cleveland, and in following weeks programs originated from state fairs in Kansas, Illinois, Tennessee, Minnesota, California, Iowa, and the Eastern States Exposition in Springfield, Massachusetts. After three months it was switched from Sunday afternoon to Saturday noon, and the roving stopped; Stookey broadcast most of the programs from KMOX: news, talks, interviews. Soon two field reporters were added, Chuck Worcester of WNAX, Yankton, South Dakota, and Woodrow Hattic of WWL, New Orleans.

By the fall of 1942, it was apparent that the most significant agricultural information was originating in government, and CBS decided to move "Country Journal" headquarters to Washington. Stookey wanted to stay with his daily programs in Saint Louis; so CBS hired Chuck Worcester to direct "Country Journal." Worcester had moved from WNAX to United Press in

Donald Lerch (L) interviewing Australia's Director General of Agriculture on Columbia's "Country Journal" in 1946.

Washington in 1941, and then became farm director of WEAF, New York, for about one year before joining CBS's "Country Journal" in November 1942.

In contrast to the "Farm and Home Hour," the guests on "Country Journal," as Worcester handled it, were on the program to answer questions, not to make speeches. About sixty-five to seventy stations carried the program each week. Worcester stayed with the program until 1946, when he moved to WMT, Cedar Rapids, Iowa.

Don Lerch took over direction of the program, with Mary Burnham and then Virginia Tatum as an associate. Lerch had been farm director at KDKA, Pittsburgh, worked for the USDA War Food Administration, and followed Worcester at WEAF, New York, before he joined CBS. By 1946 many of the CBS affiliated stations had their own farm directors, and Lerch set up a report schedule so each local director had a few minutes of glory on the network every month or two.

In 1952 CBS folded its "Country Journal" but assigned one of its regular newsmen, Claude Mahoney, to a feature called "CBS Farm News," a quarter hour on Saturday afternoon. It continued until 1955, when Mahoney switched from CBS to the Mutual Broadcasting System.

MUTUAL BROADCASTING SYSTEM. On the Mutual Network, Mahoney started "Mutual Farm News." For four years, 1955–1959, he reported ten minutes of farm news five mornings per week over approximately 500 stations, the biggest radio network in the country, and at the time the only nationwide daily farm program on the air.

Mahoney had grown up on an Indiana farm, and was a newspaperman in that state before he moved to Washington about 1935 as a reporter for the *Wall Street Journal*. Later he moved into radio on the CBS station in Washington, and then to the CBS network.

Mutual's interest in agriculture went into eclipse for eighteen years, but early in 1977 the network started a daily spot of farm news in its 12:30 P.M. program of general news, repeated three hours later in the West. It was sponsored by Ford, tractors division, on more than 400 stations.

The writer-announcer for the farm news spot was Bob Coker, formerly a newsman on stations in Oklahoma City, Dallas, and Indianapolis.

"AMERICAN FARMER." ABC was an offspring of NBC, and inherited some of NBC's people, programs, and philosophies. Shortly after NBC resurrected the "National Farm and Home Hour" as a weekly program, ABC came up with a competing program, "The American Farmer," which started on the first Saturday of January 1946. Both programs were aired for thirty minutes during the noon hour, Eastern time.

The program's producer, Robert B. White, had been a production director with NBC and for several years had the "National Farm and Home Hour" as one of his responsibilities. It was no surprise that the "American Farmer" was in the same mold as the "Farm and Home Hour." The new program had a friendly announcer, Chuck Bill; an orchestra; a country and western singer; a report from the USDA; and a main feature from an agricultural organization or a broadcast from some important agricultural event.

The program was never sponsored, and after eight years ABC decided it could no longer afford to pay for musicians and entertainers for a nonrevenue producing program. However, if the USDA wanted to produce the program, ABC would carry it. Jack Towers, of the USDA Radio Service, in effect became producer of "The American Farmer," and it continued each Saturday until 1969, nearly twenty-three years.

WIRE NEWS SERVICES. Several different organizations have provided agricultural wire news and market information to broadcasting stations in one form or another. Associated Press, United Press, International News Service, Transradio, Commodity News Service, and Reuters have been the principal ones over a period of a half century. United Press absorbed INS in 1952 and became United Press International.

AP, UP, and INS all started as services for newspapers. Transradio started in 1934, providing news only for radio stations, but it folded in 1951, the victim of competition from the older, better financed news services.

With the advent of the Roosevelt New Deal in 1933, UP assigned one of its staff members, Fred Bailey, to devote full time to reporting on agricultural developments in Washington. He wrote for both the newspaper and radio wires. In 1941 UP hired Chuck Worcester from WNAX, Yankton, to take over

This "American Farmer" broadcast in the late forties originated on the campus of Cornell University and included Robert White (second from the left), a farm magazine editor, a Cornell professor, and a dairy farmer.

Bernard Brenner (R) started reporting agriculture to United Press radio station clients in 1946, in Atlanta. Later, as agricultural correspondent in Washington he prepared reports for teletype and also made several daily broadcasts. (National Archives)

the radio portion of Bailey's duties. A year later Worcester was succeeded by Lee Hannify, and in 1948 Hannify was succeeded by Glenn Martz, another UP Washington reporter turned farm radio specialist. Martz was followed in 1952 by Bernard Brenner, a native of Brooklyn and agricultural journalism graduate of the University of Missouri, who went from college to army to the UP office in Atlanta. Brenner occupied the position for twenty-six years, at first writing for the UP radio wire only, and then for both radio and press wires. In 1970 his duties expanded and he became a broadcaster as well as writer, with a daily one-minute farm report which was included several times each day in UPI's voice news service. For several years, 1973–1977, he also recorded four one-minute news stories which were moved over the voice wire about 1:00 A.M. and recorded by several hundred stations for possible use by local farm broadcasters. He also wrote the long-established daily farm features, one for broadcasting stations, one for newspapers.

In 1978, Brenner resigned and UPI's daily farm services were taken over by Sonja Millegren, from Sioux Falls, daughter of a onetime farm editor of the *Argus Leader,* journalism graduate of the University of Missouri, with four years experience in general assignment reporting for UPI in the Washington area. Her daily schedule in 1979 included a newspaper column, radio feature, and a one-minute voice program.

ASSOCIATED PRESS. The Associated Press was started by daily newspapers, and a few years after radio became a reality, the newspapers refused to sell a news service to radio stations. When they did start, they set up a separate organization called Press Association to serve the radio stations. The agricultural pieces written by Ovid Martin, who was AP agricultural editor in Washington for many years, went to both newspaper and broadcast clients. The same was true of the words of Don Kendall, who succeeded Martin in the sixties. Their copy was transmitted by teletype.

On October 1, 1974 John Holliman joined Don Kendall in reporting and broadcasting agriculture from Washington, and his schedule promptly became more extensive than that of rival UPI. By 1979 Holliman's daily schedule included seven farm news broadcasts plus hourly reports on commodity prices. He made one report each day on cotton, another on cattle and hogs for the Midwest, another on cattle and calves for the western states. Each was fed to one or more of AP's regional offices and relayed to stations within the region. The total number of stations taking his reports increased from under 300 in 1974 to 730 in 1979.

Holliman said, "I've got names and telephone numbers of farmers producing every important commodity and in every agricultural region. I call some of them every day, to talk about weather, or prices, or government programs—whatever seems to be important news for farmers."

CNS NETWORK. The Commodity News Services, based in the Kansas City area, started in the fifties to provide teletype services for commodity brokers, then created "Farm Radio News," feeding a mixture of market reports and general farm news to broadcasters by teletype.

In 1977 CNS went into broadcasting with thirteen programs each day, mostly market news. CNS paid the line charges and tried to gain income by selling one commercial announcement in each program. There would be another slot which the stations might sell.

Stations that subscribed to CNS teletype service promptly yelled "Foul!" "You're competing for the same advertising dollars that we need to stay on the air." The broadcasts came to an end in 1979.

REUTERS. Reuters (ROYters) has been gathering and reporting news around the world for a long time, and in the United States in recent years it has offered U.S. clients a specialized service in agriculture, including daily trading on agricultural markets and reports from the USDA and other government agencies on production, prices, imports, exports. Reuters has stuck to the print medium, and as of 1978 had shown no inclination to get into broadcasting.

HELMING REPORT. William C. Helming of Kansas City likes to live dangerously. Each day he predicts tomorrow's prices of grains and livestock. He started doing it for makers of feed and breakfast food, for meat packers and food store chains, but in August 1977 he offered his service, predicting tomorrow's prices, to broadcasters. He hired Ralph Seeley, a veteran broadcaster who also had been a commodities broker, to develop the broadcast service.

Each morning Seeley picks the brains of a team of six economic analysts, getting their predictions of the next day's prices at Kansas City for wheat, corn, soybeans, fed cattle, and hogs. By 10:30 A.M. he has whipped the predictions into a report that runs two minutes, forty-five seconds, and has recorded it on a telephone answering service. Each station is assigned a time to call and record the report off the line and then broadcast it whenever it fits into the station's schedule. After two years the service reported fifty-nine station clients in twelve states, from Virginia to Montana, from Minnesota to Texas. Each month, the Helming organization reports on the accuracy of its predictions and they usually range between 76 and 84 percent.

FARM RADIO REPORT. Farm Radio Report went on the air in November 1978 as a nationwide, free, recorded news service offered by *Farm Journal* magazine and announced by Erny Tannen, former owner of farm radio station, WDVM, Pocomoke City, Maryland.

Each week farm directors and news directors of about two thousand radio stations in farm areas received a listing of the daily subjects, usually one story of national significance and another dealing with a single crop or geographic area. If he was interested in the day's story, the broadcaster would dial a toll-free telephone number, identify his station, and then record the fifty-second story. At *Farm Journal* headquarters in Philadelphia, Tannen kept a record of each day's calls and said that during the first year at least 300 calls were made each day with a high figure of 490. About one-fifth of the calls were made by farm broadcasters who belonged to the NAFB. One study on usage showed that every station that called on a particular day used the recorded story at least once and most used it more than once.

Technically, the news service was offered by FARMedia Corporation in which *Farm Journal* and Tannen were partners. While the magazine hoped to get its money's worth in the form of new subscribers, the corporation received some revenue from grower associations and other agribusiness organizations looking for publicity.

"AGRICULTURE USA." From national network farm radio it's logical to turn to national network farm television, and with it comes a change in tune, from melody to silence. If we stick to the simon-pure definition of "network," there never has been a farm program series on network television.

In the early days of TV, networks and advertisers alike counted the costs of production and time for live programs and turned away.

The next best thing has proved to be programs on film or videotape. The USDA's "Across the Fence" (changed to "A Better Way") and "Down to Earth" have been syndicated to stations for many years, and stations have used them because the programs were interesting enough, and the station management felt virtuous in presenting them, usually in public service time.

In 1958 American Cyanamid Company laid about a half million dollars on the line for six months of a weekly quarter hour program, "Farm Newsreel," produced by Martin Andrews, with time purchased on fifty-two stations. It was a short flight that ended in a crash landing.

Around that same time, two or three other venturesome souls tried to

John Stearns (R),
producer of "Ag-
USA," learns about
wine making at the
nation's oldest winery,
in California.

develop and sell similar programs. I had a small part in one effort called "Cross Country," backed by Chicago film producer Fred Niles and involving Bill Mason, Lloyd Burlingham, and Tex Barron. We produced a few trial run films that filled us with joy and hope but left stations and sponsors cold. As I recall, Niles lost upward of $100,000. I know of two other efforts that also fell on their faces.

Now for the good news. John A. Stearns, who was a successful writer and producer for radio and TV in New York and Hollywood, set out in 1961 to put together a program "that would tell city people, especially youngsters, about agriculture and agricultural people."

He was with NBC in Hollywood at the time and his first program "Agriculture USA," was seen only on KNBC. It took five years for the weekly half hour program to break even, with stations buying the program from Stearns's producing firm and selling time to local advertisers. In the late seventies it was seen on about sixty stations.

Part of each program originated in the studio, and often included "Agri-quiz" with a panel of 4-H or Future Farmer members firing questions at a rancher, an agronomist, or perhaps the secretary of agriculture. Each program included action scenes, such as a calf being born or following a load of hogs from farm to supermarket. Occasionally there was a fun scene, such as a goat milking contest, grape stomping, or the Paul Bunyan Olympics.

John Stearns was the program's host, and was assisted by Bill Snyder and

Don Ross. Always in the background was his wife, Mary Kay, who kept saying during the five years when "Agriculture USA" was losing money, "You believe in it; stay with it."

"U.S. FARM REPORT." One good success story deserves another. In 1975 Orion Samuelson of WGN launched a half hour weekly program, "U.S. Farm Report," which in its first three years had been carried by sixty to ninety stations from Virginia to California, Texas to North Dakota, with most of them in the Midwest. Samuelson planned the program, acted as master of ceremonies, and conducted most of the interviews, some of them with agricultural people passing through Chicago, and some with people visited in their home territories. Occasionally Samuelson called on fellow farm broadcasters to shoot and narrate stories from their areas: a champion dairy cow in Indiana, the wheat and drought situation in Kansas in 1976, a cotton story from Louisiana, grazing on government land in Utah, a tobacco story from North Carolina, and so on.

On the business side, the program was the property of the corporation that owns WGN and of which Samuelson was a vice-president. International Harvester sponsored the program by paying WGN a production fee. In return, IH received three of the six commercial slots in each half hour program, and IH designated the markets where it would like to have the program shown. Then it was up to WGN to barter with the station to carry the program. "We provide you with the thirty-minute program each week; we charge you nothing; we pay you nothing. There are three slots for commercials in each program which you may sell to advertisers."

The differences in business arrangements between Stearns's and Samuelson's programs were these: Stearns collected his money from the stations; Samuelson's corporation collected its money from a sponsor. A station which carried the Stearns program could sell all the commercial time in the program; one which carried the Samuelson program could sell only half the commercial spots.

AMERICAN FARM BUREAU FEDERATION. Almost as soon as Chicago had a radio station, in 1922, Sam Guard, information director of the American Farm Bureau Federation, helped to start a daily radio program for farmers on KYW, and AFBF speakers took part in it for several years. The organization had a once a month spot on the "National Farm and Home Hour" from its start in 1928 until the program ended as a daily series in 1944.

In 1955 Tex (his real name) Barron became the federation's radio-TV director, and he started producing taped interviews with Farm Bureau leaders and sending them to a selected list of radio farm broadcasters across the country. In 1960 Jack Angell, an NBC news reporter, moved into Barron's spot and started two tape services which were continued by Mel Woell, 1967; Patrick Batts, 1974; and John Lewis, 1977. "Newstape," a weekly service, was made

Tex Barron

up of a pair of two-minute reports by AFBF spokesmen, one in Chicago and one in Washington; it was aimed at the farm audience and went to about 230 stations. "Across the Land" was a monthly program, approximately fourteen minutes in length and aimed at consumers, with several short reports by Farm Bureau people. An exemplary program told consumers how fire ants affected farmers, and about the importance of baling wire, the latest trend in food prices, and the proposed boycott on lettuce and grapes. Lewis also started a monthly TV program on film which was used by as many as 82 stations, but it had a rather short life.

Mel Woell started a two-minute daily program for consumers called "Insight," used by 140 stations in 1976. Some of the subjects strayed away from agriculture: in one week "Insight" observed that the tourist tower at Gettysburg was not unsightly; members of Congress receive a lot of benefits besides their paychecks; and lunchstand hamburgers and pizzas are fairly nutritious.

NATIONAL GRANGE. When Judy Massabny, information director of the National Grange, wanted to start a syndicated radio program to carry the Grange message to a nationwide audience, no money was available in the National Grange budget. So she turned to the 500 county-wide Pomona Grange groups with a proposal: "The National Grange will produce a weekly radio program and send it to your favorite radio station if you will do two things: one, persuade the station to carry the program; and two, contribute $10 a month to pay the cost of production and distribution." More than 50 Pomona Granges agreed to cooperate, and the program got under way late in 1975. A year later a monthly service of five one-minute spots was added, intended for use by radio farm directors.

Under Massabny's supervision in Washington, D.C., the weekly and monthly programs have been written and recorded across the continent in Colfax, Washington, by Adrian DeVries, owner of KCLX, Colfax, and a loyal Grange member. He has rushed the tapes back to Grange headquarters where they have been duplicated and distributed by a commercial recording firm: the weeklies to fifty-seven stations, the monthly spots to forty-five farm directors at the end of 1978.

The contacts between local Grange officials and station personnel have led to many local programs by Grange spokesmen. In many instances, says Massabny, "the spin-off has been as valuable as the original series."

NATIONAL FARMERS UNION. The National Farmers Union took a radio flier in 1970 and it flew for about four years, from the union's Washington office, to about 300 farm broadcasters across the country. Joe O'Neill, a veteran Washington broadcaster, put together two weekly taped programs: one, a news summary of agricultural news called "NFU Report," about four and one-half minutes long; the other, "NFU Opinion," a two and one-half minute commentary. Steve Radabaugh assisted part of the time.

The tapes received enough use to make them worthwhile, in O'Neill's opinion, but the people who parceled out the money decided otherwise after four years; so O'Neill took a job with a congressman.

NATIONAL FARMERS ORGANIZATION. The National Farmers Organization in the sixties and seventies built up a radio tape "network" of more than a thousand stations for a three-per-week program originally called "Here's Allen," and since 1973, "Here's Info."

Phil Allen

It started with one weekly program on one TV station. In 1959 NFO's president, Oren Staley, hired Phillip A. Allen as reporter-announcer and bought time on Channel 9 in Sioux City, Iowa, for Allen to tell the NFO story. As NFO got more members and more money, Allen developed a "milk route" of TV stations in the Iowa towns of Sioux City and Ottumwa, and Saint Joseph and Jefferson City, Missouri, on which he made weekly, live appearances in time paid for by the NFO. Along with these appearances he began making tapes for radio stations, and by 1966 had tapes going to 45 stations. Their lengths ranged from five to fifteen minutes. By that time, most TV stations had wiped out farm programs from their schedules. Allen and W. W. "Butch" Swaim, NFO's director of information, decided to drop TV and concentrate on radio. They built their own recording studios in NFO headquarters in Corning, Iowa. Swaim set 1,000 stations as the goal, and mobilized NFO members to persuade and cajole local stations into carrying the three-per-week NFO programs that would be in tape format, four and one-half minutes long.

Some local organizations found NFO could be most persuasive in paid time and by 1975 about 20 percent of the programs were sponsored. The rest were carried as public service. Swaim died two weeks before the 1,000th station was added to the list. He had passed the radio torch to Don Mach, who handled production and distribution of the weekly tapes with Phil Allen, who continued as the perennial reporter and interviewer, aided by Kathy Quinn.

EARL BUTZ PROGRAM. The "Earl Butz Program" added some political pizzazz to the airwaves from September 1977 until it was terminated around the end of 1979.

Butz was secretary of agriculture in the early seventies under Presidents Nixon and Ford, and when he returned to home base as vice-president emeritus of Purdue University in 1976 he was persuaded to share his thoughts about agriculture not only by making speeches but also in a radio series. The programs were five per week, five minutes in length, with three minutes of Earl Butz commentary, plus two slots in which local stations could sell commercial announcements. Butz recorded the programs ten or fifteen at a time at a Lafayette, Indiana, radio station. The duplicated tapes were distributed to approximately fifty radio stations by the same organization that handled Ronald Reagan's radio commentaries. A few of the stations scheduled the Butz program as part of their farm program, but most classed it as public affairs and ran it in morning or evening "drive-time."

"TOWN AND COUNTRY TIME." One of the earliest regional network farm programs was "Town and Country Time," on the Mississippi Valley Network, headquartered in Minneapolis. It started in the fall of 1945 and continued for about one year. In pattern, it was much like the daily "National Farm and Home Hour," which recently had ended as a daily show, with music and other entertainment, farm news, and speakers. It was the brainchild of John Boler, head of the Mississippi Valley Network, and the actual director of the program was John Merrifield, a veteran of farm programming at WLS, WLW, and WHAS. The program was a full hour, 6:00–7:00 each morning, and during its one-year lifetime it was carried by eighty to ninety stations, mostly in states adjoining the Mississippi River, from its source to the delta country.

STATE AND REGIONAL NETWORKS. Many of the high power stations that had their own farm programs in earlier years discontinued them in the sixties. In their place a large number of networks of smaller stations were built up to provide daily farm programs. These are described in each state section.

Chapter Eight

Alabama

EXTENSION. At Auburn University the first voice radio transmitter was built by engineering students and dedicated February 21, 1923. To hold the antenna, students felled a forty-foot pine tree, trimmed it down to a pole, and mounted it on top of Broun Hall, the engineering building. The student-chosen call letters were WMAV—"We Make a Voice." The station had 1,500 watts power—that is, when all the tubes were working.

Extension editor P. O. Davis was manager of the station, which was on the air about ten hours each week, and much of the broadcast time was devoted to weather, market reports, crop estimates and other information for farmers.

In 1926 the station had a more powerful transmitter and a new set of call letters, WAPI, for Alabama Polytechnic Institute. In 1929 the station was moved to Birmingham, and in 1932 it was leased to a commercial operator but with time reserved for a daily agricultural program each noon. The program continued until the mid-forties. Louis Brackeen, who had helped establish the first farm programs on WSB, Atlanta, conducted the programs in the early years. Harwood Hull, a native of Puerto Rico who spoke Spanish and English equally well, took over in late 1937 when Brackeen became extension editor and Davis became director of the extension service. Hull quickly acquired an appropriate Alabama accent and a portable disc recorder, which he used to make on-the-spot interviews with farmers and agricultural leaders for his programs on WAPI. He then developed package programs which he circulated to fourteen stations over the state. Hull returned to Puerto Rico in 1942 and Jim Romine took over the WAPI and syndicated programs during the war years.

In the seventies the Alabama extension service provided Alabama radio listeners with several weekly tape recorded service programs, put together by Kenneth Copeland. One program, "Special," consisted of a four-minute talk about insects and how to control them, and a four-minute report on best food buys; it was mailed each Monday to thirty-eight stations. Another program called "Daily" contained five four-minute programs with general farm news, timely suggestions for farmers and homemakers, and 4-H club activities. This was sent each week to seventy-eight stations and to several county agents who have regular broadcasts. Fifty-one stations received a tape with ten short messages of the how-to-do-it variety, thirty seconds or sixty seconds long, mailed every two weeks. A similar program consisted of brief announcements on gardening and food buying by extension specialists; it was mailed every two weeks to fifty-two stations.

Lloyd Yerby, extension TV specialist, provided videotape programs used each Saturday on five TV stations, in Montgomery, Birmingham, Huntsville, Mobile, and Anniston, with segments tailored to each region. Yerby also supplied a weekly half hour program called "Dixie Digest" carried on the Alabama Public Television Network and shown later on four other stations. In addition, occasional public service radio and TV spots were provided, as well as movies, slides, and copy on spot news stories.

County extension workers throughout the state have made extensive use of the local radio stations, some of them continually for many years. G. A. Peasant started broadcasting a weekly program over WNUZ, Talladega, in 1950, continued it until he transferred to Ashland in 1972, and arranged for a weekly taped program over WANL.

ALABAMA FARM BUREAU. John Matthews, director of broadcast relations for the Alabama Farm Bureau, produces a daily five-minute report on agriculture carried by the Alabama Radio News Network to its forty stations. Matthews said about television, "In effect, we serve as agriculture reporters for the state's television stations. In 1975 we produced 12 agricultural feature stories and more than 100 spot news stories for Alabama's seventeen commercial stations. We have complete 16 mm sound on film equipment, fully equipped editing room, sound recording studio and radio production control room."

JESSE CULP. Around 1946 Jesse Culp started broadcasting without pay for WJHO while he was a student at Alabama Polytechnic Institute, but he worked weekends for pay on WKLF. When he was graduated in 1948, he went to work for the state Department of Agriculture and started a twice daily program of market reports on a network of ten stations. He moved to WAVU, Albertville, in 1950 and started a two-hour farm and home program, the first commercial farm program in the state. In 1952 WAVU became the parent station in an Alabama network that grew over the years to eighteen stations. In the early seventies, Culp became owner of the daily network program, which began as a full hour and gradually shrank to five minutes a day.

Culp's only assistant through more than a quarter century has been a rooster named "Static." He was only a sound effect, but years ago a listener was inspired to paint a portrait of him, big, white, heavily wattled, and crowing. The portrait adorns Jesse's studio in Albertville.

GENE RAGAN, WOOF RADIO AND WTVY-TV DOTHAN. In spite of what philosophers say about the difficulty of serving two masters, Gene Ragan, of Dothan, Alabama, has been doing it for years and making it pay. He runs the daily farm program on both WOOF radio and WTVY-TV, which are under different ownership. He draws no salary from either station, but earns his living from a commission on sales during 205 minutes of farm programs each week plus a weekly conservation and wildlife program, and the fifty cow beef herd on his farm near Dothan.

Ragan started broadcasting while he was a Georgia county agent, going across the Chattahoochee River once each week to broadcast over WOOF, in Dothan, Alabama. In 1953 he became farm director of the station and then of the new TV station there, WTVY: at first he had only a morning program, then morning and noon. Later he developed a conservation and wildlife TV program shown on Saturday evenings.

For twelve years he lived in Georgia and drove thirty miles each morning across the state line, but in 1966 he bought a farm near Dothan and built up his beef herd.

CRAWFORD "ROCK" ROQUEMORE. Farmers in Alabama who listened to Crawford Roquemore over a period of forty years or so might not have been sure who was paying him, but they knew he was working for farmers. When they first heard him, beginning about 1938 over WBAM, Montgomery, he was a livestock market reporter for the USDA. In 1953 he resigned from the USDA and became the full-time farm director of WBAM and its sister TV station. With 50,000 watts behind it, his voice could be heard over most of Alabama for a dozen years. "Rock" went back on the USDA market news payroll from 1965 to 1970; left the government's employ a second time, moved back to Alabama, and soon started a daily farm service on WTUB, Troy, from 1970 to 1975. For several months before his death in 1978 he had provided a daily five-minute summary of farm news on the Alabama News Network.

Chapter Nine

Arizona

FARM BROADCASTING in Arizona for a good many years consisted largely of broadcasts by Ernest Douglass, editor of *Arizona Farmer* magazine, over KOY in Phoenix. Both magazine and station were owned by Burridge D. Butler, who also owned WLS and *Prairie Farmer* in Chicago.

Joe McClelland, now retired to the mountains of his native Colorado, recalled that when he became extension editor at the University of Arizona in 1947, he rewrote each newspaper release for radio and sent these stories to every radio station in the state.

In the fall of 1954 a U of A senior, Robert Hutchinson, conducted a television experiment as a project for his journalism class. He produced "Across the Fence" fifteen minutes each Saturday at 4:30 P.M. over KTAR-TV, in Mesa, about ninety miles from Tucson. At the end of the series, Hutchinson concluded that the time and dollars for writing, rehearsing, and presenting the programs made television too costly to be practical for the extension service.

About that same time, in the mid-fifties, the director of extension appointed an information specialist to be stationed in the Maricopa County Extension office in Phoenix. Robert Halvorson was appointed to the job and was still there twenty-four years later, conducting daily radio programs and several television programs each week on Phoenix stations.

In the seventies, George Alstad, assistant extension editor, syndicated a series of taped radio programs twice each week to twelve stations over the state. His efforts plus those of Halvorson added up to 1,636 radio broadcasts during 1975.

John Burnham, another assistant editor, started a series of ten-minute segments once each week on a Tucson TV station. Editor Gordon Graham reported 911 TV broadcasts during 1975 by staff members on all Arizona stations, most of them segments of five minutes or less.

One of the most successful programs by extension workers was a TV garden program, a half hour each Monday evening on KUAT-TV, Tucson. It developed a big audience, but after twenty-six weeks the featured horticulturist, Dr. Charles Sacamano, reached the same conclusion Bob Hutchinson had reached twenty years earlier: "It takes too much time."

In the sixties and seventies, Johnny Linn conducted an early morning farm program on KTAR, Phoenix, which had a statewide audience. In 1976 Linn moved to WMT, Cedar Rapids, Iowa, for a two-year stay.

George Gatley moved in 1977 from farm director of KAPR, Douglas, in the southeast corner of Arizona, to KBLU, Yuma, in the southwest corner. Soon he developed a farm program also on KYEL-TV, with listeners and viewers in Arizona and California. In 1979 he branched out with a network of radio stations in Parker, Phoenix, Tucson, Coolidge, Prescott, and Douglas, Arizona, plus one in Brawley, California.

Other farm directors in Arizona in 1978 included John Lyon, KAPR, Douglas; Cece White, KJJJ, Phoenix; and Mark Reynolds, on both KVOY and KJOK, Yuma.

Chapter Ten

Arkansas

BROADCASTING to farmers in Arkansas seems to have started in the mid-twenties when Director of Extension Dan T. Gray instructed each county agent to submit a fifteen-minute "radio paper" each week to extension editor Gus Oehm. Kenneth Roy, who took over the editor's job in 1927 and distributed the "radio papers" to Arkansas radio stations, recalls that under Gray's orders a county agent who failed to submit his paper on time was sent a curt and effective telegram, "Either submit your radio paper or your resignation."

About 1934, with some additional money from AAA funds, Roy was able to hire an assistant editor, Anna Jim Holman, stationed in Little Rock where most of the state extension staff were located. The daily scripts were changed from fifteen-minute papers to a series of news reports; combining items from county agents, the state extension staff, and the USDA. In 1935 they went to eight stations in Arkansas and four others outside the state. On four Arkansas stations the reports were presented by county extension workers, who mixed in their own announcements and news items.

Like many other land grant colleges in the early twenties, the University of Arkansas started its own radio station, KARK, Fayetteville. But the university sold the station to commercial interests which moved the station to Little Rock and in 1940 hired Bob Buice as farm director.

Dave Ryker succeeded Ken Roy as extension editor and arranged that radio and TV stations were amply supplied with information from the extension service.

In 1974 the news director of KATV in Little Rock offered the extension staff the opportunity to do a two-minute spot each evening on the station's prime time news program 6:00–7:00 P.M. The extension's TV specialist John Philpott took on the assignment of developing the news spot.

BOB BUICE, KARN, ARKANSAS RADIO NETWORK. Probably the first thing that most people notice about Bob Buice is his voice. It is friendly, big, round, and rumbles upward from somewhere below the knees. I wasn't at all surprised to learn that Buice entered radio back in 1936 by winning a singing contest which led to an announcer's job on KGHI, Little Rock. Soon afterward Buice started a program for farmers. He had grown up on a farm, a sideline of his father who was a country doctor. In 1940 Buice moved to KARK, and farm broadcasting became virtually his full-time job, with programs in the morning

Bob Buice, 1952

and at noon, until the station was sold and the call letters changed to KARN. With that change in 1965 Buice headed up a network program called the "Delta Farm Show," fifteen minutes every morning at 6:15, and farm commodity prices four times each day on the Arkansas Radio Network News programs. In 1974 the network's broadcasts to farmers were set up as a separate enterprise with nine programs every day, each with a different lineup of stations, numbering from fourteen to thirty-four, fed by telephone line.

In 1975 Buice started a special service for cotton growers called "Moth Alert." Each day during the summer the Arkansas extension entomologist provided him with a two-minute report on the prevalence of the moths which produce cotton boll worms, warning cotton growers to spray with a chemical ovacide (egg killer). Buice put the daily messages on his network of thirty-four stations in the Delta three times each morning. Following these announcements, a chemical manufacturer advertised its ovacide product.

Buice was an early member of the farm broadcasters organization and served as its historian for many years. He made available many of the facts in this book.

MARVIN VINES, KAAY, LITTLE ROCK. Marvin Vines was chased out of his native Arkansas by his big brother, Austin. It happened this way: both brothers earned agricultural degrees from the University of Arkansas and ultimately both became county agents. When Austin was promoted to director of extension, the rules said his brother could not work for him. About that time in the early fifties a consumer education project was starting up with five state extension services cooperating and a headquarters in Kansas City. Vines was put in charge.

An important part of his job as consumer educator was broadcasting, and he developed a schedule of ten radio and four TV shows per week on several Kansas City stations. The two principal farm broadcasters in town, Phil Evans, KMBC, and Jack Jackson, KCMO, told Vines, "Hey, you're good. Why don't you go commercial?" Shortly after, he became farm director of KTHS, which had moved from Hot Springs to Little Rock and had received a boost in power to 50,000 watts, on the strength of plans to provide service to farmers.

Vines was assigned a half hour at 6:00 A.M. and twenty-five minutes at noon, a schedule that was maintained through two changes of ownership and a change in call letters to KAAY. From 1957 to 1964 Vines had a daily television show on KTHS-TV, a quarter hour at noon, but it came to an end when the station was sold.

He held several offices in the National Association of Farm Broadcasters and served as president in 1977.

Marvin Vines was killed when a tractor overturned as he was clearing land on his farm near Little Rock on May 1, 1979. He was sixty-eight years of age.

The KAAY farm programs continued, with John Philpott, longtime radio editor of the Arkansas extension service, as agricultural director.

In 1954 Bill Hadley was farm director of KRTV, Little Rock, and he reported one incident that makes a small note in history. He ran a four-minute film provided by the USDA on a rare but highly contagious hog disease known as vesicular exanthema (VE) disease. It showed that hogs with VE didn't like to walk; they limped. One farmer near Little Rock saw the show and recognized that his hogs had been acting just that way. A telephone call brought out a government veterinarian who confirmed that the hogs had VE. The next day the farm and its hogs were put under quarantine to prevent spread of the disease.

Johnny Holmes was another farm broadcaster who served a short term on Little Rock stations, KATV and KLRA, radio, in the fifties, after a stint on WMT, Cedar Rapids, Iowa.

Other Arkansas stations with farm programs in the late seventies included KWCK, Searcy; KGUS, Hot Springs; KDDA, Dumas; and KMLA, Ashdown.

Chapter Eleven

California

CALIFORNIA has long been our leading agricultural state. In recent years it also has led all others in population but it has lagged behind some other states in using radio to carry information to farmers. The earliest farm broadcast in the state was a daily series started in 1928 by M. B. Rounds, county agent in Los Angeles County, a county that at the time produced more dollars worth of farm products than any other county in the United States. He and his staff followed a daily schedule of broadcasts until 1934 when they began to participate twice each week in the "Western Farm and Home Hour" on NBC's western network.

Several other county agents began regular broadcasts in the late thirties: Frank Beyschlag, in Imperial County, was on the air four days a week over KXO, El Centro; and E. L. Stanley, in Sacramento, started a daily series over KFBK.

At the University of California, Hale Sparks, a radio director, began a series of weekly broadcasts in 1937 called "The University Explorer," which he continued for many years. It included many reports on agriculture along with other activities of the university and its research workers.

HENRY SCHACHT, UNIVERSITY OF CALIFORNIA, KPO, KGO. In the thirties the "National Farm and Home Hour" had a policy of originating once a month on the campus of a land grant college. When the University of California's turn came in 1938, Henry Schacht, the youngest member of the university's publicity staff drew the short straw. He conducted rehearsals, wrote the continuity, and did some of the announcing. It turned out to be a good show. Later he conducted a series of public service broadcasts on KPO, the NBC station in San Francisco. This led to a job as farm director of KPO in 1942 where he started the "Farmers' Digest," a half hour program, six days per week. It was sponsored by the Standard Oil Company of California for sixteen years. While he was doing the program each morning, Schacht also started a quarter hour program at noon, sponsored for many years by the Ralston Purina Company, and then by the Bank of America; and a five-minute show, sponsored by an egg cooperative. In 1958 KPO management proposed moving "Farmers' Digest" a half hour earlier, to 5:30 A.M.; so Henry Schacht and Standard Oil moved the program to KGO, also 50,000 watts. The morning show expanded from thirty to fifty-five minutes each day and took on a new name, "Standard Farm Reporter."

Henry Schacht

Schacht also started "Pacific Farm News," a quarter hour program at noon, sponsored by Pacific Gas and Electric Company. And to further demonstrate that farm broadcasters sometimes do strange things under the influence of money, he took on a news program Sunday nights at 11:00 P.M.

About that same time, in 1959, he started writing a semiweekly column, the "Farm Reporter," for the *San Francisco Chronicle,* which he continued through 1979 as a sideline through several different jobs.

For several years Schacht led one trip each year for California families to visit the Orient, South America, Europe, Australia, and New Zealand. He was called on to serve as faculty member at foreign training schools for agricultural workers, conducted by the United Nations Food and Agriculture Organization.

Late in 1960, after eighteen years of rising at 4:30 A.M., he left broadcasting to return to the University of California to coordinate an information program among state and country agricultural workers. Since 1965 he has been vice-president and secretary of the California Canners and Growers Association.

KFI, LOS ANGELES. In 1935 the U.S. Weather Bureau office in Los Angeles and KFI started a special frost warning service for citrus growers, and kept refining and improving this service through the years. They did this mainly by dividing the southern part of the state into approximately a dozen zones and providing a forecast and probable low temperature for each. During fall and winter, when freezing temperatures were most critical, the station set aside a brief period each night for the frost warning. For many years, the chief forecaster, Floyd Young, did the report direct from the bureau's office. Although the citrus areas have changed and the thousands of acres that were orchards are now homes for millions of people, the frost warning service was still a regular feature on KFI radio in 1977.

KFI carried the "Western Farm and Home Hour" until it came to an end in 1938. In 1944 KFI hired its first farm director, Nelson McIninch, who had been reared on a farm in Nemaha County, Nebraska, went to high school in Kansas City, Mo., and migrated westward. McIninch established morning and noon programs of farm news, markets, weather, and reports by county agents in southern California.

In 1951 when Jim Todd, the new KFI staff announcer, met McIninch, the farm director, they recognized each other as former schoolmates in Kansas City. There came a day in 1953 when suddenly McIninch was no longer farm director of KFI. That was on a Friday and the following Monday morning Todd went on the air with the KFI "Farm and Home Hour" and later the same day with the "Noontime Farm Reporter." Soon after he left KFI, McIninch joined KNX as farm director and went on the air earlier in the morning than Todd and came on again at noon just as Todd was concluding his program on KFI. The friendly competition continued until 1966, when McIninch left broadcasting to go into college administrative work.

Todd said, "At the start I hardly knew what an orange tree or avocado tree looked like; my problem was to keep my ignorance from showing." He got growers, county agents, and experiment station people to do the talking, visited all the fairs in southern California, and served as KFI's farm director until 1974.

In his more than two decades as farm director of KFI, Jim Todd watched housing developments take over the citrus groves and vegetable fields of Los Angeles and the vicinity, causing his programs and schedules to change. The noon program was canceled. The morning farm show was moved earlier and earlier until in the seventies, Todd was going on the air at 4:00 A.M. and off at 5:30 A.M. It was too early for his California listeners and in 1974 Jim resigned. Later, he described the last years as "a half-assed farm program and disc jockey show."

Todd left as the station was changing owners and managers. Dick Sinclair, the station's business-finance reporter and part owner of a lemon grove, volunteered to take over the farm programs, but he proposed some changes that the new KFI management approved. The program would run 5:00–6:00 A.M.

Sinclair lined up nine county agents to provide news and advice, usually taped over the phone, every week. He taped interviews with state extension workers and researchers at the agricultural college at Davis and devoted a good portion of the program to home gardening and consumer information. There was music, too, mostly popular and modern.

And every evening in winter, KFI broadcast the frost warnings from the Weather Bureau, just as it had done since 1935.

McCLATCHEY, KFBK, SACRAMENTO. The McClatchey family was firmly established in the newspaper business in the interior cities of California; so when radio came along, they started stations in Sacramento, Fresno, and Modesto to match their *Bee* newspapers. In the fifties they added TV stations in Sacramento and Fresno.

Agriculture is important in all those areas; and for more than thirty years, Hamilton Hintz was agricultural director of the McClatchey papers and the broadcasting stations. Each one operated with considerable independence, but Hintz kept a watchful eye on all of them from his headquarters in Sacramento.

The day-to-day broadcasts on KFBK, Sacramento, were handled by Ray Rodgers who had started as farm director of KMJ, Fresno in 1944, and two years later was asked to move to Sacramento to take over the KFBK farm programs that Charles Marshall had been conducting. Rodgers conducted morning and noon farm programs and twice each day switched to the federal-state market news office for reports on prices for livestock and the innumerable vegetable and fruits produced in the Sacramento area. In the seventies the market reports were cut back to a weekly summary on Saturday mornings.

Hintz also put together another weekly program that ran for over thirty years, the "McClatchey Farm Review." The program received input from stations in Fresno, Modesto, and Sacramento and was carried by all three stations. This too came to an end in the seventies. But Rodgers continued his morning and noon programs of farm news on KFBK as he had done since 1946.

The McClatchey station in Modesto, KBEE, came along in the early fifties, a few years after the stations in Sacramento and Fresno. Bert Hartcastle and then Joly Boynton served as farm director for this station during much of the time until the seventies.

FRESNO. In 1948 KMJ hired Wally Erickson, a Minnesotan, as farm director. The programs consisted of interviews with farmers and an abundance of California market reports provided by the federal-state market news service and the state livestock association.

Two years later, Erickson was lured across town to start a program on KFRE; KMJ hired Ed Sturgeon as farm director, and the rivalry began. On

KFRE Erickson expanded his farm programs from a quarter hour to an hour and a half each day, divided between early morning and noon, and expanded to a four man staff. His assistants at various times included Fred Milnes, Don Upton, Jim Miller, and Paul Nelson.

Sturgeon held forth as KMJ farm director from 1950 to 1962; and when KMJ-TV went on the air in 1953, he started a TV farm show. The competition for audience and advertisers was intense for about ten years, but in 1960 KFRE changed ownership and the station cut back on the time it devoted to farm programs. Erickson's staff was reduced to two, and then to one, Erickson himself. In 1969 he left KFRE and opened an agricultural public relations firm in Fresno.

It was ironic that the year KFRE changed hands and became less agriculturally oriented, Erickson was serving as president of the National Association of Farm Broadcasters.

Sturgeon was followed at KMJ in 1962 by John Weidert from the extension radio service of the University of Illinois. He had two assistants during his ten years at KMJ: Ed Simmons, an Iowa State University graduate who had been a broadcaster with the Massachusetts Extension Service and WMT, Cedar Rapids, Iowa; and Bill Allison, from WKAR, East Lansing, Michigan; WKJG, Fort Wayne, Indiana; and KONG, Visalia, California. Weidert went to the USDA in 1972 where he became assistant to the secretary of agriculture. Allison became farm director.

Although the KMJ farm team had been reduced in the seventies from three men to two, Allison estimated that he and his assistants, first Don Upton and then Keith Eldridge, had more than doubled the farm programs in four years. Probably the most popular was a daily called "Garden Spot," at 6:00 A.M. and 8:30 A.M. during morning "drive time." On KMJ-TV, Allison and Eldridge presented ten minutes of farm news, weather and markets each day at noon.

Besides their daily programs, they developed several documentary films. One was called "Big Farm-Small Farm"; it wound up with Allison reciting The Farmer's Creed: "We, the willing—led by the unknowing in Washington—are doing the impossible for the ungrateful. We have done so much for so long with so little that we're now qualified to do anything for nothing."

In 1977 Allison left radio to concentrate on the TV farm program and in 1978 he became manager of the county Farm Bureau. Richard Rodriquez then became KMJ's farm director.

KARK, SACRAMENTO. Ray Rodgers and KFBK provided the only voice speaking to farmers in the Sacramento area for a good many years; but in 1970 Walt Shaw started a farm show on KARK, a full hour in early morning, providing competition. Not long after, Shaw also presented a weekly half hour on KXTV-TV. The program was strictly public service, and Shaw was gladly doing it without pay! In 1975 Shaw was made program director of KARK but continued his agribusiness programs on radio and on TV.

KENNETH R. JOHNSON, KEEN, SAN JOSÉ. Kenneth R. Johnson, of KEEN, was another of the very few farm broadcasters who daily produced a farm program just for pleasure and without pay.

In 1979 Johnson was a farmer, real estate salesman, and landscaping contractor and instructor. At various times over the past thirty years he has produced cherries, prunes, apples, and many other crops on rented land.

In 1964 he was operating a pear orchard that surrounded the KEEN transmitter tower. One day while talking with the people who ran the station, the idea of an agricultural program for consumers came up. Johnson said he'd like to do it for free if the station would provide the time without commercials. He has been at it ever since, first on Sundays, daily since 1972. It goes on the air at 5:50 A.M. but Johnson tapes the program the day before, generously using tapes from the extension service, USDA, UPI, and other sources. But the spice in the program is Johnson's commentary, "somewhere to the right of right wing." For example, he once said, "EPA and OSHA are not letters on a telephone dial—they are the greatest threats to a healthy agriculture today."

KEEN's original farm show started in 1950, with a husband and wife team, Gene and Eleanor Vennum. From 1952 to 1969 Ken Wilhelm, secretary of the county Farm Bureau, had a weekly program, mostly centering around bureau activities.

CALIFORNIA FARM BUREAU. The California Farm Bureau entered radio in 1950, and hired Bert Buzzini, who had been farm director of KCBS, San Francisco, to write and broadcast a quarter hour daily program on twelve stations spread throughout the state. The program was sponsored by the Farm Bureau itself, aimed at recruiting more members and keeping present members happy, and by the subsidiaries of the organization that sold insurance and oil.

In 1957 they hired a former co-worker of mine from WLS, Albert Tiffany, who had been broadcasting to midwestern farm families for nineteen years. He broadcast daily to California farmers for three years and then became manager of the Ventura County Farm Bureau. As part of that job he started a local farm program, written for both consumers and farm bureau members. In 1976 he retired after thirty-nine years of farm broadcasting.

The California Farm Bureau decided in 1965 to parallel its radio network, which had grown to twenty stations, with a network of TV stations. But the new thirty-minute TV program was aired on a weekly basis, rather than daily, and carried by fifteen stations.

Principal spokesman for the Farm Bureau on both radio and TV in the seventies was broadcast director George Green.

In 1975 Bill Eckmann, the Bureau's director of information, started a hot line for benefit of radio stations, with a daily recorded message of one to two minutes reporting an item of agricultural news and the Farm Bureau's view of it.

JACK ROBINSON, KWG, STOCKTON. C. W. "Jack" Robinson had been
an agricultural leader in the San Joaquin Valley area for many years before he
became farm director of KWG in 1959. When he died in 1965, at age sixty-
seven, a scholarship fund in his memory was established to help 4-H and FFA
members who wanted to study at Stockton Delta College, which he had helped
to establish. Dick Holmberg was KWG farm director in the late seventies.
ties.

The roster of California farm broadcasters in the late forties included
another Stockton man, Clint Sherwood, farm director of KCGN, Stockton.

Howard Keddie conducted daily farm programs over KCDQ, San Diego,
from 1946 to 1955, and then moved to KFSD, serving approximately the same
area.

In the seventies, Buck Clausen conducted a daily program on KCEY,
Turlock, along with teaching vocational agriculture in the local high school and
managing his dairy herd.

Joly Boynton conducted farm programs on KBEE, Modesto, for several
years in the sixties, dropped out of broadcasting for a while, and in 1978
became farm director of KOSO-FM, Modesto.

Mike Snow, a student at Fresno State University, started a morning farm
program on KYNO, Fresno, in 1977.

Other California radio stations with daily farm programs in the late seventies included KCHJ, Delano; KNGS, Hanford; KTRB and KHOP, Modesto;
KPRL, Paso Robles; KONG, Visalia; KUBA and KHEX, Yuba City.

Chapter Twelve

Colorado

KFKA, GREELEY. Every Monday, Tuesday, and Wednesday, beginning in late 1921, the early morning Union Pacific train from the north would slow down to a crawl at Forty-sixth Avenue in Denver; a passenger would hop off, expertly, and catch a No. 66 streetcar to the stockyards. There he would make the rounds of the pens, looking over the animals, especially the cattle; talk with commission agents and buyers; and make notes on prices and receipts. Then he would catch a streetcar on its return trip, ride to the UP tracks, swing aboard a northbound train as it dutifully slowed for him, and ride sixty miles to Greeley.

At noon KFKA listeners heard what Harry E. Green had learned about the livestock market that day.

It was an unusual way for a radio station owner to spend his time, but Green had his reasons. In this period, 1921 to 1926, Green had made most of his living as an accountant. Many of his clients were cattlemen; thus it would be profitable for his accounting business if his newly built radio station could give cattlemen the market reports they needed, quickly and accurately.

After about five years, during which he also became part owner of the Denver livestock market paper, the *Record Stockman,* Green arranged to have a telephone line connecting the stockyards to the KFKA studio in Greeley. He assigned Carl Jordan, of the *Record Stockman* staff, to report the livestock market four times each day over KFKA.

KFKA historians credit Green with setting the pattern adopted in USDA livestock market reports, especially in comparing this Monday's receipts and prices with those of last Monday, and comparing Denver with other major markets. A big livestock auction was held in Denver, and for years KFKA carried live reports, three or four hours, from the auction ring.

For more than twenty-five years, Green personally conducted the programs intended for farmers and ranchers in his area. His noon program of farm news and editorial comment did much to foster Weld County's climb to become the biggest cattle feeding county in the nation.

In 1956 he turned over the station's farm programs to Larry Kirk, a recent graduate of Colorado State. Kirk developed morning and noon programs of farm news, markets, weather, and interviews in early morning and at noon. As the Denver terminal market became less important and local auctions increased, KFKA's market reports changed with the trend.

When Kirk left in 1965 to go to the University of Nevada he was succeeded by Don Hopkins, who had conducted farm programs most recently at KGNO,

Dodge City, Kansas, and had also been with WIBW, Topeka; KSOO, Sioux Falls, South Dakota; and several other stations. Hopkins conducted morning and noon programs until 1968 when he was succeeded by Don Nelson. In 1972 Nelson became farm director of KLZ, Denver, and Mike Flesher took over. In 1976 Flesher joined in a game of musical chairs which changed farm directors of several western broadcasting organizations. When the players were sorted out, he was with the Intermountain Network, and the director's position at KFKA was occupied by John Corbin from the KFKA news staff.

H. E. Green died in 1963 and the station was sold in 1966, but the legend of Green's daily train rides persists. KFKA's president, Joe Tennessen, pointed with pride to the station's fifteen hours of farm programs each week. "More than any other station in the state," he said.

COLORADO EXTENSION SERVICE. The Colorado extension service, headquartered at Fort Collins, started a weekly program of talks to farmers on KOA, Denver, not long after that station went on the air in 1924. The series continued until 1936. Extension editor Glenn Kinghorn planned the programs and often represented the extension service. In 1940 when KOA started a sponsored early morning farm program, "The Alarm Clock," the Colorado extension staff took part.

Rex Brown became extension editor during World War II when all state extension services were working overtime to pump out information to increase food production and conservation, using radio, press, and every other means of communication.

Mel Eckard was hired as radio specialist in 1953, and during his nine years on the job developed a series of taped programs which went to stations in the state.

Jack Dallas, who took over the job in 1962, had worked for several stations in Iowa and Minnesota. Over the next fifteen years as the station's interests changed, he said, "Most of our programs have become shorter, five minutes or less. . . . We produce daily consumer programs and garden programs and weekly programs on agriculture and on natural resources. . . . More and more of our time is spent on specials sent by phone to selected stations. . . ."

In 1975 Dallas, representing the extension service, teamed with Hollis Hoff, representing resident instruction at Colorado State University, to provide a series of one-minute actualities. Most were put on tape and sent by mail to thirty-seven Colorado stations every two weeks. About half the subjects dealt with agriculture.

KOA, DENVER. Station KOA gave the state extension service air time to present a weekly program for farmers and ranchers from 1925 to 1936. Then no farm programs were broadcast for about four years, but in 1940 word came from NBC headquarters, which owned the station, "Start a farm program." Clear channel stations such as KOA were under attack for failing to use their high power and noncompetitive frequencies to serve rural listeners, and farm programs were considered the first line of defense. KOA manager, Lloyd Yoder, asked for cooperation from the USDA and the state extension service to provide information and speakers for a proposed new program called the "Alarm Clock," presided over by staff announcer Jim Campbell. Wallace Kadderly, USDA radio chief, said the USDA would participate if certain ground rules were followed: first, the information would be used regularly, regardless of whether sponsors bought time; second, the USDA information would be put into one portion of the program identified as public service, and separated from the commercial portions by station identification or at least one minute of music; third, nothing would be said to imply that the USDA was endorsing any product or sponsor.

KOA agreed to these terms; Kadderly agreed to send the daily "Farm Flashes"; and the USDA agencies, AAA, AMS, FCA, FSA, FS, REA, and SCS all promised to have their regional offices start a flow of information to Jim Campbell at KOA. So did the state extension editors in Colorado, Kansas, Nebraska, and Wyoming.

The KOA "Alarm Clock" started May 13, 1940, and kept ticking along for four years, at first in peacetime and then in wartime. In 1944 KOA hired a county agent from Ohio, Hal Renollet, as farm director and he set up morning and noon farm programs labeled the "Mile High Farmer," and an evening summary of markets, all available for sponsors.

After several years, Renollet suddenly died from a heart attack. Don Peach took over the successful program and conducted it in about the same manner as Renollet until 1954. Then he went to work for Purina, and Chuck Muller, farm director at WJPS, Evansville, Indiana, became farm director.

About this time NBC sold KOA to actor-comedian Bob Hope and others. Don Searle came aboard as general manager, bringing with him ideas and experience gained through managing several stations that were strong in farm programming. He lengthened the farm programs and gave them ringing names: "Breakfast Bell," "Dinner Bell," and "Supper Bell." They had been great in Colby, Kansas, Searle's last stop; but Denver was more urban minded and too many listeners complained about the heavy dose of farm programming with their evening meal. So "Supper Bell" died quickly. The "Dinner Bell" rang until 1964, and Chuck Muller conducted only "Breakfast Bell" plus some market news spots until he left the station in 1976.

Chuck Muller was born in New York City but became a farm owner at the age of two when his mother died and left her Missouri farm to him. He earned a degree in agriculture at Cornell, and served as announcer and farm director on two stations, WNBF, Binghamton, New York, and WJPS, Evansville, Indiana, for a total of eight years before he moved to KOA in 1954.

In twenty-two years at KOA Muller watched and contributed to a change that was taking place in agriculture. He and KOA management worked closely with USDA market reporters as they followed the trend away from terminal markets to county sales and local auctions, and reported closing prices on grain at Kansas City to help local elevator operators in Colorado set their prices for the following day.

Following Muller in 1976 at KOA was Evan Slack. He was well known to farmers and ranchers in the KOA area because he had been serving them for seventeen years as Muller's friendly competitor, on the Denver stations KHOW, KLZ, KMGH-TV, and from 1972 to 1976 on the Intermountain Network where he was heard on sixty radio stations located over nine states.

Slack grew up on his family's mule farm near Springfield, Missouri, and before he arrived in Colorado in 1958 he had several years experience as part-time farm broadcaster on several Missouri stations while attending high school and the University of Missouri, plus one year as assistant farm director of KSOO, Sioux Falls, South Dakota.

Beginning in 1977, besides his daily programs on KOA, Slack made two five-minute broadcasts each morning over the Mountain Network stations in Montana and Wyoming.

INTERMOUNTAIN NETWORK. The Intermountain Network, headquartered in Salt Lake City, used telephone lines to link together some sixty stations spread over nine states, emphasizing news and sports, but farm programs were a rather late addition to the service. In 1972 Evan Slack became the network's first farm director.

Four years later Mike Flesher, farm director at KFKA, Greeley, Colorado, moved into the farm director's spot. Flesher fed four programs of news and markets to the network each day between 6:30 A.M. and 12:30 P.M. The network had sold time to national advertisers, such as the Angus Association, Pfizer, and American Cyanamid; and also local advertisers. The network and its affiliated stations split returns on sales of time.

One of Flesher's biggest projects in 1977 was rallying twenty-eight farmers and ranchers from five states and leading them on a successful lobbying trip to Washington. Their concerns were farm prices, drought, irrigation—and foreclosure.

KLZ, DENVER. Station KLZ had some farm programs before 1945, but little time was spent on them until Lowell Watts was hired as farm director in October 1945 after he returned from World War II. Watts was graduated from Colorado State in 1941 and was chosen for a fellowship at WLW, Cincinnati. He stayed on the staff of the WLW farm department for a few more months until he joined the Army Air Corps and became a B-17 pilot.

At KLZ Watts started early morning and noon programs that included market information, weather, and farm news. He soon acquired a plane to enable him to interview farmers and ranchers over the entire area served by KLZ.

In 1951 Watts was called back to active duty for a two-year stint in Korea,

Lowell Watts

and Carl Herzman, who had been county agent in Denver, took over his duties at KLZ and remained after Watt's return in 1953, because of the increased work load since KLZ-TV had come on the air. The Watts-Herzman team developed for TV a daily farm program and a once-a-week garden show. They also continued the morning and noon farm programs on radio.

In 1954 Watts left KLZ to become director of information at Colorado State; and a year later Herzman left the station to become state conservationist. In 1959 Watts was named director of extension, and for a number of years Herzman was assistant director before he retired in 1976.

After Herzman left, KLZ seems to have had no farm director until Evan Slack was hired. Slack said that during his eight years on KLZ he and his farm programs survived six owners, eight managers, and fifteen program directors. When Slack moved to the Intermountain Network in 1972, Don Nelson moved from KFKA, Greeley to become KLZ farm director, and continued the morning and noon radio programs which Slack had established.

In the late seventies other stations with daily farm programs included KIIX, Fort Collins; KFTM and KBRU, Fort Morgan; KLMR, Lamar; KLMO, Longmont; and KFLJ, Walsenburg.

Chapter Thirteen

Connecticut

FRANK ATWOOD, WTIC. The history of farm broadcasting in Connecticut can best be summarized by the efforts of Frank Atwood in the years from 1939 to 1970.

Atwood became assistant extension editor at Connecticut State College late in 1938, and his first major assignment was to start a weekly radio program covering agriculture, home economics, and 4-H Club work on WTIC, Hartford.

During World War II, Atwood went with the State War Council and his weekly program was devoted to home gardens, farm labor, and helping farmers to help win the war. During the war years WTIC started a daily farm program, "The Farmers Digest," with staff announcer "Uncle Jim" Platt in charge. Soon after the war ended, WTIC invited Atwood to take over the "Farmers Digest." The sales staff had trouble selling time to local sponsors because the word "farmers" appeared in the title, and soon the name was changed to "The Frank Atwood Program." That attracted the banks, meat packers, insurance companies, automobile dealers, and drugstores that helped insure the program's survival.

For a few years, in addition to his early morning program, Atwood had a ten-minute program at noon. And during his last ten years, he had a Saturday program on home gardening, which the station continued after he retired in 1970.

Atwood entered TV in 1957 with a half hour public service farm program each Saturday noon.

The one continuing effort that gives him the most satisfaction, looking back over his twenty-four years at WTIC, was a loan program that helped farm children buy heifer calves. Over a thousand young people

Frank Atwood

85

took out loans, and many of them stayed in farming. The big event of each year was a picnic for youngsters that had loans, and their parents, on the grounds of the WTIC transmitter. In 1964 and 1965, instead of a picnic, he took the whole gang to the New York World's Fair.

Atwood was proud of the special WTIC–Travelers Insurance Company weather service. The weather staff gave soil temperatures, dew reports, and special spray recommendations for fruit growers.

After Atwood retired WTIC hired Don Tuttle, whose farm program on WGY had ended. He continued Atwood's schedule of broadcasts until 1974 when the station changed owners, causing the WTIC farm programs to come to an end.

DOUGLAS WARDWELL. Douglas Wardwell had been a radio announcer on several different stations before he became radio-TV specialist at the University of Connecticut in 1960.

It didn't happen all at once, but by the time he left the Connecticut extension service in 1966, he had produced nine programs per week, used by thirty-six radio stations, covering virtually every phase of agriculture in the state; had written two scripts per week, sent to radio and TV stations; had recorded a packet of twelve radio spots each month, sent to county agents for their use on local stations. In addition he produced about twenty-five filmed stories a year which were used on three TV stations in the state.

Chapter Fourteen

Florida

EXTENSION. Florida is a state in which the extension service took the lead in farm broadcasting and held it for many years. Radio and TV broadcasts were aired over the university's radio and TV stations; script and tape services went to stations throughout the state; and county agents provided local broadcasts.

J. Francis Cooper, extension editor, started the "Florida Farm Hour" on November 11, 1928, when WRUF, Gainesville, the University of Florida station, was only a few weeks old. He served as the regular host for several years, supervised the program after that, and was a frequent participant in the noontime programs until he retired in 1961. The programs started as a half hour three times a week, then expanded to a full hour six days a week, but in the fifties they were cut back to forty-five, then thirty, and then to fifteen minutes each day. For the first thirty years, most of the programs were intended for farmers, but in the sixties they were aimed primarily at consumers.

Cooper stated a daily script service in 1933, a Florida version of the USDA's "Farm Flashes," which went at first to five stations. By the time the service was halted in 1957, scripts were going to fifty-seven stations and to most of the county agents.

Clyde Beale was the assistant editor in charge from 1935 to 1955, with Jefferson Thomas and Jasper Joiner assisting. Harvey Sharpe and Jack McCallister were in charge in the late fifties. Assistant editor Roberts C. Smith took over in 1961 and remained until the "Florida Farm Hour" came to an end in 1964.

Beale began in 1949 to distribute taped talks and interviews; most of them were recorded portions of the "Florida Farm Hour" on WRUF. In the fifties, 3 stations received a daily four-minute tape and 12 others got a half hour tape once a week. Over the years the tape service grew to four different services, each with its own set of users, totaling more than 135 stations in 1979.

The Florida extension service entered television in 1950, one program a year for three years. In 1955 a weekly program was started over WFLA-TV, Tampa, along with two films syndicated to other stations. Bill Mitchell was the extension staff TV and film specialist then, and he increased his production the next year to eight fourteen minute films and eighteen live TV shows. The University's TV station, WUFT, went on the air in 1958, with a weekly half hour program devoted to agriculture. Mitchell began to produce a weekly film, used regularly by four stations and occasionally by four others. Associate editor Al Moffitt took over TV and film responsibilities in 1963, and changed the WUFT schedule from a weekly to a daily quarter hour program called "Sun-

J. Francis Cooper

shine Almanac," recorded about one week in advance and used by five other stations as well as WUFT thirty-nine weeks out of the year. Douglas Buck replaced Moffitt in 1965, aided by assistant editor Donald Poucher and then by Marshall Breeze, who expanded the schedule to five per week year-round, and added two more TV outlets.

Cooper said that several county agents began to broadcast weekly in the thirties, among them M. B. Moore in Orlando, J. S. Rainey in Miami, Alec White in Tampa, and Albert Lawton in Jacksonville. In later years, O. R. Hamrick in Madison, Hugh Whelchel in Homestead, and George Huggins at Starke were county agents broadcasting regularly.

Extension service annual reports show that in 1937, county extension workers gave 223 talks over five radio stations. By 1950 the number had climbed to 2,454 broadcasts by agents in thirty-seven counties, and to above 4,000 in 1958, which was the last year county extension workers were required to report how many broadcasts they made.

The first use of television by agricultural agents was reported in 1953, with agents in six counties making 93 TV broadcasts. In 1958 agents in thirty-one counties made 914 broadcasts relating to agriculture, home economics, and 4-H Club work.

Radio and TV farm programs presented by Florida stations have appeared and disappeared through the years, and so have farm directors.

On WTVT, Tampa, Dean Baxter presented a daily television program for farmers for about five years, 1965–70. When he resigned, Bruce Hutchcraft, recently discharged from the Army Veterinary Corps, covered west-central Florida in his own plane or a four-wheel-drive Scout, filming and recording farm stories in the seven county area served by the station, to use on his five-minute program each morning. He also did several thirty-minute documentary films under the general heading of "Hillsborough's Hidden Hundred Million," referring to the approximate value of annual agricultural production in Hillsborough county.

In 1978 he resigned from WTVT to run for public office, but at the end of the year he was back on the air with a farm program on WTOG-TV, in St. Petersburg.

On WFTV, Orlando, Bill Berry took over the daily farm program called

"Sunrise" in 1978, a program that had been the creation of Bill Lavinghouse, who had conducted it for more than twelve years, beginning in 1965, under the names "Florida Agriworld" and "Sunrise Jubilee." Lavinghouse had spent twenty-five years making agricultural feeds, but his company closed its Florida plant in the sixties, making him a youthful retiree. He suggested to the manager of WFTV that the station might use an agricultural consultant to put more agriculture into its news programs, and found himself in charge of a weekly half hour farm program. It grew to an hour once a week, then to a daily.

Lavinghouse helped to build a following among farmers by reporting on carlot prices of frozen orange juice and by getting late night phone calls from each of the livestock auctions markets in central Florida. Lavinghouse said, "I have the prices on the air before they get to the USDA office in Thomasville."

In Milton during the late seventies, farm director Byrd Marpoles conducted two hours a day of farm news and market reports over WXBM.

Other stations with daily but shorter farm programs included WGRO, Lake City; WMFL, Monticello; WKIS, Orlando; and WSUN, St. Petersburg.

Chapter Fifteen

Georgia

EXTENSION. One of the longest "marriages" in radio was the daily participation of the Georgia extension service on the "Dixie Farm Hour" on WSB, Atlanta. It started in 1926, and was still going strong more than a half century later with only one interruption of about three years from 1933 to 1936. But like some other happy marriages, this one started out of jealousy.

In 1926 the Sears Roebuck Foundation sent agricultural director George Biggar to Atlanta to start a farm program on WSB similar to those he had inaugurated on WLS, Chicago, and WFAA, Dallas. The foundation would provide the programs; WSB would provide the time free. Biggar lined up participants and information from the USDA and from the state extension services in surrounding states, but the president of the University of Georgia, Andrew Soule, resented the notion of agricultural specialists from other states coming to a Georgia station and broadcasting to "his" farm people. So he negotiated with WSB for a daily quarter hour, to originate on the university campus at Athens with the extension service paying the cost of phone lines.

For about two years WSB carried both programs, but in 1928 the Sears Foundation decided to get out of broadcasting, and the Georgia extension service had the WSB farm audience to itself.

Georgia extension people broadcast every day over WSB until 1933 when budgets were cut and the university decided it could not afford to pay the phone line charges. But in 1936 money became a bit more plentiful and the extension service resumed broadcasting over WSB one day each week.

In 1940 the Georgia extension broadcasts were absorbed into WSB's newly established "Dixie Farm and Home Hour." Georgia extension editor Jack Wooten became coordinator of information and speakers, provided by four other state extension services and USDA agencies.

The cooperative arrangement between the agricultural agencies continued until near the end of World War II. During that time the Georgia extension service acquired its first radio specialist, Ronnie Stephens, who became a regular broadcaster on the program, along with WSB's farm director—a position that was to have many occupants over the years.

Stephens remained as radio specialist until 1960 when he was succeeded by Roland Brooks who was still on the job at the end of 1979, after more than 6,600 broadcasts over WSB, plus uncounted programs in other series.

In the fifties Stephens started "Extension Calls," a tape recorded service of agricultural information, gathered by phone from extension specialists and from county agents. Brooks continued the daily series, but gradually shortened them from the original thirteen-minute length until each feature in 1976 was two minutes. He and his assistant Joe Courson started a companion series called "Inquiry," which included home economics, home gardening, and 4-H.

In another service Brooks initiated telephone news features to more than 28 stations' news editors, plus the Georgia News Network of more than 100 stations, and the Georgia Farm Bureau Network of about 50 stations.

Besides the reports by phone and tape, there was a script service called "Broadcast Release," usually fifteen items covering agriculture, home economics, and 4-H. The service was sent to the newsroom of every radio and TV station in the state and also went to the Tobacco Network and the WPTF Network in Raleigh, North Carolina.

The Georgia extension service produced a series of filmed programs called "The Growing South" in 1960 on the state educational TV stations. In more recent times audiovisual editors Chuck Thorp and John Hoerner have provided film and tape features used by stations throughout the state. One of their notable efforts was providing county agents in five counties with a series of colored slides; each agent then recorded a series of one-minute messages to go with the slides. They estimated that these messages, carried on five TV stations, reached 80 percent of the state's population. It worked so well that USDA officials sent sample kits to extension services in all other states in the hope they would copy the Georgia idea.

Going back in history, in 1936 extension editor Ralph Fulghum reported nine county agents were broadcasting over local stations in Georgia, three of them every day. Fulghum provided the agents with a script service, seven minutes each day.

D. F. Bruce, in Macon, was on WMAZ; P. H. Ward broadcast daily on WPAX, Thomasville; and in Savannah, A. J. Nitzschke or his assistant, Bynum "Bill" Prance was on WTOC every day in the thirties.

WSB, ATLANTA. Now let us consider the other half of the long and happy marriage between WSB and the Georgia extension service which started in 1926. Around 1940 clear channel stations were being criticized for failure to provide enough programs that served rural people, and WSB decided to start its own farm program, an hour in early morning, to be called "The Dixie Farm and Home Hour." It was to be noncommercial and would be conducted by Bynum "Bill" Prance, former assistant county agent in Savannah. The USDA and state extension services in all the southeastern states agreed to provide information. The program turned commercial during World War II, but by that time the USDA had learned to live with advertisers.

When Prance served military duty, his place was taken by Jim Romine, a former extension radio specialist in Alabama, who started a second farm program at noon.

Many men followed Romine as WSB farm director, including Charley Welch, 1945–1946, Dudley McCaskill, 1946–1950, Lee Morris, 1950–1954, and Mike McDougald, who was in the job from 1954 to 1957.

His place was taken by John Farmer, 1957–1959. Jim Dunaway took over in the sixties for several years and John Moore in the early seventies. By this time the farm director's job was considered half time. An important feature in the fifties, sixties, and seventies was a daily report on broiler markets, broadcast from the USDA regional office in Atlanta, with Bill Poole as reporter for some twenty years.

WSB-TV made a gesture toward agriculture in the sixties with a half hour program called "Spade and Hoe," conducted by the Fulton County agent, Doug Strohbein. It was aimed principally at the suburban viewers but it included a weekly summary of farm markets.

At that time WLWA-TV in Atlanta had an early morning farm program, made up mostly of USDA films and television packages.

CHANNING COPE, WAGA. According to some of the senior residents of Georgia, the most colorful character among the state's farm broadcasters in a half century was Channing Cope. Cope presided in the fifties over the "Yellow River Farm Program" on WCON, Cornelia, and a small network with stations in Macon, Marietta, and Gainesville, and then on WAGA, Atlanta. He did his morning broadcast from his farm home. Guests on his program usually had spent the night. If listeners heard a rooster crowing, it was not a sound effect.

Cope depended for his weather predictions on one of his farmhands, Will Johnson; and the women listeners liked it when Susie Benton, Cope's cook, shared one of her recipes. Cope had opinions on most agricultural matters, but his great love was kudzu, which was good feed for cows and wonderful for stopping soil erosion. He planted kudzu on about one-third of his own 180 acres and preached kudzu in his writing and broadcasting. Although not everyone agreed about kudzu's merits, Cope was credited with having done more than any other one person to get the crop adopted by Georgia farmers.

GEORGIA FARM BUREAU. The Georgia Farm Bureau started making use of radio in 1965, and one year later hired Jimmy Lee, farm director of WMAZ, Macon, to become the Bureau's radio-TV director, at first on a part-time basis; full time since 1970. By the mid-seventies Lee's efforts were focused on two weekly programs, "Georgia Radio Monitor" and "Georgia TV Monitor." "Radio Monitor" was a thirty-minute program of music, news, interviews, and talks planned "to gain greater appreciation and understanding by the consumer of what's happening out on the farm." The program was taped in the Farm Bureau's studios, and put on the air each Saturday morning at 11:30 on fifty-two Georgia stations which blanketed the state. The air time was paid for by two organizations affiliated with the Farm Bureau: the Georgia Agricultural Commodity Commission and the Georgia Farm Bureau Insurance Company.

"TV Monitor" was produced live each Saturday at 7:30 A.M. over WMAZ-TV, Macon, and in the mid-seventies was also carried on the cable TV systems in Tifton and Vidalia.

Several other Georgia radio stations with extensive farm programs in the late seventies included WJAZ, Albany; WGRA, Cairo; WGFS, Covington; WCUG, Cuthbert; WLOP, Jesup; WYTH, Madison; WMGA, Moultrie; WROM, Rome; WPTB, Statesboro; and WVOP, Vidalia.

Chapter Sixteen

Hawaii

THEY named him "Fortunato," which easily translates into "Lucky"; and for about eighteen years "Lucky" Teho was *the* farm and garden broadcaster on radio and television in Hawaii, part of his job as information specialist of the University of Hawaii's College of Tropical Agriculture.

Teho was born in Manila, capital of the Philippines, but his parents moved to the territory of Hawaii when he was only three years old. He received a degree in sugar technology from the University of Hawaii in 1927, and for twenty years worked for several sugar companies on several of the Hawaiian islands.

In 1948 he took a job as publicist for the College of Tropical Agriculture. In 1957 he persuaded KGU in Honolulu to carry a daily program of farm and garden information, and he ran it until he retired in 1974. He taped the KGU programs and they were repeated by radio stations on other islands including: KMVI, Maui; KTOH, Kauai; and KPUA, on the island of Hawaii.

Fortunato Teho

With his radio program sucessfully launched, Teho branched into tele-vison, with a weekly half hour program, "The Aloha State Farmer" on KHVH-TV, Honolulu. Between 1958 and 1974 he had several other television pro-grams on Honolulu stations KGMB-TV, KHON-TV, KHET-TV, and KIKU-TV, with titles like "The Extension Line," "The Green Thumb," "Island Liv-ing," and "Talking to Plants." (He's confident that if you do talk to them you'll take good care of them.)

Teho was the big figure in agricultural broadcasting in Hawaii, but not the first. Maria Palmer, assistant to the director of extension, started a weekly broadcast over KGU in 1930, which lasted until 1936.

Chapter Seventeen

Idaho

KID, IDAHO FALLS. "How about giving up your job as program director and starting a farm program?" the station manager asked.

Bob Burtenshaw nodded his head in agreement. He didn't especially enjoy being program director of KID, but he did like the idea of a farm program since he had grown up on a dairy farm in the area.

It was in 1963 that Burtenshaw, already a veteran of ten years with the station, started his morning and noon farm programs, and they continued into the late seventies. The KID signal ranged out about 150 miles in all directions reaching irrigation farmers close to the Snake River and dry land farmers and ranchers in areas to the north and south of the river. Potatoes, sugar beets, wheat, cattle, and sheep were their major agricultural interests.

A few years ago, when KID-TV was young, Burtenshaw tried a noontime televison farm program, but it didn't succeed.

IDAHO FARM BUREAU. The Idaho Farm Bureau in the seventies had a two man information staff, Bill Whittom, director, and Ed Blaser, market specialist. They provided radio stations with three daily programs and a monthly TV documentary. Bill Whittom produced the "Voice of Idaho Agriculture," six three-minute reports gathered from all parts of the state and mailed weekly to thirty-four Idaho radio stations. Blaser produced two daily reports of livestock sales made by farmers and ranchers. At least two commodity reporters in each county telephoned reports of what was sold at what prices to county farm bureau offices, and these reports were relayed to Blaser, who worked in Pocatello. He tailored one of his daily reports for the Pocatello area, the other for the Boise area; each was available by Code-phone in each city. About twenty-five stations called one or the other telephone number, dubbed off the report, and put it on the air.

Blaser and Whittom produced a monthly, hour-long documentary "Idaho RFD," used by KIVI, Nampa-Boise, and KPVI, Pocatello at 10:00 P.M. Blaser said, "Farmers appreciate being able to tell their story through a Farm Bureau representative."

IDAHO EXTENSION. The Idaho extension service began making use of radio about 1947, when tape recording equipment became available. Agricultural editor Archie Harney started sending tape recorded programs to radio stations in Idaho and to stations across the line in Spokane, Washington. Jim Johnson joined him in 1960 as assistant editor and continued the radio service after Harney died. Jim Holderness, who had worked with an agricultural consulting firm in the Midwest, returned to his native Idaho as agricultural editor, responsible for agricultural recordings plus news and publications. Johnson recalled that the weekly radio output was six programs each week, three minutes each, sent to about forty stations.

Bill Stellman became Idaho's assistant editor and radio specialist in 1964, and Scott Fedale took over the job in 1977. Besides providing agricultural news to the state's radio stations, Fedale also shot agricultural stories on videotape which he sent to stations in Boise, Idaho Falls, and Spokane.

Chapter Eighteen

Illinois

WDZ, TUSCOLA. James L. Bush put his radio station, WDZ, on the air in March 1921, the third station in the U.S. to receive a commercial license (with no number in the identification). But he broadcast only grain market reports. Bush was a grain dealer in Tuscola, and he telephoned grain prices to elevator operators in his area several times each day. He figured if he could convey the same information by radio, it would lower his telephone bills.

The broadcasting schedule was a very simple one: each day the station would sign on at 9:00 A.M., broadcast the grain market reports for five minutes, and then sign off. Throughout the day it would continue to broadcast this way every half hour until 3:00 P.M., then go off the air. Mark Spies, now retired in Arlington, Virginia, recalled that the station operated on this schedule when he joined WDZ as chief engineer in 1929, but soon after, the station began to broadcast continuously during the daylight hours. In 1934 Edgar Bill of WMBD, Peoria, bought a half interest in WDZ, put in Clair Hull from the WMBD staff as program director, and started a farm program that included information from the state extension service, the USDA, and other sources. He also included grain market reports every half hour. The station changed ownership and was moved to Decatur around 1950.

CHICAGO. In the early twenties radio stations popped up like wild onions across the country and the biggest weedpatch of all was in Chicago. Westinghouse put KYW on the air in 1921, and in March 1922 it started a daily program for farmers at 6:30 P.M. Several organizations and people shared in planning and presenting the programs: Wilson Weatherbee was director of KYW and Steve Trumbull was chief announcer. Samuel R. Guard represented the American Farm Bureau Federation and was succeeded in 1923 by H. R. Kibler; Edgar L. Bill represented the Illinois Agricultural Association; spokesman for the National Livestock Producers Association was J. D. Harper, NLPA editor; the U.S. Grain Growers Association also participated regularly. In 1923 the Farm Bureau started a separate program on KYW, aired each Saturday evening, called "Voice of the Farmer," with Edwin Borroff of the KYW staff as announcer.

The Chicago stockyards put WAAF on the air in 1922 to broadcast its livestock prices, and the market reports were continued after the *Drovers Journal* bought the station in 1924. The Chicago Board of Trade bought WDAP in

1923 and began broadcasting grain prices. The Sears Roebuck Agricultural Foundation put WLS on the air in 1924.

All the stations before 1927 went on and off the air several times a day.

The man heard most frequently on the air was James E. Poole, who worked for the Chicago Livestock Exchange and reported Chicago livestock prices several times each day over WAAF, WLS, and later over KFKX. His gravelly voice was one his listeners could immediately identify, and they heard it until Poole retired in 1943 when he was replaced by Bill Morrisey.

Phil Evans, who became dean of the farm broadcasters in Kansas City in later years, recalled that in 1927 when he was selling livestock for the Producers Livestock Commission in Chicago, he broadcast daily over WJJD, WBBM, and WIND, once a week on WENR and WLS. While Poole reported prices that had been paid, Evans predicted prices that would be paid the next day or next week.

Chicago stations competed for farm listeners. KYW staged a special farm broadcast just three nights before WLS came on the air. James Evans, in his book *Prairie Farmer and WLS*, said the KYW broadcast was publicized as "the biggest farm community meeting ever held in the world and the first one to be held by radio." KYW sent word to farm organization leaders in twenty to thirty states urging them to mobilize groups of listeners. President Coolidge telegraphed congratulations and said he hoped to listen; Secretary of Agriculture Henry C. Wallace did listen and heard about two dozen speakers from the KYW studios.

KYW scored another publicity coup in 1925 by persuading *Country Gentleman*, the leading farm magazine at that time with nationwide circulation, to publish an article, "Behind the Microphone at KYW," describing KYW's daily and weekly farm programs.

Chicago's position as the farm broadcasting capital of the nation was clinched in the fall of 1928 when NBC and the USDA started the "National Farm and Home Hour" with Chicago as home base.

The "National Farm and Home Hour" is discussed in more detail in Chapters 5 and 7 but Everett Mitchell, the program's announcer from 1930 until it went off the air in 1960, must be recognized in this section on Chicago stations since he started one of the earliest farm programs, "The Farmers' Exchange" on WENR in 1926 and conducted it for about two years. A few years later he began an early morning farm radio program on WMAQ, added a morning TV program in the fifties, and continued them until he retired from broadcasting in 1968, after forty-two years on the air.

Other programs on other Chicago stations had their day in the sun and then faded—all but WGN. Individual stations, their programs, and people will be examined separately.

WLS, CHICAGO. Almost from the day it went on the air in 1924 until 1960, WLS was *the* farm station in Chicago, with thousands of loyal listeners in Illinois, Indiana, Wisconsin, Michigan, and Iowa. During much of that time,

WLS was a halftime station, sharing the frequency with WENR. But virtually all its hours were directed to rural people.

The Sears Roebuck Agricultural Foundation started it that way in April 1924. Samuel R. Guard, director of the foundation, who had been information director of the American Farm Bureau Federation, hired Edgar L. Bill, publicity director of the Illinois Agricultural Association, to be director of the station. Bill then hired the young man who had been his assistant at the IAA, George Biggar.

Biggar arranged for market and weather reports from the USDA and negotiated with *Prairie Farmer* for a weekly summary of agricultural news. He lined up Ed Heaton, the foundation farm adviser, for a question-answer period twice each week and welcomed speakers from the agricultural colleges in the area to broadcast on the noon or evening programs.

He invited listeners to suggest a name for the noon program and out of several thousand suggestions the judges chose "RFD Dinnerbell Time." The "RFD" stood for "Radio Farmers Democracy." That part of the name was dropped after a time, but "Dinnerbell Time" survived.

After a few weeks, "Dinnerbell Time" was supplemented by reports from the Chicago stockyards at midmorning and from the Board of Trade at midafternoon. WLS came on the air to broadcast these farm services and then went off until it was time for the next program. Radio was like that in 1924.

After little more than a year, the foundation sent Biggar to Dallas to start a farm service on WFAA, and the WLS farm programs were taken over by Fred Petty, formerly an assistant editor of *Orange Judd Farmer*. In later years Joe Naylor, then Malcolm Watson directed the programs.

In 1928 the new Federal Radio Commission decreed that a station must broadcast continuously if it was to keep its license. Sears did not want to sell time to other advertisers and knew continuous broadcasting without advertising revenue would be too costly.

So the Sears Roebuck Agricultural Foundation decided to leave broadcasting. It terminated the farm and home programs it had been supporting in Dallas, Atlanta, and Memphis and looked for a buyer for WLS, one who would continue the station's policy of serving rural people. *Prairie Farmer* magazine was a leading candidate, and a 1928 survey of *Prairie Farmer* readers showed that 25 percent of them had radio receivers. Within that group 59 percent indicated WLS as their favorite station.

Prairie Farmer writers and editors had been broadcasting once each week over WLS while it was owned by the Sears Foundation, and owner Burridge Butler had negotiated for a daily farm broadcast on WMAQ, presented by *Prairie Farmer* staff members. Also, the coverage of WLS was about the same as *Prairie Farmer*'s circulation: Illinois, Indiana, southern Wisconsin, and western Michigan. Butler bought WLS for $250,000, effective October 2, 1928.

Most of the WLS people responsible for entertainment programs went to work for the new owner; Edgar Bill remained as station manager. But *Prairie Farmer* people took responsibility for the agricultural programs and Dave Thompson, a field editor of *Prairie Farmer,* became program director. George

Thiem, Floyd Keepers, Arthur Page, and, most often, Charley Stookey conducted the "Dinnerbell" program.

In 1930 Stookey left WLS and Arthur Page became host of "Dinnerbell Time," in addition to his duties as assistant editor of the magazine. Three years later he was joined by a Methodist minister, Dr. John W. Holland, who concluded each noontime program with a three-minute devotional service. To WLS listeners they were a beloved team for the next twenty years, ended by Page's death in 1953. "Doctor John," as he was known on the air, continued for several more years.

"Dinnerbell Time" was never available to sponsors. It was the time of day when WLS and *Prairie Farmer* talked to their audience about things that affected rural people: the hazards of fire, price support programs, good neighbors, soil conservation, and how to keep robins out of the cherry trees. Each year the "Dinnerbell" staff and a troupe of entertainers broadcast from the state fairs in Illinois, Wisconsin, and Indiana for one week; the program reported "Farm and Home Week" at the University of Illinois and at Purdue, the International Livestock Exposition and 4-H Club Congress, plus the corn husking contests in Illinois and Indiana. I was part of this routine, as assistant farm director from 1935 to 1938, followed by George Menard and by Al Tiffany.

Arthur C. Page

After Arthur Page's death, Dix Harper became WLS farm director, and except for "Dinnerbell Time," WLS farm programs became more oriented to the business side of farming and to the business side of farm broadcasting, in the pattern of programs Harper had developed as farm director of stations in Kokomo and Indianapolis. He created more farm programs with more spots available for advertisers. Harper was assisted by a team that, at various times, included Maynard Bertsch, Harry Campbell, Ray Watson, Bill Mason, and others. In 1958 Bill Mason became head of the farm department, and the team expanded to five men.

Then, in 1960, came the end. ABC bought WLS, combined it with WENR, and converted programs to rock and roll. Except for a token farm program tucked away in the early morning hours, WLS forgot about the rural audience.

One Chicago farm program shone brightly for a time in 1929 as a spin-off of WLS. It was started by Sam Guard who had been director of the Sears Roebuck Agricultural Foundation, the person most responsible for building

WLS and a frequent participant in the station's programs. Lloyd Burlingham, prominent in agricultural editorial circles in Chicago, was also a frequent speaker on WLS farm programs. With the sale of WLS to *Prairie Farmer,* both men broke their connections to the station and teamed to buy a ninety-eight-year-old farm magazine, *Breeders' Gazette.* To help promote the magazine, they negotiated for time on KFKX, which Westinghouse had built in Nebraska and then moved to Chicago. They established a schedule of four programs totaling two and one-quarter hours each day, including livestock market reports by the inimitable Jim Poole. The broadcasts lasted only about one year.

WJBC, BLOOMINGTON. When farmers in McLean County wanted to know what the county farm adviser, Eugene Mosbacher, had to say, they could find out by tuning in on WJBC. He was a regular on the station for more than thirty years. In 1975 the station held a ceremony in his honor and gave him a plaque to put on the wall and a travel certificate that would take him and his wife almost anywhere they wanted to go. But a year or so later, when I talked with him, they hadn't gone anywhere yet. "Who wants to go to London or Rome? I'm looking for a good agricultural trip somewhere."

The man who arranged the award was WJBC's farm director at the time, Ken Behrens, who had developed an extensive farm service around the long-time farm adviser broadcasts. Behrens had started as morning announcer on the station and little by little began to work in market reports, weather, and then interviews with farmers. Then station management added an hour at noon, and Behrens was made full-time farm director.

His place was taken in 1976 by Kelly Lenz, who added an evening farm program to the schedule, before he was succeeded by John Hawkins in 1977. Lenz also added a direct Weather Service wire to provide timely agricultural advisories.

Hourly reports on commodity trading were a longtime service feature on WJBC and presented by Paul Bates, a local broker.

Kelly Lenz was an Iowa farm boy who joined WIOK (which in 1972 became WAKC) in Normal as a disc jockey in 1970. Dick Green had a well-established program of farm and general news on the station, but he broke a hip in 1974 and Lenz took over, expanding the farm services to morning, noon, and evening programs. He moved to WSBC, Bloomington, and in 1977 moved to WIBW, Topeka, Kansas.

DICK HERM, BOB RANKIN, WPEO, PEORIA. Most farm broadcasters think they have a full-time job putting on a daily program, and most livestock commission men think selling livestock keeps them busy enough; but in Peoria, Dick Herm and Bob Rankin for about twenty-five years found the two occupations made a happy combination. From the Herm livestock commission office in the Peoria stockyards, they broadcast a half hour farm program at 6:00 A.M. over WPEO, including a daily five-minute report from the local county agent. Then they went out to the yards to sell the cattle, hogs, and sheep consigned to them by their clients.

During the morning, they telephoned market reports to thirty-one other stations distributed over the northern half of Illinois. When their selling tasks were over, they went on the road to get interviews and stories from farmers for their daily broadcasts and to encourage farmers to send their animals to the Herm commission firm. Is there a possible conflict of interest between soliciting business and gathering news? None at all, insists Rankin. "We have the producers' interest at heart; and if we think the market is going to get better, we advise them to hold back their animals; we do it on the air and in person."

Between them, Herm and Rankin devoted about seven hours each day to their radio programs, local and network; and they found enough hours during the year to plan and stage a two-day event each July, the "Dick Herm Steam Show," in which the heroes were old-time steam engines and threshing machines.

CHUCK KUPPLER, WTAD (AM), KHQA-TV, WQCY-FM, QUINCY.

Chuck Kuppler could have given lessons in how to fill a schedule to overflowing with programs early morning, mid-morning, and noon on WTAD radio; morning and noon on KHQA-TV; and a series of market reports every fifteen minutes from 9:15 A.M. to 3:30 P.M. on the SAC band of WQCY-FM.

Not bad for a guy who claimed to know nothing about broadcasting when he was hired in 1970. Dick Failor had been news reporter and farm director on WTAD for about thirty years, and when his health forced him to retire in 1970, the station management decided to replace him with an agricultural man with the hope he could develop into a broadcaster. Kuppler was just down the street at the Adams County Farm Bureau office, and his agricultural credentials were impressive. Coming from a strong farm background Kuppler became a county farm bureau executive, first in Kendall County and then in Adams County, for a total of nine years. What he needed to know about broadcasting he learned quickly enough.

In his regular farm program on WTAD (AM) Kuppler started at 5:30 A.M. with a one-hour mixture of farm news, general news, music, and taped interviews. His favorite was a continuing series called "Pepsi Spotlights the Farm Family of the Week." It was a series of five interviews with members of one family, five minutes each day, Monday through Friday.

The television audience on KHQA and several CATV satellites received Kuppler's farm news twice each day. The noon show, up to the close of 1975, included only cash prices for grain and livestock, but Kuppler's conversations with farmers lead him to the conclusion: "Farmers are getting more and more interested in futures prices, and we need to find time for them on television."

The market news service on WQCY-FM called "Agricasts" was a service for subscribers only, and was broadcast on two FM stations, one in Quincy and one in Davenport, Iowa, about 120 miles north. Subscribers were provided with a receiver capable of receiving only one station, and they heard market reports, usually three to five minutes, every quarter hour from 9:15 A.M. to 3:15 P.M. Kuppler in Quincy and a colleague in Davenport shared the "Agricast" reports at fifteen-minute intervals.

GEORGE MENARD, WBBM, CHICAGO. After studying journalism at Notre Dame, George Menard got a job as announcer on WROK, Rockford, in 1935, and soon afterward he started a program for farmers with whom he had grown up.

In 1938 he moved to WLS as assistant to Arthur Page and stayed for nine years, conducting the "Dinnerbell" program at noon, the early morning "Farm Bulletin Board," doing staff announcing duties, acting as master of ceremonies on the "Barn Dance," and often singing, when WLS wanted a number sung well and on key.

Toward the end of his term at WLS, Menard teamed up with Chuck Acree, a WLS alumnus turned free-lancer, to produce a farm quiz program called "Man on the Farm" sponsored by Quaker Oats, and originating in a barnlike auditorium on the company's research farm at Libertyville. For a time the show was on the Mutual Network, but most of the time it was recorded, first on discs and later on tapes, and syndicated nationwide for a total of seventeen years, 1947–1964. Menard was producer, commercial announcer, and vocalist, while Acree handled the audience participation.

In 1950 Menard inaugurated "Farm Town USA" on WBKB, Chicago's pioneer TV station, which became WBBM-TV. This farm program was principally aimed at the city audience and presented each Sunday afternoon for three years. The typical program set the scene with filmed views of the farm, home, barn, and the family at work. Then the family was interviewed, live, in the studio, usually accompanied by some of their animals, up to and including a 2,500 pound bull.

For a time WBBM's morning farm radio program was conducted by farm director Harry Campbell and then by Lloyd Burlingham, who was a Guernsey breeder, farm magazine editor, agricultural commentator, and one-time manager of the "National Dairy Show." In 1953 Menard succeeded Burlingham on the "Country Hour," and started a daily TV program which was christened "Farm Daily" but later was called "Chicago Farm Report."

In 1964 his fellow farm broadcasters elected Menard president of their national association. The WBBM farm programs went off the air about a year later, but Menard's services to agriculture were not through. In 1967 the USDA and U.S. food manufacturing firms joined forces to stage an American Foods Festival in Tokyo, and Menard and his wife, Martha, were invited to be host and hostess. They came home exhausted but delighted.

WGN, CHICAGO. WGN was the last of the clear channel radio stations in Chicago to start a farm program, waiting until 1945; then for about fifteen years a four-way competition existed for farm listeners and advertising dollars among WLS, WBBM, WMAQ, and WGN. In the sixties, the others dropped

George Menard and his wife, Martha, were ambassadors of good will in 1967 at the American Foods Festival in Tokyo.

out, first WLS; then WBBM; then WMAQ. For ten years WGN was the only Chicago station with a daily farm radio program, but in early 1979, WCFL hired Bill Mason as its first farm director.

The WGN finger pointed in 1945 at Hal Totten, the station's veteran sports reporter and broadcaster, and suddenly he was a farm broadcaster. His approach was that of the consumer, which represented most of the listeners. Totten recalled that in the late forties, farm broadcasters met in Washington, visited the White House, and shook hands with the president. When it came Totten's turn, Harry Truman said, "So, you're Hal Totten. I listen to you almost every morning while I'm shaving."

I came in contact with Totten shortly after an FCC hearing early in 1946 when one USDA senior official chided broadcasting stations for not presenting farm programs in the evening. A few days later, Hal Totten wrote to me, as USDA radio chief, and said in effect: "We'll set aside a half hour every Saturday evening at 6:30 for USDA. Fill it any way you want to." This was not an opportunity; it was a burden! Somehow the program was aired each Saturday evening with the help of two market information specialists in Chicago, Walter John and Paul Ostendorf, who carried most of the work load. About a year later, the program mercifully ended.

After about four years, Totten moved into station management away from Chicago; and Norman Kraeft, who had been his assistant, took over the WGN farm programs. Over a period of about eleven years during which the programs

Orion Samuelson conducts daily farm programs on WGN, Chicago, and produces a weekly farm TV program syndicated to 75 or more stations.

went commercial, Kraeft added market reports throughout the morning and farm news at noon; carried his tape recorder to farms, experiment stations, and agricultural events over a wide area; and built a large audience.

In 1960 Kraeft moved to Washington and Orion Samuelson, farm director of WBAY, Green Bay, Wisconsin, became the new WGN farm director. Samuelson began as station announcer in Sparta, Wisconsin, and two years later he moved to WHPY, Appleton, Wisconsin, where he ultimately became program director. WHPY was under the same ownership as WBAY, Green Bay, which in the fifties had a four-man farm department. Samuelson was named head of the WBAY department in 1956. Four years late he was ready for a bigger audience and found it at WGN.

John Almburg was his assistant in the early sixties, and in 1967 Almburg was followed by Bill Mason, who worked closely with Samuelson for ten years. For several years they had morning and noon programs on radio and a daily televison show. In the seventies the daily broadcasts were limited to the morning radio show, but in the meantime Samuelson had developed the weekly syndicated televison program, "U.S. Farm Report"—a reflection of agricultural methods and farmer opinions nationwide. It was sponsored in part by International Harvester and syndicated to more than eighty television stations. The television program was the property of the parent company which operates WGN, and in the mid-seventies, Samuelson was named a vice-president of the company.

Max Armstrong became WGN's assistant farm director in 1978 after several years of producing radio programs for the Illinois Agricultural Association.

Samuelson was president of the NAFB in 1965, and Bill Mason held the same office ten years later.

In the seventies the Chicago Board of Trade decided for the first time to step outside the grain business and choose two public members for its board of directors. One public member was the former chairman of General Motors; the other was Orion Samuelson, farm director of WGN.

BILL MASON, WCFL, CHICAGO. Bill Mason started a farm program on WCFL, Chicago, at the beginning of 1979, bringing much experience to a

50,000 watt station that never before had had its own farm director in more than a half century on the air.

Mason had grown up on a farm in northern Illinois and wanted to be a radio announcer. He did short hitches on several stations in Illinois and Wisconsin and was married in the late forties before his wife, Priscilla, persuaded him to enroll at the University of Illinois. He earned his way by working as student assistant to Jack Murray, radio specialist on the Illinois extension staff, helping conduct daily farm programs on the University station, WILL.

Mason was graduated from the University of Illinois in 1953 and conducted the farm programs of WIBC, Indianapolis, for a year before moving to WLS, Chicago, where he became farm director. In 1960 Mason moved to WBBM, Chicago, for three years. Its farm programs were cut back and Bill freelanced for four years before joining WGN and Orion Samuelson for ten years. In 1975 Mason served as president of NAFB.

His programs on WCFL included ten minutes at 5:20 A.M. and a half hour of farm news, weather, markets, and farmer interviews at noon.

MICHAEL ROSS, WGLC, MENDOTA. Mike Ross of WGLC was one farm director who could get as much time as he wanted for his farm programs. He owned the station, and had been its only farm broadcaster since he bought it in 1969.

He had an hour and a half each day of programs with farm news and markets in early morning, midmorning, noon, and midafternoon. WGLC had 250 watts, and reached into about four counties, three of which were in the nation's top fifty in farm production. Cattle and hogs, corn and soybeans were the major products.

Ross stressed the local angle in everything, general news as well as farm news. Most farmers in his area sold their livestock and grain locally, and so it was local prices that the station offered.

Ross grew up on a dairy farm near Milwaukee and broke into radio after World War II as a fiddle player on WLS, and later did many different things on stations in Ottawa, Streator, and Dixon, Illinois.

His farm programs made money for the station, Ross believed, not because they were sensational or exciting—but because they were local.

WMBD, PEORIA. Edgar Bill, WMBD owner, hired Emil Bill (no relation) as farm director in 1935 and nicknamed him "Farmer Bill." He had been a newspaper reporter, vaudeville performer, musician, and actor before he went into farming; and by 1935 he was well established as a Guernsey breeder, poultryman, horseman, and beekeeper. Bill continued his daily programs for thirty-five years, retiring in 1970, about a year before he died at eighty years of age.

With coverage of about ten counties, Bill knew almost everyone in the area and they saw him often. By his own estimate, he attended about 150 meetings each year.

With all the respect and affection he had accumulated on the air, "Farmer Bill" was a tough act to follow, and WMBD management looked for his replacement for two years.

Then they hired Colleen Callahan, fresh out of the University of Illinois, who had grown up on a four hundred acre farm, won ribbons with her Hampshire hogs at the state fair and the International livestock show, and had been the only woman on the university livestock judging team.

Colleen Callahan

When the WMBD manager wondered "What will the audience think when they hear a woman giving market reports?" Callahan had an answer:

"When dad turns on the radio for markets, he's looking for information. If I can build a good program, it isn't going to make any difference if I'm a man, woman, or dog barking out the facts."

She was hired.

Within a short time her schedule included a market summary at 6:20 A.M., music and talk at 7:00, and forty-eight minutes beginning at noon with market, farm news, and features aimed at the housewife, all on radio, plus a noon market report on television.

A year later one farm wife said, "We didn't think anyone could replace Farmer Bill, but Colleen is warm, knows her stuff, and is down to earth."

JOYCE CUTRIGHT, WIAI, DANVILLE. Joyce Cutright grew up on a farm not far from Danville, Illinois, studied agricultural communications at the University of Illinois, saw one of her friends, Colleen Callahan, get a job as farm broadcaster at WMBD, Peoria; and two years later she started as farm director of WIAI-FM, Danville, October 1975.

Cutright provided her listeners with an hour of farm news, interviews, and markets in early morning and another twenty-five minutes at noon. Morning, afternoon, and evenings, she covered her territory of several counties talking to farmers, farm advisers, and others.

With three years experience behind her, near the end of 1978, she moved to KWTO, Springfield, Missouri, as farm director, and was succeeded by Patty Jeckel, another Illinois farm woman.

"HANK" HAYNES, WSOY, DECATUR. Soybeans were still a novelty crop in most parts of the Midwest when WSOY went on the air in 1925, but the call letters told the world that Decatur was the soybean processing capital of the United States. Since 1955 WSOY's farm director had been Harrington "Hank" Haynes. The early morning program had grown to two hours, a mixture of news, market reports, weather, a few musical numbers, and of course commercials to pay the way. On the midday show Haynes shared time with the news staff in a program of markets, weather, news, and a special agricultural weather analysis.

In 1975 he was joined by Warren Meyers, who had been the local farm adviser for twenty-five years. He went into broadcasting when he retired from extension work.

WTAX, SPRINGFIELD. Two men with a total of about eighty-five years in front of a microphone conducted farm programs on WTAX, from 1928 to 1979, and were followed by a young woman who never lived on a farm, never attended an agricultural school, but had been thoroughly indoctrinated in farm broadcasting.

The first of the veterans was "Spizz" Singer, who started the programs with a farm hour in early morning in 1928, along with entertainment programs during the day. In 1969, around the time of his seventieth birthday, he went into semiretirement, dropping the farm program but continuing for another ten years to handle commercial announcements for some longtime sponsors.

WTAX management chose as his successor another veteran broadcaster, Marty Roberts, who had been announcer, newsman, and farm director over a period of a quarter century on stations in Tuscola, Cincinnati, Springfield, and Peoria, before returning to Springfield as WTAX farm director in 1969. Over the next nine years Roberts expanded the morning farm program to two hours, added an hour and a half at noon and several market reports during the period when livestock and grain markets were open. Besides conducting interviews with farmers and agricultural officials himself, each year for several years he chose a 4-H Club member and an FFA member to report on activities of their organizations in central Illinois.

When Roberts resigned in early 1979, Tim Christ, the station's newsman and Roberts's part-time assistant, filled in for a few months and then joined a family farming enterprise in Texas. Peggy Kay Fish then became the station's farm director. For two years she had worked with her stepfather, Leland Glazebrook, on his Corn Soybean Network, a tape recorded and live market service used by many central Illinois stations. With several years' experience in local business firms in their home town of Sullivan, Fish handled her stepfather's sales and accounting, and when he had to be away, she broadcast the market reports. The network was a sideline to Glazebrook's salaried jobs, first with WLBM and then with WDZQ. When he decided the network was too burdensome and should be discontinued, Fish was ready to take on a farm program of her own. She found it on WTAX.

WSPY, PLANO; WCCQ, JOLIET. I submit that every hired man should have a boss like Larry Nelson, owner-manager of WSPY and WCCQ. The two stations simulcast an hour of farm news in early morning, another hour at noon, thirty-five minutes each evening, and seven five-minute market programs during the day. Bob Cramer was farm director of the stations, but his boss handled the full hour farm program that goes on the air at 5:30 A.M.

The two stations, both FM, went on the air in the seventies, and chose WGN's farm programs as their competition, offering three-county coverage versus WGN's three hundred counties. Nelson said, "The WGN men can't get to many of the farm events in their big territory. We can and we do. When there's an important farm meeting, we do our noon show from the meeting; we broadcast from the county fairs. We're getting recognized. It used to be that the WGN boys used to be invited to speak at farm meetings in our area; now the invitations are coming to Bob Cramer or Larry Nelson, and we almost never say 'No.' "

MAX MOLLESTON, KHBC, ROCK ISLAND. Max Molleston was raised in a city, was a political science and economics student at Iowa State University and the University of Iowa, and then a radio news reporter for about ten years before he became farm director of KHBC in 1973. He believed such training and background were about right for a farm director today. He said, "Today's farmer needs to know how politics works, and he needs to have a better understanding of the economic forces affecting his prices in the marketplace. That's what I try to include in my programs."

In addition to an early morning program of farm news, Molleston increased the number of market reports on KHBC: every hour when the principal livestock and grain markets were open. On Saturday at noon he had a half hour summary of farm news and an interpretation of trends in marketing during the week.

WLBH, MATTOON. WLBH had a full-time farm director from the start in 1946: Calvin Pigg, 1947–1952; Howard Miller, 1952–1969; and Leland Glazebrook, 1969–1975.

Most often the program schedule included morning and noon programs of farm news, farmer interviews, weather, and market information including county agents from the ten surrounding counties reporting on a regular schedule. Glazebrook added more market reports, including opening grain and livestock markets at midmorning, and a summary in late afternoon. For many years the station had a mobile unit, and both Miller and Glazebrook used it to broadcast from county fairs and other important agricultural events.

CORN SOYBEAN NETWORK. Leland Glazebrook spent thirty years farming and doing other kinds of agricultural work before he entered broadcasting in 1969. He found he had many human interest stories that he couldn't find time for in his daily programs on WLBH, Mattoon, and in 1971 he started putting those stories on tape and sending the tapes to stations in central and southern Illinois, about twenty-nine stations. Ten minutes a day, five days a week, with tapes mailed once a week. He continued his network after he became farm director of WDZQ, Decatur, in 1976.

He sold time in the programs to sponsors such as Monsanto, DeKalb, Du-Pont, Funks, Agrichem, and Wayne, and paid the stations for air time.

ILLINOIS AGRICULTURAL ASSOCIATION. The Illinois Agricultural Association (Illinois Farm Bureau) entered radio in 1922 by participating in a daily program on KYW, Chicago for several years until the program was discontinued. After an interlude of more than forty years, the organization started a daily farm broadcast, "R.F.D. Illinois," over a statewide network which grew from about twenty to more than forty stations carrying the half hour program in early morning. Each program carried a Farm Bureau commercial with other time slots to be sold by local stations.

By 1979 the radio services had been expanded to include a four-minute program, "Latest News in Agriculture," used by sixteen stations; "Farm News at Noon," used by forty stations; a daily five-minute program on KMOX, St. Louis; and six market reports each day, two minutes each, used by eighteen stations.

Art Sechrest was radio director during most of the year, assisted by Max Armstrong. In 1978 Sechrest moved to the Corn Soybean Network, made up of Illinois stations, and Armstrong became assistant farm director of WGN, Chicago. Allan Jarand became radio director and announcer for the several series of programs.

Clarke Steigerwald was involved in the IAA radio programs beginning in 1968, and a few years later was designated as television director, producing a daily videotape feature, "Town and County," used on WMBD-TV, Peoria, and WCIA-TV, Champaign. Steve Johnson soon joined the staff as cameraman and tape editor, and in 1979 Mike Stanton from WMBD was added as writer and announcer. The three-man team in 1979 produced the daily "Town and Country"; ten minutes of agricultural features for WGN-TV, Chicago; and videotape with four to six features covering a wide range of agricultural subjects sent biweekly to fifteen stations, including several in neighboring states.

ILLINOIS EXTENSION. Ted Mangner believes he was the first radio specialist in the Illinois extension service and first farm director of the University radio station. He was hired in 1937, fifteen years after WILL went on the air. He stayed in radio for more than thirty years.

From 1937 to 1944 Mangner conducted the daily one-hour program each noon on WILL, interviewing staff specialists and also roaming around the experimental farm, broadcasting live from a mobile unit. In addition he wrote the Illinois version of "Farm Flashes," which went to thirty-eight stations over the state and to county agents. When Mangner moved to KMOX, replacing Charley Stookey in 1944, his place at the university was taken by E. H. "Duke" Regnier, followed in 1946 by Bob Beeler, each with the title, radio specialist.

Extension editor Hadley Read in his book *Those Times Remembered* reviewed the radio and TV activities and people of his office from the time he came aboard in 1947 until he retired in 1974. It makes a long and impressive list. For a short term in 1949, the WILL farm programs were handled by Bob Goralski, then a student, who became an NBC-TV news announcer. Shortly after in 1948 the job was taken over by Claude Gifford, who became USDA director of communications. After a year Jack Murray took over WILL radio and in 1949 he arranged for twice-a-week programs on WGN. In 1950 Bill Mason, who was a student assistant, began taping the WILL talks and sending them to other radio stations over the state, replacing the scripts from "Farm Flashes." The Illinois extension service probably became the first to offer a syndicated tape service to stations in its state.

In 1952 WBKB-TV, Chicago, asked the extension staff to present a half hour live farm and home hour program each Saturday noon. Staff members and props went to Chicago for the show for thirty-two weeks. Out-of-pocket costs for all shows during the year totaled less than $100.

In 1953 WCIA-TV in Champaign came on the air, and Don Schild, extension TV specialist, produced a fifteen-minute farm show daily for six months but reduced the schedule to once a week for two years. He also produced a series of thirteen half hour kinescope TV productions on "The Story of Agriculture," for distribution by the University of Michigan TV center.

In 1956 David Phillips took over TV and Robert Nemcik took over the radio tape service and the daily radio show on WILL. They started a half hour evening show on WILL, and a half hour weekly TV show on WCIA. In 1958 Jon Greeneisen replaced Nemcik, and the staff added a fifteen-minute weekly tape, "Illinois Farm Time," for radio and a second television show, "Farm Forum," on the local station.

In 1960 J. J. Feight filled Nemcik's job, and the next year Greeneisen moved to the USDA. Meanwhile the staff started a daily "Farm News Report" on WCIA and trimmed the daily radio program on WILL from forty down to fifteen minutes. In 1962 John Weidert became farm radio specialist. When he went to the USDA in 1963, the daily WILL program was stopped, but the tape service was continued with changes of producers and announcers every few years: Glenn Broom in 1964; Cliff Scherer in 1966; Ron Scherer in 1968; Dave Warner in 1973; Gary Beaumont and Sandra Casserly in 1978. More than one hundred different stations, including those affiliated with two networks, received the radio tapes three and one-half minutes per day.

The staff turned out a series of public service announcements for television, about 100 per year covering a wide range of agricultural and consumer interests. Not all stations used every spot, but many stations used the spots several times, totaling approximately 40,000 each year.

A telephone call-in service was started in 1970, at first with the message changed only once a week, but later a new message was used every day by forty to fifty stations each week.

In the late seventies, twenty other stations in Illinois listed their own farm programs, ranging from a half hour to two hours per day.

Chapter Nineteen

Indiana

PURDUE. I doubt if there ever was another farm broadcasting effort quite like the "Purdue Threshing Ring." It started in 1927 when officers of the Purdue Agricultural Alumni Association formed an idea for a "radio meeting"—a combination of reports on the latest in farming and propaganda that would make the alumni feel good.

The creators were also extension workers: Assistant Director Harry Reed; Fay Gaylord and Roscoe Fraser, vegetable specialists; J. R. Wiley and Claude Harper, livestock specialists. They dreamed up a "threshing ring" with several characters who might interrupt the talks with humor, and they rigged sound effects that imitated a separator, steam engine, and of course a whistle. They took the idea to Fred Petty, agricultural director of WLS, and the upshot was "Purdue Week" on WLS: a half hour each noon, another half hour each evening, and a two-hour broadcast on Friday evening.

The "Purdue Threshing Ring" became an annual feature on WLS for each of a half dozen years and also from 1934 to 1940 on stations in Indianapolis, Fort Wayne, Gary, Terre Haute, and Evansville. It was a traveling feast of fact and frolic.

Purdue's radio station, WBAA, was licensed in April 1922, and the scant early records indicate some broadcasts of agricultural statistics. In my two years, 1929–1931, as an assistant extension editor, we did two news programs each week containing some agricultural information, and we did a daily program during the annual Agricultural Conference, which most schools called "Farm and Home Week."

Glenn Sample, who became assistant editor in 1936, recalled that as a student he helped with "Farm News," a weekly quarter hour farm program on WBAA. When he went to work full time, he made it three times a week, and about 1940 he made it a daily program, which has continued since with talks, interviews, market reports, and weather forecasts.

About that same time, the extension service acquired disc recording equipment and Sample began to record some of the WBAA talks and send them to stations over the state, with each platter remailed to several stations before it got too scratchy for broadcast.

In 1942 the Indiana State Fair was canceled. Purdue and WLS, both of which had made a big thing of the fair, got together to stage a "State Fair by Radio," a half hour each day for a week on Art Page's "Dinnerbell Time."

113

Horace Tyler (C) during a 1953 broadcast over
WBAA, Purdue University.

In another wartime effort, two Purdue poultrymen and Sample turned back the clock twenty years to put together a poultry school: a series of talks recorded on platters and played by a dozen stations over the state on schedule, twice a week for five weeks. The radio talks were supplemented with printed material sent by mail to 3,995 people who signed up.

In 1943, Jim Miles, a "reader" for the Ohio State legislature, joined the Purdue staff as farm radio specialist, taking over the daily program on the university station, the now-and-then platters, and inaugurating a daily script service. Miles became manager of WBAA about 1947, and Harold Schmitz, who had started as a student broadcaster, took over the services to Indiana radio stations. He was followed in 1949 by Harry Leckrone, who had been announcer-farm director at WILY, Centralia, Illinois. He increased the WBAA programs to two a day, "Farm Fun and Farm Facts" at 7:00 A.M. and "Farm Forum" at noon, six days a week. He set up a regular transcription service used by about twenty stations and converted the script service to mimeographed "Work Tips" sent out once each month.

Leckrone's place at Purdue was taken in 1951 by Horace "Ace" Tyler, who had spent a year as assistant county agent in southwestern Indiana where agents in a half dozen counties took turns in daily farm programs on WGBF and WEOA, Evansville. During that year a new station opened in Princeton and the county extension staff started a daily program. The owner, Ray Lankford, gave his own name to the station, WRAY, but he did more than that: he converted his hatchery into a studio and acoustically treated the walls with egg case dividers.

Soon after he became radio specialist on the Purdue staff in 1951, Tyler discontinued the script service and converted the recorded programs from platters to tapes. Around 1970 the taped services were divided into two categories, one dealing with farm production, the other with home gardening and landscaping. Davonna Oskarson took over these services in 1977 when she joined the Purdue staff from the WLW farm department, and at the end of 1979 she provided a daily farm feature to seventy Indiana radio stations. The gardening program was sent to fifty stations, with each program about two minutes in length. She also provided a daily seven-minute program on tape to the university station, WBAA, which was broadcast during the noon hour. In 1979 she arranged for a telephone call-in service, with a daily agricultural story.

In 1952 Tyler and assistant extension editor Ralph Hamilton began for the first time to provide scripts and black and white slides to TV stations serving the state. In 1954 Ed Ferringer took over the TV services and replaced the slides with black and white movie film, which he changed to color film in 1957. The films went to farm broadcasters on stations in Indiana cities, plus Chicago, Cincinnati, and Louisville.

Tyler and Ferringer started a weekly videotaped series, "Ag Comment," in 1965, intended for inclusion in farm programs and used by eight stations during most of its life, ending in 1976. Tyler changed partners several times: Gary Nugent in 1968; Gary Godspeed in 1974; and John Totten in 1975.

Totten was a veteran radio and TV newsman on WFBM, Indianapolis, and other stations in South Bend, Evansville, and Columbus, Ohio, and was the son of Hal Totten, WGN's first farm director. In 1979 he provided two short features, one to two minutes in length on color videotape, to farm directors on four Indiana stations; two horticulture features to seven stations; and an agricultural economics story several times each month to ten news editors.

In 1950, a survey of Indiana county extension workers showed that 110 were broadcasting on a regular schedule but only 65 had not been on the air at all. They made 8,008 broadcasts, averaging eleven minutes each on fifty-five stations. Only 18 had microphones in their own offices. Also, 3 of 5 extension workers thought there was no better way to use their time than in broadcasting; 1 in 5 wasn't sure, and a few thought they might better be putting their efforts elsewhere.

A survey made twenty years later showed 108 Indiana county extension workers had made about 13,000 radio broadcasts during 1970, most of them by tape recording.

WFBM, INDIANAPOLIS. New Palestine is a tiny dot on the map of Indiana, south of Indianapolis, but 2 of its 863 citizens together spanned more than fifty years of farm broadcasting over WFBM. Henry Wood was WFBM farm editor from 1926 to 1946; and his successor, Harry Martin, continued the daily programs until 1976. From his home in New Palestine, Martin also ran the Rural Radio Network which blanketed Indiana through forty-three radio stations with three short farm programs each day.

Wood was farm editor of the *Indianapolis Star* when he stopped by the WFBM studios one day in 1926 and suggested that he do farm features.

Woods's offer was quickly accepted and he stayed for twenty years, presiding over the "Hoosier Farm Circle" each day during the noon hour. His program gradually grew from ten minutes to thirty minutes each day and included live country music.

When management decided to add a morning farm program to the noon broadcast, and Wood decided to give up radio to concentrate on newspaper work, his mantle fell on the staff announcer who usually assisted on the noon farm program, Harry Martin. Wood continued writing until shortly before his death in 1977.

Henry Wood

Martin had farmed with his father in central Indiana, attended Butler University, and became an announcer on WLBC, Muncie, before he went into the army during World War II. All this time he went by his legal name of Harold Modlin. On WFBM he became "Harry Martin," a name easier to remember.

Martin took over the noontime "Hoosier Farm Circle" in 1946 and added a ten-minute farm program each morning. The noon program continued until 1965 while the morning program lasted until 1974. Two years earlier Martin branched out on his own by starting the Rural Radio Network, made up of small stations scattered over Indiana.

He continued his daily radio and TV programs on WFBM for about two years after he started his network, but in 1974, under new ownership, things came unglued. The radio programs were canceled, but on TV Harry recorded five programs each Sunday evening that were aired each morning, Monday through Friday. That series was halted late in 1976.

RURAL RADIO NETWORK. The Rural Radio Network was operated like a family farm.It was started in 1972 by Harry Martin and his wife Marian. Two years later their son Dan, who had worked part-time on the programs, asked for a full-time job with the network. He was known on the air as Dan Bradley. In 1977 Ned Arthur, a hog farmer and tractor mechanic with electronics as a hobby, joined the staff to take charge of equipment. A few months later he became a son-in-law.

All four were on the air and shared in other duties involved in providing forty-five stations each day with a ten-minute recorded program of farm news and interviews plus two live programs of market news. The live broadcasts traveled from studios in the Martin's home in New Palestine to WSMJ, a high power FM station in Greenfield. Other stations over Indiana rebroadcast the WSMJ signal.

On the business side, the network paid each station for the commercials it carried and collected from the sponsors.

As of 1979, the Martins had no plans to expand 'outside Indiana where they had interests in two farming operations. "Indiana is home; that we're successful means that we're meeting a need."

Harry and Marian Martin

HARRY (LECKRONE) ANDREWS, WIBC, INDIANAPOLIS. On his doctor's advice in 1946, Harry Leckrone began another line of work after he sustained a back injury handling freight at the railroad station. The local radio station in Centralia needed an announcer and hired him. A year later Leckrone joined the extension staff at Purdue as radio specialist. Over a three year period he expanded the farm programs on WBAA and the transcribed services to Indiana radio stations.

In 1950 when he joined WLW as assistant farm director, the station decided Leckrone's name would not be understood on the air. So he changed it to Andrews. He worked for four years with farm director Roy Battles, broadcasting from the WLW farm and from agricultural events all over the WLW area. In 1954 he moved to WIBC, Indianapolis, where Dix Harper and Bill Mason had established farm programs a few years earlier, and where the station owned a 200-acre farm.

Andrews moved into the farm house and took over the farm's operation along with broadcasting each morning and noon. For many years Tom Cockram was the announcer handling commercials and acting as foil for Andrews's witticisms, and from 1969 to 1979 Al Pell, county 4-H Club agent, served as Andrews's assistant and substitute. In 1979 Andrews's health was at a low point and Pell conducted the early morning program with the noon program conducted by the station's operations manager Jack Morrow.

Near the end of 1979, Pell resigned as county 4-H Club agent, to become a full-time broadcaster, with two employers: on radio, he was designated farm director of WIBC; on television, he was farm director of WHMB-TV, Noblesville, a few miles north of Indianapolis. Pell started a full hour noon farm program on that station in May 1979 with the familiar combination of farm news, weather, market reports, and interviews. By the end of 1979 the program was paying its own way and management was considering shifting it to an evening hour.

BOB BUIS, WLBC, MUNCIE. Bob Buis (BICE) ran the farm programs of WLBC, Muncie, from 1960 to 1965, an hour in early morning on radio and a quarter hour at noon on TV. He produced the programs and also sold most of the announcements they carried.

Even more gratifying was the 4-H Broadcasters Club he started, which grew from 11 to more than 50 youngsters. They met every week at the WLBC studios and learned about radio and TV by staging practice broadcasts. When they got to be expert enough, Bob put them on the air, on both radio and TV.

JOE JARVIS, WCVL, CRAWFORDSVILLE. Joe Jarvis was a gray-haired rookie in farm broadcasting. He didn't begin until 1974, after a dozen or more years as a disc jockey, which followed two dozen years working for the B&O railroad. In 1974 he took over the two, half hour afternoon farm programs on WCVL. The WCVL signal covered about two counties, and Joe knew most of the farm people, especially the 4-H and FFA members.

AL BISHE AND GENE CRAWFORD, WGBF, EVANSVILLE. When World War II came along and brought gasoline rationing with it, the county agents down in the "Pocket" of southwestern Indiana decided they ought to use radio to reach their farmers more regularly and more often. With the assistance of Glenn Sample, Purdue extension radio editor, they arranged for fifteen minutes during the noon hour each day on WGBF, Evansville, with agents from counties taking turns broadcasting. Over the years some of the agents dropped out, but the Evansville agent, Al Bishe, continued until he retired in 1965. The next day he went on the WGBF payroll. He talked a lot about flowers, shrubs, fruits, and vegetables, and over the years he built up a big following in the city, suburbs, and small towns, as well as among the farm people.

In the fifties, Gene Crawford, an Illinois farm boy, became part-time farm announcer on the station and developed a commercial farm show that was profitable for sponsors and station.

By 1975 Crawford and Bishe had expanded their farm programs to an hour in the morning and a half hour at noon. In March 1975 Bishe died after thirty-three years on the air.

Crawford continued the programs on WGBF for two more years but in 1977 he moved to another Evansville station, WIBX as full-time farm director. He broadcast three, three-minute spots in early morning and six around noon.

WTHI, TERRE HAUTE. Farm programming on WTHI radio and TV didn't

Wayne Jenkins (R) and Ralph McHargue.

just expand in 1976—it exploded. For years it was only a half hour in the morning and quarter hour at noon on radio and a quarter hour at noon on TV. To keep busy, farm director Wayne Jenkins also handled the weather on the evening TV news program. but in 1976 Jenkins was given an assistant, Ralph "Cork" McHargue, who had been an outdoor writer for newspapers and magazines. In the same breath he was assigned on radio a full hour in the early morning and an hour at noon, plus ten market news spots during the morning and early afternoon. On television, besides a noonday farm and evening weather shows, they were told to produce four agricultural stories each week for the evening news programs.

Behind the scenes was the principal owner of the station, Tony Hulman, who also owned the Indianapolis Speedway and each year started the annual "500" automobile race.

Jenkins received an engineering degree from Purdue and was a student announcer on WBAA, the university station. After serving as announcer on several Indiana stations, he engineered, built, and managed a radio station in Brazil, Indiana, before he went to WTHI in 1961 as director for news and weather, and then farm director.

Jenkins organized a junior showmanship contest for farm youngsters in the WTHI area, which includes several counties of Indiana and Illinois, held at the Clay County fair each year, beginning in 1975. Each boy and girl showed cattle, hogs, and sheep raised by someone else, and the judging was based on how well the young people showed them in the ring. Station WTHI put up the prizes.

JAY GOULD, WOWO, FORT WAYNE. It was in 1941 that the manager of WOWO, sent an off-the-air recording, with an apology, to a major advertiser. The manager explained he had lost his farm director and the recorded program had been done by the director of children's programs. He said the station would have a regular farm director shortly.

The advertiser replied that it would be unnecessary to make any change. The substitute would do. Jay Gould changed from children's program director

"Hello, World." That was the way Jay Gould greeted his listeners each morning on his "Little Red Barn" program.

to farm director and kept the title until he semiretired in 1978 as he approached his eightieth birthday. His schedule expanded from fifteen minutes each week to three and one-half hours each day, the "Little Red Barn" each morning and "Dinner on the Farm" each noon.

His programs were wide ranging in subject, for Gould said, "To me agriculture encompasses the whole complex of nature and of living."

He raised funds for many causes, and he conducted tours for his listeners to nearby events, such as the annual livestock show in Chicago, and to far away places such as South America, Europe, Australia, and Asia.

Working with him throughout the years was Bob Sievers, whom Gould described as "the best farm commercial man in the business." Dugan Fry of the WOWO news staff was Gould's assistant and substitute for several years and succeeded him as farm director in 1978.

ROBERT JENKINS, WIRE, INDIANAPOLIS. Station WIRE went against the trend of stations in metropolitan areas by starting a farm program in 1973, when many other stations of its age (50 years at that time) had turned their backs on farm listeners. Rob Stone was the station's first farm director and Bob Jenkins took over in 1975. Jenkins's schedule involved several market news segments of five minutes or less in the early morning, three more around noon, closing market reports at midafternoon, and a market review at 5:15 each evening.

WSLM,SALEM. Not many Indiana towns of 5,000 had a radio station, but Salem had AM, FM, and cable TV, complete with a company plane and a farm director who flew it.

WSLM was the dream of Don Martin, high school speech teacher and licensed radio operator. When the station went on the air Valentine's Day 1953, it had a half hour farm program at noon, conducted by a vocational agriculture teacher, Erwin Eisert. Two dozen years later, Eisert was still teaching and still broadcasting. The station's power had increased from 250 to 5,000 watts; its coverage had broadened to about eighteen counties; and the original half hour farm program had been expanded to a full hour in the morning and another at noon. The first sponsor, the county farm bureau, was still on board along with many others. When the station's cable TV went on the air in 1975, Eisert started an evening news and weather program.

WAYNE ROTHGEB, WMEE, WKJG-TV; FORT WAYNE. How would you like to baby-sit for 4,000 children? Wayne Rothgeb does it once a year and loves it. For four days in May he presides over a Farm Day for all the kindergarten children in Fort Wayne.

He finds a friendly, courageous farm family with a diversified operation, lines up about ten FFA chapters to help as explainers, and about a thousand children each day get a close-up look at cows and calves, sows and pigs, sheep and lambs, hens and chicks.

Farm Day is a major offshoot of Rothgeb's four daily programs on WMEE radio and one daily show on WKJG-TV.

Rothgeb worked as student announcer at Purdue on WBAA until 1948. He became farm director of WKJG in 1957 and started his TV program two years later.

LARRY SCHUMAN, WCMR, ELKHART. When Larry Schuman of WCMR outlined his daily schedule, I immediately felt tired. He rolled out of bed in time to drive forty-seven miles to be on the air at 5:45 A.M. with an hour of farm news, market reports, weather, and interviews. He also had eighty minutes over the noon hour and sold all the commercial spots in his programs and the ones surrounding the midmorning and midafternoon market reports. He filled his morning and afternoons gathering stories, doing interviews, and keeping clients happy; then he went home to his family and worked on his farm.

There seemed to be a formula for becoming farm director on WCMR: get an agricultural degree from Purdue and sell feed and fertilizer for the Farm Bureau Co-op. The station had had two farm directors and they both went through that process. Bill Day was the first, beginning in the late fifties and continuing until 1972 when Larry Schuman succeeded him.

WIOU, KOKOMO. WIOU hired two Iowa State graduates in succession who became recognized as top men among farm broadcasters. The first was Dix Harper in 1948 when the station went on the air. For the first year WIOU refused to sell time in its farm programs, but afterward Harper and his programs made a good profit for the station.

Harper moved in 1951 from WIOU to WIBC, Indianapolis, which covered a much larger share of Indiana, and he was replaced by Bob Nance.

INDIANA FARM BUREAU. The Indiana Farm Bureau started a tape service in 1968, four short interviews each week sent first to twenty-seven stations and then gradually extended to eighty-two Indiana radio stations. In the seventies, Gene Wilson, radio editor, started a second tape service called "Crossroads Commentary," two and one-half minutes of Farm Bureau slants and opinions used by about fifty stations.

A great many farm broadcasters have to get up at some ridiculous hour like 3:45 in the morning, and probably all have worked out their own methods of waking up—really waking up—after the alarm goes off. One Indiana broadcaster, who shall be nameless, found the system that worked best for him. It was to crawl out of bed, shut off the alarm, and then doze for a few minutes on a leather couch. The leather was cold enough that it brought him to life, gently but surely. He started this system when he was a bachelor and continued it when he married. Soon afterward his bride's younger sister came to visit, and she bedded down on the couch. Next morning the alarm went off; the bridegroom went through his usual routine of turning off the alarm, groping his way to the couch for his wakeup nap, and then EEEEEEK! It took a lot of explaining to his bride and her sister. A lot of explaining. But in time he could laugh and tell about it.

Chapter Twenty

Iowa

WOI, AMES. Any account of broadcasting in Iowa that pays attention to the long-range calendar must start with WOI at Iowa State University and Andrew (Andy) G. Woolfries.

Born in Ireland in 1904 but raised in Waterloo, Iowa, where he built an amateur station, Woolfries enrolled at Iowa State in 1921 to study electrical engineering and promptly got a part-time job as one of a three-man team helping to build a radio-phone station to replace the eight-year-old wireless telegraph transmitter. In a few weeks the new transmitter was ready and the seventeen-year-old Woolfries pushed the button that put station 9YI on the air and broadcast a "CQ" call to anyone listening. Within minutes he had a response from the station at Pennsylvania State College. That was the night of November 21, 1921.

The following April, 9YI was licensed as WOI and authorized to use up to 1,000 watts of power although its transmitter at the time was only 100 watts. Woolfries recalled (more than a half century later), "We had a potent medium of communication but nothing to communicate." At the suggestion of Dr. R. K. Bliss, director of extension, Woolfries and his associates began to copy opening and closing prices on the Chicago hog market broadcast in code by the Great Lakes Naval station and rebroadcast the reports in voice over WOI. Soon came daily reports on butter and egg prices provided by the USDA office at Stevens Point, Wisconsin. "By midsummer or fall," Woolfries wrote, "Director Bliss began to assign extension specialists to broadcast over WOI in their free time. Only after a year of bickering was USDA willing to count broadcasting as useful employment for the staff."

In 1928, after the FCC ordered all stations to broadcast continuously, the extension service talks were regularly scheduled in an early morning half hour. Extension editor Blair Converse scheduled the speakers, and Woolfries, who was then chief announcer, acted as host. In the thirties Samuel H. Reck moved from being an extension editor in South Dakota to one in Iowa. He also became a regular participant in the WOI program called "Farm Facts."

One event in 1936 made a note in history. A blizzard in February wiped out a series of county 4-H Club meetings, one hundred of them. So the 4-H leaders arranged a series of broadcasts over WOI, two 4-H programs each week for several weeks covering the topics that would have been talked about during the meetings.

The early forties brought World War II and some significant changes.

Richard B. Hull

Reck acquired disc recording equipment and started sending a series of platters to stations throughout Iowa under the title "Keep 'Em Eating." The series was well launched in 1942 when Reck moved to New Jersey as extension editor and Woolfries moved to WMT, Waterloo, as farm director.

The position of extension editor was taken by C. R. "Dutch" Elder, an Iowa State alumnus who had been a newspaper editor at Osceola. He continued to take part in one of WOI's several daily farm programs. Dick Hull, another alumnus and who had been radio specialist of the Minnesota extension service, replaced Woolfries. In 1943 Hull was named manager of WOI, and the farm broadcasts of the extension service and WOI were taken over by Dale Williams, who had been county agent in Minnesota.

On WOI radio he conducted early morning and noon programs until 1970 when the early morning show was discontinued. When WOI-TV came on the air in 1950, Williams teamed with assistant editor Dick Cech to start a daily television farm program, which became a fixture in the station's schedule.

Besides the programs on the university's own stations, in the seventies Williams taped eight, four-minute radio programs per week and distributed them to fifty other stations. He also sent a series of four-minute videotape features to four other Iowa stations. He provided two programs each week via telephone recording to radio stations that called in for them. Williams retired in 1980.

From its very beginning WOI presented market reports. In 1933 Congress threatened to cut out the USDA appropriation for market news, and in forty-eight hours, 35,000 Iowa farmers had signed petitions to keep the market reports coming. Congress heeded the message.

I recall visiting WOI in 1940 and thinking that the schedule of market broadcasts was very good. In 1943 Ronald Charles "Cap" Bentley, extension marketing specialist, took over the WOI market programs and made them even

Dale Williams

more useful by reporting on more commodities, interpreting markets, and giving indications of future price trends. During the next twenty-one years the market reports grew from from twenty minutes to more than an hour each day. When TV came along, he added a noontime program. Each week he taped a market summary used by twenty-six radio and fourteen TV stations.

Along the way he trained a number of assistants, including Dallas McGinnis, who was farm director of KXEL, Waterloo, from 1950 to 1955 and then returned to help Bentley with his daily broadcasts for ten years. McGinnis became markets director when Bentley retired in 1965. In 1979 McGinnis and three assistants broadcast fifteen programs each day totaling eighty-one minutes plus three recorded reports available by telephone, one each on livestock and meat, feeder cattle, and grain futures.

Besides its broadcast services, WOI has been a training ground that has

R. C. "Cap" Bentley and
Dallas McGinnis

Henry Field

turned out more farm broadcasters then any other college station. Some found jobs on Iowa stations, but the many who moved to other states have constituted one of Iowa's most valuable exports.

KFNF AND **KMA,** SHENANDOAH. Shenandoah was the home of radio stations KFNF and KMA, rivals from 1925 to 1978 and each the creation of the imaginative, articulate seed dealers named Henry Field and Earl May.

Henry Field and his seed company staff built the KFNF transmitter and put it on the air February 18, 1924, with broadcasts every day from 12:30 to 12:55 P.M.

Henry Field was his own program and farm director even after the station began full-time broadcasting around 1928. KFNF was operated by Field seed house employees, all of whom were encouraged to take a turn announcing. Field's son, Frank, was a regular on KFNF and liked broadcasting better than the seed business.

Henry Field died in 1949 and the family sold the station. The new owners continued farm programming but with a number of changes in farm directors during the fifties. Royce Wills was farm director for several years in the sixties and seventies; and he was followed by Cliff Adams, the station's last farm director. In 1976 the station was sold to a religious organization which completely changed the program format and wiped out the farm programs. Cliff Adams then moved to KSO, Des Moines.

If Henry Field could do something, his crosstown rival could do it too; so the next year in August 1925, Earl E. May put KMA on the air. He said the call letters stood for "Keep Millions Advised." At first KMA was on the air only

Earl May

from 11:00 to noon; 6:00 to 7:00; and 9:00 to 11:00 P.M.; but within three months, May started going on the air each morning at 6:00 A.M. and then at 5:00 A.M. May himself was the announcer; and the following year, he was awarded Radio Digest's Gold Cup as the "world's most popular announcer." His wife, Gertrude, was a popular soloist, especially on the Sunday religious programs. They wouldn't let their son, Edward, go on the air doing commercials for a couple of years, until he was seven years old. The station acquired a sizable staff; but May was on the air at 10:00 A.M., 12:30, and 7:30 P.M. with general news, farm news, weather, and market reports for many years until his death in 1946.

After May's death, perhaps the most popular personality on KMA was Frank Field, Henry's son, who began broadcasting for KMA after his family sold KFNF. His title was a bit vague, but he talked about farming, gardening, and the weather in an inimitable fashion until he retired in 1975, after fifty-one years of broadcasting.

The first man to be given the title of farm director on KMA was Merrill Langfitt, who had been a county agent in the area. He held the position from 1946 to 1960 with farm news programs morning and noon. Jack Gowing, Langfitt's assistant for several years, took over the program in 1960 continuing with about the same schedule until 1971. He had two associates in the farm department, Tom Beavers and Jim Lightfoot who was known on the air as Jim Ross. Cliff Adams, a Minnesotan, became farm director in 1971 and was assisted by Jack Mihall and then by Steve Hoefing. Hoefing took over the reins in 1974 and brought in Lynn Ketelsen as his assistant.

In 1976 Ketelsen moved to a farm network in Minnesota, and Hoefing was lured away by the Purina Company. Station KMA cast a vote for experience in the person of Craighton Knau, who returned to farm broadcasting for a third time after working at advertising agencies.

WHO, DES MOINES. There it was, a 50,000 watt clear channel station with a signal that blanketed the leading state in production of corn, soybeans, fed cattle, and hogs. After a dozen years, in 1936, the management of WHO decided the station should have a farm director and a daily farm program. The *Davenport Times Democrat,* also owned by the Palmer family, had an enthusiastic young farm editor, Herb Plambeck. After one year on the paper, Plambeck was transferred to WHO and went on the air at 6:30 the next morning. He, in effect, read the stories he had written for that day's newspaper.

With his 6:30 A.M. farm news program well established after a few months, Plambeck was asked to start a half hour program each day at noon. In 1937 a weekly review program was started, "The Corn Belt Hour," each Saturday at noon.

When television began, Plambeck and his assistants launched a daily, noon TV program which built a substantial audience, but it survived only a few years.

Besides the daily programs, the WHO farm staff staged a series of events which lent excitement to their programming. One of the earliest was a plowing match started in 1939, a regional event at first, and then national. The plowmen entered, farm families showed up, and then the presidential candidates followed every four years to speak to crowds of up to 200,000.

For many years, WHO invited farmers to locate the tallest stalk of corn in their fields and send it to the station. During World War II, photos of the Tall Corn Sweepstakes became a form of pinup to boost the morale of Iowa farm boys in military duty.

WHO also started a Master Swine Producers Recognition in 1942 as a wartime project and continued it for many years.

During World War II, the station promoted Victory Gardens and established the Victory Farm Volunteers, an effort that brought several thousand young people to work on farms. Following the war, a GI Farm Family Contest was held, turning the spotlight on GIs who returned to farming after military service. For years farm safety and fire prevention were two themes that had almost daily reminders on the farm programs.

Plambeck did a hitch as a war correspondent during World War II in Europe. Later he broadcast from more than fifty countries, including Mainland China.

He also was one of the founders of the National Association of Farm Broadcasters and its first secretary, second president, and longtime historian.

As WHO's farm service expanded, Plambeck was able to hire assistants and about forty of them worked with him in his thirty-three years. Many of them moved to farm director jobs on other stations, including his first assistant, Mal Hansen, who became farm director of KRNT, Des Moines, and then WOW, Omaha; Ed Bowman, to KOA, Denver; Jim Chapman, to WTAM,

Herb Plambeck (third from left) started the National Plowing Matches which attracted crowds as large as 200,000, and every four years also attracted candidates for president. Ike was there in 1952.

Cleveland, WRFD and WOSU, Columbus; Howard Langfitt to WJDX, Jackson, Mississippi. Other used their credentials earned at WHO to move to jobs in advertising, agricultural trade associations, and elsewhere. But two of Plambeck's assistants, Keith Kirkpatrick and Lee Kline, stayed on to continue the WHO farm programs after Plambeck left the station in 1970 to become assistant to two secretaries of agriculture.

Kirkpatrick joined the WHO farm department in 1950 after graduating from the University of Iowa where he had conducted farm programs on WSUI. In 1966, while he was still the assistant farm director, his fellow broadcasters elected him president of the NAFB.

Kline came along in the early fifties, after learning farm broadcasting as a WMT, Cedar Rapids, scholarship winner while he was a student at Iowa State University, and then as a broadcaster from the Chicago stockyards. For about eighteen years, the trio of Plambeck, Kirkpatrick, and Kline represented the solid foundation of WHO farm programming, augmented for a dozen years by

Keith Kirkpatrick editing film for WHO's short-lived TV farm program in 1954.

Chet Randolph. Since 1970 Kirkpatrick and Kline have continued the programs and are institutions in the state.

When Plambeck closed out his career at WHO he counted 107 awards that he and his department had received from all the major farm organizations, Kiwanis, the Hoover Commission, and the governments of Norway and The Netherlands.

When WHO observed its 50th anniversary in 1974, Plambeck returned as a guest speaker. Among other things, he said "Through war and peace, in good times and bad, traveling far and wide, interviewing thousands, I've walked with kings and talked with presidents, and worked daily with the progressive farm families of Iowa and the Midwest. Few men have had a higher privilege."

WMT, CEDAR RAPIDS. WMT can trace its beginning to 1922; its call letters to a newspaper, *Waterloo Morning Times,* forty-five miles away; and its farm programs to "Tall Corn Time," conducted in the thirties by "Neighbor Bob" Leefers. His official title was chief announcer, and "Tall Corn Time" was remembered as friendly and entertaining.

In 1942 the station hired Andy Woolfries away from WOI, Ames, and made him full-time farm director. Then the farm programs got down to business. Woolfries was followed by Chuck Worcester, 1946–1955; Bob Nance, 1955–1973; Ron Michaelson, 1973–1975; Jack Crowner, 1975–1976; Johnnie Linn, 1977–1978 and Jerry Passer, 1978. Three of them, Worcester, Nance, and Crowner, were elected president of the farm broadcasters' organization.

The farm director usually had one, and often two full-time assistants. In more or less chronological order since 1943, they have included Johnny Holmes, Warren Kester, Bob Simmons, Bill Alford, Greg Michel, Dean Borg, Lyle Borg, Jerry Bretey, Bob Pritchard, Dave Etzel, Walt Adams, Jim Burt, and in the mid-seventies Jerry Passer, Mark Oppold, and Rich Balvanz, virtual-

Chuck Worcester
broadcast regularly
from his farm home
over WMT Cedar
Rapids, 1946–1961.

ly all Iowa State graduates. Bill Alford became sales director for all the Orion stations; Jerry Bretey became manager of WMT radio; others sought careers at other stations.

In 1947 Chuck Worcester, who directed CBS's "Country Journal," and WMT started offering one scholarship each year to a student just finishing his junior year in communications at Iowa State. The winner worked full time during the summer in the station's farm department and as a campus correspondent during his senior year. Many of them have become farm directors of other stations.

The preceding year Worcester left Washington, D.C., where he reported agricultural information, and moved to WMT where he could "get out and walk the corn rows and talk to farmers rather than bureaucrats."

At WMT Worcester continued the Clean Plowing contest which Woolfries had started; and in 1949 he began a mechanical corn picking contest, which became a national event. With the help of other cooperating stations it lasted into the seventies. A "farm gadget" contest grew so big it was moved to the state fair. Another perennial event was the "Favorite Farmer's Daughter" contest, which he credited his assistant Bob Simmons with starting.

In 1952 Bob Nance moved from WIOU, Kokomo, to join WMT and when Worcester was named station news director in 1955, Nance took over as farm service director. Among other things, Nance and Worcester had started television farm shows when WMT-TV went on the air. The WMT audience then had its choice of farm programs in early morning and at noon on both radio and TV.

On his way home from a cattle sale, Chuck Worcester was killed in a car accident March 1961.

WOC, DAVENPORT. J. R. Underwood reached his seventieth birthday in September 1966 and started his third career by becoming farm director of WOC. He had been a frequent broadcaster on WOC radio and TV during the twenty-one years he was county extension director (his second career) in Davenport. As farm director he was on the air six times each day on radio and twice on TV. Instead of traveling over one county, he now covered a dozen counties, in Iowa and Illinois. In his first career he spent twenty-two years as a vocational agriculture teacher and then school superintendent.

Underwood was not the first county extension agent or director in Davenport to use radio to reach farmers. In 1937 the director of extension reported seven county agents in Iowa had regularly scheduled radio programs, and R. W. Combs in Davenport had a microphone on his desk. He and his assistants took turns broadcasting five minutes every day. The county budget paid for the telephone lines; the station provided the time, without commercials. In the late seventies, after a dozen years as WOC farm director, J. R. Underwood was happy to have sponsors buying time in his programs, since that was what kept the programs on the air.

KXEL, WATERLOO. KXEL hired Hugh Muncy, a former Minnesota farmboy, as farm director almost as soon as the station went on the air in 1942. In addition to reporting news and markets to farmers he hired a student correspondent to report regularly on agricultural news from Iowa State College. One of Muncy's popular programs during the wartime years was a "Buyer's Guide" for homemakers. He said that at the time he was unable to answer one request: "Where can I buy black market sugar?"

Dallas McGinnis conducted the farm programs from 1950 to 1955, and on KXEL he added more market reports than had been included earlier.

Jerry Urdahl occupied the spot for several years, followed in 1975 by Bryan Roberts. Roberts established a schedule of farm news in early morning and again at noon with four market reports through the morning and early afternoon. Besides the markets provided by the regular news wires, he subscribed to the Commodity News Service wire and to Jerry Urdahl's weekly report on the feeder pig market. About a year later, Hal Hanna was added to the farm department, and the two of them traveled over about eighty counties. Roberts said he was not responsible for selling time, but he collected a commission on any sales he made.

KSO, DES MOINES. Cliff Adams may not be the only farm broadcaster who served one term as mayor (Mankato, Minnesota) but surely he was the only one who started his radio career on a station in Greenland, a sideline to a job as a construction worker in the late fifties. After several years on KYSM, Mankato, and four years conducting farm programs on both stations in Shenandoah, Adams moved to KSO. The station had had no farm information since Vince Caudle had conducted a daily broadcast in the sixties.

Adams established a schedule of short programs. Seven of them were broadcast between early morning and midafternoon, mostly weather and markets, including one spot where grain prices from several elevators in central Iowa plus prices on the major terminal markets were reported. He said, "It's a change from the longer programs I had been used to on KFNF and KMA, but listeners seem to like it; so I like it."

KWMT, FORT DODGE. Dave Sylvester of KWMT says he didn't know a horse from a cow when he took over the farm programs at his first station, KROS, Clinton, in 1947. The management wanted a farm program and Sylvester, the morning announcer, was elected to do it. He relied heavily on the county extension staff, local farm bureau, and farmers to supply the needed information. Over the next twenty-three years he combined farm programs with other announcing jobs on KROS and KWDM, Des Moines, and KOIL, Omaha. In 1973 he moved to KWMT, following in the footsteps of Jerry Brady, who established the station's farm programs before joining the farm department of WMT, and Fred Lark, who became a station owner in Montana. In 1976 Sylvester acquired an assistant, first Mike Morse, and then Jerry Struck.

Their schedule included early morning and noon farm programs and five market reports during the morning and noon hour, including direct reports from stockyards at Omaha and Sioux City. Even when he was working alone Sylvester figured he flew 60,000 miles and drove 30,000 miles in a typical year.

Sylvester's most memorable mistake occurred when he was combining farm programs with general announcing and news. On a news program he was reporting on a trial and referred to the "prostituting attorney." As he tells it, "a couple of lines later the same phrase appeared again and I was determined to do it right, so I almost shouted 'PROSTITUTING ATTORNEY.' Some days you can't win."

CHUCK CONGER, KBIZ, KTVO; OTTUMWA. Chuck Conger went from Iowa State University to KRVN, Lexington, Nebraska, in 1959 where he directed farm programs for seven years and expanded the station's services to its farmer owners and other listeners. But he wasn't completely happy because he didn't have a herd of beef cows. After a couple of years of farming and part-time broadcasting over KAMI, Cozad, Nebraska, he found what he had been looking for: a farm well suited to a cow-calf operation and farm programs on both radio and television on KBIZ and KTVO, Ottumwa.

On the air, Conger started broadcasting over KBIZ at 5:00 A.M., serving as disk jockey and farm reporter. Later in the day he presented a half dozen market reports and a quarter hour of farm news during the noon hour. On KTVO, the television outlet, he had a quarter hour of news and markets beginning at noon.

Bob Quinn, another Iowa State and WOI graduate, took over the programs in 1978 when Conger decided to devote himself full time to farming.

DALE HANSEN, KWWL-AM, -TV, WATERLOO. U.S. Highway 20 runs east and west across Iowa, and Dale Hansen did a great deal of traveling along it from one farm broadcasting job in Webster City to others in Fort Dodge and Waterloo where he directed farm programs on both KXEL and most recently on KWWL, radio and TV. There also was a side excursion to Alexandria, Minnesota, for four years. In the late seventies at KWWL he was responsible for a farm program beginning at 6:15 A.M. on radio, a quarter hour of farm news and markets on TV at noon, a videotaped summary of markets for the evening news program, and three feeds of farm news during the morning on a network of eighteen stations covering Iowa and southern Minnesota. He said, "We've got the regular news wires available, but we seldom use them. We're interested in our own area, and our own news gathering facilities are better than anyone else can offer."

KIWA, SHELDON. Frank Luepke grew up on a Wisconsin dairy farm; worked as a radio repair man, radio station engineer, staff announcer, and insurance salesman before he became farm director of KIWA in 1962. In the late seventies, he was presenting an hour of farm information at 6:00 A.M. and sharing the noon hour in a program of general news, farm news, market reports, and weather.

KIWA also had a mobile unit that could shoot a signal for twenty-five miles, and Luepke used it to broadcast live from fairs, farm meetings, field days, and other agricultural events in northwest Iowa.

KCBM, SIOUX CITY. A new station plus a new farm director should add up to a new pattern in farm programs. In the case of KCBM (FM) and farm director Art Blair they added up to something like 150 different farm programs per week, most of them only about two minutes long. Starting in 1976 Blair reported farm news thirteen times a day following each hourly program of general news. He broadcast three livestock reports from the Sioux City stockyards and four other livestock reports from the surrounding area, five reports on grain prices, and two daily bulletin board spots, called "AG Reminders."

Blair, who grew up in suburban Chicago, had been a war correspondent in Viet Nam, news reporter on a Sioux City TV station, and candidate for the news director job at KCBM. He observed that no Sioux City station was paying much attention to the interests of rural people; so he was hired, not as news director, but as farm director.

He said many farmers told him they liked the FM signal because it picked up less static from a tractor or electric motor, and they liked the flow of farm news and market reports throughout the day.

Steve Saunders took over the KCBM farm director's spot in 1978 when Blair returned to straight news work on a California station. Saunders was a native of Iowa and a graduate of Mankato State College.

CLETUS PAUL, KBUR, BURLINGTON. Cletus Paul's farm programs on KBUR were mixed with general news, weather, and music from 6:00 to 7:00 A.M. He also had fifteen minutes during the noon hour, market reports at mid-morning and midafternoon, and a five-minute market summary during the evening news program. He got a direct report from the Peoria livestock market and reported other midwest markets from the AP news wire.

His farm programs were on both AM and FM, with a radius of about fifty miles in Illinois and Iowa, and he spent most of his time interviewing farmers in that area.

He entered radio as an announcer on KBUR shortly after World War II. Ten years later he was named farm director, the only one the station ever had, or wanted.

OTHER IOWA STATIONS. The Sioux City stockyards for years had a working relationship with KSCJ radio and KVTV-TV for receipts and livestock sales. In the mid-forties Chep Schafer was spokesman for the yards, followed by Harry Aspleaf and Warren Kester. Kester started evening market reports on KVTV, and he aired photographs he shot of animals sold a couple of hours earlier. In the seventies Al Welding and Jim Rodenburg made an early morning report on the day's receipts over KMEG-TV.

Al Heinz, KGLO, Mason City, began as farm director in 1950, took a few years off about 1965, and then returned to the station. Don Meinert filled the job during his absence.

AT KSIB, Creston, Ray Heinen was probably that station's earliest farm director; Chep Shafer took over in 1948, moving from KSCJ, and said he was on the air fifty-four hours each week with farm news, markets, weather, and music.

In addition, about eighteen other Iowa stations reported they had farm programs in the late seventies.

IOWA FARM BUREAU. In the mid-seventies Lyle Borg, of the Iowa Farm Bureau, presided over three weekly radio programs which were all taped and all long established. "Voice of Agriculture," started in 1955 and consisted of five stories that could be used as one quarter hour program or as five separate stories, "telling the farm story to nonfarm audiences." It was sent to sixty-two stations. "On Capitol Hill" started in 1959 and featured interviews concerning legislation with members of Congress, the state legislature, and the officers of the Farm Bureau. They were five minutes or less and used by fifty-nine stations. "Accent" was the title of a weekly commentary in which Borg reflected Farm Bureau attitudes, usually as outlined by the organization's resolutions, but without mentioning the Farm Bureau by name. Forty-two stations received this weekly tape.

IOWA RADIO NETWORK. The Iowa Radio Network comprised seventeen stations that owned the network, and fed varied news programs to its member stations all day long, including eight programs of market news between 6:35 A.M. and 3:45 P.M. and a two-minute capsule of agricultural news by the UPI farm correspondent in Washington. The market news reports were voiced by the network staff announcers, using information from the market news services of the USDA and Iowa State University.

According to C. Ross Martin, network manager, the stations paid an annual fee which covered all the network services, but no special fee was given for the farm services. When a station sold a spot announcement adjacent to a market report or the farm news summary, the station pocketed the money.

Chapter Twenty-one

Kansas

KSAC, MANHATTAN. Almost as soon as the *Kansas City Star* put its radio station on the air in 1922, Sam Pickard, extension editor at Kansas State Agricultural College, arranged for speakers from the college to deliver lectures on the air one night a week. But it was a 200 mile round trip from the college in Manhattan, Kansas, to Kansas City, Missouri. Traveling expenses for the speakers during that year cost $250.

In 1923 Pickard organized more speakers into what he called the "College of the Air" over KFKB in Milford, Kansas, owned by Dr. John R. Brinkley. The program included two speakers each night, five nights a week, for ten weeks, covering subjects such as poultry, dairying, beef cattle, cooking, sewing, and child care. Students were invited to sign up, listen, and take an examination in the subjects of their choice. A total of 967 signed, and 311 took examinations at the end of the ten-week term. At first speakers traveled twenty-five miles from Manhattan to Milford, but then Pickard arranged for them to speak from the campus. He and two associates put up their own money as assurance that Kansas State College would pay the bill for telephone lines to the station.

Meanwhile, the President of Kansas State, William L. Jardine, and others had persuaded the legislature to appropriate $29,000 for a 500 watt transmitter and two towers to hold the antenna. KSAC went on the air December 1, 1924, and its early programs included the "College of the Air" and a "Farm Hour" each day at noon. Pickard was in charge of programs and their principal announcer. Occasionally he had help from a young journalism instructor, Morse Salisbury, and George Gemmell, head of the college home study projects.

In 1925 President Jardine moved to Washington as secretary of agriculture in the Coolidge cabinet, and he took with him his English department head, Nelson Antrim Crawford, as USDA director of information. He named Milton Eisenhower, a Kansas State alumnus, as his assistant. Soon after he also had Pickard set up a nationwide radio service, and Kansas State philosophy began to be felt nationwide.

KSAC shared time with other stations from the start, and since 1929 with WIBW, Topeka. Beginning in 1961, the KSAC share was from 12:30 to 5:15 P.M. Monday through Friday plus time for the college football games each Saturday afternoon in the fall.

The "College of the Air" faded into history, but the daily "Farm Hour" continued into the seventies.

Many different people have presided over the KSAC "Farm Hour" including Kenneth Gapen, who became USDA Radio-TV chief in the forties and fifties. In the years of World War II, Miriam Dexter conducted the "Farm Hour" and also produced a weekly platter service which replaced the script service to other Kansas stations that had been started in 1932. In 1948 Grant Salisbury was named radio specialist, directing the daily KSAC "Farm Hour" and changing the recorded service from platters to tape. He was the younger brother of Morse Salisbury, the second USDA radio chief.

In 1937 Lyle Longsdorf, extension editor, reported that the year's schedule of talks on KSAC had been laid out in advance, 3,500 talks by 370 different speakers. By the time the syndicated tape service was started a dozen years later, the talks were shorter and not scheduled so far in advance, permitting the subjects to be more timely. For a quarter century, the number of stations receiving the service had stayed in the range of sixty to seventy.

It was about 1939 that editor Lyle Longsdorf and radio specialist Jim Chapman took me around Kansas, calling on county agents and radio stations. We found only a few county agents who knew anyone at the local radio station; most stations carried the "Farm Flashes" out of duty, rather than pride; and I don't recall meeting anyone at a commercial station who called himself a farm director.

By the mid-seventies things changed and 106 county agents reported they were appearing regularly on local radio stations and thirty were on TV stations. About three-fourths of the radio programs were taped in advance, but on TV most of the appearances were live. From KSAC, Paul DeWeese taped six programs per week, five minutes each, and a series of two-minute spots called "Farm Talks."

Up to 1952, KSAC was operated by part-time staff members and students under the general supervision of Longsdorf. In 1953 Kenneth Thomas was named manager and given a budget for a full-time staff. In the late seventies Jack Burke was manager of television and radio operations which included KSAC radio in Manhattan, the Kansas State University Radio Network, KSET-TV in Wichita, and a film production unit.

In the mid-seventies, Lowell Kuehn was the lone Wichita outpost of the extension service and presented three TV programs per day, Monday through Friday. Some were aimed at farmers, others at homemakers and home owners. A survey of viewers showed that less than one-fourth lived on farms; two-thirds watched the extension programs two or three times a week, regardless of topics; and more people were interested in gardening than any other subject. He offered a garden calendar that brought 2,780 requests.

WIBW, TOPEKA. As was mentioned earlier, KSAC and WIBW shared the 580 KHZ frequency since 1929 although WIBW operated for profit. In recent years, KSAC had operated principally in the afternoon, giving WIBW plenty of air time to sell, and to develop a substantial farm service. In the seventies WIBW had a three-man farm department, headed by George Logan, then Rich

Hull, then by Kelly Lenz. The farm staff goes on the air at 5:30 A.M. with a half hour of farm news, followed by an hour of news, conversation and live music by the Pleasant Valley Gang, which was on the station with no change in personnel for more than thirty years. Hull said, "When the Gang goes off the air, we're going to lose something important."

The station presented market reports every hour throughout the morning, including reports on livestock at St. Joseph, Missouri, and Omaha; futures trading in grains and other commodities in Chicago, Omaha, and Kansas City; and a summary of hog trading at eleven terminal markets.

The farm department was also responsible for a half hour television program, "Midday in Kansas," which included general news, weather, and consumer information.

It was in the forties that Gene Shipley became the station's first full-time farm director. Shipley was one of the first farm broadcasters to cover his listening area in a company plane. It was called the "Red Rooster." The plane crashed and he was killed April 1, 1949. Wes Seyler succeeded him, continuing to 1953; Wilbur Levering then became farm director, broadening the scope of service, until he left in 1965, and George Logan became WIBW farm director. His diploma in agricultural journalism from the University of Missouri carried his real name, George Loesing. He was a summer trainee in the USDA Radio-TV Service; and after graduating in 1957, he took a full-time job there. In 1960 Loesing joined Bob Miller in WLW's farm department, and became "George Logan," a name easier for listeners to understand. He has kept the name ever since, through five years at WLW, ten years as head of the WIBW farm department, and more years as general manager of KGNC, Amarillo, Texas, and of WIBW-TV.

Rich Hull was an Iowa farm boy (no relation to another Richard Hull, Iowan and broadcaster a generation earlier). Hull had an extensive farm broadcasting background before he joined WIBW in 1974, and the next year he was promoted to farm director. Late in 1978 the Stauffer organization named him general manager of KGBX, Springfield, Missouri.

George Logan

Lenz was named farm director to succeed Rich Hull. Lenz had moved to WIBW in the summer of 1978 from WJBC, Bloomington, Illinois. In the seventies Dan Hoffman, Kendall Frazier, Jim Allison, Sam Knipp, Terrie Imer and Mike Miller were farm staff members. Sam Knipp was the first Kansas State University student to be awarded the scholarship that Rich Hull and WIBW started in 1975. The scholarship involved working a summer with the WIBW farm staff and then during the following school year working as a WIBW campus reporter. The next year's winner was Suzanne Parker.

The three-person staff averaged about 100,000 miles each year taking part in meetings, reporting them, and making speeches.

The WIBW farm department people were paid straight salary, but the top man had a bonus arrangement; if the year's sales of time on farm programs were above those of last year, he receives a commission on the increase.

The April 1976 *Reader's Digest* carried a reprint from New York Magazine called "One Day on a Kansas Farm." It was about Wilford Lindbloom and his two sons, who farm 7,000 acres in eastern Kansas. Their day started, according to author Stephen Singular, at 5:00 A.M. with radios in all three houses tuned to WIBW, Topeka." WIBW bought reprints and distributed them generously, especially to people who might be wondering where to spend their advertising dollars.

KXXX, COLBY. KXXX had been on the air three years without a farm show when the new owners brought in Ed Mason, of WIBC, as general manager in 1950. One of his first moves was to start special programs for farmers in the early morning, noon, and evening. It didn't take long for Mason to discover that he could not do justice to overall management and also to farm programs; so he hired C. R. Clem as farm director. About 1953 Guy "Doc' Embree took over and continued until 1963 when Rich Hawkins became farm director, the position he occupied until 1979, when he moved to KRVN, Lexington, Nebraska. Over the years, the station added market reports, weather forecasts, and farm features throughout its schedule in addition to the morning, noon, and evening blocks of time that were distinctly labeled "farm." These programs were supplemented by a daylong schedule planned to interest farm and ranch people.

One of Mason's innovations in 1950 was the "KXXX Sale Ring"; and twenty-nine years later, it was still going strong with reports from livestock auctions throughout the area. The auctions telephoned their prices to the station and paid for the announcements.

Another innovation was the station's own weatherman, equipped with meteorologic instruments comparable to those used by the government forecasters. The same forecaster had been on the job for more than a quarter century, so he was simply known as "Weatherman Snider."

A major change in agriculture was fostered by KXXX in the introduction of irrigation, promoted through several station-sponsored clinics and resulting in the gradual diversification from wheat alone in the KXXX area. By 1978 corn, sorghum, potatoes, and other crops were produced on more than 3 million irrigated acres.

Mason was born with the name Wallace Mosier on a farm in Iowa; was graduated from the University of Iowa; and was later to become farm director on KFRU, Columbia, Missouri; WLW, Cincinnati; and WIBC, Indianapolis.

When Mason went to Colby in 1950, he was general manager of one station and farm director for four stations owned by Farm and Home Radio. After a few years the organization broke up and Mason concentrated on one station, KXXX.

Richard Hawkins, KXXX farm director from 1963 to 1979, grew up on a ranch just one county north of the KXXX transmitter. He earned a degree from the University of Kansas and worked summers at KXXX, which led to his becoming full-time farm director after graduation. He continued to manage the family ranch while working at the station and his boss said, "It helps keep him in touch with the listeners."

DON HOPKINS. Don Hopkins, now in Winona, Minnesota, is one of the most enthusiastic raconteurs among farm broadcasters, and he has a long record of experiences in many stations, in many states.

Hopkins was farm director of KGNO, Dodge City, at the time President Kennedy was inaugurated, and Hopkins was one of the mounted posse from Dodge City which took part in the inaugural parade. Dressed in his black and white cowboy outfit, he went to the inaugural ball and was discreetly informed that all guests were supposed to be in formal dress. He replied, "Out where I come from, this *is* formal dress." He got in, big hat, boots, and all.

KFRM, WICHITA. If cattle prices had been higher when Larry Steckline sold his 4-H Club calves in the sixties, maybe he would have realized his first ambition to become a CPA. But the money ran out, so he took a job as bookkeeper at the Wichita stockyards. In time he was made publicity director of the yards, and as part of that job he started a daily market show on KTVH, Wichita.

For five years he broadcast as an employee of the stockyards, but in 1968 Steckline became a full-time farm broadcaster on KTVH, KFRM, and KICT (FM). About 1970 he gave up TV to concentrate on radio with morning and noon shows, and six market reports distributed throughout the day from 9:30 A.M. to 5:05 P.M.

The combined pattern of the AM and FM signals covered parts of five states, and so did Steckline in a twin engine plane. He estimated he made about one hundred speeches each year, and attended many other meetings. His assistants Bob Givens and Jerry Minshall shared the morning and noon shows and the market reports.

Yearly, KFRM promoted the Great Plains Country Fair in a different location each year. The main attraction was a big name entertainer, but many people came to see the tractor pulling contests. Steckline said, "You don't need much except space for an event of this kind. We had one fair at the airport in Great Bend; no grandstand. We asked people to bring their own seats, and 70,000 people turned out.''

In 1978 Steckline was succeeded by Paul Pippert, who moved from KCMO, Kansas City, and Howard Tice came aboard as second-in-command.

SONNY SLATER, KSAL, SALINA. Earlin D. ''Sonny'' Slater started as an entertainer in 1945, and in 1971 became farm director of KSAL. He was on the air for two hours each morning, beginning at five o'clock, and then again for an hour at noon. He also broadcast market reports several times each day from the Chicago Board of Trade, the Salina Board of Trade, the local grain elevators, and local livestock auctions. His market reports were all short. ''We figure a farmer operating a $50,000 tractor can't afford to sit around listening to lengthy reports.''

Slater said that county agents from a half dozen counties back in the thirties began taking turns in a daily program on KSAL. ''We've gone through a lot of different agents in the years since, but the same counties still take part in the program, one of them every day.''

RON HAYS, KFH, WICHITA. Farmers in a dozen Kansas and Oklahoma counties received programming filled with news, markets, and weather between 5:20 and 7:00 A.M.; markets at midmorning; twenty minutes during the noon hour; more markets again in midafternoon, and a summary at 5:15 P.M.

Bruce Behymer established the pattern of the KFH programs in 1934 and conducted them until 1974. He had been a livestock owner all his life and served as secretary and as publicity director of the Wichita stockyards. It was his stockyards job that led him in 1934 to KFH.

Ron Hays succeeded Behymer. He received the top award, American Farmer, from FFA in 1973 while attending the University of Kentucky. Besides his schedule of broadcasts, Hays established a telephone service, the KFH Hotline. Anyone who was interested could call the hotline number and get a recorded summary of markets and highlights of farm news.

KFDI (KFBI), WICHITA. Lester Weatherwax was one of the Four Weatherwax Brothers, Iowa farm boys who played about a dozen musical instruments and sang very good harmony in the Chautauqua during the early twenties.

After the Chautauqua ended, Weatherwax became a radio announcer. Early in World War II, KFBI had him broadcast a one-hour farm program each morning for Kansas farmers.

Weatherwax retired as farm director in 1955 and KFBI's farm programs retired with him. About ten years later the station changed owners and besides changing one letter in the station identification to KFDI, the new owners reinstituted a farm program with "Dusty" Herring in charge. He continued the program until his health failed in 1972.

Rex Childs took over the farm programs and was in charge into the late seventies. His schedule included agricultural news segments scattered throughout two hours in the early morning, fifty minutes at noon, separate reports on opening livestock and grain markets at midmorning, closing reports in midafternoon, and a farm market summary in the general news program at 5:00 P.M.

Before becoming KFDI farm director, Childs had sold farm implements, raised quarter horses, auctioneered, and owned a grocery store.

As KFDI's farm programs expanded, he acquired an assistant: Bruce Behymer, by then seventy-nine years old and retired after forty years on KFH. But he was not content to rest in his rocking chair; not content, even, to take a day off when he fell down a flight of stairs at the stockyards and broke his arm.

In addition to the stations discussed above there were farm programs on radio stations at Great Bend, Iola, Liberal, Pittsburg, Pratt, and Wellington in the seventies.

Chapter Twenty-two

Kentucky

ALTHOUGH a series of broadcasts was started on April Fools' Day 1929 by the Kentucky extension service over WHAS, Louisville, it ran for more than thirty years. Assistant extension editor Lawrence Brewer was in charge. The noncommercial programs originated on the university campus at Lexington and were fifteen minutes long during the noon hour, three days a week. By 1931 the series had become six days a week and mostly on agriculture although the other university colleges also took part. According to records unearthed by longtime editor J. Allen Smith, the extension people "radiocast 237 educational talks" in 1931 and 356 talks in 1932, with one program each week devoted to questions and answers on agriculture and homemaking.

In 1936 extension editor C. A. Lewis started a weekly news report which he called "Doings of Kentucky Farm Folks."

Brewer resigned in 1945, and Roy Hunt, a student, handled the interviews until Robert Ford was named assistant radio editor at the start of 1947. In the same year WHAS cut the farm time from fifteen minutes to eight minutes Monday through Friday and five minutes on Saturday. In 1950 Ford proposed switching from live programs to tape recordings because the tone quality was better on tape than on a Class C phone wire. When the programs were taped, he found other stations that would use them and began a syndicated service. He also started a Saturday livestock program on WAVE in Louisville. This new program may have irked the WHAS brass hats because in 1951 the university programs were cut from daily to Saturday only.

In 1952 the university relaxed its policy against broadcasting commercial shows, but maintained its stance against alcoholic beverages, cure-alls, religious or political sponsors, and endorsements of any product.

Ford lined up thirty-two stations for a five-minute tape Monday through Friday, and fourteen stations for a nine and one-half minute livestock program scheduled for each Saturday. WHAS was one of the first stations to accept the week-long tapes and continued to use them until about 1960.

The tapes were produced in the university's, not the extension service's, studios. About 1956 the extension service acquired its own studios, complete with recording and dubbing equipment. It was presided over by Ford until 1963 when he was succeeded by Bob Rees. In 1979 Garvin Quinn, Oscar Day, and James Hazeline were radio-TV specialists on the extension staff. They provided Kentucky radio stations with three weekly tapes, each containing several

John Merrifield talking seed corn with a Kentucky farmer.

five-minute farm features. Another radio tape series dealt with consumer tips, and the same weekly tape included a 4-H Club feature.

For TV stations, they provided a videotape once each month with five, three-minute features on various phases of agriculture plus the same features edited down to one and one-half minutes.

Kentucky had a state-supported educational TV network, and in 1975 the extension service produced a series of thirteen half hour programs on marketing of different farm products.

With tobacco such an important crop to so many Kentucky farmers, one of the extension tobacco specialists, Ira Massie, had his own weekly series on WKYT-TV in Lexington, and on WAVE-TV in Louisville.

WHAS, LOUISVILLE. His diploma from Oklahoma A&M College read Burnis Arnold, but for a total of eight years listeners to KVOO, Tulsa, and to the extension service recorded programs knew him as Barney.

When he moved to WHAS in 1952, Arnold found some well-established program patterns he might follow since WHAS had had a full-time farm director after 1939 when John Merrifield migrated down the Ohio River from WLW Cincinnati. In 1945 Merrifield joined the Mississippi Valley Network and was replaced by Frank Cooley, a Kansas farm boy with a degree from Kansas State University and six years as vocational agriculture teacher. Cooley continued the morning program of farm news and traveled over Kentucky and Indiana with recording equipment interviewing farmers, county agents, and agricultural leaders.

Don Davis, who had been Cooley's assistant, took over the programs late in 1949 and continued as farm director until 1952.

Up to that time the farm programs had been limited to radio and to early morning. But Arnold added a noon program and then a daily TV program.

Most farm broadcasters promoted Farm-City Week, and in 1968 **Barney Arnold** received a trophy for his efforts. Charles Dana Bennett (L) conceived the event and Larry Hapgood (R) presented the trophy on behalf of Kiwanis International, which sponsored Farm-City Week.

Hayden Timmons signed on as assistant farm director in 1953 and stayed for seven years. Fred Wiche joined the staff in the seventies.

The schedule in the mid-seventies included an hour on radio beginning at 5:30 A.M. and then ten minutes each noon. On TV they broadcast a farm news spot on the general news program each day at noon, with half hour features each Wednesday and Sunday.

When the yearly Kentucky State Fair rolled around, Arnold moved his programs to the fairground and reported on what was happening and who was winning. Persuading people to write to a radio station was not as important as it was a generation ago; but in 1975 one of the station's sponsors made an offer that required listeners to write in, and in five weeks they received 26,000 replies.

WAVE, LOUISVILLE. WAVE radio and TV launched its farm service in 1955 by hiring Shirley Anderson, who had just retired as county agent in Jefferson County (Louisville) after thirty-four years. He presided over a weekly series of one-hour TV programs called "Farm" that originated each Saturday noon from the station's own 900 acre farm. The station estimated 154,000 farms with 632,500 farm residents in the eighty-county area covered by the WAVE-TV signal, and 83,701 farm homes had TV sets in 1955.

About two years later, Anderson retired, and WAVE management called an air base in Alaska where Jack Crowner was about to complete a two-year hitch as a pilot in the air force.

Crowner was a native of Michigan, student broadcaster on WKAR, and graduate of Michigan State University. He then spent a year in New Zealand in the International Farm Youth Exchange where he met his future wife who was from Kentucky. He, of course, didn't hesitate to accept the WAVE offer.

He promptly expanded the WAVE farm programs from weekly to daily on TV and radio. At first he flew often to visit farmers and to attend farm meetings, but he gave it up because the inconvenience of relying on others for ground transportation was a nuisance.

One of the things Crowner did to keep listeners' interest was to talk about the people he met in his travels through Kentucky and Indiana. Every day he pulled a card or two from his file and talked from the notes he had made about these people, their farms, and their activities.

Crowner's programs on WAVE were interrupted for about a year when in 1975 he moved to WMT, Cedar Rapids, Iowa. But Kentucky remained more attractive, so the Crowner family returned to Louisville where Jack became director of the Kentucky Beef Cattle Association, and before long he arranged to resume his TV programs on WAVE-TV and WFIE-TV, Evansville, Indiana.

As a personal project, Crower started the Farm Radio Service Network, tape service for stations in Kentucky, Indiana, and Illinois, five minutes each day. In the seventies he offered specialized programs on cattle, hogs, tobacco, and grain. Some stations used only one; others used two or three. In total, about sixty stations used the programs.

DINK EMBRY, WHOP, HOPKINSVILLE. Drury "Dink" Embry grew up on a farm in Butler County, Kentucky, learned to play a guitar at an early age, and was successful as an entertainer on WHOP with an occasional appearance on the Grand Ol' Opry over WSM, Nashville before World War II. When he returned from the army in 1945 to WHOP, management asked him to add some farm information to his early morning songs and conversation. Before long he also had a farm show at noon. He still broadcast them thirty years later in the early morning and noon, serving listeners in a half dozen counties of southwest Kentucky and Tennessee. Occasionally he met them as a speaker and as an entertainer.

KENTUCKY FARM BUREAU. The Kentucky Farm Bureau started a weekly taped service for state radio stations in 1955; and throughout the years, Larry May, Richard Griffin, and Paul Everman did the planning, announcing, and the other duties more normally associated with being information director. Mike Feldhaus was named the organization's first radio-TV director in 1974. In 1975 the weekly service was produced in two versions, "Farm Bureau News and Views," five minutes; and "Farm Bureau Roundup," fifteen minutes and aimed at consumers as well as farmers. Feldhaus said, "The program is concerned with farming—but occasionally we'll do interviews on home gardening, canning and freezing, to balance the hard farm news that we present. Since May, 1974, the number of stations carrying our programs has grown from 32 to 96. The Farm Bureau newspaper carries a complete listing of all stations carrying the programs, where to find each station on the dial, day of week and hour or day."

In the seventies stations in Ashland, Bowling Green, Cadiz, Maysville,and Somerset also had farm programs.

Chapter Twenty-three

Louisiana

THERE'S SOMETHING about the woodlands of Louisiana. . . . On a deer hunt in 1939, extension director J. W. Bateman told extension editor Bentley Mackay to start getting Louisiana extension information to radio stations. A few months later, they and a USDA representative from Washington named Baker met at a vacant, wooded 4-H camp to develop a plan for parish (county) agents to become regular broadcasters on Louisiana radio stations. The agents would be supported by a steady flow of scripts from Mackay's office, written by Mackay and his assistant, Marjorie Arbour. Three years later, after the outbreak of World War II, Gordon Loudon was hired as the first radio editor. In 1943 he was followed by Charles Price.

During the war years parish agents increasingly used radio to build up to about 1,000 broadcasts per year, and state specialists often took part in the early morning farm program on WWL, New Orleans.

Shortly after the war ended, G. J. Durbin succeeded Charlie Price as extension radio editor. Station WLOU, Lake Charles, hired farm director Charley Collett, and three stations stepped up their schedule of county agent broadcasts to five per week while fourteen others had weekly broadcasts.

In 1949 Gordon Loudon returned to the extension service as radio editor. He noted that local agents were broadcasting regularly on twenty-four stations; in several parishes black extension agents shared time with the white agents; and in three parishes, the agents' programs were in French. On ten stations the agents were in time paid for by sponsors; and since the sponsors insisted on the better times of day and promoted their programs, these agents had larger audiences. Agents in five parishes were using wire recorders in 1949, but two years later they all had switched to tape.

Loudon and the extension service set up a daily program on the university's own station, WLSU, and it was carried simultaneously over WNOE, a fifty kilowatt station in New Orleans. This, too, was the year when Louisiana extension workers began broadcasting monthly on WDSU-TV, New Orleans. By 1954 the extension service was providing film clips and special art work to local agents for use on seven of the state's eight TV stations, and the extension editors estimated about 30 percent of the farm families in the state had TV sets. All fifty-three radio stations in the state were using scripts or had live programs, and about 60 percent of the agents were participating in radio programs, live or on tape.

A major event in Louisiana in 1957 was Hurricane Audrey, and extension agents worked night and day to help farm people prepare for the hurricane; they later gave helpful information after the hurricane passed. Other hurricanes hit the state in later years, notably Hilda in 1964 and Betsy in 1965, and each time radio and TV were vital methods of communication.

By 1960, when Pat Morgan succeeded Jim Colvin as radio specialist, agents in forty-eight parishes used radio, thirty-eight of them daily, while forty-eight used TV, with daily programs on four stations involving agents from several parishes.

In 1963 while Morgan continued his production of about 1,300 radio tapes each year, sent to seventy stations, he started a weekly agricultural TV show called "Agriscope," aimed at the city audience and shown on five Louisiana stations.

The number of stations receiving extension service radio reached a high point of eighty-three in 1967 while sixteen stations carried live or taped extension TV programs. In that year John Lienhardt started a six-year stretch as radio specialist.

Henry Red Hebert (AYbare) took over as broadcast specialist in 1973, and the next year he was joined by Wiley "Mike" Futrell. They were both Louisiana natives with masters degrees from LSU and several years experience as radio and TV news reporters on commercial stations.

In the late seventies this team provided a weekly tape service to forty-two radio stations, a weekly script packet to all the ninety-eight radio and eighteen TV stations in the state, and a monthly TV film in which extension director Cox answered questions sent in by Louisiana farm people.

Three television stations carried weekly programs by local agents: Bill Greene in Orleans Parish produced "Town and Country," principally aimed at the urban audience and on WWL-TV and WVUE-TV, New Orleans; on KSLA-TV, Shreveport, agents from four parishes combined their efforts. A Nielsen Survey in 1976 credited the Shreveport program with 52 percent of the urban audience and 39 percent of the rural people watching at the time.

WWL, NEW ORLEANS. Station WWL made a gesture toward "public interest" during the mid-thirties by setting aside a quarter hour each Saturday afternoon for talks to farmers and homemakers by Louisiana extension specialists. In 1939 the station established a daily farm program, a full hour beginning at 6:30 P.M. with Woodrow Hattic in charge and backed by a live orchestra. Hattic arranged to receive information from extension services in Louisiana, Mississippi, and Alabama and also to set up a schedule of speakers from the three state extension services and the USDA agencies in the area.

When Hattic invited listeners to name the program he got more than 25,000 suggestions. The winning name was "Dixie's Early Edition." In its first ten months, the program drew 33,000 requests for USDA and state extension publications. During the war years, the program was an important channel for telling farmers about production goals, rationing, manpower, and other wartime information. In 1943 Hattic left the program and was replaced by Gordon

Loudon. The starting time was moved earlier and earlier so that by the time Loudon left in 1949, he was going on the air at 5:00 A.M. George Shannon then took over the program. After Shannon, Shull Vance became WWL farm director in 1962 and continued until 1969 when the program ended.

KWKH, SHREVEPORT. KWKH had provided time for county agents to broadcast during the forties, and in 1952 the station hired its first farm director, Jack Timmons, a native of Texas, graduate of Texas A&M, and radio assistant in the Texas extension service. Timmons started farm programs in early morning and at noon and continued them until he went into sales work and then into station management. He was president of the farm broadcasters organization in 1957 and ten years later, when he was general manager of KWKH, he received the organization's annual award for meritorious service.

Jack Dillard became the station's farm director in 1959. He was a native of Oklahoma, graduate of Oklahoma A&M, and had spent several years in extension work before he joined KWKH. He conducted the morning and noon farm programs alone until 1968 when he was joined by James Duncan, a Texas farm boy. In their ten years as a farm broadcasting team, 1968–1978, they complemented each other in many ways: their voices sounded much alike; it was not unusual in a conversation for one to start a sentence and the other to finish it; both lived on Texas livestock farms just across the state line from the station; both were active in 4-H, church, and community affairs. One key to their success as they saw it was, "We get happy about things, or sad, or sometimes we get angry, same as our listeners might."

Together they traveled about 100,000 miles each year in rented cars, visiting farmers at home or at agricultural events and talking on the air about the people they had met. "We use lots of names, and every day we have a proverb dedicated to the people having birthdays that day."

Dillard left KWKH at the end of 1978, and Duncan continued the daily farm services.

In 1959 Gordon Loudon left the extension service for the second time to ply his trade commercially, this time on WJBO radio and WBRZ-TV, Baton Rouge, and conducted farm programs on those stations until 1972.

Farm listeners around Lafayette in the mid-seventies could watch a daily farm program on KATC-TV, directed by Floyd Cormier, those around Alexandria could tune their radios each morning to Bill Day, farm director of KALB.

Chapter Twenty-four

Maine

THE EXTENSION SERVICE at the University of Maine introduced farm broadcasting to Maine farmers in 1935, when Bruce Miner was hired as extension
radio specialist. He started writing a Maine version of the USDA "Farm
Flashes" and distributed them to radio stations spotted up and down the
Maine coast. For several years the state extension service presented a weekly
farm program live over WCSH, Portland. Several county agents also used local
stations once each week.

In 1945 WCSH established its own daily farm program and formed a
mini-network with WRDO, Augusta, and WLBZ, Bangor, with Linwood
"Jake" Brofee as farm director. Brofee was from Maine, was graduated from
the state university in 1931, and was a vocational agriculture teacher. He wasted
no time in lining up agricultural authorities of all kinds. He visited fairs and
farmer meetings, and built a substantial audience. The program continued until 1962.

One experiment in agricultural TV was attempted in 1961, but a year later
it came to an end, perhaps because the experiment was too successful. The
potato growers association offered to buy a half hour time slot on WAGM-TV,
Presque Isle, if the extension service would produce the programs. The extension service hired Jim Mills away from Ohio State and planted him in Presque
Isle. Mills and his guests from the extension service, growers association, and
the agribusiness community did an extensive potato campaign. Surveys showed
they had more than 40 percent of the audience from 6:30 to 7:00 P.M. on Saturday evenings. At the end of six months, the growers organization signed up for
another twelve months.

But as Mills reviewed the situation more than a dozen years later, he said
the university president "decried the fact that everywhere he went in the state
he was reading, hearing or seeing stories about Maine agriculture, and he concluded that this was to the detriment of the University and the rest of the
economy." So after a year and a half, the potato programs on WAGM-TV
came to an end.

Mills spent several years on the staff of the USDA Radio-TV Service and
several more as communications director of the National Agricultural
Chemicals Association. In 1979 he joined the sales-marketing team of the National Association of Farm Broadcasters.

Chapter Twenty-five

Maryland

EXTENSION SERVICE. From 1945 to 1951 Ted Kangas, radio specialist of the University of Maryland extension service, was the only farm broadcaster in the state with a weekly program on WBAL, Baltimore. When some special agricultural event occurred, he served as the station's reporter.

Lest other stations feel slighted, Kangas started a daily agricultural script service that was made available to all stations in the state and used by most.

The script service was replaced by tape in the fifties when the radio programs were handled by extension radio specialists Don Dickson and Andy Feeney: a weekly tape that included a series of five-minute interviews with agricultural specialists for daily use.

Then John Wagner entered the scene in 1962. Wagner was graduated from the University of Maryland with a degree in radio in 1957 and was later in the USDA Radio Service from 1959 to 1962. He remained with the extension service through seventies.

Wagner gave the radio programs a suburban slant. In the late seventies he produced four separate series on tape: a fifteen-minute weekly program used by twenty-eight stations; a thirty-minute tape produced and mailed weekly to thirty-five stations, containing five five-minute talks or interviews, one of them on farming but with the others aimed at the urban or suburban listener; a monthly tape made up of twenty-eight one-minute reminders or tips on gardens, lawns, or pets, used by thirty-five stations; and a "Waterman's Report," five minutes each week, providing information useful to commercial fishermen and recreational boaters, and used by ten stations in the vicinity of Chesapeake Bay.

At intervals during the sixties and seventies, Wagner said he had asked Maryland radio stations, "If we provided you with a farm program—strictly farm—would you use it?" Not enough "Yes" answers were heard to warrant starting the program.

County agents in a half dozen Maryland counties were using radio regularly in the mid-seventies, and some of them had been broadcasting for twenty years or longer. Ray Muller, in Elkton, had a daily and a weekly show for approximately two decades, and in 1976 his associate, Richard Baverle, took over. Bob Miller had had a weekly radio program for most of the quarter century he had been county agent of Wicomico County. It was around 1960 that agents in Baltimore and Anne Arundel counties joined forces in a half hour home horticulture program on WBAL-TV. The agents changed with the years, but the program was presented every week with Dave Hitchcock and Russ Balge sharing the responsibilities in 1979.

WFMD, FREDERICK. Mention Frederick and perhaps the first name that comes to mind is Barbara Fritchie, who was supposed to have said, "Shoot if you must this old gray head. . . ." But in the several counties around Frederick, Fritchie probably took second place to "Happy Johnny." In the late fifties, Happy Johnny Zufall was on the air over WFMD for three hours every morning and two hours at noon with his fiddle, guitar, banjo, and seemingly endless repertoire of songs and tunes. He also supplied news from the county agents, Farm Bureaus and Granges, livestock auctions at Boonesboro and Hagerstown, and Baltimore stockyards. At night Zufall, his wife, son, and two daughters were entertaining live audiences almost anywhere within a radius of 150 miles, something he started in 1929 and continued until he became ill in 1973.

WBAL, BALTIMORE. For about seventeen years, 1951–1968, Conway Robinson, WBAL, had farmer listeners all over Maryland and in portions of neighboring states, providing them with farm news, interviews, prices on the Baltimore livestock market, and broiler prices in DelMarVa.

During most of those years, Robinson conducted "Morning on the Farm" as the sun came up; "Dinnerbell" at noon, five days a week; and two quarter hour programs called "Country News," mostly about interesting people he had met, and "This Business of Farming," both on Saturday during the noon hour. Each Sunday noon he presided over a quarter hour on TV, primarily aimed at the urban audience.

Robinson was a newspaper reporter in Annapolis when he heard WBAL was looking for a sports reporter; so he applied. It was not long before the program director remarked during the interview: "You're really not interested in sports. What would you *really* like to do?"

"I'd like to do a farm program," Robinson answered.

The program director said, "We'll have an audition, but first let's have a cup of coffee. What would you like in yours?" Robinson replied, "The way this interview is going I think I'd like a shot of brandy in mine." "You're hired," the director shot back.

Robinson was close enough to Washington to be on the scene when important agricultural news was developing in Congress or the Department of Agriculture. He also made regular visits to the USDA experiment station at Beltsville and the University of Maryland. But the stories he liked best were those he picked up from farm people themselves, whether in the mountains of western Maryland or in the flatlands along the shore. Robinson left broadcasting in 1968.

"UP ON THE FARM." In the summer of 1976, the educational television network, operated by the Maryland Center for Public Broadcasting, introduced its first farm program, "Up on the Farm," in prime time, 8:00 P.M. on Monday evenings.

Producer Dick Hoffman approached the program from the sporting side of agriculture, thoroughbred racing. Host Ron David was a news reporter and film maker; market news on the program was reported and analyzed by George Roche, market specialist for the Maryland Department of Agriculture. Don Sarreals, an experienced weather forecaster, related his reports to growing and harvesting conditions. A ten-minute feature on each show dealt with how-to-do-it in agriculture and was handled during the first two years by Jan Eliassen, who grew up on a poultry farm on Maryland's eastern shore, got a degree in broadcasting from the University of Maryland, and worked as assistant to John Wagner in the extension service radio shop. He was succeeded in 1978 by Jay Nicholson, who also grew up on an eastern shore farm.

The programs were well filled with timely and useful information for farmers and with an occasional quick gesture in the direction of consumers.

WDMV, POCOMOKE CITY. For about twenty years after it went on the air in 1955, WDMV called itself the "DelMarVa Farmers' Station" and presented a farm report of some sort every hour on the hour from 6:00 A.M. to 6:00 P.M. The station never had a full-time farm director, but the program director and the news director both paid as much attention to farm news, weather reports, and markets as to any other kind of progamming. Mike Salter, who became program director in 1975, reshuffled the program schedule so the information for farmers in this cradle of the broiler industry was concentrated in early morning, noon, and early evening.

The station used AP audio reports, tapes from Maryland and Delaware extension services, and telephone interviews with agricultural authorities. Broiler prices received a major share of attention because several thousand people in Delaware, the eastern shore of Maryland, and Virginia were in the broiler business and probably turned out more broilers per square mile than any other part of the nation.

WBOC, SALISBURY. In contrast to WDMV a few miles away, WBOC doesn't report broiler prices at all. Why? Because there is no longer any open trading in chickens. Tom McGuire, farm director of the station, said, "The broiler grower knows the price he's going to be paid when he starts raising the chicks. The industry is almost completely integrated, from the hatching egg to the dressed bird."

In his daily morning and noon programs totaling one and three quarter hours each day, McGuire reported local prices for grain and livestock and also prices at the Midwest markets on which local prices were based.

McGuire was a native of Maryland's eastern shore and a thirty-year radio veteran, announcer, and news reporter. He was named farm director in 1974.

Chapter Twenty-six

Massachusetts

WHEN WBZ went on the air in the late summer of 1921 at the Westinghouse plant in Springfield, its inaugural program was from New England's major agricultural show, the Eastern States Exposition. That was a one-time shot, however, and agriculture got little attention on WBZ until 1924 when extension editor Robert Hawley and the poultry department of Massachusetts Agricultural College conducted a poultry school of the air. Listeners were invited to enroll by paying a one-dollar fee and in return each listener received a printed outline of the course and several extension publications.

The Massachusetts radio poultry school was so successful that in 1925 Hawley started a weekly program on WBZ called "Farm Forum," where he read questions from farmers who had written to the agricultural college, and one or two experts from the college staff gave the answers. After about a year, William R. Cole took over the programs, as a sideline to his regular job as food preservation specialist, and changed the format to a series of talks by extension specialists.

The "Farm Forum" audience was increased substantially when the Westinghouse Company built a new transmitter close to Boston, but the old one remained operational in Springfield with programs aired simultaneously over both stations.

In 1928 the program was absorbed into the daily program of the New England Radio News Service described in Chapter 6.

The Massachusetts extension service cooperated with WGY, Schenectady, New York, when "Farm Paper of the Air" began, at first by providing two or three scripts per month. About 1930 extension speakers began to travel to Schenectady to deliver their talks in person.

In the summer of 1931 the Massachusetts extension service decided to provide a daily manuscript service to radio stations in the state by localizing USDA Farm Flashes and supplementing them with Massachusetts information.

The daily script service was started in July by G. O. Oleson, who had been extension editor for some five years, but I took over about one month later and cranked out six scripts each week for the next four years.

At first the scripts were ten minutes each, and they were used by just four stations in the state. After a few months they were stretched to fourteen and one-half minutes, and by 1935 they were used by a dozen stations. In 1933 we made a survey of listeners and found that "Farm Flashes" had many more townspeople than farmers listening, so we changed the title to "Farm and Garden Chats" and began to include more gardening information.

In 1932 I was asked to take responsibility for the three live programs per week which Massachusetts extension speakers presented on the daily program over WBZ and the fifteen to twenty speakers per year who took part in the WGY programs.

The programs were all done from scripts except for the weekly 4-H Club program on WBZ with George L. Farley as the central figure. Big, rawboned "Uncle George" lost his eyesight about 1933 and was hospitalized for many months. But when he regained his strength, he was more dynamic and more magnetic on the air, before an audience, and in private than he had been when he could see.

In 1934, I was given a student assistant named Charlie Eshbach, who wrote many of the scripts in the "Farm and Garden Chats" series during the next year and a few years later became director of the New England Radio News Service.

In the summer of 1935 I moved to WLS, Chicago, and Oley Oleson switched from news and bulletins to radio. He stayed with radio until he retired from the extension service in 1956. He continued the daily script service until June 1941, by which time county agents in eleven counties had local programs, most of them once each week.

Oleson had become the principal spokesman of the Massachusetts extension service on the Yankee Network "Farm Journal," which was the successor to "New England Agriculture"; and also on the WBZ "Farm Hour," which went on the air at 6:00 A.M. His schedule frequently involved two or three 180 mile round trips each week between Amherst and Boston for broadcasts. In 1946, with the pressures of wartime ended, Massachusetts extension service dropped out of the Yankee Network series but provided one speaker each week to a new farm program on WHDH, conducted by Joe Kelly, and a steady flow of information to Frank Atwood on WTIC, Hartford. Oleson acquired a tape recorder in 1950 and started providing taped talks and interviews to WTIC, WBZ, and other stations. Bill Alford was imported from Iowa State College as assistant radio editor in 1952, stayed for two years, and was followed by another Iowan, Bob Simmons. These teams produced thirty to forty tapes each week.

Television came to the Massachusetts extension service in 1951 when the service was invited to produce a weekly half hour program on WBZ-TV. The responsibility for planning the program fell to the exhibits specialist, Earle S. Carpenter. The program was a combination of agriculture, homemaking, gardening, and food shopping. It was hosted by Plymouth County agent Joe Brown. He conducted the program for three years, until the major responsibility was taken over by the staff of the university's experiment station at Waltham. Carpenter also scheduled one speaker each week for a WBZ-TV series called "Homecoming" which ran for about a year beginning in 1954.

Beginning in 1957 the next big venture was a gardening series on the educational station in Cambridge, WGBH. Alfred Boicourt was the presiding horticulturist for the first four seasons, followed by Harold Mosher. Both were from the Massachusetts State University staff. In 1962 Massachusetts dropped out and New Jersey horticulturists took over. This series was the forerunner to "Crockett's Garden" which ran strong on public TV stations until 1979.

County extension staffs in Worcester and Springfield started a TV series about 1954; the former lasted for two years, but the Springfield agents were still on the air more than twenty years later.

Among the county agents who made use of radio, I doubt if any were more enthusiastic than George F. E. Story, in Worcester County. He may have been the first county agent in the United States to adopt radio as an extension tool. He started in 1921 on the experimental station of Clark University in Worcester, then irregularly on WCTS; and in 1931, he started a daily program at noon on WTAG, Worcester. The program was a mixture of farm, home, and 4-H, reflecting the extension activities. Story presided over a staff of about ten persons and they all used radio to help do their jobs.

Two stations in Massachusetts had farm directors as early as 1940: Jesse Buffum on WEEI, Boston, and Malcolm McCormick on WBZ-WBZA, Boston-Springfield. NERNS provided much of the information on the WBZ program, but Buffum gathered his own information from sources throughout New England. Following World War II, Joe Kelly, who had been a staff announcer, started a program on WHDH which also drew on many sources for speakers and information. In 1947 Don Tuttle, a staff announcer, started a farm program on WHAI, Greenfield, which served Massachusetts, Vermont, and New Hampshire. It continued until Tuttle moved across the Berkshire Hills to WGY, Schenectady.

The WBZ and WEEI programs came to an end in the fifties, but Kelly continued on WHDH until the late sixties when he was succeeded by Ken Stahl. The program ended in the early seventies.

MASSACHUSETTS FARM BUREAU. As the extension service was getting out of broadcasting, in 1969, the Massachusetts Farm Bureau got into it for the first time by hiring Gregg Finn, a former disc jockey, as information director. Finn started a recorded five-minute radio program called "Farm People of Massachusetts." It was aimed at urban listeners, telling them about the people who operated Massachusetts farms (6,000 of them in 1969), food prices, pesticides, the effect of environmental laws on farming, and so on. In 1976 the program was used regularly by fifteen stations in Massachusetts and one in Kansas. In the early seventies, at a Farm Bureau meeting in Kansas, Finn was a guest on Bruce Behymer's program on KFH, Wichita, and told about his efforts to bridge the gap between farm people and city people. Behymer said, "If you'll send me your tape every week, I'll put it on the air."

On television Finn was host on "Countryside," a live, half hour program presented each Sunday morning on WBZ-TV, produced by the Massachusetts Department of Agriculture, featuring farm families and their work. In 1976, after seven years on the air, it seemed to be firmly fixed in the station's schedule at 7:00 A.M. each Sunday.

Chapter Twenty-seven

Michigan

WKAR, EAST LANSING. When WKAR, Michigan State College, East Lansing, went on the air in 1922, James B. Hasselman, extension editor, started a farm program.

Hasselman continued to broadcast or supervise WKAR's daily broadcasts to farmers until 1934 when he joined the USDA in Washington.

The extension service kept its responsibility for WKAR farm programs until 1948 when the station itself received an increased budget and offered to pay half the salary of a farm broadcaster, with the extension service paying the other half. The first person to hold this position was Grant Salisbury, who had been station manager and farm director of KSAC at Kansas State College.

At WKAR Salisbury had three farm shows each day and wrote a daily script service mailed to two dozen stations and to county agents using radio.

One of his unique services was the "Flying Bull Report." The Flying Bull was a plane that carried semen to artificial inseminators, dropping each batch by parachute at a certain spot where the inseminator would be waiting to pick it up. Each morning WKAR reported whether the plane would be flying and its schedule.

Salisbury left the extension service and broadcasting to enter magazine journalism in 1951 and was followed by Howard Hass, from WOI and WHO, Iowa.

On WKAR Hass continued the morning, noon, and late afternoon broadcasts; and for the extension service he started a series of taped programs, fifteen minutes per week, sent to about twenty-five stations, and a series of one-minute scripts, eight to ten per week, sent to county agents for use in their broadcasts.

When Hass left WKAR and Michigan at the beginning of 1955, Arthur Burroughs, who had been a student assistant, took over the WKAR farm director spot; he was followed by other Michigan State and WKAR alumni Robert Worrel, 1960–1964; Dick Arnold, 1964–1973; and by Dick Littleton, whose job was ended in 1974 as a result of a budget squeeze caused by the reduced sales of Michigan-made automobiles. Dick Estell, a veteran WKAR staff member, took over the WKAR farm programs as a part-time job from 1974 to 1979.

There were years during the sixties when the extension service had no radio-TV specialist but student assistants, including Jim Harrison and Tom Bare, kept radio tapes going to Michigan stations. Roger Brown was named radio-TV specialist in 1969 after earning two Michigan State University degrees and serving as broadcast director of the Michigan Farm Bureau.

He developed several taped services sent to Michigan stations: "Ag Extra" was a weekly radio tape of five three-minute interviews with agricultural extension specialists sent to 100 radio stations over the state. On WKAR he presented two weekly, fifteen-minute programs about food. These programs were taped and distributed to most of the stations in the state. He also provided the Michigan Farm Radio Network with five "actualities" each week, most of them one minute in length.

On TV he presented a daily series of nine-minute programs aimed at consumers on WJIM-TV, Lansing, and portions of the programs were rebroadcast on thirteen other stations.

Brown estimated that in the late seventies about seventy of the eighty-three county extension staffs in the state were taking part in radio programs in their home areas, most of them weekly, but with a few on a daily basis. The extension staff in Wayne County (Detroit) for several years had a weekly program on WWJ-TV called "Country Living," presented each Saturday morning from 7:00 to 7:30, aimed mostly at city and suburban residents.

On WNEM-TV, Saginaw, county agents in three counties combined their efforts to produce a weekly half hour program, aimed at farmers.

WJR, DETROIT. The most powerful radio voice speaking to farmers in Michigan and adjoining areas was that of clear channel station WJR, and for thirty years, 1944–1974, the program was conducted by Marshall Wells, who died January 1975, at the age of 63. Wells went on the air at 5:10 A.M. with "Town and Country" and again at noon with "Farm Roundup," six days each

Marshall Wells

week, often broadcasting from his home. He opened and closed his programs by ringing an old farm dinnerbell.

He traveled over his listening area in his Cessna plane, and it was taken for granted that when there was an agricultural event, Wells would be there.

In a memorial program on WJR following Wells's death, one of his colleagues said, "He was stubborn sometimes, but that was part of the beauty of the man's character. He didn't avoid controversy, and he always maintained, 'If there's an argument, I'm on the side of the farmer.' "

For about two years after Wells's death, staff announcers Tom Campbell and Jim Garrett, backed by news director David White, wrote and announced the farm program. In 1977 Scott Kilgore, who had been assistant farm director of KFEQ, Saint Joseph, Missouri, was named farm director of WJR. In addition to handling the early morning farm program he added farm market reports to the station's news programs at noon and 6:30 P.M.

But WJR's farm programs began in 1939 with Duncan Moore who was the station's first farm director. He had been raised on a Virginia plantation, became a newspaper reporter, and then a highly respected news broadcaster. The emphasis was on talks by experts from the Michigan extension service and the USDA but they also had a sprinkling of market news.

WWJ, DETROIT. WWJ was a forerunner in broadcasting political events when it reported results of the Michigan primary election in the summer of 1920 and of the Harding-Cox presidential race in November. But the station waited until 1946 to hire a farm director. John Merrifield was chosen. He had started farm programs on WLW, Cincinnati, in 1936, and WHAS, Louisville, in 1940. He then became farm director of the short-lived Mississippi Valley Network 1945–1946.

On WWJ he had a full hour each morning on radio, and he also wrote a farm column for the *Detroit News,* which owned the station.

In 1947 WWJ-TV went on the air and Merrifield started a TV program which survived for several years. But the radio program and the newspaper column served Michigan farmers with up-to-date information for thirteen years.

HAROLD SPARKS, WLKM, THREE RIVERS. In the twenty-four years that he was a county extension agent in Michigan, Harold Sparks became accustomed to facing a microphone or TV camera. As early as 1947 he was a regular guest on John Chase's farm program on WHFB, Benton Harbor; he frequently went across the state line to appear with Jay Gould on WOWO, Fort Wayne, Indiana, and for nine years was a regular on WSBT-TV, South Bend, with Bob McDermott. When he was county extension director in Niles, Sparks had a microphone on his desk and did a daily radio program on WNIL. He left extension work in 1966 to become full-time farm director on WNIL, and in 1970 switched to WLKM at Three Rivers with two farm programs Monday through Friday, 6:35–7:00 A.M. and a quarter hour at noon.

HERB SCHMIDT, WBCM, SAGINAW. If you were interested in the history of farming in the Saginaw Valley, all Herb Schmidt had to do was to go through his own family records of five generations on the same farm.

Schmidt began telling farm stories occasionally on WBCM's farm program about 1965, when Bob Driscoll was farm director. In 1974 he took over full responsibility for the farm program, three spots of four minutes each in the morning and a half hour of markets, weather, and farm news at noon. The Saginaw Bay area produced most of the beans used in the baked bean industry, and reports on bean prices were a regular part of WBCM's farm programs.

WKZO, KALAMAZOO. Farm programs on WKZO, from 1945 to 1978, were run by Carl Collin and later by Karl Guenther. Collin was from Toledo where he worked as a newspaper reporter. He broke into agriculture in 1937 with the Agricultural Adjustment Administration in Washington and then in Michigan. In 1945 the AAA state information offices were abolished, and Collin sold himself and the idea of a farm service program to John Fetzer, who owned stations in Kalamazoo and Grand Rapids. Collin then went on WKZO each morning and noon until he retired in 1973. For several years his morning show was fed to WKZO's sister station in Grand Rapids, which greatly expanded its coverage. During the last six years, in addition to his two-a-day radio programs, he had a half hour each morning at 7:00 A.M. on WKZO-TV, which included a substantial amount of consumer information.

In gathering information for his programs, Collin arranged for a direct report each morning from the Chicago stockyards, called several hog buying stations in southwest Michigan for their prices, got grain market reports from a local broker, and studied daily reports from the fruit market at Benton Harbor. He also arranged for weather reports direct from the local weather bureau office at the Kalamazoo airport even though they were denied to other stations for several years.

Karl Guenther had a farm background and had been a general news reporter on WKZO for ten years when Collin retired in November 1973.

The half hour spot in the morning remained as it had been for many years, but under Guenther the noon program was expanded from a quarter hour to three quarters of an hour. The TV programs were cut from five days each week to only a Saturday evening, but it was filled with features about farmers for a consumer audience.

Jim Bernstein, who had been broadcast director of the Michigan Farm Bureau, took over the WKZO farm programs for about one year in 1978 but Guenther returned to the farm director's job in 1979.

HOWARD HEATH, WPAG, MICHIGAN FARM RADIO NETWORK. Howard Heath had been farm director of WPAG, Ann Arbor, for twenty-five years when he and another WPAG staff member, John Stommen, formed the Michigan Farm Radio Network in 1970. From a studio in the Heath farm home

Howard Heath and **Bob Driscoll**

near Milan, Heath continued his daily programs on WPAG and broadcast market reports and farm news to an ever-growing number of Michigan stations. Soon the network became a series of subnetworks, an apple network, an onion network, a dairy network, and so on, with each station receiving several programs each day out of the total of more than one dozen daily broadcasts which Heath provided and carried by a total of more than fifty stations.

At first Heath and his wife Eva, often aided by daughters Mary, Sue, or Kathy, broadcast all the programs. In 1974, Bob Driscoll joined him. Driscoll was an Iowa farm boy, and graduate of the Brown Institute. He started the farm programs on WBCM, Bay City, in 1965, and served as publicity director of the Michigan Farm Bureau for eight years. Roy Olson joined the staff in 1976, at about the same time the network moved out of the Heath's basement to its own building in Milan.

In its relations with member stations, the network paid the phone line charges and sold time to advertisers, sharing the income from sales with the stations.

The farm network spawned the development of a parent firm, the Great Lakes Radio Network, which also produces news and sports programs.

Howard Heath recovered from heart surgery in 1977 but suffered a fatal attack in 1979 at fifty-four years of age. His partners established a memorial fund to provide scholarships in agricultural communications at Michigan State University, from which four of the Heath daughters had graduated.

Mary was a broadcaster of the Agri-Network in Ohio before joining the staff of the Michigan Soybean Association; Sue was a farm broadcaster at KGNC, Amarillo; and Kathy was working in agricultural information with the Oklahoma Farm Bureau.

Driscoll succeeded Heath as president of the farm network.

MICHIGAN FARM BUREAU. The Michigan Farm Bureau in 1977 provided about forty state radio stations with a total of four taped program series each week, three aimed at farmers and one at consumers, plus a daily agricultural story provided to the Michigan Farm Radio Network.

Many of the services were started in the sixties by Bob Driscoll, and continued by Walt Olson, Eric Levine, Jim Bernstein, and then Michael Rogers beginning in 1978.

OTHER MICHIGAN FARM PROGRAMS. For several years beginning in the late forties, Frank Harmon had a farm program on WTTH, Port Huron, serving the farming area north of Detroit.

Across the state, in Grand Rapids, Dick Richards conducted a farm program on WZZM about the same time.

Station WHBF, Benton Harbor, started its farm program in 1946, with John Chase as farm director, presenting programs in early morning and at noon. County agents in western Michigan were regular guests on the program, and spray services and frost warnings were broadcast for the particular benefit of peach and apple growers in the area. Another important service was a daily price report for Michigan fruits on the Benton Harbor market. Jack Kelly conducted the WHBF farm programs for several years in the sixties and seventies.

Chapter Twenty-eight

Minnesota

MOST of the know-how needed to build a radio telephone transmitter arrived in Minnesota during the summer of 1920, when C. M. Jansky joined the electrical engineering staff at the University of Minnesota, a year or so after he had helped put a station on the air at the University of Wisconsin. Late in 1920 the station that was to be called WLB was on the air. One of the regular items that entered its irregular schedule was weather. The next year, in the fall of 1921, the station became the third station to broadcast USDA market reports.

In 1924 WCCO (Washburn Crosby Company), Minneapolis, came on the air with more power than WLB; and for a dozen years the university and the Minnesota extension service had programs on WLB, or on WCCO, or both, including a series of radio courses in poultry and dairying for which about 2,000 people signed up. In the thirties a daily series of talks by agricultural experts was carried on both WLB and WCCO simultaneously. There was a two-year period with no agricultural broadcasting beginning in 1936, but in 1938 WLB was given an increase in power to 5,000 watts, so the signal could be heard over most of the state. Extension officials then decided to give radio another try.

They hired Richard B. Hull, an Iowa State graduate who had handled farm programs on WOI, Ames, Iowa, and also at WOSU, Ohio State University. He set up a schedule of market reports twice each day and began the "University Farm Hour," Monday, Wednesday, and Friday 12:00–1:00 P.M. Hull started making platters of the WLB talks and syndicating them to stations around the state. Before long he established a Tuesday and Thursday morning noncommercial program on WCCO which was divided into two segments: one was news from the Minnesota extension service, announced by Hull; the other dealt with general farm news, by Val Brenner. The two reporters sounded very much alike because they were both Dick Hull.

"Val Brenner," presumably a station employee, could talk about events and occasionally express opinions that might be inappropriate for an extension service spokesman.

Hull left the Minnesota extension service in 1941 to become manager of WOI, Iowa State College.

During World War II no one stayed in the Minnesota radio specialist job long enough to establish a claim to the title, but in 1945 Maynard Speece was appointed. He was reared on a northern Minnesota dairy farm, was graduated from the university agricultural college in 1943, and was a county agent for two years before becoming a full-time broadcaster for three years with Minnesota extension service and then for four years with USDA. He was farm director of WCCO from 1952 to 1977.

Speece was succeeded in 1948 by Ray Wolf, a former vocational agriculture teacher and county agent. At the Minnesota extension service, Wolf continued the daily half hour on the university station (changed from WLB to KUOM) and developed several series of taped programs syndicated to Minnesota stations. When he retired in 1976, four programs were being broadcast: "Agricultural Business Reports," four and one-half minutes, six per week to fifty stations; "Garden and Consumer Tips," one minute, six per week to sixty stations; "4-H Chats," four minutes, one per week to forty stations; and "Veterinary Talks," three and one-half minutes, one per week to forty stations.

Wolf had the Minnesota extension service enter television in 1950 with a weekly program, "Town and Country" on KSTP-TV and later moved the show to WTCN-TV. In 1958 the university's own TV station KTCA came on the air and "Town and Country" went there. Leo Fehlhafer came aboard as assistant on both radio and TV programs. In 1970 TV had taken on a life of its own, and Norman Engle joined the extension staff as TV specialist. In time he acquired an assistant, Mike Harris. Engle came to Minnesota from the Pennsylvania State University extension office as did Harris from Ohio State University. One of their major productions in 1976 was a weekly "Yard and Garden" program presented live on KTCA and circulated on videotape to about six other stations over the state. They produced several other short-term series on specific subjects, such as 4-H, the handicapped, and safety, which were given similar distribution.

WCCO, MINNEAPOLIS. For the first eighteen years of its life, WCCO devoted a considerable amount of time to farmer interests as long as someone else provided the programs: speakers from the Minnesota extension service; daily reports on Minneapolis grain and South Saint Paul livestock prices by USDA market reporters. Farm leaders used the station to help form Land O'Lakes and Farmers Union Grain Terminal cooperatives.

Soon after Pearl Harbor, CBS, which had bought the station in 1932, ordered the station to hire a farm director.

WCCO hired Larry Haeg, a young local farmer who had worked for the AAA in Washington and was a member of the state legislature in 1940. He started as farm director in May 1942 with an hour in early morning and a half hour at noon. He broadcast farm news, market reports, weather, and interviews with farmers, farm leaders, and government officials. Haeg's term in the state legislature enabled him to get answers to questions about labor, fertilizer, chemicals, and other things that concerned farmers in that period more easily since he knew most of the informed people.

A year later he was the key man in organizing the farm broadcasters into a national organization and was their first president.

Haeg's farm programs were started as public service shows, but they had

Maynard Speece

not been on the air long when he was approached to sell seed corn. He later said farm programs became a very strong part of the station's sales.

In 1952 WTCN interests bought out WCCO radio and TV and chose Haeg as general manager of WCCO radio. Later he was to become president of the radio-TV firm.

When Haeg became WCCO manager he hired Maynard Speece to take his place as farm director. Over the next twenty-five years, Speece expanded the farm programs, starting at 5:50 A.M., continued the noon show, and added a "Sunday Morning Farm Hour." He also mixed in poems, puns, jokes, and other contributions from listeners, along with farm news and analysis.

For several years in the fifties and sixties, he shared the farm programs with an associate director, James Hilgendorf, who used the name Jim Hill on the air. In the seventies, Chuck Lilligren was his assistant and became WCCO farm director when Speece retired at the end of 1977.

DAVID STONE, KSTP, MINNEAPOLIS. David Stone was an announcer of the old school. He spoke with measured phrases and every syllable was artfully carved out of polished marble. He was the station's farm director for thirty-five years, from 1943 until 1978. But Stone wasn't the first farm director on KSTP. He was preceded in the thirties by Harry Aspleaf, Cal Karnstedt, and Val Bjornsen.

In 1948, television became part of the KSTP operation, and the first day's programming started with Stone's farm program. It has been on five days each week to the present. By the late fifties, KSTP radio had gone to rock-and-roll, and the radio farm program was discontinued although the program was still going strong on TV as was Stone, who observed his seventy-eighth birthday in 1979. He was out with a film or taping crew virtually every day, visiting farms and attending meetings and fairs.

KDHL, FARIBAULT. Dean Curtis has conducted farm programs on KDHL since 1947, with only two years off in the seventies to develop a broadcasting service for the state Farm Bureau.

When the station went on the air in December 1947, Curtis had a farm program at 6:45 A.M., and it had remained in the same time period since, although it had been expanded and was later joined by a quarter hour at noon and an evening program. The latter was sponsored by Purina for twenty-one years.

KDHL covered about thirty-six counties in Minnesota and Wisconsin, and so did Curtis. Many of his trips meant driving home late at night and going on the air with little or no sleep. This lack of sleep caused him a problem one time. On one of his programs Curtis dialed a telephone number, asked a question, and if the listener gave the right answer, a prize of $10 was awarded. One morning he made a call and a woman complained from her bed that she had been awakened. Curtis said sympathetically, "I wish I was there with you." She did not think it was funny. He killed the microphone while he apologized to her over the telephone.

David Stone

Curtis's travels were broadened considerably in 1971 when he was president of the NAFB, and was on the road about half the time.

When he was working for the Minnesota Farm Bureau from 1973 to 1976, his farm programs on KDHL were taken over first by staff announcers Joe Braham and Peter Kempner, and then by Earl Miller, who had spent four years in the radio division of the National Farmers Organization.

MINNESOTA FARM BUREAU. On his programs for the Farm Bureau, Curtis said he kept doing what he had done for more than twenty-five years in Faribault; reporting farm news. By 1975, 113 Minnesota stations were receiving his programs on tape, either five-minute programs six days each week or a weekly fifteen-minute program. Each program contained a blank spot where the station could insert a local sponsor's commercial. Curtis insisted he tried to keep away from anything resembling Farm Bureau viewpoints on controversial issues.

He believed the Farm Bureau's taped programs, which demonstrated that farm programs could pay their way, inspired farm programs on several small stations and two networks in Minnesota.

RICH HABEDANK, WJON, WWJO; SAINT CLOUD. Rich Habedank led a fairly complicated life by directing and announcing two similar farm programs on WJON (AM) and its sister station across the hall, WWJO (FM). He had six ten-minute programs on both stations in early morning, and at noon a twenty-five–minute farm program on the AM station, almost immediately followed by seven minutes on the FM station. But his life became simpler at 6:00 P.M. when he simulcast a fifteen-minute wrap-up of the day's markets and farm news on both stations. He received the Farmers Union livestock report from the South Saint Paul stockyards, the local livestock report from the Granite City market, and reports on the Chicago Board of Trade from Dick Reinerts of Farm Radio News.

Habedank started studying agriculture at the University of Minnesota, broke away to learn broadcasting at the Brown Institute, and in 1975 he succeeded Jim Key as farm director. Key had succeeded Jerry Urdahl.

Mark Kreuger joined him as assistant farm director in early 1977, and they promptly planned a special series about the benefits and pitfalls of irrigation.

KWOA, WORTHINGTON. Jim Wychors, general manager and part owner of KWOA, did a daily farm commentary on his station, a reflection of his years as a farm broadcaster, and planned the station's programming to meet the needs and interests of his farm listeners. With Bruce Lease as farm director since 1966, the station went far beyond the traditional morning and noon programs of farm news and interviews. In response to requests from farmers, the station presented grain and livestock market reports every half hour during the day's trading and hourly weather reports, provided by a teletype connection to the Weather Service office in the Twin Cities.

MINNESOTA'S FOUR FARM NETWORKS.
For 117 years Minnesota struggled without a farm network. Then in about three years, it acquired four of them: three in radio; one in TV.

First came the Dick Rogers Farm Radio Network, which began broadcasting in 1975. Rogers was a radio news reporter from Minneapolis, who became interested in agriculture only after he had married Lorraine who came from a farm near Hutchison. He operated his six-station network from KYSM, Mankato, which hired Rogers as the station's farm director after he had started his network program. He fed four programs each day to the other stations that rebroadcast the KYSM signal. He sold half the commercial spots and the stations sold the other half.

Originally the Rogers Network included two stations that belonged to the Linder family; but in November 1976 the Linders hired Lynn Ketelsen from KMA to be farm director of WKLM, Willmar, and fed his ten daily programs, totaling three hours, by wire to all four Linder-owned stations, in Marshall, Montevideo, and Mankato.

The third radio network called Rural America Farm Network was started in 1978 by Mark Vail and Roger Strom. Vail had been on the air over KOLM, Rochester, and Strom had handled farm programs on KXEL, Waterloo, Iowa. They linked nine stations in southern Minnesota and in Wisconsin, feeding the programs of farm news, markets, and interviews from their headquarters at Wanamingo Minnesota.

Minnesota's television network farm program was named "Country Day" and was started in April 1977 by KSTP-TV, St. Paul, hosted by Steve Edstrom, a veteran radio personality from WCCO, Minneapolis. In the early months only stations close enough to receive and rebroadcast the KSTP-TV signal carried the program, five days per week, 6:30 to 7:00 A.M. By late 1977 several stations outside the rebroadcast range had joined the network and they were provided with videotapes which they broadcast several days after the live program. In 1978 the production pattern changed: "Country Day" was taped for all stations one week in advance of the broadcast date, with a spot for a live market report by an announcer or farm director at each station. By the end of 1979 the network had expanded to twenty-nine stations in ten midwestern states.

The expansion of the network was accompanied by an expansion in staff. Gary Schendel, with news experience on several Iowa stations, became host and director in the summer of 1979; Don Buehler was assistant director and local market reporter; June Lindsay, recruited from Pennsylvania, joined the staff near the end of 1979 as a field reporter. A video cameraman and a sound technician accompanied each reporter as he or she reported rural stories from anywhere in the Midwest.

Several other Minnesota stations had their own farm programs in the late seventies, including KWMP, Wabasha, with Don Hopkins, a veteran of approximately forty years on the air; KAUS, Austin; WVAL, Sauk Rapids; KOLM, Rochester; KBRF, Fergus Falls; KFEE, Rochester; and KEYL, Long Prairie.

Chapter Twenty-nine

Mississippi

EXTENSION. Jack Flowers, extension editor in Mississippi, started the weekly quarter hour "Mississippi Farm and Home Hour," WJDX, Jackson, in 1949, a few months before he left to take a position with the USDA in Washington. His successor, Duane Rosenkranz, arranged to record the program and send tapes to twenty-four stations, but to save money he reduced the programs to five minutes per week.

In 1952 he hired Tommy Wilkerson, an Air Corps veteran and recent graduate of Mississippi State College, as radio specialist, a position he would fill for the next quarter century. Wilkerson offered the stations five minutes per day of farm and home programs, and the number of cooperating stations grew in the next few years to thirty-six. In 1956 he divided the service, offering a farm service and a home service, five minutes per day, a pattern that he and his successors continued at least through 1979. Nearly eighty stations carried the programs, and most persuaded sponsors to buy time in or adjacent to the programs. Wilkerson also provided the same stations with a weekly quarter hour summary of crop and market conditions.

Beginning in 1976 the Mississippi extension service started a seasonal "Moth Alert" broadcast telling cotton growers in each section of the state when it was time to spray to prevent cotton bollworms. The radio specialist obtained information each day from the county agents and the extension entomologist and prepared a two-minute report which was recorded on a telephone "hot line." A chemical company bought time for the alert and a commercial message on eighteen stations, each of which recorded the daily message and broadcast it on regular schedule.

When Wilkerson retired in 1977 his duties were taken over by Kal Ruppel, who had worked on several Mississippi stations. A year later he was followed by Bruce Johnson, who had studied broadcast journalism at the University of Missouri. In 1979 Johnson moved to the Oregon extension service and was succeeded by his assistant, Tyson Gair, a Mississippi State University graduate.

WLBT-TV, JACKSON. There was a period of about twenty years beginning in the early fifties when WJDX was one Mississippi station with a farm director, and for several years it was a two-man team, Howard Langfitt from Iowa, and Forrest Cox from Texas. They shared an hour and a half of farm news and features in the morning on radio and for about three years, 1953–1956, they had a farm news and market program on television at noon. Langfitt left broadcasting about 1962 while Cox continued the radio program and the TV market report until 1972 when WJDX-TV was replaced by WLBT-TV. Besides regular news programs, his assignment on WLBT-TV in the seventies included a daily agricultural markets summary at noon.

PROGRESSIVE FARMER NETWORK. For years Jim Yancey heard too many Mississippi radio stations broadcasting yesterday's prices for cotton and soybeans on their noon news programs, and in 1978 he decided to offer a better service. His Mid-South Agricultural Network went on the air in March with four Mississippi stations being fed market reports from the network studio in Starkville. Eighteen months later Yancey sold the network to the Progressive Farmer Company, publisher of farm and consumer magazines, but he remained as head of the renamed Progressive Farmer Network. By the end of 1979 it served twenty-six stations in Missouri, Tennessee, Arkansas, Louisiana, and Mississippi.

Yancey and his assistant Mike Windham broadcast four programs each day to their client stations: opening cotton and soybean prices at 9:45 A.M.; noon prices at 11:45 A.M.; closing prices at 2:30 P.M.; and a summary of the day's trading sent over the wires in late afternoon for broadcast next morning. Although the emphasis was on cotton and soybean prices, the five-minute programs noted changes in prices of oil and gold, trade agreements, and developments in the international situation as they might affect cotton and soybeans.

Until he started his network, Yancey, who held an MBA degree from Mississippi State University, had spent fourteen years in marketing and communications with several organizations, including the Mississippi extension service, the Cotton Council, and the American Soybean Association. Windham, also a University graduate, had been a broadcaster with the extension service and news reporter on several Mississippi radio and TV stations.

Yancey's programs contained three spots for advertisers, one to be sold by the network, one by the station, and the third under option to the network but sometimes sold by local stations.

Chapter Thirty

Missouri

"EARLY SOWING increases the yield of oats. The University of Missouri College of Agriculture reports that oats sown on March 17 last year came safely through the April freeze and yielded 48 bushels per acre. Oats sown two weeks later yielded 37 bushels and a month later only 25 bushels."

That message on March 7, 1922, broadcast over WOS, Jefferson City, put the Missouri extension service into broadcasting.

Extension editor A. A. Jeffrey followed with fifty-word "Radi-Agrams" each day through the spring and summer of 1922.

Live broadcasts by agricultural experts started in the spring of 1923. Each Wednesday for about two and a half years an extension worker would make the thirty-mile trip, usually by train, from Columbia to Jefferson City. Around the end of 1925, Christian College (now Columbia College) in Columbia paid for a leased telephone line to WOS, and invited the agricultural college staff to make use of it. Another Columbia institution, Stephens College, started its own radio station, KFRU, about that same time, and invited the extension service to put on a twenty-minute program each Tuesday and Friday evening. The three broadcasts per week on the two stations continued until 1930 when Jeffrey started a daily manuscript service of about 1,200 words, "Missouri Farm Broadcast." In 1963 a second script service of questions and answers was added, five each week. The script services continued until 1969.

A gap of about four years began in 1930 when the state extension staff broadcast no live radio programs, but in 1934 Jeffrey arranged for a daily broadcast on KFRU, Columbia, each morning. Around the same time county agents started local programs over KFEQ, Saint Joseph; KMBC, Kansas City; KFVS, Cape Girardeau; and KWTO, Springfield.

By 1940 agents in fifty-four Missouri counties were appearing on radio regularly, and in several counties the local staff had a daily program. Throughout the fifties, sixties, and seventies, about seventy agents broadcast at least once each week, mostly in commercial time.

The development of portable recorders made broadcasting much more attractive to county agents. For example, C. C. Keller, in Springfield, acquired a wire recorder and in 1948 wrote, "I think it is one of the best investments we have made."

The state extension office started providing recorded programs about 1948, first on discs and then on tape. The daily "Farm and Home Chats," went to twenty stations during the first year and over the next quarter century,

173

reached a peak of seventy stations before falling back to about fifty-five. Along the way, the program developed several weekly companions: "Point of Interest," a public affairs program; "Missouri Forum," dubbed from the audio portion of a TV show on KUMO-TV; "Yard 'n Garden"; "A Look at the Weather"; and during the growing season, the "Insect Situation."

In 1973 "Report" was started, four minutes once each week giving highlights of research at the college experiment station; the program had forty-four subscribers.

In 1970 the extension radio office acquired an "electronic secretary" and used it to record the daily "Insect Situation" report. About two dozen stations called in each day, dubbed off the recorded message, and put it on the air.

A. A. Jeffrey, a pioneer in radio use, retired in 1951, and was followed by Elmer Winner for five years and then by Richard Lee. Howard Dail, who fostered the script services and the expansion of county agent broadcasting in the thirties and forties moved to the California extension service. The syndicated tape services were increased in number and provided to more stations, largely through the work of James Hodgson, William Mackie, Richard Bailey, and later Harlan Lynn.

KMBC, KANSAS CITY. Not long after the Missouri Bureau of Markets and the Missouri extension service launched their daily broadcasts on WOS, extension workers from Kansas Agricultural College began crossing the state line once each week to broadcast over WDAF, Kansas City. This continued from 1923 to 1924. During the four years that followed, Kansas City was without farm broadcasting programs.

In 1928 Sears Roebuck opened a new store in Kansas City and brought in George Biggar to start a farm service on KMBC similar to the programs Biggar had developed under the auspices of the Sears Roebuck Agricultural Foundation in Chicago, Dallas, and Atlanta. The three daily programs originated in the bungalow studio in the Sears store, and they brought thousands of visitors to the store during the year they were aired.

Another brief effort to serve the farm audience began in 1932 when KMBC hired its own farm director, Phil Evans, a Chicago livestock commission salesman and frequent broadcaster. After two years Evans dropped out of radio, but returned to broadcasting in 1936, as Midwest reporter on the series of regional network programs sponsored by Goodyear. A year later he returned to KMBC for a long stay, twice each day on KMBC (and KFRM) from 1937 to 1965, and two more years on WDAF, until illness forced him to retire.

Besides his daily broadcasts, Evans operated his own farm and two others near Stanley, Kansas. Many of his broadcasts originated from his home.

Evans was one of the few farm broadcasters willing to stick his neck out. For example, each day he predicted what he thought livestock prices would be the next day. On one occasion, when cattle prices at Kansas City had been below those at Omaha and Saint Joseph for several days, he told his listeners "Hold back your cattle. Don't send them to Kansas City." Cattle receipts dropped; prices at Kansas City jumped to the level of other markets and stayed there.

In a drought year, a Kansas congressman introduced a bill that would provide financial help to farmers in only the congressman's part of the state. A hurried thousand-mile survey showed Evans that the remainder of the state was in even greater need. He telephoned the congressman, "If I'm not notified before noon tomorrow that drought relief money will be available for the entire state I'm going to tell the story on my noon program." The congressman called at ten o'clock the next morning to say he was amending his bill to include all of Kansas.

KCMO, KANSAS CITY. KCMO started a service for farmers in the late forties, which continued until 1978.

The station's first farm director was Chester W. "Jack" Jackson, who had been spokesman for the Texas extension service on the daily "Texas Farm and Home Hour." He established morning and noon farm programs on KCMO, set up a studio in the Exchange Building at the stockyards, and hired Bruce Davies, a recent University of Missouri graduate, to report the markets several times each day. In 1953 Jackson was given another assistant, a Kansas county agent named George Stephens.

All three men were chosen by their fellow broadcasters as president of their national association; Jackson in 1954, Davies in 1963, and Stephens in 1966.

One of the KCMO special promotions in the fifties was the 100-Bushel Corn Club and corn clubs were formed in about 150 Missouri and Kansas communities. The clubs continued until yields of 100 bushels became commonplace.

Davies moved to Chicago to report livestock markets there and was replaced by Jack Wise. About 1958 Jackson returned to extension work as editor in Maryland. Stephens became farm director and Paul Pippert moved from the news staff of KCMO to the farm department. Pippert took over as farm director in 1973 when Stephens moved to an advertising agency in Kansas City.

In reviewing their combined service as KCMO farm directors, covering more than twenty years, Stephens and Pippert noted they changed from script to ad lib, shortened the talks and reports, lessened the amount of instruction broadcast, and gave more attention to news—especially the markets. In the fifties most sponsors bought a ten- or fifteen-minute segment of the farm program while in the seventies a sponsor usually bought one or two spots in one program.

In 1978, KCMO ended its farm programs, the last in Kansas City, and Pippert became farm director of KFRM, Wichita.

KFEQ, SAINT JOSEPH. It was the stockyards and the grain people in the city who were most influential in creating KFEQ in 1923, and livestock and grain market reports became fixtures in the daily schedule. County agents in nearby counties arranged a program schedule laden with the kinds of things county agents tell farmers. In 1950 KFEQ hired its first farm director, Harold Schmitz, a soft-spoken Indiana farm boy who had gone to Purdue where he broadcast as a student and then as extension radio specialist.

At KFEQ Schmitz continued the traditional reports from the stockyards and the grain exchange but also established a morning farm hour beginning at six o'clock. About two years later, KFEQ-TV came on the air and he bid for evening air time and got it. He also acquired an assistant, Ralph Mellon, who later was replaced by Jim Sprake.

One of Schmitz's favorite radio features was called "Just Wonderin'." "I used a portable recorder, and I'd find someone in a feed store or in the corner of a hog pen or in a milking parlor and 'just wonder' about what he was doing, whether there might be a better way to do it, what he thought about while he was doing it—almost any topic. More listeners commented about 'Just Wonderin' than anything else."

Early in the game Schmitz began to arrange trips for farmers to Europe, to South America, and to Mexico, and in 1964 he left broadcasting to become a travel agent.

Schmitz was succeeded by Jim Sprake. Sprake hired Gene Millard, a young farmer in the area, as his assistant. Both men made up the KFEQ farm team for nine years until 1973 when Sprake resigned, and Millard became farm director, assisted at first by Scott Kilgore, a young Missouri farmer, and then by Bob Azleton, who had broadcast markets from the Saint Joseph stockyards. In 1976 Millard was promoted to general manager of KFEQ, and Azleton became farm director. Azleton was joined in 1977 by Bryce Anderson, farm director of KDTH, Dubuque.

KMOX, SAINT LOUIS. In 1932, the same year that KMBC hired Phil Evans as farm director on the western side of the state, KMOX balanced the state by hiring Charley Stookey to start a farm program serving eastern Missouri and across the Mississippi River into Illinois.

For Stookey it was a return to his homeland since he had grown up near Belleville, Illinois. He had gone to the University of Illinois, taken a job with *Prairie Farmer*, and then conducted the "WLS Dinnerbell Time" for three years, from 1929 to 1932.

On KMOX Stookey went on the air for an hour and a half, starting at 5:30 A.M., with country music and pipe organ (the WLS music pattern). He frequently took his recording equipment to the stockyards and talked to farmers who had tried new crops and chemicals of the time like soybeans or high nitrogen fertilizer.

In 1939 CBS tapped him to conduct a weekly half hour program called "Columbia's Country Journal," in addition to his daily programs on KMOX, and he presided over the CBS program until 1942.

Two years later he moved his daily show from KMOX to KXOK, Saint

Louis and added one new feature: he began to invite listeners to go with him on one-day bus trips to see interesting agricultural activity, such as the cotton harvest in the Missouri "Bootheel" or the apple country in southern Illinois. Later came week-long trips to New Orleans, to the lower Rio Grande valley of Texas, and across the border into Mexico. When Stookey acquired his pilot's license in 1946, he used a plane to visit farmers and attend farm meetings. He also joined with soil conservation specialists to arrange for farmers to fly over their own land so they could see the effects of erosion and the benefits from terracing, contouring, and other soil conservation measures.

His farm broadcasting in Saint Louis included nine years at KMOX, eight years at KXOK, two years at KWK, and a year at WEW. In 1952 he gave up farm programs. For a number of years, he and his wife have kept both their typewriters busy as free-lance writers from their home in Florida.

One of Stookey's successors at WEW was Paul Vogel, who had been farm director of KWOS, Jefferson City, and then WDAF, Kansas City. When he joined the USDA as an information specialist in 1961, he returned to his legal name of Paul Schrimpf. He too was free-lancing from his home in Kansas City in the seventies.

Stookey's successor at KMOX in 1944 was Ted Mangner who had been extension radio specialist and farm program director of WILL, University of Illinois, for seven years, 1937–1944.

Over the twenty-four years he was on KMOX Radio from 1944 to 1968, Mangner usually had two half hour programs each day, one in the early morning and the other with market reports during the noon news program. He also broadcast "Sunnydale Acres" each Saturday noon, "Country Columnist" on

Ted Mangner

Sunday, plus a country music program on Saturday evenings. There was a period of about eight months in 1958 when he broadcast on both radio and TV, up to the time he literally fell on his face from exhaustion.

Mangner was the principal salesman for time on his programs; and between making speeches to farm groups over Illinois, Missouri, Arkansas, and Tennessee along with calling on his clients, he said, "I all but lived on the road."

Amazingly, he found time to do a few other things. For several years he wrote and published a monthly house organ for the milk producers' organization in the Saint Louis area; and also he wrote a weekly column in the newspaper at Vandalia, Illinois, a city he had called home for many years. He then bought a farm, moved to it, and for a few years did his programs from his farm home.

KMOX did not name Mangner's successor as farm director in 1968, but it continued to carry livestock reports from the USDA market news office in East Saint Louis.

SPRINGFIELD. Until after World War II, most broadcasting to farmers in the "Ozark empire" was done by the county extension staff in Springfield, unofficial capital of the empire. Then came two commercial farm broadcasters whose careers intermingled like spaghetti.

Lloyd Evans and Jim Kendrick were co-workers for about eight years and competitors for twelve. Kendrick also followed Evans as farm director on two different stations in Springfield. Evans was the first farm broadcaster in town, starting on KWTO (Keep Watching the Ozarks) in 1948. He also managed the station's farm. Three years later Kendrick moved from KWFT, Wichita Falls, Texas, to join him as an assistant. In 1959 Evans moved to the rival radio station, KGBX, and its sister television outlet, KTVY; Kendrick then moved into the farm director's slot at KWTO, and Lewis Miller came aboard as an assistant. The two farm departments were on the radio each morning and noon and competing for listeners. But Evans had the TV audience. In 1972 Evans moved out of farm broadcasting and his place at KGBX was taken by Roy Lee. In 1977 Kendrick moved to KGBX as farm director where he continued until late 1979 when Rich Hull added the farm programs to his duties as general manager of the station and Kendrick became a news reporter on KBUG, Springfield. On KWTO Joyce Cutright became farm director in 1979, moving from WIAI, Danville, Illinois.

In the summer of 1952, the Ozark area was hit by drought, and farmers ran short of hay. Evans called several of his fellow farm broadcasters to the north and they went on the air informing other farmers of the situation and asking them if they had hay to sell. The pertinent information was passed to Evans who told Ozark farmers by radio and phone where hay was available. Dozens of farmers drove their own trucks to the north or west and came back loaded with hay.

By the time a similar USDA project began that summer, Ozark farmers had been feeding hay from the north for several weeks.

MISSOURI FARM BUREAU. Terry Buker of the Missouri Farm Bureau reported that his organization began to use radio in 1974 with an actuality service whenever newsworthy events occurred. One of the Farm Bureau officials would record a few pertinent quotes on tape; then, one at a time, Buker or an assistant would call each station and feed the tape over the phone line. In 1975 the MFB started a service called "Agriculture Legislation," a ninety-second weekly review of important agricultural legislation, fed to seventy Missouri stations, by automatic phone equipment.

BROWNFIELD NETWORK. Clyde Lear wrote a master's thesis at the University of Missouri on how to form and operate a radio network. In it he made a careful analysis of the contracts between the national networks and their member stations, telephone contracts, and other business aspects of network operations. Then he went to work as a news reporter for KLIK, Jefferson City, where he met Derry Brownfield, who was handling farm programs on the station. Lear suggested that they begin a farm network and in 1972 the Missouri Network was born. Clyde Lear was responsible for the business while Brownfield would handle the programming.

Their first thought was to link the network stations by rebroadcasting the programs of KLIK-FM. "I offered to keep on doing my programs on KLIK without pay," Brownfield recalled. "Instead, I got fired. It forced us to use telephone lines, and that turned out to be a good thing. Our telephone bill is about $12,000 per month, but we know the programs are going to get to all the stations."

As the Missouri Network spread across state lines, out-of-state affiliates objected to being part of a network labeled "Missouri"; so the name was changed to the "Brownfield Network." Some of the stations in the Mississippi Delta of Arkansas and Tennessee wanted more cotton and rice markets. The need was recognized and Brownfield and Lear created the Delta Network. Some stations were interested in general news reports, so the partners created a third network for that purpose. By 1978 there were more than seventy stations drawing from their three networks.

Three men handle the farm programs: Brownfield, Don Osborne, a former Indiana county agent, and Dan Coons, a Missouri farmer. "We're analysts, not mere reporters," Brownfield said. "We study the reports that move over our two market news services; we call elevator operators and local livestock market people all over our area; we take notes and then we talk about prices, receipts, what is happening, why we think it is happening, and what is likely to happen tomorrow and next week."

They started their day at 6:05 A.M.; and in the next eight hours they made

Derry Brownfield

fifteen "feeds" to one or the other of their networks from headquarters on Brownfield's farm near Centertown, Missouri.

DICK McHARGUE NETWORK, HANNIBAL. Lear and Brownfield began to receive competition in the fall of 1976 from Missouri Farm Broadcasting, Inc., operated by Dick McHargue and Dale Hastings. MFB had ten stations located in Hannibal, Jefferson City, Marshall, Boonville, Lexington, and Chillicothe. It carried seven farm programs each day, beginning at 6:25 A.M. and wrapping up the day's markets at 2:10 P.M. The first program of the day was made up of farm news and interviews; the others were market reports, principally from the Commodity News Service ticker.

The programs were fed by telephone line from Hannibal to stations in Jefferson City and Marshall. Stations in the other cities were fed by FM broadcast. On the business side, McHargue sold time in the network programs, and paid each station for carrying them.

McHargue and Hastings learned their agriculture on farms in Missouri and Illinois, and each worked on several stations before migrating, separately, to KHMO, Hannibal, in the sixties where they worked together on farm programs and where McHargue operated a 190-acre farm.

The network started with five stations and within a year had expanded to ten, all in Missouri.

"We're not interested in expanding into the cotton country in the Missouri Bootheel, or into other states. We have some opportunities to expand to other stations in Missouri, in corn-soybean-cattle-hog country. Those are the things we know best and we plan to stay with them and the people that produce them."

Chapter Thirty-one

Montana

NORTHERN BROADCASTING NETWORK. Conrad Burns was a commission man on the Billings livestock market and began broadcasting reports from the market in 1969. In 1974 he started a daily program on a local TV station, but after one year a new station manager came aboard and changed the programs and staff. Conrad Burns and Daile Fairly, an experienced salesman, decided to start their own network that would serve Montana radio stations with Montana news, especially farm news. Fairly would handle the business end; Burns would handle the farm programs, keeping his headquarters at the Billings livestock market.

The farm service of the new network started in 1975 with a program of farm news and interviews plus six market reports during the morning and afternoon, transmitted to a handful of stations in Montana. Over a period of a few months, Fairly extended the network's coverage to stations in Wyoming and western North Dakota, totaling twenty-six stations in twenty markets. To keep pace, the network made a deal with Evan Slack, KOA, to make two five-minute reports each morning from Denver, reflecting activities in Wyoming and Colorado. Both Burns and Slack used their own planes in gathering stories and interviews, but Conrad said he received most of his stories by telephone.

The programs were transmitted to all stations by wire, and the network paid the stations for commercial time.

Chapter Thirty-two

Nebraska

EXTENSION. Long before soap operas had earned their name, Elton Lux, extension editor, created one over KFAB, Lincoln, which in the twenties was operated by the University of Nebraska. The program had a cast of three, was fifteen minutes in length, and was on the air one day each week. On the other days of the week, one of the agricultural experts from the university would talk to farmers.

In 1927 the extension service issued a press release announcing that "Hiram Highpockets, well-known Nebraska farmer, will be tried on charges of stealing and wasting the soil, in Judge Stickem's court at 7:30 P.M. on March 12. The trial will be broadcast over KFAB. The verdict will be in by 8:30 P.M."

Elton Lux talked about those early KFAB programs in an oral history of the University of Nebraska, recorded in the seventies. The interviewing was done by George Round who had worked with Elton Lux as a student and then as an assistant extension editor. He later succeeded Lux as extension editor.

In 1934 Round went to WOW, Omaha, and proposed a weekly radio program for farmers. WOW tossed in some additional ideas plus talent to create "Farm Facts and Fun," which went on the air each Saturday noon and continued for more than forty years. It was expanded to a network of five stations by 1939, and in the mid-seventies it was taped and distributed to thirty Nebraska radio stations, with James Randall, extension radio specialist, presiding over the production.

When television came to Lincoln in 1953, Round was ready with a weekly program aimed at urban residents, "The Back Yard Farmer." Jack McBride was hired as the first extension TV specialist and helped in production of the program, first on KFOR-TV and then on the statewide educational network. When Round retired as the university director of information in 1973, Tom Bare became host of the program.

WOW, OMAHA. When World War II ended, WOW decided to start a daily farm program and hired Mal Hansen fresh out of the navy, with two years experience as assistant to Herb Plambeck at WHO, Des Moines, Iowa, and another year as farm director of KRNT, Des Moines.

On WOW Hansen started with a half hour of farm news, weather, and markets in early morning. At first it was noncommercial, but before long sponsors began to sign up, and the station, for the first time, was making a profit on

Mal Hansen

its farm programs. Hansen added a noon program, which proved even more popular with farmers and with sponsors than the morning program.

WOW-TV came on the air in 1949, and Hansen started a quarter hour farm program each noon, and then an evening garden program, "In Your Own Back Yard."

On his noon TV farm program, he set up a schedule of one extension specialist each week from Nebraska and one from Iowa. This led to establishing a farmers' short course on television, one hour each day for a full week in January with a procession of extension specialists supplying information. The short course was an annual event until Hansen left WOW and broadcasting in 1959 to become a travel agent.

For eleven years Hansen had invited his listeners to take a tour with him each year and found he liked being a tour conductor even more than being a broadcaster.

On his first tour the British Broadcasting Corporation provided two mobile units with engineer, producer, and announcer, along with their promise to relay Hansen's broadcasts to New York from anywhere in Europe. In New York each program was recorded and then flown to Omaha for broadcast over WOW. "Seems pretty dull stuff now," Mal observed, "but in 1948, it was something."

The account of WOW farm programs switches to Arnold Peterson, a Nebraska farm boy, who earned a degree from the University of Nebraska and worked for the Land Bank in Omaha before World War II, became the county agent in Douglass County (Omaha), had a regular program on a rival station, and also was a frequent guest on Hansen's radio and TV programs. In 1952 Hansen invited him to join the WOW staff. Peterson shared the radio and TV programs until Hansen left seven years later and then became farm director. Over several years, Peterson was assisted on radio and TV by Frank Arney and then by Gary Kerr. In 1974 the TV station was sold and Peterson had to make a choice between radio or TV, and he chose WOW-TV which had satellite stations that covered the state.

Pat Kelly continued with a morning farm news program on radio as a function of the station's news department.

KMMJ, CLAY CENTER AND GRAND ISLAND. Station KMMJ had a two-man farm team during most of its fifty-five years on the air, with Jack McConnell as farm director and Doug Samuelson as his assistant in the late seventies. McConnell became farm director in 1978 after several years with KEYL, Long Prairie, Minnesota, and KCLN, Clinton, Iowa.

The two men conducted a full hour of farm news in early morning and presented sixteen market reports during the day, a total of twenty-five hours per week. The station frequently bought space in the *Nebraska Farmer* to list their programs. George Kister began broadcasting livestock and grain market reports on KMMJ almost as soon as the station went on the air in 1925, in Clay Center, Nebraska, He continued broadcasting from 1939, when the station moved from Clay Center to Grand Island, until he retired in 1968, a total of forty-three years.

Kister was joined in 1936 by Elvin "Dutch" Woodward, who went to KFNF, Shenandoah, Iowa, for a short time, and then came back to KMMJ where he worked on farm and public service programs until 1966. He then moved to KHAS-TV, Hastings. At his new location, his schedule in the mid-

George Kister

seventies included two five-minute cut-ins in the "Today" show, and a daily half hour farm program at noon. He retired in 1978 and died in February 1979.

Gene Williams served briefly as farm director of KMMJ in the early seventies, and was followed by Rich Balvanz.

BILL McDONALD. It would be hard to persuade the people who listened to Bill McDonald on KFAB from 1942 to 1958, and on KFOR, Lincoln, for the next ten years, that there was no such road as Blackbird Road. "That's where Bill McDonald lives and does his broadcasts. Everybody knows that."

Actually, Blackbird Road started as a joke, in 1947, when Bill and Thelma McDonald moved to an acreage within the city limits of Lincoln so their son and daughter would have room for their 4-H projects. Three years later, when they moved to a farm, "Blackbird Road" moved along with them.

McDonald had interrupted his studies in electrical engineering at the University of Nebraska in 1926 to take a job with the Henry Field Seed Company, in Shenandoah, Iowa, to be as he said a "seed analyst and other things."

Almost every employee of the seed company broadcast on KFNF, Field's station. McDonald said, "One day after lunch, one of the fellows said, 'Let's turn on the radio station and do some broadcasting.' We talked for about an hour, turned off the station and went back to our regular work." When the radio commission ordered broadcasters to stay on the air continuously during the day, McDonald spent more time in radio and less in seeds. In the thirties he became program director of KFNF.

In 1942 he went to KFAB, Lincoln, as program and farm director. He began morning and noon farm programs on KFAB and also joined George Round of the Nebraska extension service in co-hosting the weekly "Farm Facts and Fun." That connection may have led to KFAB's offering an annual scholarship to the university. When McDonald was asked several years later to choose between being full-time program director or full-time farm director, he

George Round and **Bill MacDonald**

chose the farm programs. In 1950 he had an AP teletype installed at his home and began doing virtually all his programs from there. Thelma recalled, "That teletype was a member of the family."

In 1958 KFAB moved from Lincoln to Omaha, but McDonald was too strongly wedded to his farm. He resigned from KFAB and became farm director of KFOR, Lincoln, and other stations owned by the Stuart interests. He broadcast live over KFOR and sent daily programs on tape to other Stuart-owned stations in Grand Island, Salina, Sioux City, Oelwein, and Springfield, Illinois. He also continued his weekly contributions to "Farm Facts and Fun."

In the sixties, the doctors discovered McDonald had cancer. He was in and out of the hospital several times, but when he was home, he was on the air. Thelma remembered, "When he faced that microphone, something happened; his voice always had a lift and enthusiasm that fooled the world."

William E. McDonald died in July, 1968. The "squire of Blackbird Road" had been on the air for forty-two years.

KFAB, OMAHA. When KFAB moved from Lincoln to Omaha in 1958, and Bill McDonald decided to stay on his farm near Lincoln, the station hired Bruce Davies as farm director. This was an opportunity for Davies to return home since he had done part of his growing up in Boys Town near Omaha where he learned to like farm work. Davies was graduated from the University of Missouri and was an announcer for KCMO, reporting livestock prices from the Kansas City stockyards for several years. He then reported livestock prices on radio and on television for the Chicago stockyards and also for WLS for several years.

On KFAB he maintained the pattern of morning and noon farm programs that Bill McDonald had established, and was regarded so highly by his fellow farm broadcasters that he was elected president of NAFB for 1963. But his career was cut short when he died in 1965 after open-heart surgery. He was forty-two years of age.

Davies' post of farm director of KFAB was taken by John McLaughlin, an Iowa State University graduate who had been radio specialist in the North Dakota extension service and farm director of WDAY, Fargo. After a few years at KFAB, McLaughlin joined the teaching staff at the University of Nebraska, and was succeeded by Fred Lark, who moved from KMMJ, Grand Island.

KFAB's next farm director from 1970 to 1977 was a man with genuine, down-to-earth beginnings: Warren Nielson was born in a sod shanty in western Nebraska and worked at KMA, Shenandoah, Iowa, from 1945 to 1970 as "utility infielder."

Roy Dahmer became farm director in the late seventies continuing the early morning and noon programs on radio and at noon on TV.

KOLN-TV, LINCOLN AND GRAND ISLAND. When Leslie Blauvelt decided that twenty-five years of running a livestock sale barn was enough and sold out in 1956, he didn't stay in his rocking chair very long: he became farm director on KOLN-TV. After fourteen years Lloyd Oliver, a seasoned farm broadcaster who last worked for KFAB, took over as farm director and Blauvelt scaled down his activities because he had Parkinson's disease. He did no work on camera after 1973

Their service to farmers was strictly television and their news coverage was done principally on film, with both Oliver and Blauvelt covering eastern Nebraska for film stories and interviews. The programs were repeated over KGIN-TV, at Grand Island, and by eighteen satellite stations covering about half the state.

Livestock market reports had always been the backbone of the programs, with emphasis on livestock auctions. In the late seventies, the Oliver-Blauvelt team gave more time to livestock futures prices because they believed more farmers and feeders were protecting their investments by hedging on the futures markets.

They were on the air with farm news, weather, and market reports twice each morning and again at noon.

Oliver had a degree in journalism from the University of Denver before World War II, studied speech, and then farmed for five years in Nebraska. In 1952 he combined his education and his experience by starting a farm department at KRGI, Grand Island. He moved from there to KIOA, Des Moines; to KRNY, Kearney, for nine years; three years at KFAB; and brought his sixteen years of radio experience to the television programs on KOLN-TV and KGIN-TV.

KRVN, LEXINGTON. The Big Blizzard of 1949 killed several people, thousands of cattle and sheep, and cost millions of dollars to farmers and ranchers in central Nebraska. People kept saying, "If we'd only had warning in time." That feeling led to a 3,500-member, nonprofit organization that erected KRVN. The station went on the air February 1951. KRVN was owned by farmers and ranchers, was guided by a board of directors, and was run by a staff of radio professionals, almost all with farm backgrounds.

The new station arranged to receive a daily telegram from the Omaha office of the Weather Bureau providing a special forecast for western Nebraska. By the mid-seventies the station was connected to the Weather Service and its radar weather stations by teletype and received a continuous flow of weather information.

Of course, no radio station can sit around waiting for a blizzard to strike so KRVN always gave high priority to market reports. The market news schedule in the seventies included four reports each day from the USDA office in Omaha, covering all Missouri River livestock markets, a report on meat trade, reports on forty-five Nebraska livestock auctions, three reports on cash grain trading, and one on grain futures prices at Omaha.

Rex Messersmith, farm director from 1972 to 1979, and his associates including Dale Dahlberg, Jerry Bennett, and Ken Anderson, roamed over most of Nebraska gathering stories that they used in farm programs in early morning, noon, and at 9:45 in the evening. The early morning and evening programs were aimed at consumers, especially consumers in the western states because during the hours of darkness, the KRVN signal was beamed to the West to protect a New York station on the same frequency.

Messersmith earned a degree in animal husbandry at the University of Nebraska in 1952, worked as assistant extension editor for four years, and in 1956 became farm editor at WNAX, Yankton, where he served for seventeen years, interrupted by two years with a livestock marketing organization in Kansas City.

In 1979 Messersmith left broadcasting to join the Nebraska Livestock Feeders Association and was succeeded by Rich Hawkins, who for seventeen years had been farm director of KXXX, Colby, Kansas.

KRVN had several farm directors in the twenty-one years before Messersmith took over; Gordon Bennett preceded him for two and a half years; Al Schmeckley went from KRVN into farming; Mel Uphoff went into the animal health supply business; Chuck Conger moved to KBIZ, Ottumwa, Iowa, as farm director; Bruce Behner and Max Brown were other early farm directors at KRVN.

RED DAVIS, KOLT, SCOTTS BLUFF. Virl (Red) Davis stood out in almost any crowd. He was several inches over six feet tall with slightly salted red hair and beard, that is, slightly salted in the mid-seventies after thirty years in radio.

Davis started on KOLT as an engineer in 1947, but in the early fifties started a farm program at noon. In 1972 he gave up the noon show in favor of several short program segments of farm news in early morning, and market reports every hour throughout the morning and early afternoon. He received reports from six livestock auctions in the area, and called local elevators to get the prices they were paying for wheat, grain, sorghum, and Great Northern beans. Davis said, "About 70 percent of the Great Northern beans produced in the United States are grown in our area. The elevators that buy beans look to KOLT as their guidepost in determining their day-to-day prices."

WALLACE BAZYN, KVSH, VALENTINE. Wearing a white wig and a scarlet coat isn't considered a necessary part of a farm broadcaster's training, but it was part of Wallace Bazyn's experience for two years when he was assigned to the ceremonial "Old Guard" unit at Fort Myer, Virginia, just outside Washington. More pertinent to his job as farm and ranch director of KVSH was the fact that Bazyn grew up on a grain and cattle farm in eastern Nebraska and worked several years as a newsman on WJAG, Norfolk, before he was drafted into the army in 1957. He returned to the station when he took off his Revolutionary War uniform in 1959. In 1961 WJAG started a sister station at Valentine, about 175 miles to the northwest, in the Nebraska sand hills and close to the South Dakota line. Bazyn moved there as farm and ranch director and signed the station on the air on March 6, 1961. He was KVSH's only conductor of farm and ranch programs up into the late seventies, when he also served as commercial manager of the station.

Chapter Thirty-three

Nevada

EXTENSION. The state of Nevada had only one farm broadcaster on a radio station payroll. Herb Samuels started a farm program on KOLO, Reno, in 1948. It was a daily quarter hour at 12:45 P.M. and sponsored by a local livestock auction, a feed dealer, and the local International Harvester dealer. The program ran for two years, and then there was a blank in Nevada-produced farm programs for fifteen years until Larry Kirk, KFKA, Greeley, Colorado, was named extension radio specialist at the University of Nevada in 1965.

Kirk became farm director for the ten stations located in the "cow counties," meaning outside Reno and Las Vegas. He, of course, reported on research results and the advice the extension service wanted passed on to farmers and ranchers, but he went beyond that. He gathered information from the Farm Bureau, the cattlemen's association, the sheepherders' association and other producer groups, and then included their actions and opinions in his tape recorded programs.

Chapter Thirty-four

New Hampshire

EXTENSION. The New Hampshire extension service joined with other New England states, which gave about one hundred dollars each year to support the New England Radio News Service when it started in 1928, and sent one speaker each week from the state university to talk on WBZ, Boston, until 1946 when the live programs ended. From 1946 until 1952, when the project ended, the area-wide script service included stories based on New Hampshire extension service news releases.

In 1953 Henry Corrow, a former Vermont newspaper editor, became New Hampshire's extension editor and started a daily tape service of agricultural information which was used by fifteen New Hampshire stations. For several years the program was fifteen minutes in length, but at the suggestion of many stations it was cut to five minutes each day. This lasted until 1965.

Because of limitations of budget and manpower, no regular radio service was produced for the next eleven years. In 1976 Corrow hired a radio specialist, Curtis MacKail, a 1975 graduate of the university's school of agriculture who had been an announcer on radio stations in Rochester and Dover. MacKail started a tape service of one-minute announcements, twenty-five of them on a single reel, representing one month's supply. He described them as "consumer tips" and in 1979 they were used by twenty-four New Hampshire stations. On television MacKail also provided a monthly consumer program broadcast by the New Hampshire public television service.

WKNE, KEENE. For twenty-two years, 1943–1965, New Hampshire had one commercial farm broadcaster: Stacey Cole, WKNE. During most of his years on the air, he produced two programs in early morning and another at noon, all labeled "Down on the Farm" and all originating from his home, "Red Crow Farm," in West Swanzey.

Chapter Thirty-five

New Jersey

EXTENSION. When the radio big shot looks out the window onto Broadway and says, "I don't see any farmers out there," what would you do? If your state was known as the "Garden State," you could come back with a proposal for a weekly garden program. That was exactly what Wally Moreland, extension editor in New Jersey, did in 1932. The "Radio Garden Club" went on the air over WOR, New York, New York, with horticulturists from the New Jersey extension service, the New York and Brooklyn Botanical Gardens, and the Garden Club Federations of New York and New Jersey. Soon the program was aired twice each week as a public service with no sponsors. Marjorie Merritt, assistant editor, handled schedules and scripts. The program was also broadcast on the Mutual Network.

In 1939 the "Radio Garden Club" programs were transcribed in Braille and placed in libraries for the blind throughout the United States with costs paid by the New York Garden Clubs and the American Red Cross. This new service was unveiled at the New York World's Fair.

When WOR pointed a finger at staff announcer and singer Joe Bier in 1937 and said, "We're going to start a daily farm program and you're our farm director," Bier and Moreland arranged for extension staff members to go into New York once each week to talk on the WOR farm program. During World War II, usually two New Jersey extension speakers made broadcasts each week.

Moreland was succeeded in the mid-forties by Sam Reck, who had been extension editor in Iowa, and soon Reck hired Max Kirkland as radio specialist. For close to a quarter century, Kirkland provided a series of daily messages that found places in the programming of about thirty radio stations, most of them in New Jersey but with a few across the line in Pennsylvania or New York.

For about five years in the sixties, Bill Reed was on the New Jersey staff as television producer, providing live and film programs to several TV stations in New Jersey and also Pennsylvania.

In the seventies the service to broadcasting stations that had been conducted by the extension service was absorbed into the university-wide Rutgers Communication Service and disappeared.

Many county agents over the state had made use of local radio stations beginning in the thirties. In the fifties most of the twenty county extension staffs had regularly scheduled programs, and about half were still making use of radio into the seventies. County agents Milt Cowan, in New Brunswick, and

Norman Smith, in Bridgeton, had been on the air for more than twenty years. In Morris County, Carl Klotz had a regularly scheduled program on cable TV.

One of the few commercial farm broadcasters on a New Jersey station was Will Piegelbeck, who in the forties and fifties had daily farm programs on WNJR, Newark, and on WWBZ, Vineland. He was known on the air as "Farmer Will."

In the seventies, Herb Stiles presided over about an hour each day of farm news and market reports on WSNJ, Bridgeton.

Chapter Thirty-six

New Mexico

EXTENSION. The New Mexico extension service hired its first radio specialist in 1940. Jack Baird, a recent graduate of New Mexico State College, provided a New Mexico version of the USDA "Farm Flashes" to the state's four or five stations until he was called into military service and the scripts were discontinued.

Immediately after World War II, Cecil Herrell became radio specialist of the New Mexico extension service and stayed on the job for twenty-two years. During that time, he provided script services to New Mexico stations and arranged for county agents to appear on most of the stations. In the fifties, when tape recorders were first used, he substituted tapes for the scripts and provided regular services on agriculture and home economics going to all stations. When he retired at the end of 1968, Neil Stueven took his place. He was a native of Minnesota, earned a journalism degree from the University of Minnesota, and worked as radio specialist in the South Dakota extension service for nine years, 1960–1968. In 1977 he provided thirty-six New Mexico radio stations with several taped services: a daily four-minute interview, about equally divided between agriculture and home economics; and thirty spots per week of thirty to sixty seconds, also divided between agriculture and consumer information used by thirty stations. In the seventies he started a script service in both English and Spanish, four spots each week. The Spanish translations were written by Edmundo Urbina, a native of Durango, Mexico.

On television, Stueven provided a series of one-minute spots, usually on videotape, to stations over the state.

FARM BUREAU. Dorothy Sullins, information director of the New Mexico Farm and Livestock Bureau, started providing New Mexico radio stations with a weekly program in 1973. The program, called "New Mexico Insight," was used regularly by twenty stations. Another service, five interviews per week with members or officials of the organization, was used by sixteen stations.

For New Mexico TV stations she provided slides of officers of her organization and accompanying public-service messages and comments on agricultural topics.

Chapter Thirty-seven

New York

WGY, SCHENECTADY. It was acting in Schenectady's amateur theater group that made it possible for G. Emerson Markham to escape from the accounting department of the General Electric Company to WGY in 1924. About a year later, when company brass approved his suggestion of a farm program, Markham resorted again to his acting ability. He created a character called "County Agent Robbins," who knew a lot of extension workers who were happy to be daily guests on the "Farm Paper of the Air" at noon. County Agent Robbins stayed alive from the start of the program in November 1925 until some time in 1931 when the same voice became known as G. Emerson Markham.

A few months after the "Farm Paper of the Air" was born, Markham started an evening program called "The Farm Forum," dealing with broader issues affecting rural people, including politics. When WGY put out a souvenir booklet in 1946 to celebrate twenty-one years of farm programs, it made the point that every man who had been President of the United States or Governor of New York in that time had appeared on the "Farm Forum" or "Farm Paper of the Air"—so had hundreds of farmers and agricultural experts.

In the thirties about two-thirds of the speakers were from the extension services or farm organizations in New York; the other third were divided between Massachusetts and Vermont. Bob Cragin was assistant farm director in the thirties. In 1942 Bob Child, a New York farm boy, Cornell graduate, and former extension agronomist, became assistant farm director.

In 1943 and 1944, Markham was one of those who helped start the National Association of Radio Farm Directors, was elected chairman of the first regional group that was formed, and then was vice-president of the national organization when it was created a few months later. In 1944 he was named general manager of WGY, responsible for AM and FM radio and for the new television station WRGB. Markham remained as host of the Friday evening "Farm Forum" until 1949 when he joined the staff of the National Association of Broadcasters in Washington, D.C.

Child took over the responsibility of conducting the noonday "Farm Paper of the Air" in 1944 and continued until 1948, with Bill Givins as his assistant. On March 24, 1943, soon after WRGB went on the air, Child started a weekly "Victory Garden" program, with most scenes shot in an actual garden planted outside the back door of the studio. "Victory Garden" was TV's first agricultural series.

Givins became farm director of WGY in 1948 with the responsibility for the noncommercial noon program, and for a new early morning farm program called "Chanticleer," in which the station sold time to advertisers.

There was no regularly scheduled farm program on the television station, but in 1949, at the urging of General Manager Markham, Givins presided over an all-day television broadcast of a Soil Conservation Service project to remake a farm in one day. TV engineers worked for two months to set up relay stations from the farm in the Berkshire Hills of Massachusetts, fifty miles from Schenectady. On the day of the big demonstration, several crews of cameramen and reporters covered the construction of terraces, contours, and waterways, hour after hour. This all-day coverage of remaking that Massachusetts farm was claimed to be a television "first." So far as I could learn, it also was a "last."

In 1950 Givins moved to KYW, Philadelphia, as farm director. On the "Chanticleer" program in early morning, Ed Mitchell alternated with a folksy staff announcer Charles John Stevenson. Merle Galusha conducted the "Farm Paper of the Air" at noon, the weekly "Farm Forum" each Friday evening, and a television farm program each Saturday noon.

In 1952 Galusha was named program manager of WRGB, GE's television station, and to succeed himself as farm director he hired Don Tuttle who was farm director and staff announcer on WHAI, Greenfield, Massachusetts.

With Tuttle's arrival, two major changes in WGY farm programs took place. The twenty-seven-year-old station rule, "Everything from script," was discarded. Tuttle asked guests on the WGY farm program to ad lib. The other change came from top management: time on the WGY "Farm Paper of the Air" would be available for sale to sponsors. Commercially sponsored air time brought a quick negative reaction from Cornell University and the New York extension service. They ordered that no state staff member or county agent could appear on the program. A year later the director of extension retired and his successor decided on a change of policy allowing his staff to appear on sponsored programs.

Tuttle began to devote less time to speakers and more time to interviewing farmers on the farm and interviewing county agents and farm leaders wherever he could catch them, using a tape recorder.

The "Farm Paper of the Air" and the "Chanticleer" programs paid their own way, but in the late sixties, new management began to cut back on farm programs. First, the weekly "General Electric Farm Forum" was wiped out; the "Chanticleer" program was stopped; the noontime "Farm Paper of the Air" was shortened, and then in 1968, it came to an end after forty-three years. A year later Tuttle took over farm programs of WTIC, Hartford, succeeding Frank Atwood.

Ed Mitchell deserves special attention in any discussion of WGY's farm programs since he took part in them for forty years, with Markham, Child, Givins, Galusha, and Tuttle. With the title of farm adviser, nominally he was under each of the others, but Mitchell was a personality in his own right. Before, during, and after his broadcasting career he was an apple grower in Stuyvesant Falls. On the weekly "Farm Forum" he answered listeners' questions in the "Question Box," a popular feature of the program. On the "Chanticleer" program three mornings per week he radiated good humor and talked farming in a way his fellow farmers understood.

RURAL RADIO NETWORK. The Rural Radio Network was started in 1948 with unique backing and what was then a daring concept. The financial backing came from the Grange League Federation, a big farm supply organization, and from the Dairymen's League. The concept was a network without telephone lines but with a series of FM stations picking up the original signal and rebroadcasting it over most of New York State.

Headquarters and the "mother station" were established at Ithaca, and each of the original five stations was located on a mountaintop at least 2,100 feet high. Other stations at lower elevations would pick up and rebroadcast signals from one of the five key stations. In time, twenty AM stations joined the network, including one station each in Connecticut, Massachusetts, and Pennsylvania.

Bob Child was hired from WGY as director of farm service programs. He recruited three experienced newsmen—Johnny Huttar, Lee Hamrick, and Charles Hodges—from radio stations in the Northeast and Claire Banister from the Texas extension service. The five person staff shared farm programs in early morning and at noon with weather and market reports throughout the broadcast day. The network tied into the USDA market news wires and equipped each station with a set of weather instruments. After a time the farm team was provided with a mobile transmitting unit that made it possible to broadcast from meetings of the state agricultural society, the Grange, the State Fair, and other agricultural events.

From the start, the network had money problems. FM was new; not many people had FM receivers and many of those who did found they also needed a high, costly antenna to receive the programs. Sponsors stayed away in large numbers, and at the end of the first year the Dairymen's League pulled out of the agreement, leaving the GLF as the sole owner of the network stations.

TV was coming on strong in the fifties and competing for audience dollars in buying new receivers and for sponsor dollars with FM. In 1955, after seven years, the Rural Radio Network folded. Child became a marketing economist with the GLF and later helped the Census Bureau take the 1969 Census of Agriculture.

EXTENSION. In New York state, radio discovered agriculture several years before Cornell University and the extension service discovered radio. WGY's farm service had been on the air three years with state specialists and county agents taking part before Charles A. Taylor, who had been supervisor of correspondence courses, was asked in 1928 to add the job of coordinating radio broadcasts by the extension service.

Extension Director Ladd gave Taylor a goal: "the extension message in

Bob Child (R)

every home in the state every day." Taylor organized county agents for daily programs on WHAM, Rochester; WGR, Buffalo; and WFBL, Syracuse. At the same time he started sending news "briefs" to the agents and to radio stations. By 1946 Taylor had mobilized stations and county agents into daily programs on forty stations over the state.

In 1929 Cornell acquired its own radio station, first called WEAF and then WHCU, and Taylor presided over a daily farm hour. Later, Elmer Phillips became the farm director. The schedule was planned to get every agricultural department on the air each week, and copies of the schedule were mailed to people who were interested.

For a time there was a weekly program in Finnish until the Finnish student who conducted it was graduated.

Lou Kaiser succeeded Charley Taylor in late 1945. Kaiser had started a farm program on WSYR, Syracuse, in 1927 and was farm director of WBEN, Buffalo, from 1930 to 1936. At Cornell he began to make some changes.

The farm program on WHCU was reduced to fifteen minutes each day and more time was spent on producing transcriptions and scripts, with 1,560 brief scripts under the title "Farm Radio News," and 1,230 platters sent to a total of fifty-nine different stations in 1946; they brought more than 100,000 requests for printed publications. A survey showed that 77 percent were from people not on any county agent mailing list.

Cornell acquired two wire recorders in 1948 but replaced them one year later with portable tape recorders. In 1951 the extension service acquired professional quality recording and dubbing equipment and a tape library; so copies of tapes could be sent on request to stations, teachers, and county agents. Several hundred radio talks were accumulated, but almost nobody asked for them. Finally Kaiser and his associates decided the best thing to do with a tape recorded radio talk was to erase it and use the tape again.

The Cornell staff and four or five New York county agents began taking part in WRGB's TV farm programs in 1947 (General Electric at Schenectady), but it was not until 1953 that the radio section was renamed "radio and television," and the staff knuckled down to regularly scheduled TV programs on WBEN, Buffalo; WHEN, Syracuse; WRGB, Schenectady; and WNBT, New York City. One year later, assistant extension editor James Veeder was put in charge of a separate television section.

By the seventies the extension service had turned from farm families to urban families and the weekly radio tapes were labeled "New York Today," used by twenty-nine radio stations, mostly at hours outside the early morning "farm slot." The script services were sent to stations and to extension workers and covered many subjects outside agriculture. The services to TV stations dealt with subjects such as managing money, raising children, community resources, and problems of the environment. Katherine Barnes, Shirley White, and Gordon Webb were handling the writing and production.

WHAM, ROCHESTER. George Haefner put WHAM on the air at 5:00 A.M. with an hour of farm news, weather, market reports, and recorded music. He also had a forty-five minute farm program during the noon hour, a weekend summary of farm news on Sunday, and a garden program on Saturday.

He started in 1945 with a quarter hour public service program. His boss said if they could find some sponsors, he could have a half hour. The sponsors were signed up and the program was expanded to thirty minutes. Gradually it grew to one and three-quarter hours Monday through Friday, plus the two weekend shows.

Haefner reported prices from several livestock auctions as a public service, but most of the auctions bought time on his program to solicit patronage.

Haefner knew he had many listeners across Lake Ontario in Canada, but in his own traveling to gather news and to speak at farm events, he concentrated on about nine counties in New York. He also served the fruit growers of his area for years with weather reports and spray advisories at the same hour each morning during spring and summer.

FARM BROADCASTERS IN NEW YORK CITY. As stated in Chapter 35, farm broadcasting in New York City began on the impetus of the New Jersey extension service, but two other stations besides WOR had daily farm broadcasting programs.

WEAF, New York City. Frank Mullen, who had been the nation's first farm broadcaster on KDKA in 1923, became executive vice-president of NBC in 1941 and soon ordered WEAF to set aside a half hour in early morning. He brought in Chuck Worcester from United Press headquarters in Washington to preside over the new farm program.

Estelle Worcester recalled spending the early morning hours at WEAF with her husband doing his typing, and then the two would clear out of the office about nine o'clock so the cubbyhole office could be used by Garry Moore and H. V. Kaltenborn. During the rest of the day, the Worcesters would take to the road in New York, New Jersey, Pennsylvania, or Connecticut and talk with farmers, county agents, and others.

After he had been on WEAF for about a year, Worcester was hired by CBS, and he was replaced at WEAF by Merton Emmert, who had been groomed on a fellowship at WLW, Cincinnati, and then stayed for a time as a full-time farm broadcaster. Emmert directed WEAF's farm programs for about two years and in 1945 was replaced by Don Lerch from the USDA.

In 1947 Lerch became director of CBS "Country Journal" in Washington, and Tom Page took over at WEAF. In 1954 Phil Alampi moved from WJZ to WNBC (formerly WEAF) where he continued until 1958. Since that year there have been no farm directors.

Over a period of twenty-one years, New York City moved from one farm director to two, to three, back to two, then one, and since 1958—none.

TOM PAGE. Tom Page might have been guided into farm broadcasting by the master himself, his father, Arthur Page, of WLS, Chicago. But instead it was an amateur spiritualist seer who pointed the way.

Tom was graduated with a degree in chemistry from North Central Illinois College in 1937 and set out, as he said, "to make my own mistakes." Two years later in Denver, he was down on his luck, living in a church, and serving as janitor to keep a roof over his head. A friend who claimed to be tuned in to "the other world" gave him a reading. "I see you talking to a big audience. They are smiling. They like you but they can't see you. There is a microphone." Two weeks later, Page learned of a job at a local radio station in Denver, KVOD; he took the job and stayed five years. In 1944 he moved to WIBX, Utica, where his announcing responsibilities included a farm program for three years. That was enough to prompt his friends at Cornell to recommend him to follow Don Lerch at WEAF in 1947. Tom Page in New York and his father in Chicago probably composed the earliest father-son combination in farm broadcasting during 1944–1951.

Page recalled that when he first went to WNBC, he had an unsponsored hour in the morning and a sponsored half hour at noon, which was the principal outlet for market news. The nearby market reports were the last survivors as the noon program was reduced in length and finally canceled.

Page recalled that he traveled extensively over New York, New Jersey, and New England with an engineer and recorder. Interviews done on the wire recorder were usually edited into segments so the interview might be used on the air as several shorter pieces.

After he left broadcasting in 1951, Page did a brief stint with the USDA, worked for Dow Chemical, and then became a patent lawyer in Indianapolis.

PHIL ALAMPI, WJZ, WEAF, NEW YORK CITY. Phil Alampi had been a poultryman since boyhood and a vocational agriculture teacher in his native New Jersey for several years before he started an early morning farm program on WJZ, key station of the ABC network, in December 1945. His quarter hour program soon grew to a half hour, and it continued for eight years. He was a showman and he used all kinds of gimmicks to put variety into his programs. He was chosen as president of the NARFD in 1951.

In 1954 Alampi shifted to rival station WEAF. In his new location, he conducted a farm news show on radio and a comparable program on television. His wife, Ruth, joined him on a home garden show on radio and on "Home Gardener and Handyman" on TV.

In 1956 he left broadcasting to become the secretary of agriculture for New Jersey, a position he still occupied in 1980, but Ruth continued the garden programs on radio and TV for WNBC until 1968. After a brief holiday, she came back on the air with three garden shows each week on the New Jersey public television network.

WGR, WBEN, BUFFALO. WBEN and WGR have long competed for a major share of the audience in western New York, including the farm audience. WGR hired Don Huckle, a former vocational agriculture teacher and assistant county agent, as farm director in 1945. WBEN was not far behind in establishing a farm program with staff announcer Joe Wesp in charge. Wesp's occasional substitute was Alden Fox, who took over the farm programs full time in the mid-fifties and continued for more than twenty years. Fox was a Buffalo native who started as a newspaper reporter, switched to radio entertainment and news in 1939, and became acquainted with farming during World War II when he and his wife rented a house on a farm and he worked as a farmhand for some of the neighbors when he wasn't on the air.

His one hour "Farm and Home" program was a radio fixture, beginning at 5:00 A.M., for many years, and the station's promotion department modestly claimed he had more listeners than all other Buffalo stations combined at that hour. Fox spent many hours, on and off the air, helping to promote 4-H, FFA, volunteer fire departments, and the Erie County Fair where he introduced tractor pulling contests, the first in western New York.

When he retired in May 1976, the early morning "Farm and Home" program was taken over by Jack Ogilvie, a veteran announcer on the station, and the program was extended to seven days each week.

WSYR, SYRACUSE. Lou Kaiser started the farm programs on WSYR in 1927 and continued them for several years as a part-time activity. The station's first full-time farm director was Robert Doubleday who conducted the early morning programs for thirty years until his death in 1979. He always introduced himself with "This is the deacon speakin'."

Don Dauer, a veteran of twenty-eight years in radio and television and former program director of the station, took over the daily two hour program.

ED SLUSARCZYK. Ed Slusarczyk had earned three college degrees, and had been a farmer, radio news reporter, station owner, and politician before he was lured out of retirement in 1970 to become farm director of WIBX, Utica. In 1976 he switched to WTLB in the same city and in 1978 he and WTLB officials created the New York State Agricultural Network, with Slusarczyk as president, farm director, and principal salesman.

By the end of 1979 the network had expanded to sixteen stations covering New York state plus portions of New England and New Jersey. The daily program was six minutes, including two minutes of commercials and four minutes of farm commentary, as Slusarczyk described it, "the kind of thing county agents talk about." The network sold time to advertisers and paid the stations for carrying the program.

On WTLB Slusarczyk and his wife "Bunny" were on the air seven days each week with a two hour farm and home program, 5:00–7:00 A.M. Monday through Saturday, presented live, and two hours of recorded programs on Sunday. He explained, "Most of my farmer friends are dairy farmers and they have to work seven days a week, so we try to keep them company."

Besides his wife he was assisted by Joe Wilson, who was raised on a New York state farm and had more than a dozen years experience as a broadcaster before he took the job of farm editor on the WTLB and network programs.

Slusarczyk always started his program with polka music because he said his own experience convinced him that cows milk easier to polkas. He lightened his program with mechanical sound effects such as a cow and a kitten, and at some point in each program he would change his voice and become "Stash Pendowsky," who was comical, or satirical, but always opinionated.

WIBX, UTICA. Tom Yourchak followed Slusarczyk as farm director of WIBX in 1976. Ten years earlier, when he was a teenager on a northern Ohio dairy farm, Yourchak may have been the youngest farm broadcaster in the nation, with an early morning program on WWOW, Conneaut, before he went to his high school classes. During his four years at Kent State University he was a part-time announcer on WKNT, Kent, Ohio. After earning a degree in speech and political science, he became farm director of WCWC, Ripon, Wisconsin, with morning and noon farm programs.

At WIBX, he continued the time schedule established by his predecessor, 5:00–7:00 A.M. Monday through Saturday and 12:20–12:45 P.M. Monday through Friday. The early morning programs included music, general news, and sports as well as farm news, markets, editorials, and Yourchak's farm-oriented weather forecast.

WJTN, JAMESTOWN. Not many 500-watt stations (250 at night) have had a farm director, but WJTN had Robert S. Webster, known as "Doc," for more than twenty years, 1951–1972. Doc was a city boy, born and raised in Cleveland, started in radio in 1935 as announcer on WHAM, Rochester, and put on his first farm programs over WTWN, Saint Johnsbury, Vermont, in 1950. He moved to WJTN in 1951 and stayed there as morning announcer and farm director, focusing on an area of about three counties in New York and Pennsylvania.

Several other New York state stations had daily farm programs in the late seventies including WCJW, Warsaw; WBRV, Boonville; WDOE, Dunkirk; and WBTA, Batavia.

Chapter Thirty-eight

North Carolina

EXTENSION. "The Radio Is Coming." That was the heading in a newsletter to North Carolina extension workers in October 1922, announcing that North Carolina State College station, WLAC, would be on the air that fall "with the powerful frequency of 500 meters." The radio came all right, but it didn't last long as college property. In 1924 the station was sold to commercial interests, and the call letters became WPTF (Raleigh). Extension service records show that several county agents in 1927 were appearing regularly over WWNC, Asheville, and the next year three extension specialists broadcast a lecture series on poultry, field crops, and animal husbandry intended primarily for vocational agriculture students and teachers, also on WWNC.

Extension editor Frank Jeter started a radio script service for North Carolina radio stations at least as early as 1930; and in the mid-thirties, Eugene Knight, a recent graduate of North Carolina State College, was hired as radio specialist.

Knight started a daily quarter hour on WPTF consisting of news and advice for farmers plus the main item, a talk by an extension specialist. Copies were sent to stations in Charlotte, Rocky Mount, Wilmington, and Durham. Over the next year, a total of eight stations agreed to use the daily scripts. The daily talks on WPTF continued until 1940, but in 1938 Knight changed the scripts from a daily six-minute talk on one subject to a series of shorter news items. By this time he had a dozen stations as customers, including two with farm directors Grady Cole, WBT, Charlotte, and Mardi Liles, WWNC.

In 1940 WRAL, Raleigh, and the Carolina Broadcasting System proposed putting the extension service daily programs, "Carolina Farm Features," on a network of eight stations, fed by WRAL. Eight stations looked better than one, and the extension service changed its allegiance. WPTF was unhappy and started its own daily program, "Tarheel Farm Journal," with Ted Ellis in charge.

In 1943 Lewis Watson became extension radio specialist and poured ointment on WPTF's bruised feelings. Extension specialists began to appear regularly on the WPTF "Tarheel Farm Journal," and they attracted more mail than any other feature on the station.

In 1945 Jeter became spokesman for the extension service in a daily quarter hour program on WPTF. He was a natural. The midday program continued for nine years, and in 1951 he added a 6:30 morning program, three days each week until 1954 when failing health forced retirement.

Meanwhile the state broadcasters association proposed a state-wide network, with an extension program available to all stations. Within months the extension service programs were carried by forty-three North Carolina stations. The daily programs continued for twelve years, most of the time under assistant editor Ted Hyman, with Robert Bryan taking over in 1964. In 1966 Reese Edwards became radio specialist, and he decided more stations would use the programs if they were on tape; so the network program was ended and a tape service was started: five talks or interviews on one reel of tape, mailed each week. Edwards handled these programs from 1966 to 1974, when he was succeeded by Mike Gray.

In television, extension workers were occasional guests on WFMY-TV, Greensboro, in the early fifties, and in 1955 the state's university system built its own TV station. Ted Hyman, H. M. Wilkinson, and Dorothy Mulder, of the extension editorial staff, joined talents in a daily half hour, "Today on the Farm," presented first in the evening and later at noon. After five years the name was changed to "Aspect," and agriculture was only a minor part of the program fare. In 1970 the program was reduced from daily to weekly, and the name was changed to "NOW." In 1976 "NOW" became "then"—it went off the air.

Gray fed film footage to farm programs and news programs whenever a story occurred or when station people asked for help. In addition, he provided county extension workers with a brief animated cartoon on film, and agents in fifteen counties used it to introduce their programs on local TV stations.

TOBACCO NETWORK. Ray Wilkinson, Verne Strickland, and Sylvia Sutter are three of the principal reasons the Tobacco Network grew in about 12 years from one network to five and from 12 to about 300 radio stations, scattered over parts of five states.

It was in 1963 that Vestal Taylor's health forced him to resign as farm director of the network; and Wilkinson, program director of WCEC, Rocky Mount, for about twelve years, was invited to take over programs on the Tobacco Network and also on its parent station, WRAL, Raleigh. Strickland became assistant farm director in 1967 after being information director for the North Carolina Farm Bureau, and Sylvia Sutter, who was a college graduate, worked her way over a period of several years from staff secretary to broadcaster. In 1979 Ken Tanner, after three years on the farm staff of WNCT, Greenville, became the fourth member of the Tobacco Network team.

In the seventies most of the network radio programs were distributed on tape, but the farm team presented daily live programs on WRAL radio. On WRAL-TV they presented two programs each morning and two market reports each noon, including prices from twenty-two livestock markets over the state gathered by the state Department of Agriculture. Then came two syndicated television programs each week, "Tobacco Today" and "Peanut News," used by seven TV stations in the Carolinas, Georgia, and Florida.

The Tobacco Network programs won awards from the North Carolina Farm Bureau in 1976; the radio award went to Ray Wilkinson (L) and Verne Strickland (R) and the TV award went to Sylvia Sutter.

Wilkinson, Strickland, Sutter, and Tanner were in constant motion visiting agricultural workers and farmers in their area. They had been to twenty-four countries in western Europe, behind the Iron Curtain, and to Japan and China, always carrying tape recorders and movie cameras. About two days each month they were out with the network's mobile van videotaping farm stories and occasionally making a live feed to the studio in Raleigh.

WPTF, RALEIGH. There's more information about WPTF's early farm programs available from the North Carolina extension service than from the station itself, because for years there was a close working relationship betwen the two.

WPTF's first farm director was Ted Ellis, who started a morning farm program in 1945 when the extension service, fickle creature, divorced WPTF and shacked up with rival WRAL and the Carolina Network. Ralph Reeves followed in 1949, but the dominant farm voice on the station was Frank Jeter, extension editor.

Wally Ausley became farm director in 1960, guided the morning and noon farm hours for sixteen years, and started the Southern Farm Network.

Ausley was a North Carolina farm boy, active in 4-H and FFA, earned a degree from the University of North Carolina, started a sports network, and then became program director of WTIK, Durham, before joining WPTF as farm director.

On WPTF he reported markets for all the state's farm commodities and scheduled at least one guest on each daily program. With 50,000 watts on a good frequency, he and other station officials believed they were blanketing the state well. So he was surprised when representatives of some of the smaller stations around the state came to WPTF in 1974 and proposed a network to carry a daily farm program of weather and markets during the noon hour.

The Southern Farm Network came into being in 1974 with eleven stations and grew to eighteen stations, blanketing the most important agricultural half of the state. Ausley was assistant general manager of the network and producer-announcer of the daily program. Two years later he was made general manager of WPTF, and Johnnie Hood took over the network and local programs, assisted by Hap Hansen, who had worked on several North Carolina stations.

Hood, a native Carolinian, had taken charge of the "Early Bird" morning farm program as Ausley's assistant at WPTF in 1972, and he also was manager of WPTF's farm, producing tobacco, corn, and soybeans.

WNCT, GREENVILLE. WNCT entered farm broadcasting belatedly in 1974 when owner Roy Park blocked out an hour and a half in the morning and an hour at noon on radio, plus a daily slot on TV for farm programs. He also assigned a salesman to work full time on farm accounts.

The station's first farm director was Billy Yeargin, native of the area, tobacco auctioneer, farmer, and disc jockey with fourteen years experience. He held contests, arranged a tobacco plant exchange and other promotional events, besides providing some solidly planned programs of markets, news, and farm information.

Yeargin hired Charlie Slate, who had been farm director of the Carolina and the East Texas networks, as his assistant in 1975. A year later Yeargin resigned and Slate took the top spot. He soon hired as his assistant Ken Tanner, from WRVA, Richmond. In 1977 Slate moved to a station in Missouri and Tanner became farm director. John Moore, farm-raised in eastern North Carolina with ten years experience on several other North Carolina stations, moved from the WNCT news department as assistant farm director. When Tanner moved to WRAL and the Tobacco Network near the end of 1979, Moore became farm director. Over the six year period, the early morning farm program had expanded to two hours and the noontime program to one and one-half hours. The daily TV show was recorded whenever the farm director could find time, and was on the air 11:30 to 11:45 A.M.

GRADY COLE, WBT, CHARLOTTE. In his forty-one years as farm director, news reporter, and leading personality of WBT, Grady Cole became a legend. The stories of his popularity in the Carolinas and his influence with listeners and with public officials in both states are so numerous it's impossible to tell them all, but a few examples follow:

Halfway through his career someone at the station counted nearly four hundred baby boys that had been named for him. During a rainy winter in the forties, Cole's broadcasts and personal lobbying resulted in the state legislatures of both North and South Carolina appropriating money for paving a network of farm-to-market roads. When the Soil Conservation Service remodeled a run-down farm in one day to make it erosion proof, Grady Cole's promotion efforts and his personal appearance as master of ceremonies were

Grady Cole in 1961.

credited with bringing out a crowd of more than fifty thousand people. In the early days of World War II the army wanted to stage maneuvers in the Carolinas on land operated by about twenty-five thousand farmers, and most of them were saying "No." Army brass appealed to Cole and he began to tell the army's side of the dispute. Within a few days the landowners did an about-face and the maneuvers were held on schedule. In Taylorsville one room in the county hospital is dedicated to Grady Cole in appreciation of the day in 1949 when he served as auctioneer at a money raising event to help build the county's first hospital.

Cole involved himself in politics and was given credit for electing several governors of both Carolinas. Newspapers dubbed him "King Cole."

Cole was born in Montgomery County, North Carolina, did part of his growing up on a farm, and with only a high school education went to work on WBT as a news announcer in 1930. His news programs were so popular that three years later, when the station changed owners and Cole was fired, thousands of telegrams, phone calls, and letters, plus a petition with seven thousand names, persuaded the new owners to rehire him.

In 1936 he was offered three hours of morning time, 5:00–8:00, and he would receive a percentage of the revenue from the air time he sold. The program was called "Grady Cole Time." He built a program of live music, general news, farm news, markets, and weather, but mostly it was Grady Cole, commenting, wisecracking, poking fun, ridiculing, telling yarns—in other words, just being Grady Cole. In addition he did a quarter hour of farm news and weather at noon, which regularly was rated the top program heard during the noon hour in the Charlotte area.

He formed the Grady Cole Farm Club, which soon had 10,000 members. All members were sent a postcard to be returned giving information about the kinds of farming they did. Cole and his staff sorted the cards by congressional district, shipped each congressman the cards from his district with instructions that each member of the Grady Cole Farm Club was to be supplied with USDA publications relating to the kind of farming each member did. Of course the congressmen complied.

Air time on Cole's programs was perennially sold out and a waiting list of sponsors was made. But all sponsors did take a risk when they worked with him.

One time he told his listeners: "That stuff I've been telling you about won't do what I promised, and I'm sorry. I don't want you to buy any more of it. If you've still got some on hand, let me know and I'll repay you out of my own pocket." The WBT files contain a letter from a listener who wrote, "Grady was talking about something the other morning, but I can't remember what it was. Send me five dollars worth of it. Here's the money."

By 1961 Cole had been on the air for thirty years, much of that time seven days each week, but he dropped "Grady Cole Time," limiting his broadcasts to the daily noon-hour program of farm news and weather. When he went off the air completely in 1971, the Charlotte newspapers reported in front page headlines, "King Cole Retires."

WSJS, WINSTON-SALEM. The *Winston-Salem Journal & Sentinel* started its radio station WSJS in 1930, but it waited until 1945 to give its farm editor an additional job as farm director of the station. The farm editor was Harvey Dinkins, who had been on the staff of the paper since he graduated from Guilford College in 1926. In his daily farm programs he added market reports and weather to the stories he had been accustomed to writing for the paper. In 1954 he started a farm program on WSJS-TV, so the typical Dinkins story was likely to be used three times: press, radio, and TV. His writing and broadcasting came to an end shortly before his death in 1962.

Wally Williams, who had been the weather man on Dinkins' programs, took over the radio and television farm programs and held the title of farm reporter until he retired in the summer of 1979.

WILSON. The records are fragmentary and the memories have faded, but I learned that in 1949 two stations in Wilson had competing farm programs. Ted Leeper conducted a daily program on WPOP, and Clair Shadwell had two programs on WGTM, an hour in early morning and a half hour at noon. The morning program included music, but the noon show was all talk. Shadwell had joined WGTM in 1949, after several years as part-time farm director at WIS, Columbia, South Carolina.

In the seventies, several other stations had programs for farmers, including WMPM, Smithfield; WPAQ, Mount Airy; and WLAB, Saint Pauls.

Chapter Thirty-nine

North Dakota

EXTENSION. The North Dakota extension service jumped into radio during the drought and depression year of 1936 with Earl Hodgson in the newly created job of radio specialist and with recording equipment to make platters. Scripts would have been cheaper, of course, but Hodgson and extension editor Tom Gildersleeve were persuaded radio stations would be more likely to use the platters.

How could a hard-hit state afford it? One explanation, offered forty years later, was that some federal money was available, and in deciding how to spend it—well, the director and his extension editor were hunting and fishing pals.

The recordings were well established when Hodgson left in 1938 to go into agricultural advertising.

His place was taken by a South Dakota boy, Dick Burrus, who continued to provide stations over the state with daily messages on sixteen-inch platters, mailed once each week. He also established live programs over WDAY, Fargo, and KVOX, located just across the Red River in Moorhead, Minnesota.

Burrus left North Dakota and extension work in 1942 to join the USDA War Food Administration and later became a newsman on WJR, Detroit. He was succeeded by Gerald Seaman, an Iowan and former newspaperman who kept the wartime messages going to North Dakota farmers. About the end of the war, Seaman joined the Gittins advertising agency, writing commercials for Allis Chalmers on the "National Farm and Home Hour."

Bob Rathbone, a former Kansas newspaper editor, followed, in the period 1946–1950, and about that same time, the office acquired a Brush tape recorder; Rathbone used it to interview county agents, farmers, and ranchers, picking up stories he then dubbed onto the weekly platters.

Rathbone also began to persuade county agents and radio stations over the state to produce local programs, usually once each week, although in Dickinson the county agent broadcast a daily program. Many of those programs started in the late forties were still on the air in the mid-seventies, usually with a microphone and tape recorder on the county agent's desk.

KFYR, Bismarck, put out a signal that could be heard all over the state, and Rathbone persuaded the station to put him on the air from the campus of the North Dakota Agricultural College in Fargo five minutes each day at noon, including a garden program one day each week, a sure-fire mail puller. The extension service broadcast was a fixture in the KFYR schedule for many years, and the platter service was discontinued.

When Rathbone left in 1954 to join the USDA's Agricultural Research Service, he was followed by Dave Bateman from Arkansas and Iowa State College. Bateman expanded and reinforced the live programs from the campus, arranged for more of them on more stations, and started a TV program on WDAY-TV. Bateman produced and broadcast radio and television programs and branched out into movies. After twelve years in that job, totaling almost thirty in extension work in Arkansas, Iowa, and North Dakota, he became WDAY's farm director.

James Berg took over the extension radio-TV job, and in 1967, was succeeded by his assistant, James Kenward. Both men were graduates of North Dakota State and both had been county agents before becoming what the North Dakota extension service calls an ''electronic media specialist.''

WATS lines and recorded playbacks played a large part in the seventies' broadcast activities of the extension service. Each morning a marketing specialist recorded a one-minute summary of livestock and grain markets, which was phoned to ten different radio stations, along with another one-minute message on some phase of agriculture from other extension specialists.

Kenward produced a weekly tape of five messages, usually one and one-half minutes each, which was sent by mail to twenty-nine radio stations over the state.

WDAY, FARGO. Dave Bateman had become so completely identified with extension service broadcasts on WDAY that when he resigned from the extension service and became farm director of WDAY in 1966, few of his listeners recognized the difference. Besides an ambitious schedule of market reports, plus morning and noon broadcasts on WDAY, Bateman started a tape series of broadcasts, ''Better Agricultural Methods'' (BAM), carried by seven stations in

Dave Bateman

the Dakotas and Minnesota. In 1979 he turned over the daily WDAY broadcasts to Roger Strom, a native of Ontario who had been farm director of WYTL, Oshkosh, Wisconsin.

KFGO, FARGO. Larry Ristvedt, who became farm director of KFGO in 1976, may have been a forerunner of a new breed of farm directors because he was experienced in marketing rather than production. "Every farmer knows how to produce a crop, but marketing is probably the thing that he knows least about."

He was born in Fargo; earned a degree in economics from Moorhead State, just across the Red River in Minnesota; and worked as a commodities broker. As part of his job for the brokerage firm, he broadcast reports on commodity prices several times each day on KFGO. Later, the station hired him.

At KFGO, Ristvedt replaced Beverly Walters, who for several years was the only woman farm director on any station in the U.S.

Walters was a native of Oakes, North Dakota, and in 1959 was graduated from high school just as her town acquired a radio station where she landed a job. In 1965 she moved to KFGO, Fargo, as assistant in the farm department, first under Darryl Eastvold and then Doug Johnson. In 1969 Walters moved into the top spot.

Many of the items in the schedule which Ristvedt inherited were started by Walters: two hours of farm programming in the morning, one hour at noon, ten market reports in morning and afternoon, and a farm story for the evening and night news programs. One of the most valued services was a daily report in early morning on what's doing in sugar beets, who needed more workers, what were the pickup points for workers, and other needed information. Ristvedt tapped many different sources of information up and down the Red River Valley to put this service together.

Backup man on the KFGO farm programs was a station salesman, Bob Escen.

AL GUSTIN, KFYR, BISMARCK. Al Gustin got off to a running start as a farm broadcaster, while he was still a student at North Dakota State, by being chosen for a work-training scholarship financed by KXJB-TV in Fargo, where Darryl Eastvold was farm director. When Gustin received his bachelor's degree in agricultural economics in 1969, he was named farm director of KXMB-TV, Bismarck, just ten miles from the Gustin family farm. The neighbors could see the Gustins' boy Al on the televison each day at noon, talking about farming and giving the market news and weather reports. This lasted for a little over one year until the station was sold and the new owner decided "no farm programs."

Gustin then went down the street to KFYR-TV and established two five-minute programs of farm news each morning: at noon, he was the anchorman of a three-person team in a half hour show, with Gustin himself presenting fif-

Al Gustin

teen minutes of farm news, a woman explaining the weather, and a member of the news staff dealing with general news highlights.

In 1976 Gustin went with a North Dakota agricultural group to Egypt and Jordan to open markets for North Dakota farm products. He reported they found new customers for dairy calves, frozen semen, nonfat dry milk, and one of the state's increasingly important crops, sunflower seed.

Chapter Forty

OHIO

EXTENSION. It seems likely that the first Ohio agricultural workers to get in front of a radio microphone were county agents from the eastern part of the state. They occasionally traveled across the state line to Pittsburgh to take part in KDKA's pioneering farm program, conducted by Frank Mullen, beginning in 1923. When Ohio State University's radio station, WOSU, went on the air in 1928, one of the regular features was a weekly "Farm Night," with talks by extension specialists and university brass hats.

In 1935 G. E. "Jerry" Ferris was named extension radio editor, and he started a daily farm program on WOSU along with "continuity sheets" mailed to Ohio radio stations: news items, short lectures, questions and answers.

In 1936 Ferris reported that of the twenty-two stations in the state, sixteen were cooperating with the extension service by using scripts. On nine stations, county agents from thirty-three counties were taking turns in regularly scheduled programs.

In 1943 Bill Zipf took Ferris's spot, after one year in WLW's farm department. Zipf replaced the scripts with electrical transcriptions which were sent on a round robin schedule from one station to another, until Zipf acquired money and equipment to provide a platter for each station each week.

In 1944 Zipf joined Al Bond, USDA radio extension specialist, and Roy Battles, farm director of WLW, in testing the newly developed wire recorder: portable (forty-seven pounds), thirty-two minutes of recording per spool, built-in timer, easy erasing. It looked great at first, but in later years Zipf remembered losing programs when the wires snapped; Battles recalled tangles of wire; and Bond believed the so-called portable recorder caused untold numbers of hernias. When tape recorders became available a few years later, the wire recorders became museum pieces.

Zipf also experimented with recording on movie film, another idea that went nowhere.

It was during this period that Zipf and Bond collaborated on a *Radio Handbook for Extension Workers,* published by the USDA and distributed to state and county extension workers throughout the U.S. It was a revision and improvement on a booklet with the same title that I had written around 1939, soon after I had become the USDA radio extension specialist. The Zipf-Bond book still looked informative and useful in 1979.

In 1947 Zipf left the Ohio extension service and moved downtown to a two-hat job as farm director of WBNS and farm editor of the *Columbus Dispatch,* which owned the station.

Maurice White took over as extension radio specialist for several years and then moved to a similar spot at the University of Wisconsin. Larry Sarbaugh succeeded White, and he later joined the USDA and then the Michigan extension service.

In the sixties Art Smith, ex–county agent, became radio specialist. When he retired, Dick Howard, another county agent, took over. Howard's service to Ohio radio stations and county agents in the seventies was a monthly package of thirty-six tape recorded interviews with extension specialists, each about six minutes and organized in nine different series, four interviews in each: four on dairying, four on crop production, etc. Twenty Ohio radio stations and twenty county agents received a list of available subjects and speakers. They placed their order and sent a blank tape to carry the recordings. The stations and agents ordered an average of about 150 tapes each month.

Howard calculated that county agents in seventy-five of Ohio's eighty-eight counties were appearing in regularly scheduled broadcasts.

The Ohio extension service radio work was taken over in 1978 by Jack Ference, an OSU graduate with bachelor's and master's degrees in communication.

The Ohio extension service entered television in 1955 by hiring Jim Chapman, from WTAM-TV, Cleveland, a twenty year broadcast veteran and one-time extension radio specialist in his native Kansas. Chapman started live programs, aimed at consumers, on all three of the commercial TV stations in Columbus. About one year later, WOSU-TV, owned by the university, went on the air, and Chapman started both farm and consumer programs on that station and continued a daily consumer program on WLW, Columbus. From the WOSU programs, he made copies available to other Ohio stations, at first by kinescope, later by videotape.

In 1964 he went on a two-year assignment to India and upon his return became a publications editor in the Ohio extension service.

Chapman was succeeded as television editor by John Schmidt—son of an OSU professor of rural sociology, a star of several Broadway musicals, and a singer on the Arthur Godfrey CBS television program before he returned to Ohio State University in 1957 to take graduate work in communications and then join the extension service staff. As extension television editor he produced agricultural features of about four minutes in length, averaging two features per month on videotape or film, and provided to twenty Ohio television stations. He also put together special quarter hour programs for five stations and provided twenty-two stations with a videotape "library service."

WLW. Roy Battles, Bill Zipf, and Bob Miller all earned degrees in pomology from Ohio State, and if the apple business had been good enough, chances were all three would have spent their lives in apple orchards somewhere in Ohio. But all three went into broadcasting at WLW and elsewhere, and when

A group of farm broadcasters try out a wire recorder at the WLW farm in the early forties. L–R: Earl Neil, farm manager; Roy Battles, then a county agent and later WLW farm director; Ed Mason, WLW farm director; Al Bond, USDA.

Ohio State University held a banquet in 1975 to celebrate its 100th birthday and to honor one hundred of its most distinguished alumni, Bob Miller acted as master of ceremonies for the occasion, and he, Zipf, and Battles were among those honored.

Of course, not all WLW farm directors were frustrated apple growers. The first was John Merrifield, an Iowa State University graduate who started a farm program on the station in 1936, about the time WLW was licensed to experiment for three years with 500,000 watts power, ten times as much as any other U.S. station.

In 1938 the station lured George Biggar from WLS as director of rural programs, starting county and western musical programs and supervising morning and noon farm shows. He hired Ed Mason from KFRU, Columbia, Missouri, to work alongside Merrifield as farm director.

The square mile of land on which the WLW transmitter was located included a working farm. A contest had produced the name of "Everybody's Farm Hour" for the noontime program, and the farm was named "Everybody's Farm." Earl Neal, who operated the farm, took part in almost every program and became almost as well known as Mason.

The station paid for and produced a weekly dramatic program, "Fortunes Washed Away," written by Ewing Jones, information man for the regional office of the Soil Conservation Service.

In 1939 the station started a fellowship program for recent agricultural college graduates. Merton Emmert from Kansas State and Charles Grisham from Alabama Polytechnical were the first two winners. Emmert later conducted farm programs on WEAF, New York; and Grisham, after going into advertising, became owner of several radio and TV stations in Alabama. One of the 1941 fellowship winners was Lowell Watts, who became farm director of KLZ, Denver, and later director of the Colorado extension service.

John Merrifield, meanwhile, had moved downriver to become farm director of WHAS, Louisville.

Bill Zipf joined the farm department in 1943, but less than one year later he moved to the Ohio extension service. His place was taken by Roy Battles, a county agent near Cincinnati. When the team of Biggar and Mason moved to Indianapolis in 1944, Battles became farm director.

In 1943 the WLW farm staff acquired its first woman staff member, Carrol McConaha (ends *hay*). She had grown up on an Indiana farm and graduated in radio from the University of Iowa. "My part of the show was beamed mainly at women. I remember a little verse we preached: 'Eat it up, wear it out, make it do, then do without.' " When World War II was over, McConaha married and her place was taken by Betty Brady, a home economist from Iowa State University. Both women were on most of the farm shows—two or three times each day.

Battles started a series of interviews with farmers recommended by county agents, and with the help of the publicity department, he made a short-term hero of each farmer.

From these special guests, Battles developed another series, "The Farm Front," in which three or four men would be brought to Cincinnati each week for a discussion of some topic that was timely and important.

In the spring of 1946 he chose a farmer and a homemaker from Ohio and a wholesale grocer from northern Indiana to go with him at WLW expense on a trip to France, Italy, Greece, and Poland to learn about Europe's food needs.

After his return, in addition to his reports on the air, he made about 150 talks to groups of all kinds in four states of WLW territory.

"I almost didn't take the job at WLW because it was so commercial," Battles recalled years later. "I made the adjustment, but there was a time when I went to the company president and complained that we had too many commer-

Bob Miller

cials; he agreed and we limited the number we'd put into a program. I remember refusing some hatcheries that I knew had a reputation for poor chicks—and some accounts for chemicals that the experiment station said didn't work.''

Battles had several associates during his nine years on WLW. Bob Miller went to work in late 1945, still wearing his navy uniform, and left to become farm director of WRFD, Worthington, in 1947 when that station went on the air. Harry Leckrone moved from the Indiana extension service at Purdue, and WLW changed his name to Harry Andrews, a name which he carried with him to WIBC, Indianapolis. John Babcock, from Ithaca, became John Butler.

When Battles left WLW in 1952, Bob Miller returned to the station as farm director.

A year and a half at WLW and five years at WRFD had made Miller a veteran farm director. He moved into both radio and television with programs of farm news, markets, and weather, and for another sixteen years he continued the noon broadcasts from Everybody's Farm. But the 137-acre farm by then was no longer representative of a good commercial farm, and in 1968 the broadcasts from the farm were discontinued, and the nature of his programs changed.

As he described his broadcasting in the mid-seventies, he was an agricultural specialist in a two-hour program of recorded music in early morning, 5:00–7:00, and again at 11:00–noon. Most of his reports were one or two minutes in length—about one dozen shows per hour—some intended primarily for farmers, but many aimed at consumers.

On television he had a ten-minute program each day: farm news, markets, and weather, and on Saturday he presided over a half hour show carried by three of the WLW stations in Cincinnati, Columbus, and Dayton. He considered this program "the voice of agriculture to consumers."

In his more than quarter century as farm director of WLW, Miller had a number of talented assistants who moved on to other jobs. George Loesing came to WLW, changed his name to George Logan, and carried the name with him to WIBW, Topeka. Bill Alford came to WLW from the University of Massachusetts, and after two years moved to WMT, Cedar Rapids, Iowa. Jim Mills put his WLW experience to work for the USDA, then for the National Agricultural Chemicals Association, and in 1979 for the National Association of Farm Broadcasters.

In 1975 Davonna Oskarson, agriculture graduate of Colorado State University, moved from WRFD to WLW, and after two years to the extension staff at Purdue.

To help farm-city relations, Miller promoted a Farm Day at a Cincinnati Reds baseball game for many years. Besides the game itself, there was a milking contest, usually won by Pete Rose. Before the game, Miller hosted a dinner for a modest number of farm and city people so they could get acquainted.

Another facet of Bob Miller was his setting aside any money he collected from fees as a speaker and spending that money on agricultural missionary work in underdeveloped countries in Africa. The first step was a tractor, paid for by him and put to work in Sierra Leone. Then came a school in that country; then a school in Upper Volta; later, four more tractors, all put in communities where a tractor would mean more cultivated land and more food.

BILL ZIPF, WBNS, COLUMBUS. When Bill Zipf left the Ohio extension service in 1947, he took on two jobs: farm director of WBNS and farm editor of the *Columbus Dispatch*, which owned the radio station. For ten years he told each story twice. In 1957 a third outlet opened up, a morning farm program on WBNS-TV, following close on the heels of his radio show.

In 1961 his son Dick, a commercial artist and former 4-H member, joined him on the TV program, and then on the two daily radio programs. It was a two-man team on TV until 1966, when Bill dropped out of television. They then shared time on the radio program until 1970 when Bill cut back to newspapering alone.

Dick did most of his TV features on tape, and he scheduled county agents, state extension workers, state department of agriculture speakers, soil conservationists, and others to appear at the WBNS-TV studio each Wednesday evening for a marathon taping session that provided programs for each week.

WRFD, WORTHINGTON. There was an impressive list of farm broadcasters in Ohio in 1946, serving farmers with news, markets, and good advice: Jim Chapman, WTAM, Cleveland; Charles Cleaver, WRRN, Warren; Richard Merrin, WHBC, Canton; Roy Battles and Bob Miller, WLW, and Ben Werk, WKRC, all in Cincinnati; Louella Engel, next door at WMOH, Hamilton;

Stuart Wilson, WKBN, Youngstown; Bill Zipf at the university station, WOSU.

But there wasn't enough farm broadcasting in the eyes of the Ohio Farm Bureau, which in 1947 built its own station at Worthington, a few miles north of Columbus, and christened it WRFD.

The radio programs were planned to serve and to interest farm people all day long. The early claim was that the station could be heard in every Ohio county, but the primary signal covered about forty-five of the eighty-eight counties.

Bob Miller started the farm programs in 1947 with an hour in early morning and an hour and a half at noon. Later he added market reports during the mid-morning, including several reports from the co-op livestock auction. In 1951 he hired Clyde Keithley, an Ohio State University graduate and vocational agriculture teacher, to devote virtually full time to presenting, and further improving, the market news services.

In 1950 he lured Louella Engel from WMOH to talk to farm women. After a year and a half, Engel departed and Miller hired Mary Lou Pfeiffer, who stayed with the station as assistant on the farm programs through the fifties and developed several home and garden programs on her own.

Miller left WRFD in 1952 to return to WLW and he was replaced by Jim Chapman, who had been farm director of WTAM, Cleveland. In 1955 Chapman joined the state extension staff and Keithley took over as farm director after four years in charge of the station's market reports. He had studied agriculture at Ohio State and taught vo-ag for a couple of years before joining WRFD in 1951.

Keithley served as farm director for ten years, 1955–1965, and made WRFD broadcasts important events at the state fair and at about six county fairs each year. He also helped conduct the state corn picking contest and other agricultural events of every kind, including, of course, the major meetings of the Ohio Farm Bureau.

Keithley was made operations manager of the station in 1965, and in 1970 he left broadcasting to return to vocational teaching.

He had several associates during his ten years as farm director: Jim Finely, Carl Harsh, and "Pop" Hess; and a long string of successors after 1965: Lew Davis, Ed Johnson, Bob Ziegler, Davonna Oskarson, Dave Branham; and in 1976 Ron Powers became farm director, moving from WIMA, Lima. Joe Cornely became assistant farm director in 1977, and two years later his place was taken by Dave Russell, who had been farm director of WYAN-FM, Upper Sandusky.

JACK STOWER, WIMA, LIMA. One of the tidy little empires in farm broadcasting was in northwestern Ohio, where yields of corn and soybeans generally ran high and cattle and hogs were generously (and sometimes profitably) fed. It was also where only one station reported on local markets, weather, and farm happenings. The station was WIMA, and it didn't come alive to the farm audience and farm market until 1971 when new blood moved in. The new program director was Jack Stower, who had presented farm programs on stations in Illinois, Michigan, and Ohio since 1961.

He hired Carl Schlenker, a local farmer with the itch to be a broadcaster, and they worked out a schedule of morning and noon programs which found an audience and sponsors. After two years Schlenker returned to farming full time, and Ron Powers moved from the WIMA newsroom in to the farm director job. In the summer of 1976, Powers moved to WRFD, and Stower decided it would be more fun to do the farm programs himself and let someone else have the headaches of the program director's job.

A source of pride to Stower was the station's weather radar. He said, "We can pinpoint rain or snow and track it wherever it's going in our area. Farmers and listeners probably talk more about that service than any other one thing."

For market reports—morning, afternoon, and evening—Stower received prices from several grain elevators in the area, and from three daily livestock markets, as well as from the news wires which carried USDA prices.

Stower's title was agribusiness director and he was responsible for sales as well as programs.

LOUELLA ENGEL, WMOH, HAMILTON. If there ever was a first lady among farm broadcasters, it would have been Louella Engel, who for ten years, 1944–1954, was the only woman farm director of a commercial station. Most of her ten-year career was on WMOH, although she spent over one year each on WRFD, Worthington, and WPFB, Middletown. When she started, most of the men in the newly formed National Association of Radio Farm Directors were about as old as Louella's older daughter. We young squirts considered it a privilege to call her by her first name.

Several other women were broadcasting to farmers in those war years; for example, Dorothy Crandall and Helen Stubbs, of the New England Radio News Service, and Miriam Dexter at Kansas State College, but they were on the payroll of some tax-supported organization, and when the young men returned from World War II, the women went back to their peacetime jobs. Engel was hired in 1944 to broadcast to farmers on a profit-making program for a commercial station, and she continued broadcasting when the war was over.

She was a farmer's wife and a former schoolteacher, married to Carl Engel, who operated a 120-acre dairy farm not far from Hamilton, near Cincinnati. On the farm she helped milk fifteen cows by hand, raised two daughters and a son, and started the first 4-H Club in Butler County.

In her one-hour farm program, "I brought in county agents, SCS people, Triple-A officials, and farmers that the experts told me about—farmers who had tried new methods," about a hundred guests each month. A wire recorder was her companion for several years, long after tape had replaced wire on most stations. When you are used to handling a full pail of milk, maybe a forty-seven-pound wire recorder doesn't seem so heavy.

Each Saturday was 4-H Club day on her program, and after a time, she

Louella Engel

turned the program over to the youngsters themselves, to plan, write, rehearse, and then present on the air.

Besides her daily program for farmers, Engel conducted a daily show for women, particularly farm women, on WMOH.

In 1950 she became women's director of WRFD; then farm director of WPFB, Middletown. In 1952 she returned to WMOH, where she was able to do less traveling. In 1954 her broadcasting career ended when doctors found she had cancer. The surgery was successful and in 1976 at eighty years of age she said, ''We've just been notified that the state Extension Service is going to honor Carl and me with their Appreciation Award this fall.''

CHARLES MIGHT, WMRN, MARION. For six years, 1953–59, Charles Might was farm director of WMRN, with morning and noon programs. He also managed a 425-acre beef and hog farm owned by the station. He moved from the station to the advertising agency handling the J. I. Case farm equipment account. The company changed agencies several times in the next seventeen years but kept Might. In 1976 he became sales marketing director of the NAFB, joining Ray Kremer in that effort but keeping his home and headquarters in Racine, Wisconsin.

There were other farm broadcasters in Ohio, especially during the forties and fifties. Sam Steiger was farm director of WHIO in the late forties. John Hutson was farm director of WFIN, Findlay, in the fifties. He flew his plane to

Ed Johnson

visit farmers, fairs, and farm meetings, and was the only one of the Ohio farm broadcasters who used an airplane in his profession. Ben Werk was farm man on WKRC, Cincinnati, in the forties and fifties, and on WOIO, Canton, in the sixties. Frank Belmont had a daily program on WPAY, Portsmouth, in the forties.

OHIO'S FARM NETWORKS. Ohio had two farm networks in the seventies, both of them started by former farm directors of WRFD, Worthington.

Lew Davis conducted WRFD's farm programs from 1965 to 1968 when he left to establish the Ohio Farm Network, with headquarters in Jackson. Starting with nine stations, he increased the number to twenty-one over the next six years. He was reporter, announcer, and manager.

Under his agreement with affiliated stations, Davis sold time to advertisers and bought time on the stations. He provided each station with a daily tape of twelve minutes, with the understanding that the station would fill in another two and one-half minutes of farm market reports and weather from their news wire.

When Davis left WRFD in 1968, his job as farm director was taken by Ed Johnson, another Ohio State alumnus, who had been facing a microphone for the previous seven years. Near the end of 1973, Johnson left WRFD and set up the Agri-Broadcasting Network, with headquarters in Columbus. By the end of the first year he was feeding forty Ohio radio stations and in 1975 he expanded into Pennsylvania, with Ed Houck in charge of the Pennsylvania phase of the operation.

By 1978 Johnson's outlets included fifty-five Ohio radio stations, four television stations, and eighteen radio stations in Pennsylvania. Each station received two reports on livestock and two on grain markets each morning. Johnson and his staff recorded each program on tape and fed the stations by telephone.

In the late seventies, his assistants were Todd Dysle and Tami Jackson.

Several Ohio stations which supplemented the network reports with local programs included stations in Salem, Napoleon, Hillsboro, Bucyrus, and Celina.

Chapter Forty-one

Oklahoma

KBIX, MUSKOGEE. J. Kendall McClarren, the first farm broadcaster in the state, had been farm editor of the morning and evening papers in Muskogee for about four years when the Bixbee family, which owned the papers, put radio station KBIX on the air early in 1936. The station's news, sports, women's, and farm programs were handled by people from the newspaper.

McClarren was responsible for a half hour noon program, Monday–Friday, and arranged for agricultural workers and farm families in eight surrounding counties to take turns appearing on the daily noontime program. They provided conversation and entertainment. A regular feature was market reports from the stockyards in Muskogee, plus livestock and grain prices from Kansas City, which were sent over the telegraph wires.

After a few months, McClarren took a job with the USDA in Washington, and he persuaded a former schoolmate at Connors State College, Edd Lemons, to take his place on the Muskogee papers and on the KBIX farm programs.

EXTENSION. Sam Schneider was the first radio specialist on the Oklahoma extension staff, principally because he was the newest member of the staff in 1937 when KOMA, Oklahoma City, offered to set aside a quarter hour each day at noon if the extension staff would fill it. Years later, he recalled that he bought his mother a radio receiver, "so I'd be sure of one listener."

Schneider and the extension staff kept the daily program going on KOMA and also fed information to Edd Lemons at KBIX for about three years, when he left to become a volunteer intern in the farm department of WLW, Cincinnati. After two months he returned to Oklahoma to start the farm department of KVOO, Tulsa.

Several members of the extension editorial staff shared the responsibility of keeping information flowing to farmers by means of broadcasts and scripts during the war years. In 1946 Barney Arnold, who had been Sam Schneider's assistant at KVOO, was named radio specialist, and for six years he provided a script service and electrical transcriptions to about twenty Oklahoma stations.

When Arnold resigned to become farm director of WHAS, Louisville, extension editor Edd Lemons kept the radio services going, along with his responsibilities for press, bulletins, and visuals. Lemons had been farm director of KBIX, Muskogee, and of WKY, Oklahoma City, before he was named extension editor at Oklahoma A&M in Stillwater. After three years of part-time attention to radio, in 1955 Lemons enticed Harold Dedrick from WKY to become radio-TV specialist.

Dedrick was an Oklahoma farm boy and was graduated from Oklahoma A&M in 1937. He then taught vocational agriculture, did a hitch in the navy, served as a county agent, became assistant to O. O. "Sandy" Saunders at WKY in 1951, and moved into the top spot for three years. At the extension service, he had his doubts about a service that sent the same information to stations in the crop-farming area of eastern Oklahoma and to the ranching and wheat areas in the panhandle, so he produced a variety of radio tapes. Each month he issued a catalog of subjects, speakers, and lengths, and sent it to all the stations and county agents. This led to county agents getting more deeply involved and soon at least half the seventy-seven county agents in the state were participating in radio programs, about fifteen of them on daily programs.

Out of each monthly production of perhaps 100 recorded talks, some would become part of a permanent library of recordings, and many of them were listed repeatedly in the monthly catalog.

For fast-breaking news, emergencies, or special events, Dedrick established the practice of telephoning stations or the Oklahoma News Service, which linked about forty-five stations statewide.

He worked out arrangements with the nine TV stations in the state to provide them with film footage of special events or agricultural features if the station would provide the raw film. Dedrick, or a staff member, would do the shooting and provide a script for narration.

Dedrick retired in 1973 to his 1,000 acre ranch, and the farm broadcasters voted him an honorary life membership in their association.

He had several assistants during his eighteen years as radio-TV specialist, including Ewing Canada, Herb Brevard, and Jim Stone, who joined in 1969 and replaced Dedrick when he retired. Stone was an Oklahoma farm boy who broke into radio in Okinawa in 1957 while he was in the air force, and later worked for a radio and TV station in Ada. Stone's assistant in the mid-seventies, Ed Wilks, grew up on a wheat and cattle farm in northwest Oklahoma and conducted a farm program on the educational station while he was earning his degree in agricultural journalism at Oklahoma State University. After a year and a half on WREN, Topeka, as a newsman, he returned to his alma mater and the extension service early in 1976.

KVOO, TULSA. Sam Schneider claimed he never had heard a radio program before he was assigned to start a daily series of extension service broadcasts over KOMA in 1937. Forty years later he wrote, "The development of fire and the electric lights are the only things worth comparing to what radio did for Americans. . . . The farmer was able to get help at appropriate times; city people began to realize they couldn't operate an industrial nation without help from the farmer."

After three years as radio specialist at Oklahoma State University and an unpaid period of work-study at WLW, Schneider started in 1941 a farm service

Wayne Liles

on KVOO, Tulsa. The service grew to seven programs each day and could be heard over most of the state. Pasture improvement was one of KVOO's major projects, and each year Schneider led fifteen pasture improvement winners on a trip to Chicago to see the International Livestock Exposition.

He also helped to found the National Association of Radio Farm Directors in the forties and served as their president in 1952. At that time he told his fellow broadcasters, "Radio is suffering from a rash of TV, but it can recover." He had programs on both radio and TV at the time.

Burnis Arnold was Schneider's assistant on KVOO during World War II and had full responsibility for the programs while Schneider was in the army.

Carl Meyerdirk, also an Oklahoma farm boy and agricultural graduate, became assistant farm director in 1951, and later moved into the top spot when Schneider left farm broadcasting in 1956 to become KVOO's promotion director. Besides fifty-nine radio programs and five TV shows each week, Meyerdirk had a cattle ranch. Soon after serving as NARFD president, in 1962, he became youth director of an oil company.

WAYNE LILES, KWTV, OKLAHOMA CITY. When he was a prisoner of war, following the Bataan "death march" early in World War II, Wayne Liles organized classes in agriculture for his fellow prisoners during their three and a half years as captives of the Japanese. After the war he spent one year in hospitals recovering his health and strength and then the following eight years as a county agent, during which he conducted a weekly program over KSWO-TV, Lawton.

In 1954 he was asked to head the farm department of KOMA and KWTV, Oklahoma City, and for two years he was on both radio and TV. In 1956 the radio station changed ownership, and Liles was concerned only with television. The station had viewers in about forty-seven of Oklahoma's seventy-seven counties.

In 1961 he was joined by Bill Hare, who was an Oklahoma farm boy, veteran of World War II, and animal husbandry major from Oklahoma A&M. From 1951 to 1961 Hare was with the Oklahoma City Livestock Exchange and provided KWTV with prices and films of livestock sold that day. Many viewers thought he was a member of the KWTV staff and hardly noticed the difference when he went on the station's payroll.

In the seventies Liles and Hare were on the air three times between 6:30 A.M. and noon, with news features, markets, and weather. In addition to their daily shows, they filmed many documentaries which went on the air in prime evening time. Some of their titles were: "Horse Country," "Cow Country," "Bacon Makers," and "Our Daily Bread."

WKY, KTVY, OKLAHOMA CITY. WKY was the first radio station in Oklahoma, established in 1920, but it waited until 1944 to hire a farm director, Edd Lemons, who had conducted a daily farm program on KBIX, Muskogee, for about eight years. He started a daily quarter hour show at noon that included farm news, weather, market reports, and an almost daily remote broadcast at various places in Oklahoma. He conducted a soil conservation contest and a pork production contest, and the station gave about $3,000 each year in scholarship awards to outstanding 4-H and FFA members.

In 1948 Lemons returned to his alma mater, Oklahoma A&M, as extension editor, and his place was taken by O. O. "Sandy" Saunders.

A year later, WKY-TV hit the air, and Saunders started a daily TV farm program in addition to his daily radio program. In 1951 Harold Dedrick became Saunders' assistant and then his successor.

Dedrick hired Jack Stratton as assistant, and they continued to preside over the radio and TV programs. In cooperation with the state extension service and SCS, they started a land judging contest which became an annual event, and still was going in the seventies.

In 1952 Dedrick became extension radio-TV specialist and his successor at WKY was Russell Pierson, who had been in charge of the state's seed certification work for several years.

In time, Pierson added several market reports each day to the WKY radio schedule, covering cotton, grain, and livestock, stressing feeder cattle.

One of his favorite TV features was the Farmer/Rancher of the Month. Pierson or his assistant, Ken Root, visited the family and filmed them at work and at home, and the film was broadcast on their morning TV show.

When WKY-TV was sold in 1975 and the call letters changed to KTVY, Pierson and Root were asked to continue as farm directors of both radio and TV.

Pierson retired at the end of 1979 after fifty years in agricultural work, twenty-eight of them as a farm broadcaster. Root became farm service director of the TV and radio stations and was joined by Arlene Tefft, who transferred from the KTVY news department. She was raised on an Oklahoma farm, had worked with Pierson and Root in the summer of 1978 between her junior and senior years at Oklahoma State University, and a few months later was awarded the annual NAFB scholarship as the year's outstanding prospective farm broadcaster.

Chapter Forty-two

Oregon

OVER a period of thirty-six years, 1923–1959, a radio listener in Oregon might have heard Wallace Kadderly broadcasting to farmers over KOAC, KGW, the "Western Farm and Home Hour," the "National Farm and Home Hour," or during his last year on the air, over KUIK, Hillsboro.

The first programs for farmers were over a 50-watt station on the campus of Oregon Agricultural College, Corvallis, which lasted only about six months. Then came talks by extension specialists over KGW and KOIN, Portland. In 1925, when the college built a 500 watt station, KOAC, Wallace Kadderly was named program director. He started a series of programs for farmers, at first three per week, then four, then noon and evening, six days each week.

In 1926 he wrote in the OAC alumni magazine, "400 lectures by 116 faculty members from 35 departments, many of them equivalent to a correspondence course." A conservative estimate placed the number of receiving sets in Oregon at 4,000 in the country and 10,000 in cities.

In 1929 the USDA ran its market news wire to the agricultural college campus, and agricultural economist, Leroy Breithaupt, began broadcasting market reports over KOAC every day.

In 1932 Kadderly was named manager of KOAC, but one year later he left Oregon to become USDA producer of the "Western Farm and Home Hour," headquartered in San Francisco and heard each day at noon up and down the Pacific coast.

In late 1937 he was transferred to Washington, D.C., as radio extension specialist. Within a few months he was named chief of the USDA Radio Service. I was hired to follow him as extension specialist and he became my boss in June 1938.

Kadderly guided the broadcasting activities of the USDA through the turbulent years of World War II; helped to bury the "National Farm and Home Hour"; and quietly maneuvered the commercial farm broadcasters into forming a national organization.

Early in 1945 KGW, Portland, invited him to come back to Oregon as the station's farm director, and he returned home. He carried his tape recorder to farms throughout western Oregon and southwest Washington; did live broadcasts from the Pacific International, the Oregon State Fair, and local county fairs; and worked with the state and county extension services and farm organizations in their many activities.

But twelve years in government service had left a mark. In 1950 Kadderly was persuaded to take a government job again, helping the agricultural ministries of other countries use radio and other methods of communication in getting information to their farmers. In 1958 he returned to Oregon and went into semiretirement by starting a daily farm program on KUIK, Hillsboro, a suburb of Portland. After about one year, new management decided that KUIK was a suburban station, not a rural one, and Kadderly's retirement became complete. In 1976, around his eightieth birthday, he and his wife moved to La Jolla, California.

KOAC, Oregon Extension. The first ten years of broadcasting to Oregon farmers by KOAC were guided by Wallace Kadderly, and in 1932 C. R. "Cy" Briggs took over the KOAC farm programs, after being county agent in the county where Oregon State College is located. At the time, no other station had a program especially for Oregon farmers, and Briggs had a following.

On one occasion when a strike at the North Portland stockyards was interfering with normal sales operations, he asked farmers to hold back on their shipments for one day or two. Shipments were reduced by 40 percent and the market could handle the loads that did arrive.

Briggs stayed with KOAC until 1937, when he moved to the USDA office in San Francisco and succeeded Wallace Kadderly on the "Western Farm and Home Hour."

Burton Hutton took over the KOAC farm programs and conducted them, noon and evening, for seven years, 1937–44, when he was succeeded by Earle Britton. In 1946 Arnold Ebert became radio specialist on the Oregon extension staff and occupied the spot for eight years. In 1950 he reported that five Oregon stations had their own farm directors who frequently came to the campus to record interviews with specialists, and in addition, county extension people in twenty counties put on seventy-seven programs each week over thirty-two stations. To give these county extension broadcasters a helping hand, Ebert started a series of recorded talks by state extension workers on platters.

In 1954 Ebert was promoted to head of the department and his place as broadcast specialist was taken by William Smith, a Nebraska 4-H worker.

Smith took over the two-a-day farm shows on KOAC, suffered a bit when the evening program was discontinued about 1962, and tried to be philosophical in 1976 when the noon farm program and the daily summary of farm markets were washed from the KOAC schedule after a half century.

The extension service continued to get out its information to Oregon farmers over other stations by means of tape recorded talks and a five-minute summary of agricultural markets, transmitted by phone to eight Oregon stations.

In most counties over the state, except in the Portland area, county agents were on local radio stations regularly. In Klamath Falls and Salem, the stations brought recording equipment to the county agent's office each week to record a series of conversations and then used the interviews throughout the week. The county extension staff in Coos County was regularly on the air over two stations.

Over a period of about twelve years, Smith spent most of his time on a weekly documentary, "Oregon at Work," reflecting agriculture, forestry, and fishing. It was a thirty-minute program used on the educational stations of the state along with five commercial Oregon stations.

In 1977 Smith and his assistant, Ken Kingsley, took on the task of using television to train people who wanted to be licensed to apply pest-killing chemicals. In an early trial, about one-fourth of the applicants had failed to qualify. Smith and Kingsley developed four thirty-minute videotapes and a training manual. The training materials were sent to everyone who applied, and the tapes were run on five commercial TV stations, plus the state's educational stations. About 5,000 people took the pesticide applicator's exam, and 94 percent of them passed and were given their licenses.

BILL DRIPS. One of the heartwarming comebacks in farm broadcasting had its final act in Oregon after playing nationwide for a good many years. The star was Bill Drips.

Drips had been agricultural director of NBC and the man behind the scenes of the "National Farm and Home Hour" for sixteen years, until in 1950 his health forced him to retire.

He and his wife moved from the Chicago area to a mountainside in Oregon, called Welches. Slowly he recovered and in 1953 he was able to start a weekly farm program on KOIN-TV. He continued it until shortly before his death in 1966.

KOIN-TV continued its weekly half hour farm program until 1974, under Oscar Haag, a dairy farmer and former dairy extension specialist.

Ivan Jones was farm director of KGW, radio and TV, with morning and noon programs from 1956 to 1965, when he suffered a fatal heart attack.

In the sixties, Bill Hansen was farm director of KWJJ, Portland, for several years.

Al Bauer was farm director of KSLM, Salem, in the fifties.

In 1976 two station owners in important agricultural areas also conducted daily farm programs. Bob Matheny, KRCO, Prineville, and Ted Smith, KUMA, Pendleton, both had programs in early morning and at noon, had county extension workers as frequent guests, and used market summary tapes from the state extension service.

Chapter Forty-three

Pennsylvania

KDKA, PITTSBURGH. The first broadcast to farmers on a commercial station, appropriately enough, was on the first station to get a commercial license, KDKA, owned by Westinghouse. On May 19, 1921, J. K. Boyd, USDA market reporter in Pittsburgh, began to broadcast prices of fruits and vegetables in Pittsburgh and other major markets each evening, along with Victor Red Seal records and the Westinghouse employees band.

About one year later, on July 22, 1922, KDKA joined hands with the *Stockman and Farmer* magazine to report agricultural information other than market news. Mason Gilpin, assistant editor, was the first and most frequent reporter. The magazine people found the daily broadcasts took many hours of preparation, and after a few months, editor E. S. Bayard created a new position, radio editor, for daily broadcasts.

On the recommendation of Glen Campbell, his advertising manager, he offered the job to a fraternity brother of Campbell's at Iowa State University named Frank Ernest Mullen. Mullen had been graduated in June and was working as farm editor of the *Sioux City Journal* at $25 a week. Bayard offered him $40, and Mullen took it. After he learned about rental costs in Pittsburgh, he talked Bayard into boosting the pay to $42.50.

The first full-time farm broadcaster went on the air March 24, 1923.

Engineers at Westinghouse had boosted KDKA's power to 4,000 watts by that time, and the station could be heard over the eastern half of the U.S.

Almost immediately Mullen arranged for more time on the air and started broadcasting market reports at 9:30 in the morning, again at noon, and again at 3 P.M., with a summary at 8:00 in the evening. In addition to the market reports, he began to schedule extension workers from Ohio, Pennsylvania, and West Virginia to appear on the programs. In August 1923 KDKA installed a microphone in the *Stockman and Farmer* office. Even after Mullen went on the payroll of KDKA in 1924, he continued to broadcast most of his programs from the *Stockman and Farmer* offices.

Listeners were also writers in those days. Mullen remembered years later that he used to get an average of one thousand letters and cards each day. Many of them requested information for faraway markets, and after two years he was reporting prices at about fifty markets.

In 1926 Westinghouse sent Mullen to Hastings, Nebraska, to start a farm program on KFKX. That turned out to be a brief stopover on his way to

Ralph P. Griffith (center, white shirt and tie) and a group of KDKA entertainers he led to the 1927 Ohio State Fair.

Chicago and the newly formed National Broadcasting Company where in 1928 he started the "National Farm and Home Hour."

The KDKA farm programs were taken over by Ralph P. Griffith, an actor, entertainer, and a man of many characters. On the farm programs he was Stockman Sam; in personal appearances and barn dance broadcasts he was Farmer Charlie; to the kiddies he was Uncle Ralph; when he read poems and essays he was Philospher Phil; with the Little German Band he was Professor Gus Schmaltz, and also a dog named Schnitzel.

One other ingredient was added to the KDKA farm programs when Griffith took over: commercial announcements. One of the first and longtime sponsors was Aladdin lamps. In the twenties only about one farm family in twenty had electric lights, and Aladdin lamps were brighter than ordinary kerosene lamps.

Griffith, as Stockman Sam, presided over the KDKA farm programs for about fourteen years until, in 1940, his Little German Band got a spot on the Blue Network which demanded all his time as writer, producer, and actor.

For several months, KDKA had no farm programs, and listeners complained. In 1941 management found a Pittsburgh boy, Don Lerch, with a booming voice and a degree in agronomy from Pennsylvania State University. Lerch conducted the KDKA farm programs for one year and was followed in 1942 by Homer Martz, who had been raised on a farm in western Pennsylvania, was graduated from Pennsylvania State, and spent three years with the Resettlement Administration plus six years as county agent in Erie County. Almost immediately he found himself the key man in a Victory Garden promotion in which KDKA joined hands with the *Pittsburgh Press*. The Victory Garden project lasted three years, and by that time Martz also was garden editor of the *Press*. He wore his two hats for thirteen years.

During the late forties, KDKA started a program of awarding a scholarship of $100 each to an agriculture student at Pennsylvania State, Ohio State, and the University of West Virginia. Each summer Martz would choose one of the scholarship recipients to work as his assistant, and near the end of the summer, he would be able to get away for a week's vacation.

When Martz resigned in 1955 to join a milk marketing co-op, he chose as his successor Bert Hutchinson, who had been one of his summer interns from Ohio State several years before. Hutchinson was competent, the programs continued to make money for the station, but times were changing and on many clear channel stations, farm programs were being replaced by music-and-news formats. In 1957 the station that paved the way for farm broadcasts on commercial stations, KDKA, folded its farm programs.

CHARLES SHOFFNER, WCAU, PHILADELPHIA. At the eastern end of the state, Charles Shoffner started a daily farm program on WCAU in 1924. He was well known as a writer in *Farm Journal* and other magazines before radio came into being.

He was one of the small group that organized the National Association of Radio Farm Directors in 1944, and one of the early newsletters of the association noted that he had completed twenty years of daily broadcasts to farmers. The next newsletter expressed sympathy over the death of Charles Shoffner's wife. Some months later Shoffner, well into his seventies, married the young girl who had been his secretary. His new father-in-law was unhappy with the marriage, and in 1945, during a violent quarrel, his father-in-law shot him in the throat. Shoffner died a few months later.

Amos Kirby was fifty-six years old when he took over the WCAU farm program on May 15, 1945, about the same age that Charles Shoffner had been when he started in radio twenty-one years earlier. He had been a roving reporter for *American Agriculturist* magazine for twenty years.

Kirby recalled that he tried to brighten the program with cheerful items, as well as the hard facts about markets and so on. Weather was important, and he began to stick his neck out by predicting the Philadelphia area's weather several days in advance. He claimed he went 67 days without a miss, had an off day, and then went another 107 days with correct forecasts.

Shoffner's programs were noncommercial, but when Kirby took over, the programs went commercial. Kirby became the principal salesman and had International Harvester, International Minerals, Ralston Purina, and Campbell Soup as longtime sponsors.

Soon after he became a farm broadcaster, Kirby started a Saturday garden program and continued it for thirteen years. One flower breeder honored him with the Amos Kirby dahlia, with blossoms twelve inches across.

Kirby was sixty-nine when he retired from broadcasting in 1959, and he continued to write for *American Agriculturist* until 1973, when he was eighty-four.

The WCAU farm programs were turned over to Hugh Ferguson, who had been morning announcer on the station for twenty years. Ferguson's agricultural experience had included some summers working on relatives' farms in New Jersey.

He became a busy farm reporter, visited farmers and rural leaders in the area served by WCAU, and sold advertising just as his predecessors had done. But the farm audience was decreasing as corn fields became housing developments, and in 1966, Ferguson signed off the WCAU farm radio program for the last time.

Officials of WCAU-TV decided in 1956 that they wanted a farm show and hired a young vocational agriculture teacher named Bill Bennett to start a daily, live half hour farm program.

Bennett soon accumulated an assortment of chickens, ducks, sheep, goats, and pigs which were housed in a shed behind the studio. Each morning he scattered feed on the ground and opened the door on cue so the first thing viewers saw was Bennett's "Grand Parade" of poultry and animals going after their feed. It kept city viewers interested while farmers could read the market reports flowing across the screen.

Unless the weather was very bad, Bennett stayed outdoors to report the news and to interview his guests with the feathered and furred scene stealers wandering around.

Bennett had the support of camera crews in covering fairs and other events in Pennsylvania and New Jersey, visiting farms, research centers, and some of the fabulous gardens in the Philadelphia area.

In this 1966 photo are **Bill Bennett** (R) and his guest, Phil Alampi, New Jersey secretary of agriculture and a former farm broadcaster.

When he offered a free recipe booklet, 4,000 requests came in, mostly from city and suburban viewers.

In 1967 several major changes were made: the show went to color, from daily to one day each week, and it was taped in advance.

The weekly half hour show continued for seven years, with Bennett presenting his last program on November 16, 1974, after eighteen and one-half years of television farm programming. All this time he had continued to teach animal husbandry at the Walter Biddle High School of Agricultural Science, part of the Philadelphia public school system. After 1974 he was a full-time teacher once more.

Bill Bode, writer and producer of the farm show, kept a semblance of farm programs on the station with five-minute spots on Saturday and Sunday mornings.

EXTENSION. It was in the fall of 1939 that Les Hartwig, assistant editor, reported in the agricultural college editors' newsletter that the Pennsylvania extension service had started a daily radio script service. ''We try to work enough short items to fill five minutes. KDKA uses it in connection with their early morning broadcast of songs, market news, etc. In one instance we send it to the county agent.''

In 1943 the extension editor's staff was expanded to include a full-time radio specialist, Elton Tait, who had been a member of the county extension staff in Williamsport and took part in a daily radio program. He expanded the daily scripts to about ten minutes each day, and he also provided outlines for radio programs to agents in about twenty-eight counties who were appearing in regularly scheduled programs on local stations.

When wire recorders became available, Tait used a wire recorder to record interviews with farmers and researchers in their test plots, laboratories, and other locations away from the studio. He sent duplicates of the wire recordings to six stations. Later he used a tape recorder and paper tapes to provide the same kind of service.

From the annual Farm Show in Harrisburg, Tait started a system of telephone broadcasts to radio stations over the state, reporting to each station on residents of its area who had won awards at the Farm Show. By the seventies, more than a dozen people served as reporters, and more than 100 broadcasting stations received localized broadcasts during the week. Television stations were provided with footage shot at last year's Farm Show to use as background when the telephones reports of today's prizewinners were put on audio.

In 1960 Cordell Hatch succeeded Elton Tait as radio specialist. He had started doing radio work at the University of Tennessee and brought some programming ideas with him.

He offered a series of five-minute interviews and another of short, one- to two-minute recorded statements and interviews, suitable for news programs, disc jockey programs, or almost any kind of format. By the end of the first year,

1960, the new service was requested by 117 stations, and the number has remained above 100 since.

Hatch started a companion series, "Home and Garden," also composed of one- to two-minute segments with script introduction and conclusion. This program was used by about 100 stations.

As an aid to county agents, he began sending a weekly set of stories written in broadcast style and a minimum of eight pages.

In 1957 Hatch started a daily half hour TV program, "Farm, Home, and Garden," on WTAJ-TV, in which state extension specialists took part. The program was transferred to Pennsylvania State University's own station, WPSX-TV, when that station went on the air in 1965 and continued until 1978 when it was absorbed into a daily program with broader scope. Hatch and his associates excerpted farm, home, and garden features from the daily program and packaged them into a weekly series called "Extensions," used by eight other publicly owned stations covering the state.

Hatch took time out in the sixties to earn M.A. and Ph.D. degrees from the University of Wisconsin. In 1979 his staff included three people who planned, wrote, and took part in the extension service radio, TV, and audiovisual productions. All were graduates of Penn State and had worked elsewhere before returning to the campus and the extension service staff. Paul Ruskin did his first broadcasting in the Armed Forces Radio Service before joining the staff in 1973 to specialize in TV production. Keith Stevens spent several years as a commercial photographer before becoming a radio writer in 1978. Nancy Miller joined the extension staff at the end of 1979 after fifteen years on the broadcasting staff of Pennsylvania State University.

Some of the county extension workers entered radio and then television earlier than the staff on the college campus.

Several county agents in western Pennsylvania became regular participants on KDKA's farm programs soon after Frank Mullen became the farm broadcaster in 1923.

Max Smith, county agent in Lancaster, started broadcasting once each week over WGAL almost as soon as he went to work in the county in 1937. In 1979 his staff of seven was broadcasting a four and one-half minute report each day on five radio stations by a telephone recorder-playback which they installed early in 1976. The Lancaster County staff began on WGAL-TV in 1950 with a weekly fifteen minute program. It later became eight minutes and had continued throughout the years. Smith's personal string of forty-two years of broadcasting, and still going, seems like a record for extension workers.

No sooner was WEEZ, Chester, on the air in 1947 than Harry Wilcox, county agent in Delaware County, started a weekly half hour program each Saturday noon, which lasted for twelve years until he retired in 1958.

Probably the longest-running county extension program in the U.S. is "Farm, Home, and Garden" on KYW-TV, Philadelphia, started in 1951 and going strong at the end of 1979. The program started as a weekly half hour program presented by Philadelphia's county extension agents Pat Landon, Alan

Scott, and Eleanor Tompkins. In 1953 staff announcer Gary Geers became host of the program and he continued through the end of 1979, while the station call letters changed from WPTZ to WRCV and then to KYW-TV. The local agents invited participants from other counties, from state extension services of Pennsylvania, New Jersey, and Delaware, and from the National Farm School. The program became daily in 1954.

The schedule was laid out six months in advance and the participants were brought together twice each year to make up the schedule and have luncheon at station expense.

Each Thursday afternoon the performers for the next week came to the studio and videotaped all the programs for the week. There were no scripts or rehearsals. "If we make a mistake, it stays in the program on the air and we try to laugh about it or explain it."

A Nielsen rating in November 1975 gave the "Farm, Home, and Garden" program 51 percent of the audience at 6:45 A.M., about 150,000 viewers; two-thirds were female.

The program was listed as public service, but each morning, the announcer said, "We'll bring you "Farm, Home, and Garden" in just sixty seconds, following this message."

The success of this cooperative venture in Philadelphia led to a similar weekly program by agents in three counties on WJAC-TV, Johnstown, in the late sixties. Chick Young, staff announcer, was host in the late seventies.

WFIL, PHILADELPHIA. WFIL started its farm programs in 1947, with Howard Jones, a farmer, broadcasting from his home, about fifty miles from Philadelphia. Bill Givins moved from WGY in 1952 and conducted farm programs on both radio and TV for several years. Milton Bliss took over in 1960, when the "National Farm and Home Hour," which he had produced, came to an end, but after a few months he moved back to his home farm in Wisconsin and a job with the Soil Conservation Service.

Dr. George Webster, an agriculture teacher at Delaware Valley College took over the radio and TV programs, morning and noon, and continued them for eight years, roaming a three-state territory with tape recorder and camera.

In 1968 the station changed management and its ideas about programming; the farm programs went off the air and Webster went to work for the New Jersey Farm Bureau.

HERMAN STEBBINS, WSBA, YORK. Herman Stebbins ran a 600-acre dairy farm, which had attracted visitors from all parts of the U.S., Canada, Sweden, and Brazil, especially those interested in grassland farming and Holstein cows. But thousands of farmers in southern Pennsylvania and nearby Maryland knew Stebbins best as the farm director of WSBA, a position he had held since the station went on the air in 1942.

He had moved from teaching vocational agriculture in his native Ohio to

Herman Stebbins, farm director of WSBA, York, Pennsylvania, is also manager of a showplace dairy farm.

become manager of Sinking Springs Farm near York the year before WSBA went on the air.

Since 1942 he had been on the air each morning at 5:30 with a half hour of farm news, weather, markets, and interviews. Usually he recorded his program from the farm the afternoon before, so he could listen to himself while he was milking each morning.

Several other Pennsylvania stations had farm programs and farm directors throughout the years. For several years in the fifties, John Smith was farm director of WHP, Harrisburg, with morning and noon programs.

In the sixties, Don Oesterling was farm director of WISR, Butler. C. W. Bradford had a similar job on WEEX, Easton, and Colson Jones was farm director of WFBJ, Altoona.

Other stations with daily farm programs were WKAP, Allentown; WBYO, Boyertown; WPDC, Elizabethtown; WMIP, Milton; and WKOK, Sunbury.

Chapter Forty-four

Rhode Island

WHILE several Rhode Island stations carried network programs of the New England Radio News Service during the forties and fifties, one station in the state, WPBJ-FM, Providence, had its own farm director and daily farm programs for approximately three years, 1948–1951. The farm director was Sue Bailey Reid, who had an agricultural degree from Rhode Island State University and lived with her husband and family on an apple farm near Providence. Before she became a farm broadcaster she had conducted a women's program on WLIV, Providence.

On WPBJ-FM she had a half hour program each morning that included market reports, weather, farm news, interviews with farmers usually recorded on their farms, and talks by agricultural extension people and farm leaders. Two Saturday programs each month were devoted to the Grange, the principal farm organization in the state. During one period she had to be hospitalized and was off the air for a few days but soon began to broadcast from her hospital room and then from her home.

Chapter Forty-five

South Carolina

STATION WAIF had a life of only about two years on the campus of Clemson College in South Carolina, but in those two years the Director of Extension, W. W. Long, went on the air each working day to talk to farmers.

At the same time, he encouraged county agents over the state to get on local radio stations in their areas, and he instructed editors A. B. Bryan and James Eleazar to provide the stations and the agents with scripts, which they did for many years.

Around 1940 Bryan acquired a disc recorder and a graduate student assistant, Stiles Stribling, to use it, and they began to send weekly discs to about twelve stations, six five-minute programs on one platter. During World War II, Paul Seabrook, a recent graduate of Clemson College, took over, and then in 1945 J. R. Mattison changed from a tobacco specialist to a radio specialist, a position he held for the next thirty-two years. In 1974 Robert Austin, educated at Emory College and the University of North Carolina, joined the staff and took charge of radio and TV output. Mattison then moved down to the second spot of the two-man staff.

In 1977 Austin resigned and was replaced by Bob Townsend, who had been a disc jockey and newsman on several radio stations and most recently news anchor on WFBC-TV, Greenville. Mattison retired about the same time and was replaced by Albert Littlejohn, former news reporter on WRET-TV, Charlotte.

The new team continued the recorded radio and TV services that Mattison and Austin had provided to South Carolina broadcasting stations and county agents. They included one weekly tape of three-minute interviews on poultry science that went to about fifteen county agents, and another on dairy science went to twelve agents for use in their local programs. A second series, on 4-H club activities, was narrated by a member of the 4-H staff and distributed to agents in all forty-four counties. A third series, called "Dialogue," consisted of five two and one-half minute programs, sent to sixty-five stations. A fourth series, most popular of all, was called the "Plant Professor," with horticulturists talking about home gardens and house plants; one tape each week containing five talks or interviews, none longer than two and one-half minutes was used by eighty-five stations.

Almost all the forty-four county agents and their staffs in South Carolina were broadcasting regularly in the seventies, most of them five days each week on a local radio or TV station.

Cliff Gray

CLIFF GRAY, WSPA, SPARTANBURG. Quite a few farm broadcasters have broken into radio as country and western singers, but Cliff Gray, WSPA, once aspired to the opera. But when he discovered he would have to learn several foreign languages, he gave up a music scholarship at Louisiana State University and became cameraman for a crew of portrait photographers that moved to a new town every few weeks.

Gray developed the practice of going to the local radio station, offering to sing a few songs, and possibly getting a little publicity for the photo business. "Sometimes I'd get paid three dollars for a half hour of songs." He and his photography crew worked their way through the South and up to Lancaster, Pennsylvania. When he sang on WGAL, he was invited to join the staff as announcer. He stayed for almost ten years. Meanwhile he had married a girl from South Carolina, and in 1940 he moved to WSPA as morning man and farm director. Soon he started a half hour farm show at noon, "Takeout Time," sponsored by the local Ford dealer. As part of the deal, Gray was given a new car every year—for eighteen years. "Payola scandals put a stop to that," he said.

The station owner dubbed him "Farmer" Gray, and the name stuck.

Gray generally limited his farm coverage to about five counties surrounding Spartanburg, and he saw peaches, beef cattle, and soybeans take over most of the farmland that was once used for cotton.

In 1973, after more than four decades in front of a microphone and working closely with county extension people, Gray dropped his responsibilities as WSPA morning announcer but continued as farm director, with a daily program at 5:45 A.M. and a weekly one hour program at seven o'clock each Saturday.

WFBC, GREENVILLE. When WFBC radio went on the air in 1953, Ben Leonard began to report to housewives on the produce farmers had brought to the Greenville market which he managed for the county government. His one minute noon program also reported livestock prices for the benefit of farmers. On TV he conducted a weekly half hour farm program aimed primarily at farmers, with guests from the extension service, USDA, and farm organizations.

WDOG, Allendale, and WTND, Orangeburg, also had local programs to serve farmers in their areas.

Chapter Forty-six

South Dakota

WNAX, YANKTON. In 1921 (John C.) Chan Gurney and his friend, Al Madson in Yankton, followed plans in *Popular Mechanics* to assemble a 50-watt radio transmitter set up in the ice cream parlor of a local drugstore. It was great fun at first, but after a few months, with no money coming in, broadcasting became a burden. They dismantled their transmitter and put the parts in a flour barrel in a corner of the Gurney seed house.

In the mid-twenties Gurney's business slacked off. He theorized that many Gurney customers had been lured away by Henry Field and Earl May in Shenandoah, Iowa, two rival merchants who each had his own radio station. The way to meet radio competition was to get back into radio.

He bought out Al Madson's interest, reassembled the transmitter, beefed it up to 250 watts, and set it up in his father's living room. WNAX went on the air for the second time in February 1927. Gurney was engineer, announcer, and program director. All seven members of the Gurney family went on the air, one specializing in feed grains, another in wheat, another in garden seeds, and so on.

Soon the broadcasting equipment was moved to the company building, and Gurney hired announcers, engineers, and entertainers to keep WNAX on the air all day and into the evening. Initially, all the advertising was for Gurney merchandise and business began to boom.

Gurney recalled a half century later that during five years, 1927–1932, he made thirty-two train trips to Washington in efforts to get more broadcasting power, and he succeeded, in several stages, in getting authority for 5,000 watts power, day and night, and permission to build what was then the highest antenna tower in the nation.

He left the station and the family business in 1932, and a few years later was elected to the U.S. Senate. His father, brother, and uncles continued to talk to farmers until they sold the station in 1938 to the Cowles interests, owners of newspapers in Des Moines and Minneapolis.

The Cowles management hired Chuck Worcester in 1939 as farm director. He was a Minnesota farm boy, an agriculture graduate of the University of Minnesota, and then farm director of KYSM, Mankato, Minnesota.

WNAX had a studio in Sioux City, primarily to pick up reports from the Sioux City stockyards, broadcast by Harry Aspleaf, who moved from the extension service to the stockyard's payroll. A half hour each Saturday afternoon was

244

set aside for a broadcast by county agents from South Dakota, Nebraska, Iowa, and Minnesota.

Worcester and Jack Towers of the South Dakota extension service developed a close working relationship and often used Worcester's plane and Tower's recording equipment to gather farm stories and to report on events far removed from Yankton or Brookings. WNAX used the recordings first and then they were distributed to other stations.

When Worcester left the station in 1941, Chris Mack took over as farm director. With time out for navy duty during World War II, he occupied the position until he was made assistant manager around 1950.

Chet Randolph, who had worked at WOI, Ames; KGLO, Mason City; and WHO, Des Moines, became farm director and was followed by Craighton Knau, from WBAY, Green Bay. They maintained the same kind of high level service to farmers that WNAX listeners had come to expect, but they added plowing contests, corn picking contests, and tours to faraway places. In 1956 Knau left the station, and Rex Messersmith moved from the staff of the University of Nebraska to stay until 1972.

When Messersmith moved to KRVN, Gene Williams took over as farm director at WNAX. He was raised in Nebraska where he farmed for three years before studying agriculture at the University of Nebraska for two years. He became farm director of WJAG, Norfolk, and three years later he moved to KMMJ, Grand Island.

Williams made two gradual changes in the WNAX farm programs in the seventies:

First, where his predecessors helped to conduct big events for farmers, such as plowing and corn picking contests, William's whoopla efforts were aimed at consumers: "Guess how many pounds of dressed beef will go into the freezer from the 1123 pound steer we bought yesterday. The one who comes closest gets one quarter for his own freezer." Same thing with a 225 pound hog. There were four winners, one each in South Dakota, Minnesota, Nebraska, and Iowa.

Second, more market reports were given, especially more reports on futures trading and more reports from local livestock auctions. In 1979 the station broadcast twenty-seven market reports during the day, in addition to half hour programs of farm news and interviews in early morning and during the noon hour.

Along with several farm directors at WNAX was the station's "inquiring farm reporter," George B. German. German started on WNAX as a country singer in 1928. During his fourteen years as a singer making innumerable personal appearances he talked with thousands of WNAX listeners and recounted many of the stories they told him. In 1942 the station gave him a noontime spot, six days each week, and assigned him a husky engineer to carry a disc recorder and a generator. He then went on the road and invited people to talk about whatever was on their minds. When electricity became more widespread and recording equipment became lighter, he traveled without the engineer.

When Chris Mack was in the navy and later when Rex Messersmith tried his hand at nonradio work for a time, German took over as farm director.

Besides his daily interviews on "RFD with George B," he was tour promoter and conductor. Over the years, he led planeloads of WNAX listeners to Europe and South America. He also led eight trips each to Hawaii and Mexico.

He retired from WNAX in 1968, but kept busy with a book based on his radio interviews and another of his favorite cowboy songs. He became director of the Dakota Territory Museum.

EXTENSION. The South Dakota chapter of Epsilon Sigma Phi, extension workers' honorary fraternity, in 1974 published a "History of Extension," which includes the highlights of broadcasting activity by the South Dakota extension service over the years. The radio portion of the history begins in 1931, when Steven W. Jones was hired by extension editor Samuel Reck as half time radio specialist. Jones helped college engineers rebuild the transmitter for KFDY, owned by the college but silent for the previous two years for lack of money. When the station went back on the air in 1931, its budget was $400 per year, all of which went to pay for electric power.

Steve Jones conducted a daily farm broadcast over the college station, reaching out with minimum power over about six counties, for the next six years. Press releases sent to the news director made up the principal service to other stations in the state.

In 1937 extension editor Harry Aspleaf bought a disc recorder, and hired a student named Jack Towers to produce live programs on KFDY and to make disc recorded programs, which were sent to stations at Yankton, Watertown, Sioux Falls, and Pierre. Once the recordings were established on a weekly basis, they replaced scripts and news releases.

When Chuck Worcester was farm director of WNAX, Yankton, he owned a plane that he and Towers flew to many different locations to record interviews and describe events. Worcester used each platter first on WNAX; then it was circulated to other stations.

Gerald Doyle took over as radio specialist when Towers moved to the USDA in 1942, but during most of the war years the position was vacant. Extension editor John Ryan kept recordings going to radio stations, and late in 1945 he began to use a wire recorder, although at first only WNAX, Yankton, was equipped to broadcast wire recordings.

The extension service switched to tape equipment in 1950. John Gerken handled much of the radio work; and about this time, length of recorded interviews was cut to a three-minute maximum, and programs went on request to about twenty stations over the state.

Gerken reported to other agricultural college editors in 1950 that he had hitched together six recorders to make that many dubbings at one time, and the stations said the quality was good.

Bob Parker took over as radio specialist in 1951, moving from WMT's farm department, and soon organized the South Dakota State Farm Network, with stations in Sioux Falls, Mitchell, Huron, Watertown, Aberdeen, and Pierre, carrying a half hour farm program each morning at six o'clock. Parker moved to the Connecticut extension service in 1953, just about the time South Dakota extension specialists were beginning to make use of TV, taking part in farm programs on KELO-TV, Sioux Falls, and KVTV, Sioux City, Iowa. The KELO talks and demonstrations were recorded on film and were sent to other South Dakota stations on request. In 1968 the college acquired its own educational TV station on the campus at Brookings, and assistant extension editor Dan Johnson started a daily noontime farm program.

Johnson was followed by Neil Stueven, who moved to the New Mexico extension service in 1973. Cal Willemssen followed in 1973 and Mark Eclov in 1976.

In 1979 Mark Eclov and a student assistant produced five weekly series of radio tapes and had plans for a series of live one hour programs on the state's public television station.

SIOUX FALLS. There have been at least two Sioux Falls stations with farm programs since the forties. KSOO was the first with its own farm director, G.D. Warland, who was later replaced by Ralph Wennblom in 1946. Two years later Red Stangland became farm director and remained until 1961, when he built his own station in Sheldon, Iowa. He had at least one assistant, Russ Bailey, during that time but he created a fictional character, Zeke the Hired Man, to provide some comedy.

Orrie Kerwood took over the KSOO farm programs for about ten years, 1961–71, and was succeeded in order by Denny Oviatt, Joe Morrison, and in 1976, Tom Steever, fresh out of South Dakota State University but with two years experience as a KSOO announcer while he was a student. Steever had two hours of farm programming in early morning and an hour and a quarter at noon, with two reports on grain futures during mid-morning.

Les Harding, a former county agent, became farm director of KELO in 1949 and remained until he retired from broadcasting in 1971. He also served as secretary of the Sioux Falls Livestock Foundation during that time, had the job of officer of the Sioux Empire Fair, and operated his own farm. His assistant during many of his years on KELO was Karl Storjolhann, who flew his own plane to many agricultural events in the area.

KELO farm programs were discontinued in 1971 but another Sioux Falls station, KXRB, started an extensive farm program, more than three hours each day and conducted by former KSOO farm director Denny Oviatt.

VERNE SHEPPARD, KOTA, RAPID CITY. Why would a good hand milker from Wisconsin migrate to the Black Hills of South Dakota? One main reason, according to Verne Sheppard: live country music.

After serving in the air force and earning a degree from the Stevens Point State Teachers College, he stepped into an announcer's job on WTWT, Stevens Point, and a year later moved to WVNJ, Fargo. On both stations he used his

Verne Sheppard (L)

real name, Verne Lotz. In 1950 he learned that KOTA, Rapid City, was one station that still broadcast live country and western music, and he signed on as announcer, newsman, and market reporter. With the change in location he also changed his name for broadcast purposes to Verne Sheppard. He said, "It was a lark, but the name stuck."

KOTA's first farm program, an hour at noon, had been started in 1945 by Ed Denslow, who had worked for a local livestock auction. Gene Taylor, who had been a staff announcer, took over the farm programs in 1952 and added a farm hour in early morning.

The live music programs which had lured Verne Sheppard to KOTA were gradually phased out and came to an end in 1958. Sheppard devoted more time to news and had increasing responsibilities for market reports in the farm programs. He was named farm director in 1961, and then lengthened the morning show to four hours of farm news, general news, and recorded music, and in 1967 he started a half hour farm program on KOTA-TV. He was still conducting the radio and TV programs at the end of 1979.

He was time salesman and secretary in his one-man farm department.

KKAA, ABERDEEN. It looked as though it was inevitable, but it took a long time for the *Dakota Farmer* magazine to enter the radio business.

It appeared inevitable because the chairman of the publishing company was Frank Mullen, a pioneer in farm broadcasting; and the president of the company, Vern Laustsen, had written commercials for Allis Chalmers on the "National Farm and Home Hour." But it was not until 1974 that the *Dakota Farmer* station, KKAA, Aberdeen, went on the air. Mullen came from his home in California to help dedicate the station.

It took over one year and at least two farm directors to begin to establish the farm department. In September 1975 manager Dave Laustsen hired Ray Smith and things became more stable.

Smith said, "When Dave first talked to me I just laughed. I'd been in radio 20 years, been manager of stations in Nebraska and Illinois. From manager to farm director looked like a big step downward." But he took the job, including the responsibility for sales as well as programs, fifty-five minutes in early morning and forty minutes near noon. "Business is great, and after three years on the job, I love it."

Over the next four years he expanded the farm programs to sixty minutes in early morning and eighty minutes during the noon hour, increasing the amount of farm news and market reports in each program, and of course providing more time for commercial announcements.

In 1977 manager Dave Laustsen and a partner bought the station, making KKAA independent of the publishing company which had founded it.

Chapter Forty-seven

TENNESSEE

EXTENSION. Hiram Hicks was a fictitious radio character, but he started something that lasted: county agents talking to farmers by radio. (George Story in Massachusetts might have been a bit earlier on an experimental station.) Soon after WREC, Memphis, went on the air in 1922, W. M. Landess, county agent of Shelby County, started a weekly broadcast. He was introduced as "Hiram Hicks," a farmer. The number of years he played Hiram Hicks is uncertain, but Landess continued to broadcast every week over WREC until 1934, when he joined the newly formed Tennessee Valley Authority. Leonard J. Kerr, his successor as county agent, took over the radio programs and continued them for twenty-eight years. When he retired as county agent in 1962, he went to WREC and directed farm programs on both radio and TV. His successors as county agent, E. E. Permenter, 1962–1973, and Ray Wilkinson, 1973–1979, continued the tradition of broadcasting to farmers but over different stations, WMPS, WMC, and WHBQ, Memphis.

In 1936, WMC, Memphis, entered farm broadcasting by beginning a daily program in which county agents in Tennessee, Arkansas, and Mississippi took turns as guest speakers, with the local agent, Leonard Kerr, as host. WMC put a microphone in his office, and the agents from out of town did their broadcasting there.

In 1946 Ernest Brazzle became the first black assistant county agent in Shelby County, and one year later he started a weekly program for black farmers on WDIA, Memphis. He was also one of the first county agents to take portable recording equipment to farms and homes to interview farmers and their families. After about fifteen years with a weekly program, he was invited to go on the air every day. Until he retired in 1978 he made a tape of three to four minutes each day, with a live half hour show each Saturday. His successor, William Vasser, continued the daily programs on WDIA.

Landess was the only extension worker in Tennessee making use of radio for about eleven years, until in 1933 extension editor A. J. Sims began to adapt the USDA "Farm Flashes" to Tennessee and distributed them to seven stations which fairly well blanketed the state. On WSM, Nashville, J. R. Millikan of the Tennessee Department of Agriculture started a daily program; and on WNOX, Knoxville, county agent R. M. Murphy also began to broadcast. Several years later the station manager of WNOX said Murphy's daily farm program had the biggest audience of any on the station. One reason: his program was the only

Ernest Brazzle (R)

way farmers could learn when to come to the AAA office to get their government checks.

Later in the thirties, several other county agents started regular programs: M. D. Brock on WTJS, Jackson; G. C. Baker on WOPI, Bristol, on the Tennessee-Virginia border; and W. J. Lovelace on WDOD, Chattanooga.

In 1937 the state extension service headquarters on the University of Tennessee campus at Knoxville arranged for a twice-a-week program, via leased wire, over WSM, Nashville. This was destined to be a long distancer runner; it ran as a live program until 1949, and it continued into the eighties on tape. In its early years, assistant editors Sam Carson and Joe Elliott were in charge; beginning in 1946, Fletcher Sweet took over. Cordell Hatch, a University of Tennessee graduate, had charge for a few years, and George Mays became radio specialist in 1966 and was still on the job in 1980.

In the mid-seventies, the state extension service had several series of programs, distributed on tape:

The program prepared for WSM also went to seventy-six other stations. "Better Farming in Tennessee," a fifteen-minute weekly program made up of two or three interviews was distributed to sixty-eight stations. Another weekly, "Tennessee Home and Garden Show," went to fifty-four stations. In the sixties, George Mays started a service of spot announcements, one to two minutes long, with about ten spots on one reel of tape and used in 1979 by thirty-four stations. A script service of similar one-minute announcements went to nearly ninety stations.

In 1978 the University of Tennessee established a call-in service of recorded messages for the benefit of radio stations, with messages changed twice each day. The agricultural extension service provided ten to fifteen messages each month for this service.

WMC, MEMPHIS. Derek Rooke was almost ready to join his father's pharmacy in England when he was caught up in the Royal Air Force and assigned to American planes. He then met a girl named Louise from the Memphis area, married her after the war, and became a Tennessee farmer. In 1951 he was invited, English accent and all, to start a farm program on WMC-TV. "I didn't sound like a hick, and growers took that as a compliment."

Walter Durham was conducting a farm program on WMC, radio, and also writing farm news for the *Memphis Commercial Appeal*. But soon he decided to limit his work to the newspaper, and the English pharmacist added the daily full hour of radio to his daily quarter hour on TV.

In 1971 a union election forced him to decide whether he wanted to be classed as an announcer or as a salesman. He chose sales and went off the air, after what he believed was the first twenty-year record on a farm television program. Buddy Sanders, who had been assistant county agent in Memphis, took over the WMC radio and TV farm programs.

In the seventies farmers became much more interested in market prices than they had been for years, and Sanders scheduled several market reports during the trading hours, with New York and Memphis prices on cotton and Chicago prices on soybeans, plus the USDA summary of livestock prices at the principal markets.

In 1977 Edward Winston "Buddy" Sanders left broadcasting and opened a farm supply business. His place at WMC was taken by David Warner, who had been broadcaster on the staff of the Illinois extension service for about four years.

WSM, NASHVILLE. Beginning in the thirties, WSM made its time available to the Tennessee Department of Agriculture for a daily program, and beginning in 1937 the station set aside two periods each week for agricultural talks by extension service people. These were public service programs, free of commercials. In 1944 the station began to put some of its own talent into farm service by assigning staff announcer Louie Buck to read farm news as it came from extension services and over the news wires. In 1945 the station hired its first and only farm director, John McDonald, who stayed for more than thirty years.

He grew up on a farm in western Tennessee, earned a degree from the University of Tennessee in 1932, and taught vocational agriculture for thirteen years before he became a broadcaster.

"Within a hundred miles of Nashville you can't find a county agent, vo-ag teacher, soil conservationist, FHA or ASCS official who hasn't been on a WSM program." John estimated he received one million cards and letters.

When "Noontime Neighbors" came to an end in 1972 and McDonald planned to retire, the sponsors wouldn't let him. So he developed a series of five-minute programs, spaced through the early morning. In 1977 he became a sponsor himself, "John McDonald Sausage."

He made several trips to other countries, including western Europe, Russia, the Central and South American nations, Canada, Cuba, and to the Far

John McDonald was backed up by ample musical talent, especially in the early days of his "Noontime Neighbors" program. McDonald is seated closest to the dinnerbell.

East, sometimes as tour leader for WSM listeners, sometimes accompanying a secretary of agriculture. One result was that his wife, Evelyn, became a professional tour director and arranged "Agricultural Seminars," on the Queen Elizabeth II, under the auspices of the farm broadcasters organization, which John served as president in 1956.

MURRAY MILES. Murray Miles led several lives as a farm broadcaster beginning in 1955, and in the seventies he was living three of them at the same time.

His bread-and-butter job for twenty-five years was as publicity director of the Tennessee Farm Bureau. In that role he started a weekly radio tape program in 1955 which he sent to ten Tennessee radio stations. By the late seventies the number had grown to around fifty-five stations.

In 1975 he launched a daily five-minute program, "Accent Agriculture," on the Tennessee Radio Network, with thirty stations carrying it. The program included a commercial spot to be sold by the network and another to be sold by the participating stations.

In between he became involved in television on WSM-TV, handling a weekly program "Town and Country," and the program was still on the air twelve years later. The program had something for consumers and farmers but it always had teenagers in mind.

WNOX, KNOXVILLE. The county agent in Knoxville, B. M. Murphy, began a daily program on WNOX about 1933 and stayed with it for so long many people must have thought he worked for the station.

In the early fifties, the station designated Cliff Allen as its farm director for a three-per-week program, but the assistant county agent H. P. Wood reportedly spent as much time producing the program as Allen.

The Tennessee Radio Network, including ninety Tennessee stations, carried ten farm shows each day plus some weekend specials. Dan Gordon, formerly of KWTO, Springfield, Missouri, was farm director of the network in the late seventies.

Chapter Forty-eight

Texas

EXTENSION. The "Texas Farm and Home Hour" was launched almost as soon as Texas A&M University put its station, WTAW, on the air in 1922, and in 1928 the program was fed to the Texas Quality Network made up of WFAA, Dallas; WOAI, San Antonio; and KPRC, Houston.

The guiding light on the "Texas Farm and Home Hour" for many years was Dr. E. P. Humbert, head of the genetics department at the college, who added the radio program to his regular duties for ten years, up to 1939, when the extension service hired its first radio specialist, John Rosser, who had been on the NBC staff in New York. Rosser died in 1943, in his thirties; and the radio job was taken over by Chester W. "Jack" Jackson, a Texas A&M graduate, onetime vocational agriculture teacher, and county agent. Soon he acquired as an assistant Claire Banister, a Texas rancher's daughter.

B. A. "Andy" Adams joined the team in the late forties, and in the fifties he began a syndicated tape service to Texas stations. Around that same time, Jackson moved to KCMO, Kansas City, while Banister moved to the Rural Radio Network in New York state. Richard Hickerson, who had been pest control expert on the extension staff, joined the broadcasting team and continued until the late sixties. He and Adams continued the daily "Texas Farm and Home Hour" on the Texas Quality Network until 1958 when the extension service ended the program. By then many Texas stations had their own farm directors; and the extension service decided to concentrate on a tape service to these broadcasters and to county agents who were broadcasting. A copy of each tape went into a tape library, so it could be used again next year or whenever it was timely.

Larry Quinn became broadcast specialist in 1970. He was from Oklahoma, attended Panhandle A&M, working part time as announcer on his hometown station at Guymon, Oklahoma.

About the first thing Quinn did at Texas A&M was to erase all the radio tapes in the library. He set out to produce twelve new tapes each week, from one and one-half to four minutes in length, with the understanding that each one would be erased after three months, "to be sure that there would be a fresh approach and up-to-date information." He notified county agents, farm broadcasters, and news directors of all stations about the subject, speakers, and lengths of each week's supply and provided a form on which they could request the tapes they wanted. Twice each year he sent each extension specialist a report on the tapes he had made and which stations and county agents had requested them.

For TV Quinn set up a schedule of short instructional films that went to county agents and farm directors on stations where the information would be pertinent. For newsworthy events, such as a 4-H Roundup, he provided spot news coverage for as many as twenty-five TV stations, with original footage for each one. He shipped the unprocessed film to each station and left it to the station's staff to do the editing.

When Quinn joined Layne Beaty in the USDA Radio-TV Service in 1974, he was followed briefly by Monty Reese and then by James Hedrick, from the Mississippi extension service. Hedrick, with the help of Manuel Pina, who had a doctorate from Texas A&M, started a radio tape service in Spanish, three or four tapes per week, for the several Texas stations that broadcast in Spanish.

In 1976, largely through Pina's efforts, they extended the radio tape "cafeteria" to include home economics, 4-H and community development, as well as agriculture. Every radio station and every county extension service received a weekly list of about twelve programs, thirty seconds to three and one-half minutes. The usual output was 1,000 to 1,200 recordings per week.

In December 1976 a new radio-TV specialist, James Whitman, took over after two years on the information staff of the USDA Agricultural Research Service.

He had the assistance of Ethel Galvan in developing a weekly quarter hour program in Spanish used by ten Spanish language radio stations. Several of Whitman's staff and members of the 4-H staff turned actors to produce a series of two and one-half minute skits dealing with energy conservation; eight skits were recorded each month and sent on tape to every radio station in the state.

For television Les Palmer—and later Suzanne Black, formerly of KTBX-TV, Bryan—with James Hunt, cameraman on the extension staff for twelve years, produced a series of videotaped interviews with farmers and ranchers, sent one per month to the state's farm directors, and a monthly half hour "magazine type" program focusing on research in progress at the Texas agricultural experiment stations. The latter program was sent to program directors, rather than farm directors, of twenty-eight Texas TV stations.

WOAI, SAN ANTONIO. When Bill Shomette started as farm director of WOAI in 1941, the first in the state, his programs were noncommercial, and the station carried the "Texas Farm and Home Hour." Around 1946 the station began to sell time on Shomette's programs. He continued as farm director until 1951, when he was made program director of the station, and one of the announcers, Bill McReynolds, became farm director. McReynolds was raised on a Texas farm and earned degrees from the University of Texas and the University of Florida. His programs changed occasionally, but usually there was a farm program in the morning and one during the noon hour which was heavy on market reports.

On four different occasions, he promoted overseas tours for his listeners.

Bill McReynolds

He always did a a thorough job of reporting livestock shows in his listening area, especially the annual San Antonio Livestock Show and Rodeo. He served as manager of that show from 1970 to 1974.

WBAP, FORT WORTH. Layne Beaty, who later was chief of the USDA radio and television service from 1954 to 1980, was the first farm director of WBAP, hired from the Farm Security Administration in 1943.

He was a native of Ardmore, Oklahoma, graduated from Eastern State University in Durant, and worked several years for the Oklahoma Department of Agriculture.

At WBAP he had an hour of farm information in early morning, which at the start was heavily loaded with wartime messages but became somewhat less so about late 1945.

He began to feel that he had company and competition beginning in 1947 when WFAA, Dallas, hired Murray Cox as farm director. The two men were good friends and often exchanged information. But it had to be done on the sly because the top management of both stations wanted no fraternizing with the enemy.

Television came to WBAP in 1948, and Beaty started a weekly garden program. His mainstay was the county agent, W. A. "Doc" Ruhmann.

In 1951 Beaty left WBAP to work in Europe for four years with the Economic Cooperation Administration, and he was succeeded by Ruhmann, who earned his nickname at Texas A&M when one day he went from the barnyard to biology class and on impulse he scraped some manure from his boots and put it under a microscope. The instructor gave him a compliment and his fellow students gave him a nickname, "Doc."

Ruhmann conducted the WBAP farm programs on radio and the farm-garden programs on TV for several years, before he was followed by a succession of farm directors. First to follow was Calvin Pigg and then Bob Etheredge, who moved from KFYO, Lubbock.

In 1970 Etheredge returned to Lubbock, as farm director of KDAV, and Bob Walsh, who had been a county agent, took over at WBAP. In 1972 Dick Yaws became farm director.

Yaws had been an announcer for the armed forces radio service in Japan following World War II, and then was a member of the Fort Worth Police department for twenty years. He joined the staff of WBAP in 1970 as traffic reporter. He lived on a farm thirty-eight miles from Fort Worth where he raised horses and had a small beef herd.

In the late seventies his radio program of farm news, weather, interviews, and market reports was on the air from 5:00 to 6:00 A.M. During his first two years as WBAP farm director he also conducted the television farm and garden program, but in 1974 WBAP-TV was sold and became KXAS-TV. Management of the newly christened station hired Ed Pewitt as farm director.

Pewitt was graduated from Texas A&M College in 1941, was in the Army Air Corps during World War II, and was with the Soil Conservation Service from 1946 to 1963. The last fifteen years of that period were spent in Dallas where he appeared each week on the farm programs of Murray Cox on WFAA and A. B. Jolley on KRLD. He often substituted when one or the other was on vacation or conducting a tour.

He went on active duty with the air force for ten years and had retired when he was asked to take over the KXAS-TV farm program each morning 6:30 to 7:00.

Pewitt presided over a program of farm information, general news, and weather. In 1978 the format changed and Pewitt presented fifteen minutes of farm news beginning at 6:25 A.M.

WFAA, DALLAS. Murray Cox was the first farm director of WFAA and for thirty years, 1947–1977, he was the only one.

He was a graduate of Oklahoma A&M, county agent, and veteran of World War II before he became a broadcaster with a daily sponsored quarter hour program on WFAA, which also carried the noncommercial "Texas Farm and Home Hour." The quarter hour grew to a half hour in the morning plus a quarter hour at noon. In the early fifties he started a daily TV program at noon, a schedule he followed for about twenty years. In the seventies his TV program was moved to morning and the noon radio show was canceled, so his broadcasting day ended at 7:00 A.M.

One of the highlights of his year was broadcasting from the Texas State Fair, and Cox was regarded as one of the major attractions. Also, hundreds of

Murray Cox

his listeners traveled with him on tours which he arranged and conducted, one each year. For the first eleven years, the trips were within the U.S. and by train. In 1958 he took to the air, and his airborne tours visited more than sixty foreign countries around the world.

In 1974 he was offered a daily quarter hour farm program on seventy-five stations of the Texas State Network in addition to his WFAA radio and TV programs.

Cox retired in November 1977; John Johnson, a recent graduate of Texas Technical University took over the WFAA radio and TV farm programs for a year and then took a job with the American Soybean Association. County agent Steve Wheelis conducted the programs for a few months until WFAA management worked out an arrangement for Texas A&M to provide a series of students to serve as farm program interns for six month periods. The intern did most of the interviewing, recording, and videotaping under the direction of Jess Smith, WFAA news director, who served as host of both the radio and TV programs. The first intern was a graduate student, Kevin Hamilton, from July to December 1979; he was followed by Randy Green, who expected to return to the campus for his junior year in July 1980.

On the Texas State Network, Joe Brown moved from KDAV, Lubbock, to take over the network's farm services. After about one and one-half years he returned to Lubbock, this time with KFYO, and Murray Cox came out of retirement in the summer of 1979 to once more conduct the daily farm programs.

KRLD, DALLAS. A. B. Jolley had been county agent in Dallas for about twenty years when extension editor Louis Franke and I called on him one day in

1940 and persuaded him to broadcast once each week on KRLD. He stayed with his weekly program until he retired as county agent in 1953 and immediately became farm director of KRLD, with morning and noon programs on radio and a noon program on KRLD-TV. He stayed in his second career for another nine years and retired in 1962.

PERRY BOWSER, KVOP, PLAINVIEW. Perry Bowser's world came to an end, he thought, in 1950 when he was hit by polio. But his life was restored two years later when he began to broadcast to farmers over KVOP, sometimes from his wheelchair, sometimes from his bed.

Bowser grew up in Dallas County, earned degrees from Texas Tech and Michigan State, helped develop new varieties of lettuce and tomatoes, and promoted Victory Gardens during World War II. After the war he moved to west Texas and farmed a section of land. He set up and ran a small vegetable processing and marketing plant and also taught veterans' classes in agriculture. Exhaustion from a twenty-hour day undoubtedly made him susceptible to polio.

Broadcasting at first was a form of therapy; then it became his life. In time he became strong enough to drive an all hand-controlled car, and he gathered stories over a fifty mile radius for about twenty years. When his health deteriorated he resorted to telephone and tapes for his four daily programs. Usually he took the precaution of taping each program in advance, while he was feeling well, in case he felt ill near time to go on the air. Perry Bowser died July 22, 1977.

Mike Wiseman, assistant county agent in the county where Plainview is located, was named KVOP's farm director. He added one and one-half hours of farm programming beginning at 5:00 A.M., as well as continuing the noon program which Perry Bowser conducted for twenty-five years.

KKYN, PLAINVIEW. The management of KKYN decided to compete for a share of Perry Bowser's audience in 1976 and hired Spike Wideman from KFYO as farm director. He did morning and noontime shows, plus three market reports. After two years, Wideman returned to KFYO, this time in the No. 1 spot, and Doyle Patton, a native of the area, became KKYN farm director.

HORACE McQUEEN, KLTV-TV, TYLER; KTRE-TV, LUFKIN. They called him "Hoss." Horace McQueen put on the half hour "Farm and Ranch News" over the two TV stations in east Texas, KLTV-TV and KTRE-TV, Monday through Friday mornings at 6:30. His programs were filled with cattle information because east Texas is cattle country and McQueen had his own cattle operation, but he didn't overlook the vegetable growers, timberland owners, poultrymen, rose growers, and the general farmers in his area. The two

Perry Bowser

stations covered about one dozen counties to the southeast of Dallas, but cable TV satellites gave him an audience that extended from Dallas to Shreveport.

McQueen earned a degree in agricultural journalism from Texas A&M in 1960, spent a few years on farm magazines, worked with the extension service, raised cattle in Australia and New Zealand, and entered broadcasting with the West Texas TV Network, based in Lubbock. He started his program on the Tyler-Lufkin stations in 1974.

McQueen said he brought the first Murray Grey beef cattle to the U.S., from Australia. Murray Greys have not replaced Herefords, but McQueen believed they had possibilities here.

THE LUBBOCK QUARTET. In the early years of broadcasting, Chicago had a handful of stations with at least one farm director, and was sometimes referred to as the farm broadcasting capital. In the mid-seventies that title had been taken over by Lubbock, Texas, which had farm programs on four stations: KFYO, KDAV, KLBK-TV, and KCBD-TV.

KFYO, LUBBOCK. KFYO had had five farm directors since Jack Creel started the first farm program in 1946. Bob Stevens followed a few years later, and then Bob Etheredge. Ed Wilkes took over the farm programs in 1962 and continued them until the fall of 1978 when he left to become part owner of KDAV. He was succeeded by his former assistant, Spike Wideman, who had spent two years at KKYN, Plainview. Wideman joined a seed association in 1979 and Joe Brown became the KFYO farm director.

Wilkes was graduated from Texas Tech in 1955 and was a peat moss salesman for several years. He wanted to do less traveling and KFYO wanted an agricultural man with no previous experience in broadcasting so he was hired. He worked alone for eleven years, with morning and noon programs; he also found time to run two farms and produce albums for several country-style comedians.

He acquired his first assistant, Spike Wideman, in 1973 and then Wideman's replacement, John Johnson, in 1976.

Spike Wideman (Morris Haney Wideman, Jr.) grew up on a High Plains farm, drove a tractor when he was four years old, and became a radio disc jockey when he was sixteen. He became farm director of KCBD-TV in 1972, succeeding Walt Olivo, but after one year took a part-time job in charge of the KFYO morning farm program so he would have the day to study agriculture at Texas Tech. He earned his degree in 1975, and one year later moved to Plainview for about two years.

KDAV, LUBBOCK. Bob Etheredge started the KDAV farm programs in 1971 and conducted them for one year before he moved to another Lubbock station, KCBD-TV. Joe Brown took over, after a long period of learning the farm broadcasting craft at KGNC, Amarillo. He spent six years, while in 4-H, as part-time assistant on that station's radio and TV shows and five more years as full-time assistant, under Cotton John Smith and Royce Bodiford.

In five years at KDAV, Brown expanded the farm programs to a full hour in early morning, fifty-five minutes at noon, several brief market reports during the day, plus a summary in the evening. He had two assistants in that time, Helen Brown, an animal husbandry graduate of Texas Tech; and then Jim Stewart, from KLBK, Lubbock.

When Brown became farm director of the Texas State Network in late 1977, Stewart was named farm director of KDAV.

KLBK. Horace McQueen carried the torch of "Texas Farm News" on KLBK and the West Texas Network for about eight years, 1966–1974; and when he moved to the eastern side of the state, Woody Fritsch continued the daily half hour, feeding stations in Monahans, Big Springs, and Abilene, While Fritsch was farm director a new farm product was introduced to West Texas: domestic rabbits. A processing plant opened in 1975 to process 20,000 rabbits per week, under USDA inspection, and some of Fritsch's listeners went into the rabbit business.

In 1977 Jim Stewart conducted an early morning full hour farm program on KLBK-TV.

KCBD-TV, LUBBOCK; KSWS, ROSWELL, NEW MEXICO. The farm broadcasting activities of KCBD-TV and Bob Etheredge had separate histories for several years before they came together in 1973.

Joe Brown

KCBD-TV had been on the air for seven years when, in 1960, the station hired Gene Linn as its first farm director, with a daily program of farm news and markets. He was followed a few years later by Neal Johnson. In the late sixties Walt Olivo became farm director, after several years in a similar spot on KVII-TV, Sherman. Olivo held the spot until 1972 when Spike Wideman took over for a short time before he moved to KFYO, and Bob Etheredge took over the farm programs.

Etheredge grew up on a west Texas farm-ranch, earned a degree in agricultural economics in 1955 from Texas Tech, and became a county agent. Bob Stevens, then farm director of KFYO, Lubbock, hired him as an assistant in 1958. Etheredge said, "It was the first time I'd ever faced a microphone and I was so frightened that when Bob asked me where I was born I couldn't remember." He stayed with the KFYO farm department until 1962, when he moved to WBAP, Fort Worth, for another four-year stretch on radio and TV. After a three-year sabbatical from broadcasting, in 1969 he became farm and ranch director of KDAV, Lubbock, for radio. But in 1971 he moved to a combined radio-TV farm service on KFEL. After two more years he moved out of radio and into television on two stations, KCBD-TV, Lubbock, and KSWS-TV, Roswell, New Mexico.

Etheredge, trained as a farm economist, didn't use much show biz in his daily forty-five minutes starting at 6:30 A.M.. "I try to be objective and factual; not much detail on any one subject, but a shaker of this and a shaker of that on many different subjects in each program."

HOUSTON. It is possible to list at least five broadcasting stations in Houston that have had farm programs over a period of almost a half century, but usually not more than two of them at the same time.

KPRC radio carried the "Texas Farm and Home Hour" from the agricultural college for thirty years, 1928–1958, but waited until 1955 to hire George Roesner as its own farm director. KTRH radio and TV listed Roesner, Dewey and Ronnie Compton, and Ben Oldag as farm directors from 1946 to 1979. Jeff Jeffries started on KENR in 1972; and Roesner had a farm program on KDOG-TV in 1976.

Roesner went on the air first in 1942 for Uncle Johnny feed mills with a daily program on KTRH, "Poultry Conservation for Victory." This was after he had earned two degrees from Texas A&M and spent several years teaching vocational agriculture. After four years on the air, he switched from Uncle Johnny's payroll to that of KTRH.

Roesner hired Dewey Compton as his assistant in 1953; and in 1955 Roesner moved to KPRC, leaving Compton in charge of the KTRH programs.

On KPRC, among other things Roesner organized several tours of listeners to Mexico, Europe, and Asia. He was president of the farm broadcasters' organization in 1961. He retired from KPRC in 1972, but late in 1975 he returned to broadcasting with a television show on KDOG-TV. It was about agriculture but aimed at consumers, showing farm people at work and at home, showing them how agriculture has improved to benefit consumers. The program ended when Roesner died following a heart attack in early 1977.

COMPTONS OF KTRH. Dewey Compton grew up on a vegetable farm in east Texas and joined the army in World War II. After the war he earned a degree at Texas A&M and was a county agent for about four years before going to KTRH.

Compton was turned down for pilot training during the war because he was color-blind, but his son Ronnie qualified for a pilot's license after he too

Dewey Compton
and his son
Ronnie

graduated from Texas A&M and joined his father at KTRH in 1972. Often Ronnie would fly to one agricultural event while his father drove to another; if they were going to the same event, usually they flew.

Six farm programs each week weren't enough to consume Dewey's talents, and about 1960 he started "Garden Line." Listeners were invited to call in their questions and problems, and as he said, "Ol' Dew sat in the hot seat" and offered to answer them.

The garden program led to *Ol' Dew's Gardening Almanac,* which sold a quarter million copies each year for several years. Ronnie was sales manager. Another offshoot was a gardening newsletter, with son Kerry as managing editor, starting when he was in high school and continuing while he studied at college. Still another sideline was a long-play record of *Aggie Jokes.*

Late in 1976 Dewey, Ronnie, and their wives were killed when they attempted to take off in a rainstorm from the airfield at Texas A&M.

KTRH continued the farm programs, with Ben Oldag in charge. He returned to KTRH after several years with the Texas Department of Agriculture.

JEFF JEFFRIES, KENR, HOUSTON. Jeff Jeffries' daily farm program on KENR was different from most: he did not talk to farmers or ranchers or report markets or weather. Jeffries was not on the KENR payroll for tax purposes since he was a one-man corporation. His corporation contracted with the station to present two programs each day and engage in public relation activities.

In training and experience, Clarence Blucher Jeffries fits the mold of most Texas farm broadcasters. He was raised on a farm near Laredo; was graduated from Texas A&M in 1952; was manager of nine ranches, including one in Guatemala, for one owner. He also spent two years ranching in Australia and then returned to Texas.

Since 1972 Jeffries has had two five-minute programs each day aimed at city and suburban people to tell them about agriculture. Occasionally he asked them to learn about agriculture by trying it. For example, he conducted a short campaign to persuade people to put a tomato plant in a pot and raise it as a house plant. He told them, "If you have problems with one plant, how would you like to take care of a hundred acres of tomatoes? That's what the farmer has to worry about."

RANKIN—VOICE OF VALLEY AGRICULTURE. Charlie Rankin chose the roughest approach known to get into farm broadcasting—the back of a bucking horse. He grew up in Dallas and liked to ride in the open spaces north of the city. After serving in the navy in World War II, he enrolled at Texas A&M, studied agriculture, and helped start a campus rodeo group and then the Collegiate Rodeo Association. Rankin wrote its constitution based on the FFA constitution and was elected first national president. When the first national collegiate rodeo was held in the San Francisco Cow Palace in 1948, he won the bucking horse championship.

In 1954 Johnny Watkins of KWTX told him that a rival station in Waco wanted a farm director, and Rankin became a broadcaster on WACO. Watkins stayed in Waco on radio and TV until the late sixties, but Rankin moved within a year to KRGV, Weslaco, in the lower Rio Grande Valley, heavy in citrus, cotton, and vegetables.

On KRGV radio he established a half hour program at noon, which attracted sponsors and expanded to one hour. Rankin sold most of the commercials on the program and wrote copy for many of them. In 1956 he started a half hour farm program on KRGV-TV, at first in the evening, then at noon, and then early morning.

In 1967, after the third change in KRGV ownership, he resigned and worked out a three-way partnership with two rival stations KURV and KESI. All the income from Rankin's program went into the pot; his expenses and those of the stations were taken out, and the rest was divided with 50 percent going to Rankin and 25 percent to each of the stations. He said his income doubled in the first year of the partnership. He bought a citrus grove in 1965. "When I endorse product on the air, listeners know that if I wouldn't be willing to use it, I wouldn't put it on the air."

One of the changes that he helped to bring about was the rebirth of the sugarcane industry in the Lower Valley, which disappeared in the twenties and staged a comeback in the seventies. Rankin and others used his programs to organize a co-op which started research, built a refining plant, and contracted for about 35,000 acres to be planted to cane.

In 1977 he hired Jim Hearn, a native of Ranger and a 1975 graduate of Texas A&M, as his assistant.

When Rankin left KRGV in 1967, the station hired Ken Jackson as farm director; in the early seventies he was followed by Bob McDonald.

KGNC, AMARILLO. In October 1939 the state extension services in Texas, New Mexico, and Oklahoma; the USDA people in the area; and the officials of KGNC met to start a daily noncommercial farm program.

In 1946 KGNC started a farm program intended to pay its own way. The station hired Johnnie Linn, a rancher's son, as its first farm director, which ended his law studies. He ran the programs for six years until Cotton John Smith took over in 1952. In 1957 Smith branched out into TV and continued daily programs on both stations until shortly before he died in 1968.

One of his assistants recalled that Smith never edited a tape on radio or film on TV. "If it's said, it's said, and if a farmer said it, it's important."

One of his early assistants was Royce Bodiford, who joined KGNC in 1959. He was winner of the FFA American Farmer award and national vice-president of FFA. He earned a college degree while helping Smith with the daily radio and TV programs. In 1965 Bodiford moved to KEEL, Shreveport, where he established morning and noon farm programs which ran for three years. When Smith died, Bodiford returned to KGNC to replace him. Joe Brown remained as assistant in the farm department until he became top man at KDAV, Lubbock.

In 1974 KGNC was sold to Stauffer Publications, Inc., of Topeka, Kansas, and the farm department concentrated on radio, two hours beginning at 5:00 A.M.. About one-half hour was broadcast between 7:00–9:00 A.M.; thirty-five minutes were part of the noon hour; grain and cattle prices were broadcast every hour from midmorning to midafternoon; and a roundup of farm news and markets was broadcast each evening. This kept Bodiford and his assistants Ernie Houdashell and John Burrell busy. In 1976, Bodiford was president of NAFB, and the next year he was named station manager. Ernie Houdashell then became farm director.

BEDFORD FORREST, KVII-TV, AMARILLO. Bedford Forrest spent quite a few years as a schoolteacher, and he said he thought, acted, and talked like one when he presented his morning and noon farm news and weather programs on KVII-TV. In particular, he tried to talk to farmers in such a way that consumers could understand what was said. He was not worried about farmers and ranchers understanding his style because they knew he was actively involved in operating 1,500 acres of irrigated wheat and grain sorghum, along with his father and brother-in-law.

He became farm and ranch director of KFDA-TV in 1967, with morning and noon programs. In 1972 he moved to KVII-TV, which had a satellite in Sayre, Oklahoma, and which was also picked up by several CATV systems over a wide area.

EARL SARGENT. Earl Sargent, farm director of KWFT, Wichita Falls, was usually accompanied to the NAFB convention by his wife; sales manager Les Pierce; and one, two, or three members of the owner-management team: Ben Ludy, and Forrest and Don Whan, father and son. Top management not only went along to the farm broadcaster conventions; they also went along with almost anything that improved their service to farmers.

As proof, Sargent's five daily programs had been on the air without a change in schedule from 1958 to 1979.

When Ludy and Whan arrived as new owners of the station about the end of 1957, Sargent had been conducting a farm program on the station for five years as part of his job with the Wichita Falls Chamber of Commerce. The new bosses put him on the station payroll, gave him more time on the air, a commission on sales, and much moral support.

He had grown up on a central Texas farm; spent seven years in the air corps; and earned two degrees from Texas Tech, the second one in 1952, before he moved to Wichita Falls and began broadcasting.

In one of his successful promotion efforts, he started a stubble mulching contest, and dealers bought time on KWFT to tell farmers where they could buy stubble mulching equipment.

In the sixties and seventies, Sargent began to promote the idea of root plowing to get rid of mesquite and to convert the land into good grass pasture.

RAY VILLANDRY. "The Ragin' Cajun" was Ray Villandry's nickname and trademark on the air. Cajun he wasn't, although he was of French descent and lived in Louisiana for a time; but ragin' was his stock in trade. Beginning in 1971 he did his raging on two radio stations in San Angelo and on TV in Corpus Christi; taking on middlemen, bureaucrats, boycotters, anybody and anything that didn't favor farmers and ranchers.

He entered radio by marriage—his daughter's marriage. Her father-in-law owned KPEP, San Angelo, and her husband was station manager. In 1971 Villandry's son-in-law was short of help, so he stepped in as sales manager, consultant, news director, and announcer. He then said, "Son, we need a farm program, one that's different; telling the farm and ranch story to city folks; telling it like it is." Villandry went on the air with farm news, markets, and weather in plain talk, butchered grammar, and plenty of opinions. Listeners tuned in to hear what target the Ragin' Cajun was going to shoot at next. "I always wound up with, 'God bless the farmers and ranchers for what they've done for the rest of us.' "

He moved his ragin' to KRIS-TV, Corpus Christi, for about one and one-half years, 1975–1977, then returned to San Angelo. His in-laws had sold KPEP but he found a welcome at KTEO as farm director—still ragin'.

TEXAS FARM BUREAU. The "Farm Bureau Roundup," a weekly quarter hour program, originating in Waco, was started in May 1954 by Bill Hoover, information director of the Texas Farm Bureau, and at the end of 1979 it was used regularly by about 110 stations each week.

Hoover pulled a reverse maneuver when he started the program: he persuaded professional broadcasters to become regular reporters for his weekly recorded program. The original group of three grew to ten, divided into two teams which reported in alternate weeks. In 1979 they included Roddy Peeples, Jack Dillard, Charlie Rankin, Clark Bolt, Ben Oldag, James Duncan, and Joe Brown, plus three former farm broadcasters who had changed to other kinds of work: Royce Bodiford, broadcast station manager; Bob Walsh, bank executive; and Spike Wideman, seed association publicist.

Hoover produced the programs for twelve years. In 1966 Charles Manley joined the staff, moving from Waco TV station KWTX-TV, and took over production until 1974. Joe Fields followed him and in 1977 moved to the headquarters staff of the American Farm Bureau Federation. He was succeeded by Keith Garrison, who had been a news anchorman at KFDX, Wichita Falls. In 1978 Garrison was joined by Gene Hall, who moved from the news staff of KFBM-TV, Beaumont.

From the beginning, 1954–1979, Goodson McKee, a recording contractor in Waco, served as moderator of the programs, and his recording firm also handled duplication and distribution of the tapes.

In 1975 the Texas Farm Bureau established a radio WATS line with a recording device carrying a daily one-minute farm item for radio stations. In 1978 a second recorded message was added, stressing consumer interests.

Layne Beaty (L), **Roddy Peeples** (R)

For TV stations, Garrison and Hall produced two news clips each week, one intended for farm programs, the other for general news programs.

RODDY PEEPLES, SOUTHWEST AGRICULTURAL RADIO NET-WORK. When the big moment of a 4-H kid's life is shaking hands with a farm broadcaster, you can almost predict his future. Roddy Peeples got to shake hands with Murray Cox, WFAA, about 1949, and never recovered. He studied agriculture at Texas A&M and became a farm broadcaster in the fall of 1952, his senior year, when he was put in charge of the daily farm program on WTAW. From college he went to KADA, Ada, Oklahoma; then to KGNO, Dodge City, Kansas; KLIK, Jefferson City, Missouri; and KWFT, Wichita Falls, Texas, where he was for five years assistant to Earl Sargent. Twelve years of experience gave him a three-part idea: he wanted to be his own boss—he wanted to have a farm program network—and he wanted to be in west Texas.

He started the Southwest Agriculture Radio Network in 1964 with a forty-five-minute early morning program on two stations, in Midland and San Angelo. Later he cut the length of the program to thirty minutes and expanded the coverage to eleven stations in west Texas and New Mexico, fed from San Angelo. The daily program moved over leased wires; some of the commercial spots in the program were Peeples' to sell and some were sold by the station.

In 1964 he didn't know of another operation like his, so he followed his own hunch concerning financial arrangements with stations. Since then quite a few other farm network broadcasters have followed his plan.

In the early seventies he started two daily syndicated programs, on tape, with six programs mailed weekly. "Cow Country" dealt strictly with cow-calf operations, and by 1976 it had built up to forty-four stations. "Fiber and Grain Update" started in 1975 and a year later was on thirty-three stations.

Roddy's son Rick started helping him in 1974, when he was eighteen. "Folks hardly know the difference; Rick sounds just like me."

Chapter Forty-nine

Utah

EXTENSION. Two bright young men at Utah State University earned master's degrees by tracing the history of educational broadcasting by the university. A. L. Marble wrote his master's thesis in 1935, and James K. Randall did his in 1969. Randall gave credit to Marble and I've borrowed from both of them.

Beginning around 1931 some of the extension service people from Utah State went occasionally to the studios of KSL to broadcast on the "Western Farm and Home Hour" heard throughout the western states. The Utah people probably were scheduled about six times each year until KSL changed networks.

In the meantime, Lester Pocock, director of information at the college, worked out arrangements for agricultural specialists to broadcast each Tuesday and Thursday afternoon at 11:30 over KSL, which meant they could be heard over most of Utah. Usually the fifteen-minute talk was followed by an offer of a copy of the talk, and on the average about thirty-five people wrote in to ask for copies. In 1936 the schedule was shifted to once each week, on Saturday afternoons, and it stayed that way until 1959 when the program got the title of "USU Digest" and university professors began talks about history, literature, drama, and many other subjects. It died out at the end of 1963 after thirty-two years.

As Utah acquired more radio stations, state and county extension workers began using them. Stephen Brower, extension radio specialist, reported about 1,800 extension service broadcasts in 1946; more than 2,000 in 1956; and J. K. Randall, who was radio-TV specialist in 1968, reported 8,328 programs in that year. He and the extension specialists prepared, via tape recording, nine programs per week, three minutes each, for every station in the state.

TV had been around for several years before the Utah extension service jumped into it in the summer of 1953 with a once-a-week appearance on a daily farm program on KSL-TV, Salt Lake City. Burrell Hansen, a speech professor, produced the series and acted as host. A year later KDYL-TV asked the university to produce a series of ten Saturday programs at noon featuring baby chicks and pigs, lambs, and other farm animals. Elwood Shaffer, extension editor, and Eldon Drake, audio-visual specialist, alternated as host for the series.

In February 1955 the extension service started a TV series called "Farm Frontiers," one hour at noon each Saturday on KDYL's successor station, KTVT, Salt Lake City; it ran for about one and one-half years. Each program featured a farm family, usually shown on film. It also presented county agricultural and home demonstration agents, and one or more state extension specialists, live from the studio. Brower reported the average cost of producing each program was fifty-six dollars, including travel, meals, properties, and materials.

The KSL-TV series labeled "RFD-5" went to a "magazine" format in 1957 with a section on pest control; one on country living, which had the suburban viewer in mind; another on whatever the USDA had provided; and next week's weather.

In 1957 the extension service began providing KUTV, Salt Lake City, with some filmed spots to be inserted in the station's Saturday afternoon movie. In the same year, consumer information specialists in Salt Lake City and in Ogden arranged for programs of marketing tips on TV stations in the two cities.

KSL, SALT LAKE. Like many other stations in the early days of radio, KSL was willing for many years to set aside public service time for farm programs if someone else would provide the talent.

The station hired its own farm director, Elvon Orme, and started a daily farm program some time in the early fifties, with the Kennecott Copper Company as sponsor. Ted Kegner moved from the news staff to become farm director in 1957 and continued until 1965. He was followed by Lynn Adair, who was farm director until he was named state director of the ASCS programs in late 1977.

Lynn Adair was born and raised on a small farm in southwestern Utah where his father ran a sheep-shearing business. Adair studied electronics at Utah State University and in 1957 acquired a job at KSL as a radio engineer, but he prepared to face a microphone by taking Dale Carnegie courses in speaking and oral reading. In 1963 he became assistant to Ted Kegner in the KSL farm department, and two years later Adair stepped into the top job.

KSL radio claimed a radius of about 400 miles as its territory, and he spent much of his time away from the station, attending meetings and talking to farmers, ranchers, and agricultural officials. He averaged about 30,000 miles each year, sometimes piloting a rented plane.

His fellow farm broadcasters elected him president of their national association in 1974, and the travel in connection with that office bore heavily on the KSL one-man farm department. Near the end of his term as NAFB president, Adair acquired an assistant, Clint Warby, who had worked in the KSL newsroom.

In his daily programs he usually included items on beef, eggs, and milk—aimed especially at consumers, and he had a half hour program each Saturday, intended exclusively for consumers.

In 1977 the morning and noon farm programs were canceled, and the farm director was limited to short reports, usually in the scheduled news programs. When Adair was invited to become state director of the Agricultural Stabilization and Conservation Service, he accepted.

Chapter Fifty

Vermont

EXTENSION. It was in 1924 that engineering teachers and students at the University of Vermont built a radio transmitter and found an angel in the person of Thomas Bradlee, director of the extension service. He took part in the first broadcast over WCAX (for Cooperative Agricultural Extension) on October 10, 1924, and found money to finance the station for several years, including a daily program for farmers. In 1931 the station was sold to the *Burlington News* with an agreement that the extension service would continue to have time on the air. Harry Mileham, extension editor, scheduled the agricultural and home economics speakers during the thirties. At the same time, the station started its own morning program for farmers, which continued into the mid-seventies.

In addition to its daily broadcasts on WCAX (now WVMT) speakers from the Vermont extension service took part about once a month in the daily "Farm Paper of the Air" on WGY, Schenectady, New York, from 1928 to 1970.

On the day after Christmas 1945, Jack Spaven came out of the navy to become the Vermont extension editor. He was a New York farm boy, and between his Cornell degree in 1936 and his navy duty, he had been assistant extension editor in Massachusetts and New Hampshire.

He recalled that one of his duties was doing a weekly quarter hour program on WCAX, "with only one voice—mine," at 6:00 A.M. and at the same time cutting a disc of the program. As soon as the program was over, Spaven took the disc to the bus station and sent it to WDEV, Waterbury. From there it was passed along from one station to another until at the end of about ten days it had been used by all six Vermont radio stations.

In the ten-year period from 1948 to 1958, New England state extension services promoted a Green Pastures contest, largely by radio. "As a guess, we influenced 80 percent of all commercial dairymen to make needed changes in their roughage operations."

In 1960 Tom McCormick became radio specialist of the Vermont extension staff and continued as radio specialist until 1978 when he was named head of the communications office. He was succeeded by William Soule, who had worked on Vermont newspapers, taught journalism, and worked in public relations.

McCormick soon reduced the length of the syndicated programs from a quarter hour to five minutes, and later to three minutes. McCormick and later Soule produced about two hundred programs per year plus sixty one-minute spots. In 1979 they were used by fifteen stations in Vermont plus two each in

New Hampshire and New York. Twelve of the state's county agents had radio stations in their counties and all had regularly scheduled programs, most of them produced on tape.

When WCAX-TV went on the air in September 1954, the extension service began a daily farm program, "Across the Fence." Lloyd Williams, formerly with the Connecticut Department of Agriculture, presided over the program for the first two years. A couple of years later, Layne Beaty chose the same title for the USDA's weekly TV program which was distributed on tape to stations throughout the nation.

When Williams left Vermont in 1956, Jack Spaven promoted Karin Kristiansson, a professional writer who had been staff secretary, to the job of TV specialist. She produced the programs for the next twenty years, doing the planning, writing, and much of the photography, with WCAX-TV staffer, Tony Adams, serving as host on the program.

Kristiansson moved to other work in 1975 and Lynville Jarvis, who had worked on the Vermont educational television station, became extension TV specialist, continuing the daily "Across the Fence" on WCAX-TV. Two of the programs were repeated three times during the week on WETK, the educational station. A 1979 survey estimated the audience at 60,000 sets. Jarvis also started a monthly one hour program on WETK, a weekly five-minute program on WEZF-TV, Colchester, and thirty spot announcements per year which ran on WCAX-TV.

At the time he retired from his Vermont job in 1976, Spaven counted twenty-three foreign countries in which he had served as teacher and consultant on how to get information to farmers.

WCAX, BURLINGTON. During the thirties WCAX started its own daily program for farmers in early morning to supplement the midday program by the extension service. Jim Platt was farm director for several years before moving to WQDM, Saint Albans, and later to WTIC, Hartford, Connecticut. In the late forties, Al Sutherland took over the station's farm program. There were some years in which the station had nobody filling the farm director slot, but in 1963 the station chief engineer, Burtis Dean, added the job of farm director to his engineering duties. He retired from the engineering job in 1976, when he was sixty-five, but continued the farm program each morning, rising at three and going on the air at five o'clock.

The county agent in Burlington, Bob Carlson, was a regular twice-a-week visitor on the program for almost thirty years until he retired in the seventies. In the early days his broadcasts were live, but beginning around 1950, he put them on tape.

In 1940 WQDM, Saint Albans, had a program called "Farmers' Special" on the air in early morning, conducted by Jim Platt.

In 1947 WWSR, Saint Albans, had a daily program called "Milk Talks," sponsored by a local creamery. At that same time, WDEV, Waterbury, had a daily program for farmers, a full hour in the morning conducted by staff announcer Rusty Parker, sponsored by a grain company.

Chapter Fifty-one

Virginia

EXTENSION. His last name was Michael, so he was introduced as "Mike at the mike." Rudolph D. Michael began broadcasting on January 6, 1930, from the campus of Virginia Polytechnic Institute each day at noon over WDBJ, Roanoke, with the extension service paying the line charges between the campus at Blacksburg and the radio station, about twenty-five miles away. To provide some sugarcoating for the talks on agriculture, student and faculty musicians and singers were also featured. John Merrifield took over the programs in 1959 and they continued as live broadcasts until in the sixties when they were replaced by tape recorded talks and interviews, with Ken Haines in charge, 1970–1972, and then Joe Brush until the programs ended in 1975. Forty-five years was one of the longest runs on record for an extension service program on a commercial station.

In 1934 Michael negotiated with the USDA and with the state department of agriculture to help produce a daily program on WRVA, Richmond. It was labeled "The Virginia Farm and Home Hour." When the WRVA program disappeared after two years, the title was applied to the daily program on WDBJ and then to the quarter hour tapes that were mailed to about thirty stations over the state beginning around 1960. It was produced by John Merrifield up to the time of his death in 1972.

Doyle Satterthwaite was named extension radio-TV director in 1972 and, on the basis of a survey of Virginia stations, he changed the pattern to a series of two-minute features titled "Impact," about twelve each week, principally slanted toward consumers. About seventy-five stations received "Impact" and many of them used a feature two or three times each day. A quarter hour interview called "Outroads" and a thirty-minute weekly program called "Dateline Virginia Tech" usually found places in the Sunday afternoon schedules of about 45 Virginia radio stations. When there was something newsworthy, Satterthwaite or one of his associates recorded the story on the dial-in phone system, and notified AP and UPI offices that the station could get the story by dialing the VPI number.

These programs were taken over in 1975 by the university's radio-TV unit. In 1979 Christine Sykes, who had worked in the university's production unit for one year, transferred to the extension service payroll and had major responsibility for seeing that agricultural and consumer information was included in the radio and TV tapes sent to stations throughout the state.

ALDEN AROE, WRVA, RICHMOND. Alden Aroe of WRVA was probably the only farm director who ever had a pig that would squeal on cue. The pig's name was Oink Jackson. Around 1950 a farmer gave Aroe the runt of a litter. Aroe took him home, built a pen in the basement, and discovered that if he lifted Oink's left hind leg Oink would squeal. For a few months, until he got too big, Oink would squeal to open the day's farm program on WRVA.

The squealing was only a fleeting episode in WRVA's farm service over a half century. The station was only two months old when it arranged in January 1926 for a spokesman for the Virginia Division of Markets to broadcast market reports each day, and these reports became fixtures in the day's programs. Many different people served as spokesmen for the Division of Markets throughout the years; H. C. Cline was an early one, and in more recent years, E. C. Coville was the reporter, Monday through Friday, 12:25–12:30. Until the early seventies, the market reports were unsponsored.

In the mid-thirties the station helped to create the daily "Virginia Farm and Home Hour," with county extension workers from eastern Virginia, the state extension service, and the USDA—all providing speakers and J. Robert Beadles announcing. The program lasted about two years.

The station hired Alden Aroe as farm director in 1946, shortly after he stopped flying airplanes for the air force. Aroe had spent a lot of time on his grandparents' dairy farm in New Jersey and he acquired a feel for radio as a student at the University of Virginia where he was graduated in 1940.

He figured his territory was sixty-six counties of eastern Virginia. He set aside a ten-minute period in his daily half hour, 6:00–6:30 A.M. for talks by county agents, usually on discs in the early years but later on tape. In the seventies both county agents and Aroe relied on the telephone to send and gather information.

Aroe commented about another change, "I know a lot of farmers who are using computer services at VPI; maybe computers will make farm broadcasters obsolete."

Of course, a mere computer could never replace Oink Jackson.

WIP ROBINSON, WSVA, HARRISONBURG. In the Shenandoah Valley of Virginia at Harrisonburg, there is a radio station whose call letters WSVA stand for "We Serve Virginia Agriculture." The station has had a full hour of farm programming in the morning and at noon, always at the same hour of day, since 1942.

The farm director most of those years was Wip Robinson. He said Wip was his real name, passed along through three generations.

Robinson entered radio in 1939, on WDZ, Tuscola, Illinois, probably the first station to report grain prices. Three years later, after a brief stopover at a station in West Virginia, he moved to WSVA.

In the early fifties, Robinson took a leave of absence from broadcasting, and the WSVA programs were taken over by Homer Quann, an implement dealer in the area. Robinson returned to the station after two years, and was still there in 1979.

Bill Ray

Robinson concentrated on about thirteen counties of Virginia and West Virginia, some of it valley and some of it mountain country, and felt he knew most of the farmers by sight and by name.

His programs were usually sold out, but he left selling to the sales staff.

BILL RAY, AGRINET. If you are a young farmer who can't get the market information you want, don't just sit around and complain; start a farm service of your own. That's what Bill Ray did, first on WINA and then on his own Agrinet Farm Network at Earlyville, Virginia.

Ray earned a degree in animal science from VPI and took over operation of the family farm near Charlottesville in the sixties. He couldn't get the market reports on grain and livestock prices he wanted, so he approached WINA, Charlottesville, with the suggestion that the station should have some programs for farmers and he conduct them.

In 1948 WINA had named Norman Kelsey as farm director when the station went on the air, but that early effort to serve farmers evidently had a short life.

Ray became WINA's farm director in 1965, and his broadcasting activities began to spread like crabgrass. His morning program expanded until he was on the air from 5:30 to 9:00 in the morning, and again for an hour at noon. In 1970 with Charlie Earl, of the WINA staff, as a partner, Ray lined up a dozen Virginia stations to carry two quarter hour farm programs each day, early morning and noon. WINA was the key station; the programs moved by wire. There were four commercial spots in each quarter hour program, two for the network and two for the local station to sell. For several years up to 1979 Agrinet was feeding its two quarter hour programs five days each week to fifty stations, well distributed over Virginia, with national and Virginia farm news, national markets, Virginia markets, and an agricultural weather forecast localized for different areas of Virginia.

For five years, Ray produced four and one-half hours of programs on WINA plus the two network farm shows. He also was involved in news and sports programs on the network. In 1976 he bought out his partner and re-signed from WINA in order to devote full time to the network programs. In 1978 Mike Miller joined him as associate farm director.

A year later Miller moved to WIBW, Topeka, and his place was taken on a part-time basis by Rick Franklin, who also continued as a staff announcer for WEVA, Emporia, Virginia.

One statewide survey showed 56.6% of Virginia farmers listened to Agrinet programs.

VIRGINIA FARM BUREAU. The Virginia Farm Bureau began in 1960 to send a weekly quarter hour tape of talks by its officers and also interviews with farmers, labeled "The Farmer Speaks," to Virginia stations that would use it. The number of stations generally varied from twenty to forty. In 1979, thirty-four stations received the recorded program.

In 1978 the organization created the Virginia Farm Bureau Network to broadcast two five-minute programs of farm news and weather five days each week at 6:50 A.M. and 12:45 P.M. Don Fleeger, who used the name Don Lloyd on the air, was the writer and announcer of the program. He was well established as a sports announcer in Richmond and continued to broadcast college basketball and football games along with his network farm programs.

Several Virginia stations had farm directors in the forties and fifties. Tom Howell was farm director of WSLS, Roanoke, beginning in 1945; and when the TV station went on the air in 1953, he began a TV farm show.

Frank Raymond started as farm director on WDVA, Danville, in 1947; moved in 1955 to WCIB, Bristol, on the Virginia-Tennessee line; and after a few years took his ever-present corncob pipe back to WDVA before going to WKBY, Chatham. Besides his businesslike farm programs, he served as historian of the farm broadcasters' organization for several years.

WLVA, Lynchburg, started a farm program in 1948, with Eric Lund as farm director.

WXEX, Petersburg, started a farm service in 1960, with three farm programs each day, conducted by Lauren Hiddelson.

In the seventies, there were daily farm programs on WRFL, Winchester; WKCY, Harrisonburg; WMNA, Gretna; WODI, Bookneal; and WMEK, Chase City.

Chapter Fifty-two

Washington

EXTENSION. When the state agricultural college at Pullman, Washington, put station KWSC on the air in 1922, President E. O. Holland ordered the agricultural staffers to start a series of talks for farmers. Extension editor Lincoln Lounsbury reported at the end of 1923 that there were nightly agricultural talks on seventy-six of the seventy-nine programs broadcast on the station.

By the thirties, the KWSC farm programs had moved to the noon hour and the extension editor decided to put a student in charge. Extension continued this policy for more than forty years. A few of the student farm directors became farm directors of commercial stations. Glenn Lorang, 1935, became farm director of KHQ, Spokane; and Jim Hansen, 1957–1959, became farm director of KOMO, Seattle, from 1959 to 1964. Hansen had gone to college for one year in the forties, married, and "managed to lose money in dairying, beef and vegetables before I decided to go back to college. I auditioned for the KWSC farm announcer's job before I knew it paid $100 a month."

Lounsbury started a script service, "Farm Flashes," in 1932. It was used daily on the college station and on eight other stations distributed across the state, and produced about one thousand requests each month for agricultural bulletins that were offered. Lounsbury also wrote special scripts for the "Western Farm and Home Hour," averaging about one thousand words per month.

In 1934 a second script service was started, the "Poultry School of the Air." It was a weekly program, ten minutes in length and used by seven commercial stations until some time in the early forties.

Extension editor Al Bond in 1950 started a twice-a-week service of tape-recorded talks and interviews, four and one-half minutes in length, which went to twenty-four stations over the state. Later it was stepped up to three per week, and the number of stations mushroomed to eighty-five. Harold Garrett, who had been farm director of KOI, Walla Walla, was radio specialist in charge of the service from 1950 to 1952; he was followed by Ben Copeland, from the University of Illinois, and in 1953 by Jim Johnson, a Nebraska native who had graduated from Washington State in 1950 and spent the next twenty-four years alternating between extension editor jobs in Idaho and Washington, located only ten miles apart. He started the Washington extension service's first TV program in 1954, a weekly five-minute program, produced at KREM-TV, Spokane, in black and white, with a film version circulated to six stations in Washington. In the seventies the farm program had died out, but Johnson began a weekly half hour aimed at consumers, used by fourteen of Washington's TV stations.

In the late seventies radio specialist Robert Searfoss produced two weekly radio series, "Farm Report" and "Thought for Food," which were distributed on tape to seventy-two stations.

KHQ, SPOKANE. Weymeth Simpson, KHQ radio and TV, grew upon on a farm near Spokane, became a radio announcer fresh out of college in 1947, but kept the family's dairy herd going until 1976 while he was news editor of KHQ-TV, and then farm director of both the radio and TV stations.

His radio schedule in the late seventies included an hour beginning at 5:00 A.M. and a twelve-minute segment of farm news in the general news program at noon on radio. On television he had a half hour in the morning each Monday, Tuesday, and Wednesday, plus a daily five-minute cut-in during NBC's "Today" show. Many of Simpson's TV programs were directed at consumers, and he believed most consumers in his area had a good understanding of farmers' problems. "At any rate, when there were consumer flareups and boycotts in many other parts of the country in the Seventies, there were none in Spokane."

His radio audience was distributed over much of eastern Washington and the state of Idaho, but his TV audience was extended into Montana, Oregon, and British Columbia by translator stations.

Simpson was preceded at KHQ by Tom Templeton, a Hoosier who became an Idaho rancher following WW II, and was assisted in some of his twenty years at the station by Gregory Click, who had been a student farm broadcaster at KWSC.

SEATTLE STATIONS. There were times in the late thirties and the forties when Seattle had five stations bidding to serve the farm audience, although no more than three had farm directors at any one time.

Bill Moshier was the first farm director in the Seattle area, followed soon by E. W. Jorgenson, and a few years later by Al Bond.

Moshier grew up in Cleveland but moved to Seattle as a young man. He had a dairy farm and raised chickens, vegetables, and small fruits as a sideline while his regular job was doing advertising research for station KIRO. When the station decided in 1938 to start a farm program, Moshier was the logical choice to handle it.

In 1943 he moved to KJR to start a farm program on that station at 7:00 A.M. and noon. In 1944, when the farm broadcasters formed a national organization, Moshier was elected the first treasurer. After several years at KJR, he started a farm program on KOMO, also in Seattle.

The second of Seattle's farm broadcasters, Ernie Jorgenson, was born in Nebraska, grew up in Chicago, moved to the west coast as a newspaper reporter, farmed as a sideline, and had passed his fiftieth birthday before he became farm director of KFPY in 1939. Around 1948 he moved to KXLY as farm director.

The third farm director in Seattle, Al Bond, arrived late in 1943, when Moshier moved to KJR and Bond took his place at KIRO. For six years there was a three-cornered, friendly rivalry between Moshier, Jorgenson, and Bond. Bond said, "We sometimes traveled together and often traded tips on farm stories."

Bond had been a Washington state newspaperman; became extension editor at Washington State College in 1939; and in the early forties worked for the USDA in Amarillo and Washington, D.C. before he returned to his home ground as farm director of KIRO. In 1949 he went back to the college and to his old job as extension editor from which he retired in 1969.

Jorgenson and Moshier both left broadcasting in the fifties. On KOMO Jim Hansen took over the farm programs in 1959 and continued them until 1964. He had been the student director of farm programs on KWSC for three years before he joined KOMO. He was followed in 1964 by Gregory Click, KHQ, Spokane. For about three years, 1964–1967, Click was the only farm director in the Seattle area.

For eight years farm broadcasting in the Seattle area was silent, but in 1975 KIRO designated Gary L. Stewart, an Oregon farm boy, as agribusiness editor—first with a weekly program and then daily, in early morning. In 1976 Ron Hanson took his place.

While most of the farm broadcasting through the years was done in either the eastern or western end of the state, there were two short-lived farm programs in the mid-state area.

Harold Garrett was farm director of KUF, Walla Walla, for several years before he moved in 1956 to Washington State College as radio specialist.

In Yakima, Dick Passage conducted a farm program on KYAK for several years until 1955 when he was named general manager of the station, in the heart of Washington's apple country.

In the seventies, KIT, Yakima, provided an all-night frost warning service for apple growers each spring; KRSC, Othello, and KARI, Blaine, devoted about an hour each day to farm news and information.

Chapter Fifty-three

West Virginia

TRI-STATE FARM AND HOME HOUR, WWVA. The "Tri-State Farm and Home Hour" on WWVA, Wheeling, had a long and successful life, at noon Monday through Saturday from 1936 to 1963, but all that time its name was misleading because only two state extension services were involved in producing programs: Ohio and West Virginia. No doubt many Pennsylvania people listened, but the Pennsylvania extension service never got into the act.

Walter Schnopp, extension editor in West Virginia; Frank Sanders of the Oglebay Institute; and W. C. Gist, county agent in Brooke County, West Virginia, were credited with forming the organization that put the program on the air, starting September 26, 1936. About a year later, the participants met for a planning meeting, and Morse Salisbury of the USDA, who had been involved in the early planning, brought along a guest, Max Wylie, top writer for CBS in New York. Wylie suggested there ought to be more continuity from day to day. This led to creating a fictional crossroads store where the guest speakers would just happen to drop in. Sanders became the storekeeper, John Handlan also of Oglebay Institute wrote scripts, and the crossroads store format lasted for twenty-six years, from a studio in the old dairy barn on the 750 acre farm that had become Oglebay Park.

Occasionally the program would originate from a fair, a Farm and Home week, a 4-H camp, or some other event. During World War II, a second daily program was added at 6:45 A.M., aimed at helping farm people to cope with their wartime problems and produce more food.

The programs were unsponsored during their twenty-seven years.

By 1963 radio progamming had changed, and WWVA had its own early morning farm program that produced revenue for the station; most of the founders of the "Tri-State Farm and Home Hour" had disappeared from the scene. By agreement of all parties concerned the program came to an end. No tears. It had been a good one.

The early morning commercial program on WWVA was presided over during the fifties and sixties by "Hardrock" Gunter. When he left broadcasting in favor of an insurance business in Colorado in the late sixties, staff announcer Lee Sutton took on the title of farm director for a time; and in the seventies, the program became the joint responsibility of the news department and the disc jockey on duty at the time.

EXTENSION. In 1938 Gerald Genny, extension editor, negotiated a deal with WMNN, Fairmont, to install remote facilities on the university campus at

282

Morgantown, eighteen miles from the station, for a weekly program in prime evening time. Birth of the program was trumpeted, but nobody noted when it died.

The West Virginia extension service started sending tape-recorded programs to the state's radio stations in 1951. The interviews with extension specialists were five to seven minutes in length and were dubbed one at a time to provide tapes for fourteen stations. Leighton Watson, assistant extension editor, added the taping, dubbing, and mailing to his other duties.

Foster Mullenax signed on about two years later as the first radio specialist, and he expanded the programs and the number of stations using them over the next twenty years. As Mullenax approached retirement, Jack Johns was hired for the radio spot. He was a native of Morgantown, was graduated from the university in 1960, and was employed by both of Morgantown's radio stations before joining the extension staff in 1969.

For the next ten years he produced two weekly programs on tape: "Outreach Review" was a quarter hour program covering several topics, used by fifty-three stations and "Mountain State Scene," five minutes, was used by thirty-five stations.

Johns completed a master's thesis in 1974 that included a survey of the use of radio by county agents in the state's fifty-five counties. He found that agents in twenty-five counties had regularly scheduled programs, most of them once each week, and most often aired on weekends around the noon hour. Ray Brannon, in Martinsburg, recorded a number of spot announcements once each week that were heard on the air every day over WEPM. Charles Cole, Bill Frye, and Erseline Rumbach in Weston shared a daily ten-minute program over WHAW, covering agriculture, homemaking, and 4-H activities.

The West Virginia extension service entered television in the late fifties with a once-a-year program called "Springtime West Virginia," centering on home gardens and lawns. Each program was a one hour production, and as many as five TV stations, fairly well distributed over the state, were hooked together. This was an annual production for eight years.

In the mid-sixties, the extension service produced weekly features of about four minutes each put on videotape and used by seven stations over the state, usually as drop-ins for network shows, on variety programs, or at sign-off time.

Denny Godfrey became TV-radio specialist in 1969, and he began to produce shorter features, two and one-half minutes or less, which were interviews designed for evening news programs. He reported in the mid-seventies that all nine of West Virginia's commercial stations, the three public TV stations, and two out-of-state stations received these materials along with about three short features per month.

WGNT, WSAZ, HUNTINGTON. One of the county agents who caught the radio bug by taking part in the "Tri-State" program on WWVA was William Click. So he started using WSAZ to talk to farmers in his own county and any others in Ohio, West Virginia, and Kentucky who might be listening. When he retired as county agent he went on the WSAZ payroll and promptly was nicknamed "Farmer Bill." He was on the air for a quarter hour each morning and another quarter hour at noon; and when there was a farm event of any size, Farmer Bill and his corncob pipe usually were in evidence.

After Click's death in 1961 WSAZ hired John Heiskell, an Ohio native, who had worked for Allis Chalmers in the early days of TV in Columbus, and for the Ohio Farm Bureau. He videotaped the TV show so it was on the air at the same time as his live radio program. He was on the air again at noon on radio with a quarter hour of farm news, interviews, and market reports. On Saturday he had a full hour on television with guests, videotapes, and films that he had produced himself, and on Sunday he had a half hour radio program reviewing the week's highlights.

During his dozen years on the air, Heiskell was burdened by a heart problem; and in 1972, he suffered an attack that was fatal.

Chapter Fifty-four

Wisconsin

WHA, MADISON. Professor Earle M. Terry and his students at the University of Wisconsin had the technical bugs fairly well worked out of their radio telephone transmitter by 1917; and as soon as the wartime restrictions on broadcasting were lifted in 1919, 9XM began to broadcast music and talks, some of them on agriculture, each noon and evening.

The talks were often read by Malcolm Hanson, a physics student, who helped design and build the station and was its first announcer. Later he was radio engineer for Admiral Byrd at the South Pole.

Wisconsin Agriculturist reported one of the noon farm broadcasts:

> Promptly at 12:15 standard time, Mr. Hanson starts his wireless message. First, he radiates the telephone communication, which takes about 25 minutes. Then he begins all over again and sends it all by telegraph spark. At about one o'clock, the job is done, and those who have been eavesdropping along the ethereal pathway are satisfied—if their instruments are in tune.

Eric Miller began broadcasting weather reports over 9XM on January 3, 1921; and in the fall of that year, market reports became part of the daily broadcasts. On July 10, 1922, the market reports were expanded to include talks on "agricultural problems and country life."

Meanwhile, in January 1922, the experimental call letters 9XM were replaced by the permanent call, WHA.

In the fiftieth anniversary bulletin, issued in 1969, WHA stated, "Our claim as the oldest station in the nation does not diminish the achievements of others, nor do their claims diminish ours. We were all responsible for the birth of broadcasting."

Earle Terry died in 1929, but not until he had predicted "The time will come when wireless receivers will be as numerous as bathtubs." The first count of bathtubs and wireless receivers, in the Census of 1940, showed that 55 percent of U.S. homes had bathtubs and 83 percent had radios.

The daily program of market reports and talks on agricultural problems and country life on WHA came to be called the "Farm Hour." Behind the "Farm Hour" was the craggy figure of Andy Hopkins, extension editor and head of agricultural journalism, who was one of the first to see the value of the new form of communication. When he died in 1973, ninety-three years old, his eulogists said, "He was a giant of his time."

Hopkins and a committee oversaw the daily "Farm Hour" over WHA and its satellite, WLBL, Stevens Point. William Sumner and others on the editorial staff took turns on the air from 1922 until 1930 when the station acquired a part-time farm director, Kenneth Gapen, from Kansas State College and KSAC. In 1935 Gapen, M.S. degree in hand, moved to the USDA, and Milton Bliss became WHA farm director and stayed for fifteen years, during which he conducted about 3,500 programs, reporting news, advice, interviewing experts, and doing remotes from field days, livestock shows, cornhusking contests, and other events in which the college of agriculture was involved. He left WHA in 1950 to join Gapen in the USDA Radio-TV Service, and in 1952 he became director of the "National Farm and Home Hour" and held that position until the program came to an end in July 1960.

At WHA Bliss was followed by Maurice White, who moved from the Ohio extension service and WOSU in 1950 and settled in for a long stay. In 1968 he was promoted to assistant dean in charge of short courses, and Larry Meiller (MEE-ler), who in the same year had earned his master's degree, became radio specialist. Meiller grew up on a dairy farm only ten miles from Madison.

Meiller continued the "Wisconsin Farm Hour" on WHA and WLBL in much the same pattern it had followed since 1922. By the late seventies he was including an increasing amount of consumer information, and in 1979 he converted approximately half the time to answering questions from listeners over a toll-free number. If a dairy specialist was the guest, the questions might deal with dairy cows or with milk, cheese, or butter.

Through the seventies and into the eighties he produced several recorded programs which went to Wisconsin radio stations: "Agricultural Facts," twelve messages one to two minutes in length, sent every two weeks to about 50 stations; "Badger Home and Garden," twenty gardening messages and twenty consumer tips, recorded on platters and used by 100 stations; and a script service, "Broadcast News," five to eight stories sent three times each week to all county extension workers and all radio stations in the state, a total of 350 potential users.

For television he offered a film service of about ten short items each year in the seventies aimed at consumers, via evening news programs, based on research by the experiment station. One of the most widely used stories was about a red dye made from beets which might replace Red Dye No. 2, banned from use because of its cancer causing properties. Meiller did the planning and writing and Wolfgang Hoffman did the camera work.

While he was handling his broadcast chores, Meiller also completed work on a Ph.D. degree which he received in 1977.

WBKT, WKTY, LA CROSSE. There was a time when Jack Martin, who stood five feet ten, was best known for portraying Abraham Lincoln. To make him look six feet four other actors in the stock companies in which he performed had to be under five feet six. In the twenties theatrical companies suffered a mortal blow from radio, and in 1929 Martin decided he couldn't lick 'em so he joined 'em, as an announcer, news director, and farm director of WBKT. His wife did a shoppers' program on the station for six dollars per week. He was on the air seven days each week and people began to call him the "Iron Man" long before he rounded out 5,000 days straight. He cheated a couple of times by going to Chicago to see a football game but managed to be interviewed between halves. His record of being on the air was kept intact for almost fourteen years.

One of the gimmicks he started was a "Radio in the Barn Club," and its members included a youngster named Orion Samuelson, who grew up to be farm director of WGN and producer-host of a syndicated farm TV show.

In the fifties WBKT-TV came on the air and Martin expanded his farm programs into the new medium where they continued for fourteen years. He stayed on the air until 1967, when he was seventy-five years old with thirty-eight years of broadcasting behind him. Ten years later, he and his wife were living in La Crosse.

Rival station WKTY started a farm service in 1959 with Earl Hunter as farm director and programs in early morning and at noon. The station also had farm news dropped into a suppertime program of old-time music, a pattern that held with little change through eighteen years. One feature not found on many stations in the U.S. was a special weather forecast for cranberry growers, with emphasis on when to flood the cranberry bogs to prevent freeze damage. In 1970 Eric Parsons joined Hunter as assistant farm director. Among other events, they were active in La Crosse's annual "Oktoberfest" which had slightly more emphasis on agriculture and less on the brewer's art than the original in Germany. So they say.

In 1977 Hunter was made sales manager and vice-president of the station, and Parsons was upped to the farm director's spot. He hired Ken Leinen, an Iowa State University graduate, as his assistant.

FRANK MAYFIELD. When I asked Frank Mayfield to recount his twenty-seven years of farm programs on WIBA, Madison, and his programs on WIBU, Poynette, which began in 1975, he provided me with a packet of photos:

Mayfield in an alfalfa field damaged by grasshoppers, eating sweet corn and broadcasting at the annual Sweet Corn Festival at Sun Prairie, with mother and daughter in their dairy barn, interviewing winners of the beef show at Mineral Point, and at the state fair with a sign telling passersby that he would be broadcasting his farm shows from that spot each morning at 6:15 and again at 11:30.

He photographed most of the people on his programs over a span of more than thirty years. Mayfield taught vocational agriculture in several Wisconsin high schools before he became farm director of WIBA, Madison, in 1948. In 1975 he moved to WIBU, Poynette, and was on the air two hours each morning with a half hour at noon. At WIBU he succeeded Les Leonard, who also presented a daily TV program on WISC-TV.

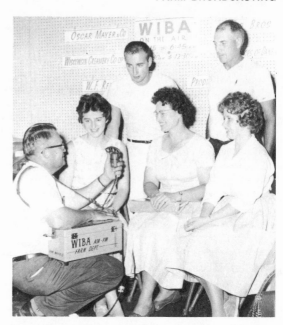

Frank Mayfield in a self-timed photo at the Wisconsin State Fair, around 1960.

WTMJ, MILWAUKEE. Hugo Murray was better known as "Hig" to his farm listeners on WTMJ. They heard him each day from 1952 to 1955, when he had a fatal heart attack. There was a gap of two years without a farm director on the station, but in 1957 Bill Hoeft branched out from his farm management business to take over morning and noon radio programs.

Hoeft provided a steady flow of farm information, picked up a report by Walt Anderson from the South Milwaukee stockyards each day, and drew on his own experiences in managing farms in the Milwaukee area.

He resigned in 1974 to start a network program of farm and conservation information, and the WTMJ programs were then taken over by Anderson. In 1977 Anderson started a series of ninety-minute programs. Each one originated on a farm, going into detail about farm operations, telling who does the work, and what the farmer spends to produce a quart of milk or a pound of beef.

WBAY, GREEN BAY. Can you imagine fellow turning his back on the Green Bay Packers in favor of farm broadcasting? That's what Les Sturmer did. He had been in the WBAY farm department for several years and was promoted in 1969 to be anchorman on the TV station's news and sports programs, which included reporting the Packers' football games, but in 1971 "the call to get back to people who work with the soil got too strong," so he returned to his farm programs on radio and TV.

Les Sturmer in 1972
(second from left)
receiving another of the
station's many awards
for farm service.

Sturmer was the lone survivor of what had been one of the largest and most active radio-TV farm departments in the nation. He summarized its history:

The WBAY farm department was organized in the fall of 1951 by Craighton Knau, from Iowa State University, who began with a two hour radio show in early morning. His first assistant was Jim Evans, who was to become head of agricultural journalism at the University of Illinois. In 1952 he hired Bob Parker, also an Iowa State graduate, as another assistant. WBAY-TV went on the air in 1953 and the three-man farm staff had a full hour TV show at noon, with a five piece band, a female singer, and live pigs, calves, and chickens. In 1954 they were joined by Dave Lindsay, and the four-man staff started a Sunday farm TV program which ran for eighteen years. In 1956 Knau left to join an advertising agency; Lindsay went to a tractor company.

Orion Samuelson joined the department in 1958 as farm director. Around this time a scholarship was established for an agricultural journalism junior from the University of Wisconsin to spend a summer in the WBAY farm department. The farm department won a Peabody Award for its "Operation Heifer Lift," in which many cows lost in a cleanout of brucellosis reactors were replaced by heifers donated by dairymen in the WBAY area.

In 1962 Parker went to work for an ad agency and Samuelson moved to WGN. Sturmer became farm director, assisted by Jim Densmoor and Don Steege. He said, "We did things like videotaping 8 hours of programming from Wisconsin Farm Progress Days, and a live broadcast of the annual Beautena Royal Calf Show with 20 to 25 calves that had been raised in dealers' stores. This took place for about eight years. We raised chickens in the building, from day-old chicks until they were laying, putting them on camera at least once a week.

"WBAY changed managers in 1966, and the farm department was reduced to one man; radio was cut to one hour in early morning. In 1974 farm information became part of a segmented morning program. On TV, farm information is given about 15 minutes during the station's noon show. Since 1967, we have been giving more attention to telling the farm story to urbanites."

An example of one of Sturmer's days runs like this: "We'll film commercials in three cheese factories in two counties in the morning; talk to a high school media class in the afternoon; MC a family party of a Purina dealership in Manitowoc county tomorrow night; and sandwich in the filming of a farm story or two and put on the junior winner of the state Soil and Water Conservation speaking contest during the live TV show at noon."

WAXX, WEAU-TV-FM, EAU CLAIRE. Pat Keliher was sixty-six years old when he received the American Farmer degree at the FFA convention in 1976, recognition of the boost he had given to FFA and vocational agriculture work through more than twenty years of broadcasting on WAXX, WEAQ, and WEAU-FM and -TV, in Eau Claire and Chippewa Falls, Wisconsin.

Keliher grew up on a dairy farm "in the Swiss cheese country," earned a degree from LaCrosse State College, spent several years with the Soil Conservation Service, and then became a professional farm manager in Eau Claire. When Jim Hill, who had been farm director of WEAU, moved to WCCO's farm department in 1953, Pat Keliher took over the daily farm programs on WEAU, which became WEAQ in 1960. In 1969 he switched to WAXX, which was under the same ownership as WEAU-FM and WEAU-TV.

At WAXX he had three programs per day, early morning, noon, and evening on both AM and FM, plus an occasional spot on TV. He also handled the sales work as well as the programs.

In 1974, he invited Jerry Urdahl, who had been at KWWL, Waterloo, Iowa, since 1960, to come to Eau Claire and take over. Keliher then cut back his activities.

The first summer Urdahl worked for WAXX, he began to get reports that army worms were coming out of the weeds and stripping the young cornfields. He learned of a helicopter service in his area and brought the farmers and chopper pilot together. The farmers who contracted to have their cornfields sprayed saved their crops.

In the late seventies Urdahl was on the air each morning for an hour and a quarter, an hour and a half over the noon hour, and a wrap-up each evening at 6:30. The FM signal, more powerful than the AM signal, covered about forty counties.

Among broadcasters and market reporters, Urdahl was "Mr. Feeder Pigs." In 1962, while he was working on KWWL, Waterloo, he began gathering information from the major feeder pig markets, and doing a daily broadcast sponsored by Ralston Purina. Later he wrote a weekly report on prices of feeder pigs which was mailed to subscribers. He took this sideline with him when he moved to Eau Claire, and he included feeder pigs in his programs on WAXX and also made a special broadcast over KXEL.

WISCONSIN FARM NETWORK, WKOW, WTSO. The first farm director of WKOW was Roy Gumtow, starting soon after the station went on the air in

1948 and continuing until 1963. John Zimmerman took over the farm programs in that year and continued them, several times each day. Meanwhile, WKOW became WTSO.

In 1973 Zimmerman and three partners formed the Wisconsin Farm Broadcasting Network, with ten stations carrying four farm features each day, which he provided on tape. Two of the three-minute segments were to be played in early morning and two during the noon hour. The network sold time to advertisers and in turn it paid the stations. Weather was an important part of the service, and the network hired its own forecaster to give weather reports with an agricultural slant. WTSO was the flagship station of the network.

MIDWEST FARM AND OUTDOOR NETWORK. Bill Hoeft had been farm director of WTMJ, Milwaukee, for seventeen years when he left that station in 1974 to start the Midwest Farm and Outdoor Radio Network. His network linked together twelve stations by rebroadcasting FM signals, with WIBA-FM, Madison, providing the original signal for a full hour from 5:00 to 6:00 each morning. The network and the individual stations divided the commercial time slots equally for sales purposes. Hoeft received estimated receipts by phone from livestock markets at Joliet, Milwaukee, and South Saint Paul; and government weather forecasts.

Besides agricultural information, his programs included many talks on wildlife, woodlands, hunting, fishing, and conservation.

DEPARTMENT OF AGRICULTURE. One of the earliest of the farm networks was started in 1951 by the Wisconsin Department of Agriculture. Frank Wing, publicity director, lined up about thirty Wisconsin stations to carry the daily half hour program, which included market reports and a series of interviews from the farm. In one form or another the network continued for about twenty years.

In the late seventies locally produced farm programs were broadcast on stations at Beaver Dam, Dodgeville, Fond du Lac, Manitowoc, Marshfield, New Richmond, Oshkosh, Platteville, Plymouth, Portage, River Falls, Sparta, Stevens Point, and Wausau. Most impressive was WSWW, Platteville, with five hours each day, presided over by Austin Baxter.

Chapter Fifty-five

Wyoming

IN the thirties the University of Wyoming was prominent in forming the Rocky Mountain Radio Council, which produced educational programs and fed them by wire or platter to stations in several states. Of course, a little agriculture sneaked its way into some of those programs, but neither the university nor its extension service ever produced agricultural scripts, platters, or tapes for use by Wyoming stations.

In compensation, however, most of the county agents in the twenty-three counties developed their own local programs, usually on a weekly schedule, and by 1979 many of them had records of twenty years or longer.

KRNK, CHEYENNE. KRNK was meteoric—meaning high, bright, and then burned out.

KRNK went on the air in the summer of 1976 with 10,000 watts power putting out a good signal over a radius of 100 miles. Its programs were all news, with fifty time periods each day for agricultural news, markets, interviews, forecasts, and commentary. The station lured Chuck Muller away from KOA after twenty-two years, and backed him with Tom Ferrell, veteran USDA livestock market reporter. On paper it looked great, but in January 1977, the station—and its farm services—went off the air for lack of advertising revenue.

Less spectacular but more durable were farm programs on KGOS, Torrington; KYGN, Wheatland; and KWOR, Worland.

Chapter Fifty-six

National Association of Farm Broadcasters

IT was bound to happen. Sooner or later some farm broadcaster would say, "We need a farm broadcasters' organization."

Wallace Kadderly and Morse Salisbury of the USDA had been saying it to each other for some time, but they felt the initiative should come from the broadcasters outside government.

The man who said it out loud was Larry Haeg, who had been farm director of WCCO, Minneapolis, for about one year when he spoke his mind in May 1943 at the annual Institute for Education by Radio, started in 1930 by Ohio State University. Most of the people who attended were from universities and public school systems, but a few agricultural people attended, and agriculture had a spot in each year's program. At the 1943 meeting Haeg presented a paper on "What Listeners and Management Should Expect from an Agricultural Program."

Besides being a broadcaster, Haeg was a dairy farmer, politician, and member of the Minnesota state legislature.

As he recalled twenty-fize years later: "The meeting in Columbus did not come off very well for the farm broadcasters. Many of us were discouraged by the lack of attention. When the regular meeting adjourned I called a meeting of the farm broadcasters in attendance and—as I recall—I made an emotional speech about the need for us to form our own organization. The speech was received with applause and cheering. I felt that for the first time the idea of an organization of farm directors had come into the open. Before this we had thought the Institute for Education by Radio would serve our purpose, but now we were sure it would not."

Haeg was already presiding; Herb Plambeck of WHO, Des Moines, was asked to take notes. The discussion boiled down to a few key decisions: Haeg was asked to serve as chairman of a Committee of Organization; a list of farm broadcasters would be compiled (the USDA had names and addresses of most of them); and farm broadcasters nationwide would be asked what they thought about forming a national organization with the tentative name of the National Society of Farm Radio Directors.

A follow-up meeting was held in Chicago, for three days in mid-December 1943 with about ten farm broadcasters present. Haeg again presided; Plambeck served as secretary. Duke DuMars, USDA, said the USDA would be holding a series of regional meetings for farm broadcasters during the winter and spring to report food production goals for 1944. He suggested groups could be organized in connection with these meetings. It seemed like a good idea, and Haeg wrote to all the farm broadcasters telling about the dream of a national organization, asking for reactions, and urging each broadcaster to attend the USDA meeting in his area.

At his home station, Haeg had some selling to do, but WCCO management gave its OK. The station would pay his expenses to attend the regional meetings. The first one was held in New York, February 21, 1944, with nine broadcasters in the northeast. They chose G. Emerson Markham, WGY, Schenectady, as chairman.

A Midwestern meeting was held in Chicago on March 5 and 6, and Larry Haeg was chosen as regional president; Arthur Page, WLS, vice-president. It was Page who suggested the name "Radio Farm Directors" because the initials "RFD" were familiar to farm people.

Just how many other regional meetings were held is a matter of some uncertainty. The USDA's schedule called for meetings in Atlanta, Schenectady, and Berkeley. Haeg recalled attending organization meetings in New York, Chicago, Atlanta, Dallas, San Francisco, and Minneapolis.

At the 1944 Institute, about thirty-five farm broadcasters held a rump caucus. They received a report from Haeg about the organization of regional groups and the response that almost every farm broadcaster thought there should be a national organization. Sam Schneider, KVOO, Tulsa, was perhaps the youngest man present at twenty-six years old and the one who rose to his feet and made the critical motion that the group form a national organization. His motion was seconded by the oldest of the farm broadcasters, Charles Shoffner, WCAU, Philadelphia, who was around his seventy-fourth birthday. The motion was passed unanimously and enthusiastically. The date, May 5, 1944; about 3 P.M. EDT. The place: Deshler-Walleck Hotel, Columbus, Ohio.

Haeg had proposed the organization, spearheaded the formation of regional groups, presided at every session; and with nobody else nominated, was elected president. Markham was elected vice-president; Bill Moshier, KJR, Seattle, treasurer; and Plambeck, secretary.

The midwestern group had adopted the name "Radio Farm Directors" and Arthur Page proposed it as the basic name for the national organization. After discussion, a vote was taken, and the chosen name was "National Association of Radio Farm Directors."

The Institute was a three-day meeting, and on the third day Haeg led another session of the agricultural group and announced a series of committees, which put most of the charter members to work.

Bylaws and Constitution: Bill Drips, NBC, Chicago; Emerson Markham, WGY, Schenectady; Bill Moshier, KJR, Seattle.

House Organ and Publicity: George Round, University of Nebraska, Lincoln; Homer Martz, KDKA, Pittsburgh; Layne Beaty, WBAP, Fort Worth; Jerry Seaman, North Dakota State College, Fargo.

Code and Ethics: John Merrifield, WHAS, Louisville; Art Page, WLS, Chicago; Mert Emmert, WEAF, New York; Jennings Pierce, NBC, Hollywood.

The first officers of the NARFD: L–R: Herb Plambeck, WHO, Des Moines, secretary; Larry Haeg, WCCO, Minneapolis, president; G. Emerson Markham, WGY, Schenectady, vice-president; Bill Moshier, KJR, Seattle, treasurer.

Directory: George German, WNAX, Yankton; Charles Shoffner, WCAU, Philadelphia; Henry Schacht, NBC, San Francisco; Herb Plambeck, WHO, Des Moines.

Membership: Phil Evans, KMBC, Kansas City; Jesse Buffum, WEEI, Boston; Hamilton Hintz, McClatchey Broadcasting Company, Sacramento; Clifford Gray, WSPA, Spartanburg.

The group adopted a general standard for membership in the NARFD: To qualify for membership, an applicant must be

a man of good character who, through background and experience can give the people he serves an understandable and independent analysis of international, national and local agricultural happenings that affect people in his listening area. He must devote the major part of his time and effort to such service. He must be engaged in farm radio broadcasting and employed by a commercial radio station or commercial radio network. (The Constitution was changed in 1949 to read, *All persons of good character. . . .*)

(The requirement that farm broadcasters work on a commercial station soon disappeared but staged a comeback thirty years later.)

About eighty-five people were engaged in farm broadcasting at the time on commercial stations and networks, on staffs of agricultural colleges and extension services, and in the USDA. Anyone who wanted to apply needed a recommendation from someone already a member of the association, and the membership committee voted on whether to accept or reject.

Bill Drips of NBC sounded a warning: "I've been urging NBC station managers to have their farm men join up. But managers are afraid this new organization will become another labor union. Unless we can convince them it is not and never will be a union, trying to raise wages for farm broadcasters, they won't let their farm men join."

The others listened, nodded, and remembered. The organization never acted like a labor union.

As the final piece of business at the May 7 meeting, Arthur Page injected a note of symbolism. He volunteered to make for the president a gavel of several different kinds of wood representing different areas of the nation, to symbolize the diversity and the unity of the organization.

As the meeting in 1944 adjourned, it was planned that the next meeting would be held in May 1945 in Columbus. It didn't quite work out that way. The war was coming to a climax; several of the charter members were in military uniforms; everyone was being asked: Is this trip necessary? So the next meeting was postponed indefinitely. But a few of the NARFD wheels kept turning: George Round, at the University of Nebraska, issued a mimeographed newsletter called "RFD," with a summary of the organization meeting and news items about the accomplishments of some of its members. A few months later he put out a second newsletter, then silence for almost one year.

Secretary Plambeck notified the approximately eighty-five potential members of the organization's existence, and that they could join for $10 if they were with a commercial station and $5 if they were in government or in education work. By the end of 1944, forty-one persons had paid dues to treasurer Bill Moshier, and each received a membership certificate for his wall and a card for his wallet.

The lineup included twenty of the thirty-five who attended the original meeting plus twenty-one others.

The war in Europe ended in the spring of 1945; in August the Japanese surrendered. Three days after the end of the fighting in the Pacific, Haeg summoned the officers and representatives from three regions to meet in Des Moines to restart the engines of the NARFD. Moshier and northeast representative Homer Martz couldn't make it to Des Moines but were consulted by telephone. NARFD's first convention "on our own" would be held in Chicago at the Stevens Hotel on December 2 and 3, 1945, simultaneously with the International Livestock Show and the 4-H Congress, which many of the broadcasters would be covering.

George Round spread the word to members and prospects through a third issue of "RFD."

When December came the clan gathered in Chicago. Arthur Page started the meeting by presenting Larry Haeg with the gavel he had made out of black

The first national convention of NARFD, Stevens Hotel, Chicago, November 1945.
Front row, L–R: C. W. Jackson, Texas extension service; Dale Williams, Iowa Extension Service; George B. German, WNAX, Yankton; Maynard Speece, Minnesota extension service; Robert White, ABC "American Farmer"; Warren Kester, WMT, Cedar Rapids; John Merrifield, Mississippi Valley Network
Second row: Gerald Seaman, Gittins agency; (unidentified); John McDonald, WSM, Nashville; Bill Moshier, KJR, Seattle; Larry Haeg, WCCO, Minneapolis, president; Maynard Coe, National Safety Council; Herb Plambeck, WHO, president-elect; Everett Mitchell, NBC "National Farm and Home Hour"; (unidentified).
Standing: Roy Battles, WLW, Cincinnati; Layne Beaty, WBAP, Ft. Worth; Harry Aspleaf, Sioux City stockyards; Gary Wiegand, KSTP, St. Paul; Harold Schmitz, Indiana extension service; Jim Chapman, WTAM, Cleveland; Marshall Wells, WJR, Detroit; Dan Thompson, National Safety Council; Merton Emmert, WEAF, New York; (unidentified); Jesse Buffum, WEEI, Boston; Homer Martz, KDKA, Pittsburgh; Carl Collin, WKZO, Kalamazoo; (two unidentified); Don Lerch, USDA; Jack Gowing, KMA, Shenandoah; T. R. Johnston, Indiana extension service; Lloyd Williams, USDA; William Drips, NBC "National Farm and Home Hour."

walnut from his own small farm outside Chicago; mesquite from Texas, osage orange from Oklahoma, both provided by Layne Beaty; and hard maple from New York, provided by Emerson Markham. It was "bonded in unity and strength."

At the close of that first meeting, Haeg passed on the organization's gavel to the incoming president, Herb Plambeck. Page then presented to Haeg a similar gavel, also made of the four woods, with rings on the handle counting out One Nine Four Five. This was Haeg's to keep. Next year Page had a gavel for Plambeck; next year for Layne Beaty, and so on until Arthur Page died, not long after the 1952 convention.

The main speaker at that 1945 convention was Secretary of Agriculture Clinton P. Anderson, who told the broadcasters how important they were in the effort to foster food production that would help write the peace. As speech writer for him on this one occasion I was shaken when he tossed aside the 6 x 8 inch cards on which it was neatly typed. I needn't have worried; he hit every brave and salient point I had written but did it much more effectively.

The membership chairman Phil Evans, KMBC, reported forty-five members had paid the $10 fee for commercial stations and six had paid the $5 fee for noncommercial people; and Bill Moshier, treasurer, said the $480 he had collected since May 1944 matched the membership figures. but Jesse Buffum, WEEI, produced receipts showing he had paid $10 in 1944 and another $10 in 1945. I tried to give Bill Moshier $5 for my dues, but Haeg ruled that the USDA chief of radio service held an honorary membership. Ken Gapen had a free ride for the years he occupied the USDA post, 1946–1954, and so did Layne Beaty, beginning in 1955. After he had been in the job about ten years, Beaty was made a lifetime voting member, one notch higher than honorary membership.

Sam Schneider, KVOO, Tulsa, Oklahoma, said years later that at the first convention he called Edward Condon, of the Sears Agricultural Foundation, and told him a group of farm broadcasters were in town; wouldn't the Foundation like to buy a lunch for some of them? Condon said the Foundation would like to buy lunch for all of them. The farm broadcasters enjoyed the meal and the Sears Foundation paid the bill.

The National Safety Council also became involved at the first session by paying for a meal and photographing the group.

In later years other organizations related to agriculture sponsored meals and cocktail parties for the organization. They included the Fertilizer Institute, American Nurserymen's Association, Foundation for American Agriculture, American Feed Manufacturer's Association, and others.

The 1945 meeting marked a separation of the farm broadcasters' business meeting from the Institute for Education by Radio. The meetings were held in Chicago until 1969, and then were moved to Kansas City at the time of the American Royal Livestock Show and the convention of the Future Farmers of America.

MEMBERSHIP. The farm broadcasters association at its peak, in the seventies, barely topped 600 members, and never more than about 250 of those devoted full time to the job of farm broadcasting.

This was in sharp contrast to the thousand or more farm directors listed in yearbooks published by *Broadcasting* and by *Radio Daily* during the fifties and the roughly 500 in *Agri-Marketing*'s yearbooks of the seventies. Those listings were honest, but misleading. If the county agent, vocational agriculture teacher, or Farm Bureau manager had a weekly program, station management was likely to list him as farm director in the yearbook. Perhaps the program director or news editor devoted five minutes each day to reading farm news from the news teletype; he also might be listed as farm director.

From its start NARFD limited its membership to those who devoted a "substantial portion" of their time to farm broadcasting. Even county agents presenting daily programs did not qualify because they spent most of their time doing other things.

From the 45 dues-paying members in December 1945, membership grew. So by December 1946 there were 108 members, and the list was marked "confidential to members." In 1949 membership was divided into two categories, active and associate. Active members, who were allowed to vote, were those devoting a "major portion" of their time and getting a major portion of their income from farm broadcasting. The actives represented about two-thirds of the 182 members the following year. By 1953 the number of active members had climbed to 225 and associates to 87, and the next year the total climbed to 449.

Beginning in 1955, when "Television" was inserted into the organization's name, the requirement for active membership was tightened to 75 percent of time and money instead of 50 percent as before. This bumped some active members into the associate membership and changed the balance of the two groups: 210 active and 195 associate members. Both categories increased for two years and in 1957 hit a peak of 240 active and 315 associate members. A jump in dues from $7.50 to $25 for most members caused a drop to 190 active and 230 associate in 1958.

The number of actives climbed to 211 in 1960, then slipped year after year to 134 in 1966, reflecting a large number of stations that cancelled their farm service programs and the people who had produced them.

Beginning in 1970 requirements for active membership were limited to farm broadcasters who were on commercial stations. This demoted radio specialists in state extension services and the USDA (except for Layne Beaty of the USDA, who had been made a lifetime voting member) to nonvoting associate members. It was a matter of stripping the decks for action because the voting members were grimly determined to revitalize farm broadcasting by more effective sales promotion and selling, and the college and government people cluttered the scene. The more stringent requirements worked. By the beginning of 1979 the association had grown to 202 active members, each one virtually full time on a commercial station or network; and 386 associate members, including at least 58 who bought broadcast time and 48 who sold it. In body and spirit, NAFB was regaining its health and growth.

OFFICERS. As in most organizations, being elected president of the NAFB was an honor, of sorts. It recognized professional competence; it recognized that the person elected had devoted much time to interests of the organization and was willing to devote even more time during the coming year.

Management of some stations refused to allow their farm director to serve as NAFB president or to hold any other office because of the amount of time it required away from the regular job. Other stations considered it a halo over the head of their farm director.

Most of the men chosen as president had served on committees, as regional vice-president, national vice-president, and since 1974, as president-elect before being elected president.

The national presidency meant adding about 100 work days each year to a schedule that already involved seventy to ninety hours per week. Something usually gave, especially if the president was the only farm broadcaster on the station's staff, as was the case with Marvin Vines, the 1977 president, Lynn Adair in 1974, and several earlier presidents. Inevitably some of the local events were slighted; family life was shortchanged, although occasionally the husband or wife of the farm broadcaster went along on a pleasant trip; but maybe the president's health also suffered. Several ex-presidents died comparatively young. The NAFB never required its president to pass a physical exam before election, but it may be a wise idea. Another essential element of being president was having an understanding station manager, who was willing to make allowances for the farm broadcaster who would be away and understood that someone else would be needed to handle weather, markets, and current farm news. In the seventies, when a president completed his year in office, the NAFB presented a plaque to the station management expressing their gratitude. It was not an empty gesture.

Almost without exception the NAFB presidents were friendly, outgoing, articulate without being painfully gabby, hard working, proficient in their jobs, and conscientious officers. At the time they held office, they ranged in age from their early thirties to about fifty-five years of age; in size, from about five foot three to six foot six, and from 135 to 280 pounds; geographically they were based at stations from ocean to ocean and border to border.

After fifteen years of electing a new secretary and treasurer from its members each year, the organization in 1959 decided to hire a professional as assistant secretary-treasurer to handle the nitty gritty record keeping year after year. Lola Barrett, who worked for the Farm Bureau, had been my secretary in the USDA, and had been a volunteer worker at NAFB conventions for six years, was appointed. She kept the records and watched over the bank account in Chicago, under the supervision of an elected secretary-treasurer. She handled the record keeping until 1969 when twin decisions were made: NAFB's annual business meeting would be held in Kansas City; and the executive committee would appoint rather than elect an NAFB member as secretary-treasurer. That person would choose someone to help with the paper work. George Stephens, KCMO, Kansas City, was the first appointee; when he left broadcasting for advertising work, George Logan, WIBW, Topeka, was appointed, and reappointed annually for several years. Several women, including Marlene Palmer of WIBW and Pat Crist and Janice Smith of KGNC, helped Logan as secretary-treasurer.

Almost as soon as they had an organization, the members began referring to themselves as "RFD's," When the word "Television" was introduced into the organization's name in 1955, the members became "TRFD's" and the directory each year carried a one-page sales promotion pitch: WHAT IS THE TELEVISION OR RADIO FARM DIRECTOR? The first letter in each paragraph always was set in large boldface type, so your eye would be attracted to the left edge of the page and you read "THE TRFD SELLS." Although the label "TRFD" was abandoned in 1965, the organization reproduced the page in the annual directory for several years. (See Appendix.)

One way to get an idea of what the NAFB organization did was to look at its committees.

The internal committees included several centering on the annual convention: facilities, hospitality, registration, program for members, and program for spouses.

There were committees on directory, auditing, membership, nominations, ways and means, and of course, on resolutions. The associate members had a chairman, and so did the several Canadian members.

There were other committees that involved reaching out to other organizations and activities, in some instances to help the other organization, sometimes to help the NAFB.

One committee maintained liaison with the Agricultural Hall of Fame, located not far from Kansas City.

Another committee was created to make awards, to decide which non-voting member would receive NAFB's annual award for meritorious service, and what awards offered to NAFB members by outside corporations or associations would receive NAFB's official blessing.

There also were committees on publicity, broadcast information, and broadcast promotion and exhibits, aimed primarily at trade publications so that they were provided with stories about successful advertising and sales efforts by the NAFB members and that meetings and officers got some recognition in the press. The NAFB also had exhibits, hospitality suites, and speakers at meetings of agricultural advertisers.

The farm broadcasters' organization and individual members gave support to observances of Farm Safety Week, Farm-City Week, Agriculture Day, and Rural Health Week, all sponsored by other organizations but welcoming the help of broadcasters.

To bridge the gap between farm broadcasters and station management, the NAFB started a management advisory committee early in its existence, and in the seventies this blossomed into a Sales-Marketing Board which put the NAFB and many of its member stations into sales promotion and created a brand new ball game.

ETHICS. The charter members of the NARFD, at the founding meeting in 1944, decided they needed a code of ethics, but evidently the first code of ethics was drawn up by a committee headed by Chuck Worcester, WMT, and was adopted at the convention in 1946. (See Appendix A.)

There have been some minor modifications in the code through the years, such as eliminating the sentence that binds farm broadcasters not to discuss controversial issues except in a forum fashion. Farm broadcasters, by nature, have opinions, but they seldom went through the formality of setting up a forum or round table.

The code was adopted shortly after the FCC had issued its "Blue Book" telling broadcasters what their obligations were, and implying that a farm program that included advertising was not a public service. The NARFD code sharply replied to the FCC with the statement, "Commercial sponsorship of farm programs does not detract from the service they offer to farm people." In 1946 many stations did not sell time on their farm programs, but ten years later strictly noncommercial farm programs on commercial stations were few and far between.

At the 1949 annual meeting there was a discussion of "Selling Your Farm Program" that was almost completely affirmative and made these points:

First, if the farm department made money for the station, the farm department was on much firmer ground within the station.

Second, farm programs that are sponsored are generally much better than sustaining shows because there is enough money to do a better job.

Third, TV was growing rapidly; the number of radio stations had doubled in four years since the war; these factors meant more competition for advertising dollars. The financial squeeze had already hit many stations; some farm directors had been fired; others had to cut down on expenses. Despite the FCC, the farm departments might be considered expendable unless they paid their own way and showed a profit.

In 1953, the editor of *Chats* posed a question: "Should an RFD be the spokesman for competing sponsors?" Chuck Worcester said, "Yes—if management and sponsors want it that way and if listeners don't object"; Phil Evans and Homer Martz both said no. Dix Harper also said yes. Ed Mason, farm broadcaster turned manager-owner, said: "For sponsors that take only occasional, seasonal spots, Yes; for accounts that want the RFD badly enough to pay for his exclusive services, No."

At the end of 1954, outgoing president Jack Jackson pointed to the sales promotion activity that had started the year before and said the organization needed to get management involved by paying part of the cost of sales promotion. This didn't happen for another seventeen years, and Jackson died about the time his ideas were being put to work.

At the 1955 convention, Henry Clay, manager of KWKH, Shreveport, and chairman of the Radio Committee of NAB, the National Association of Broadcasters, gave the farm broadcasters the viewpoint of station managers.

Clay thought the NATRFD should promote sales, but leave the actual selling to station salesman; that it was a good idea for a farm broadcaster to handle commercials for only one feed, one line of farm machinery, etc.; but not get bogged down in many extra services to any one sponsor. "It is agricultural service that makes you effective."

Incidentally, this was at a time when the NATRFD was nearing its first peak of membership, with 137 new members signed up within the next year, bringing the total over 500 for the first time.

In 1957 the organization inaugurated an annual Award for Meritorious Service, to be given to a nonvoting member who had made outstanding contributions to NATRFD or to farm broadcasting in general. The awards during the following years were given in some instances to pioneer farm broadcasters, to people who had devoted time and effort to improving sales, to others whose organizations had been longtime sponsors of events at farm broadcasters' conventions, to those who had been longtime buyers of broadcast time on farm programs. (See Appendix B.)

Early in its history, the organization's awards committee recommended that if some outside organization wanted to offer awards for outstanding work by farm broadcasters, the organization would consider and maybe approve; but the organization itself would not hand out any blue ribbons to its own members. The American Farm Bureau Federation offered an annual award, beginning in 1950, based on interpreting agriculture to the American public. The award was presented at the annual convention each year.

The Ciba-Geigy firm invited broadcasters and magazine writers to compete in a similar contest, with winners for radio, TV, and the print media. The prize was a trip for two to Europe to see Ciba-Geigy's offices, labs, and farms.

Elanco (Eli Lilly & Co.) offered a Town Crier Bell award, which also was handed out at the NAFB convention, without imposing the corporation's will on the convention for as long a time. It was also accompanied by a Foot in Mouth award to a broadcaster who was caught in some example of what should not be said on the air. This, of course, was the least coveted award.

The DeKalb Agricultural Association offered an "Oscar in Agriculture" each year.

Besides the awards that had the official blessing of the NAFB, hardly an association existed that didn't offer a certificate or trophy to farm broadcasters on a statewide or national basis. Any farm broadcaster who stayed on the job for a few years inevitably would receive certificates or plaques or recognition of some kind from the FFA, 4-H, associations of agricultural alumni, county agents, vocational agriculture teachers, cattlemen, etc. Often it's a way of saying thank you for the publicity you've given our activities in the past and don't forget we'll be around for more.

Some farm broadcasters could show and tell of awards they had won. Others claimed not to know or care.

NAFB WOMEN MEMBERS. If there were any women who attended the meeting in Columbus, Ohio, where the NARFD was formed in May 1944, they were either bashful or ignored. But the first printed directory of members, issued in 1946, listed five, two of them on radio station payrolls and three on state extension staffs: Betty Brady, WLW, and Louella Engel, WMOH, neighbors in Ohio; the extension women were Claire Banister, Texas; Mariam Foltz, Ohio; and Dorothy Smith, New Jersey. Louella Engel presented a daily program for farmers and another for farm women; Dorothy Smith presided over a garden program; the others tended to concentrate on women's interests.

Sue Bailey Reid, who had an agricultural degree from Rhode Island State, conducted a farm program and farm wife program on WPBJ, Providence, beginning in the late forties. Virginia Tatum worked on "CBS Country Journal."

Gladys Foris of the Oklahoma extension service joined NARFD in the early fifties, as did Agnes Krugh, assistant farm director of WGN.

In the early fifties, May Lou Pfeiffer became woman's director of station WRFD and joined the association.

Terry Berman was farm director of WKKD, Aurora, Illinois, in the early sixties. She had a degree in animal husbandry from the University of Wisconsin and worked at the Chicago stockyards as a market reporter before she went into broadcasting.

Helen Moore, KULB, Billings, and Beverly Walters, KFGO, Fargo, were members in the sixties, and both of them broadcast markets and farm interviews for farmers.

For several years, Beve Walters was the only woman who qualified as a voting member of the NAFB, but the seventies brought a covey of women broadcasters: Davonna Oskarson came out of Colorado State College with a degree in agriculture and became codirector of farm programs on WRFD, Columbus; moved to WLW, Cincinnati; and then to Purdue. Colleen Callahan, fresh from the Univeristy of Illinois, became farm director of WMBD, Peoria. Two years later, Callahan's college friend, Joyce Cutright, went to work for WIAI, Danville, Illinois. When she moved in 1979 to KWTO, her place was taken by another University of Illinois graduate, Patricia Jeckel.

Terri Elmer, raised on a Wisconsin dairy farm, went from the University of Wisconsin to the farm director's post at WSAU, Wausau, in 1978. She moved in 1979 to the farm department of WIBW-AM and -TV, Topeka, Kansas, and her place at WSAU was taken by Mary Beth Lang, who earned an agricultural degree from the Univeristy of Wisconsin and was an IFYE participant in New Zealand.

Peggy Kaye Fish, who had helped her stepfather Leland Glazebrook on his Corn-Soybean Network, became farm director of WTAX, Springfield, Illinois, in 1979.

Mary Heath had grown up helping her father (Howard) with his Michigan Farm Network, earned a degree in agricultural communications from Michigan State, and worked for Ed Johnson's Agri-Broadcasting Network, which served Ohio and Pennsylvania from 1975 to 1977.

Sylvia Sutter joined Ray Wilkinson and Verne Strickland on WRAL-TV and the Tobacco Network in 1974.

Helen Howe earned a degree in animal production from Texas Tech and joined KDAV, Lubbock, in 1976 as assistant to Joe Brown and helped him expand the programs.

Ellen Treimer of KAUS, Austin, Minnesota, became the station's first farm director in 1976. She studied journalism, speech, and telecommunicative arts at Iowa State and earned her degree in 1973.

There have been a few husband-wife teams of farm broadcasters in the NAFB under its several names. The earliest may have been Bonnie and Jerry Mitchell, WJOB, Hammond, Indiana, with Bonnie Mitchell broadcasting from a wheelchair, victim of a childhood disease. They were members of the NARFD, 1950 to 1953.

Ruth Alampi had achieved fame in NARFD by presenting a poem, "The Lament of the Forgotten Woman—RFD's Wife," at the 1947 convention annual banquet. In 1954, she and husband Phil started a matched pair of home garden shows on WEAF radio and TV, plus a handyman show on TV. When Phil dropped out of broadcasting in 1956, Ruth continued her garden broadcasts for twelve years on WNBC-TV and then on the New Jersey educational network.

In the seventies Marian Martin joined her husband Harry in starting and conducting the Rural Radio Network, covering Indiana.

Most of the NAFB members through the years have been married, resulting in what seems to be a friendly social network that stretches nationwide.

What it's like back home is suggested in Ruth Alampi's poem early in her experience as a broadcaster's wife.

The Lament of the Forgotten Woman—RFD's Wife

I never thought that I would be
The wife of some old RFD
Who leaves the house before it's light
And staggers home in the dead of night
Who tells of meeting a guy named Joe
Who maybe'll buy a spot on the show!

Life's not so drab for the RFD
There's always a lot for him to see.
Potato Queens are mighty cunnin'
For the gals he'll always go a-runnin'
Miss Tomato Blight—Miss Appleseed, too
He wants them all—for an interview!

When the program's put to bed for the day
And the county agents are out of the way
All the bulletins sent and the letters signed
The RFD—no appointments to keep
Of course comes home—*he* wants to sleep.

ASSOCIATE MEMBERS. Associate membership of the NAFB, a nonvoting category, was established when the organization was only five years old, and it had always been a mixed bag. Part-time farm broadcasters who couldn't qualify for active membership; college, government, and farm organization people; people who sold broadcast time and others who bought it; and some who were looking for a free ride for their organizations made up the associate membership.

The last category has been looked on with considerable suspicion. It was in the late sixties that John McDonald, WSM, Nashville, a former president, told the executive committee: "We ought to throw out half our associate members. My station used to have International Harvester, Pfizer, Cyanamid, and Armour fertilizer; I've seen those accounts go down the hole. Some PR man has said to the sponsor, 'Why buy time on a station? We can get it for you free.' I got some publicity material from International Harvester with a return card. I sent it back to the president of the company, saying, 'I no longer have an IH account and so I don't need your publicity material.' "

Horace McQueen, WACO, chimed in, "We did the same thing with New Holland, and it worked."

The organization did not vote to throw out the public relations people who were associate members, but enough of them did send back the free publicity material so it was reduced from a flood to a trickle.

For a long time the associate members floundered and wandered, with no particular objective. In one meeting in the fifties when Dene Raterman, of the National 4-H Committee asked the group, "Just what is the purpose of this group?" No one had a good answer. Each associate member may have had his individual reason for belonging, but no central purpose existed other than to fill in time while the voting members held their business sessions.

Then the associate members who sold farm broadcasting time found a target to shoot at: improved sales. They led the officers of the NAFB to the mountaintop and showed them the promised land and the pathway that led to it. That started a new era in NAFB history, for the organization and most of its members and their stations.

SALES. In 1953, under President Mal Hansen of WOW, the NARFD dipped its toe in the waters of sales promotion by holding three "clinics" for prospective advertisers in Kansas City, Chicago, and New York, persuading those who attended that farm broadcasters could sell things to farmers as well as farm magazines could.

In 1955 NATRFD ("Television" was added to the name that year) issued a leaflet headlined "FARMERS HAVE MORE RADIOS THAN ANYBODY—AND TELEVISION IS GROWING TOO."

Then a series of success stories:

A hybrid seed producer started advertising over a station in western Iowa. Elsewhere his sales increased by 12 to 15 percent, but in the territory covered by the farm show his sales jumped 82 percent.

A firm manufacturing agricultural chemicals started advertising over a station in Oklahoma. Their sales increased in that area by 20 percent in the first week.

A steel-building manufacturer began advertising on a station in northwest Missouri, five minutes at 7:10 A.M. once a week. The first five-minute show sold a $20,000 building.

A Texas farm radio director announced a new variety of cantaloupe had been developed by the college. In five weeks he received 40,000 inquiries.

NAFB members organized several teams that went to New York, Chicago, and Atlanta where they called on corporation and advertising agency people in their offices and handed out several hundred copies of the leaflet. Several thousand more were sent to prospects by mail.

Two years later NATRFD came out with another booklet, "Is Your Farm Advertising Balanced for Best Results?," and accompanied it by a slide presentation, prepared by Don Lerch who left farm broadcasting and entered public relations work. Jack Timmons, president of the NATRFD, Bob Miller, vice-president, and several other members of the organization arranged showings in New York, Chicago, and other advertising centers.

A new NATRFD insignia was adopted in 1958, and members were encouraged to twist the arms of their station promotion people to use it in their advertising, so the station that had a farm broadcaster in NATRFD would appear to be a cut above other stations.

The NATRFD urged each of its member stations in 1958 to issue a four-page farm market fact sheet with the number of farms, figures on production of major products, gross and net farm income in its area, and a biography of the farm director. Copies were sent to each major company and advertising agency buying farm time. Some stations followed through and some didn't, but advertisers regarded this as a giant step forward.

Sponsor magazine of October 25, 1958, had its annual special section on agriculture and reported,

> One advertiser has been waiting four years for a spot on one leading station, but competing accounts prevent his doing so. Isn't radio missing a good bet by not making more programs available?
>
> The typical advertiser a few years ago bought a 15-minute program perhaps three times a week, for 52 weeks. Today he probably uses spots rather than programs, on an in-and-out basis, rather than 52 weeks.
>
> The number of AM stations has more than quadrupled since World War II, and many new stations are in small communities closely identified with the farm. So far as farm audience research can discern (admittedly; there's not enough of it) the power-house stations still have a firm grip on the farmer, with their crack farm staffs the big stations provide a potent service to advertisers. But don't get the idea that the small town station is not getting national and regional business. Keystone, the sales network for 1,040 small stations, numbers Purina poultry feed, Armour hog feed, and Chilean Nitrate among its clients.

In the late fifties, TV was the big menace to radio. *Sponsor* magazine of November 24, 1959, published a chart showing that in the ten years, 1949–1958, radio dropped from 23 percent of all advertising down to 5 percent while TV had grown from 5 percent to 40 percent and was over the $1 billion mark.

In 1959 a group of "station rep" firms, each selling time on many different stations, issued a brochure that noted the average farm family in 1941 spent $800 on family living items, but by 1955 this had increased to $2,160. A 1955 survey showed that in one week, 52 percent of farm families bought ice cream; 62 percent bought lunch meats; 43 percent bought margarine; and 42 percent bought soft drinks. This survey revealed foodstuffs can be sold on farm shows, as well as fertilizers and tractors.

About fifteen general managers or sales managers of stations paid dues as associate members of the organization, and three or four usually showed up at the meetings in the fifties and sixties.

From the late forties through the sixties, *Sponsor* magazine ran a special section almost every year, with a lengthy and informative feature on agriculture and farm broadcasters. *Sponsor*'s publisher, Norman Glenn, had developed a warm affection for agriculture by working several years at WLS, Chicago, when it was a farm station and his name was Norman Goldman.

In 1961 an NAFB committee sent a questionnaire to the 300 stations with members in the association asking what share of the station's total revenue came from farm programs. About 100 stations replied, and their figures indicated farm programming provided 28 percent of revenue for radio and 24 percent for TV stations.

In 1966 Stan Torgerson, manager of WMC, Memphis, headed a team that developed a sales promotion package of slides and literature, entitled "The Name of the Game Is Sales." Each station with a voting member in the NAFB was urged to use the slides and literature to charge up its own sales team and its prospective clients. The next year Jack Timmons of KWKH, Shreveport, Louisiana, a farm broadcaster turned station manager, presided over a survey involving 1000 commercial farmers. It showed that 83 percent listened to radio some time during the week before the survey, and their listening was concentrated on about 150 stations with farm directors. About 75 percent could identify at least one farm director by name, and a similar proportion could name the director's station. Of farmers in the survey, 97 percent had radios in the house, 20 percent in the barn, 76 percent in the car, 31 percent in the truck, and 7 percent on tractors. The survey cost $40,000 and most of it was paid by 75 participating stations. The NAFB spokesmen told advertisers at a meeting of the National Agricultural Advertising and Marketing Association that the survey figures proved that NAFB farm radio was four to five times as effective in reaching farmers as other radio.

In the early seventies some of the organization's associate members from station management began to be heard more loudly, and a sales marketing committee was formed, composed of farm broadcasters, station management and sales people, station representatives, and advertising agency people. Ray Senate, national sales manager of WIBW, Topeka, and Bill Alford, agricultural sales coordinator of Orion stations, headquartered at Cedar Rapids, were the spearheads. Their major recommendation, adopted by the NAFB, was to hire a

Ray Kremer

full-time sales promotion manager; the stations would pay an extra fee for his services.

They hit it lucky. Ray Kremer had retired to Mount Dora, Florida, and after the excitement of watching the oranges grow in his back yard, by 1972 he was ready to work again.

He was well qualified for the job. One of his minor claims to distinction was handling the sound effects on Orson Welles's "Invasion from Mars," broadcast on Halloween in 1938. He also bought farm time as an agency account executive and had produced commercials for Phillips Petroleum, DeVilBiss sprayers, Hotpoint appliances, and others and had sold time as sales manager of CBS. He had been one of the founding fathers of the eastern chapter of the Agricultural Advertising and Marketing Association, which became NAMA. He knew most of the people who bought and sold agricultural advertising, and they knew him.

In the first year, 1973, a total of ninety-eight radio, ten TV stations, and ten radio networks signed up to support the sales marketing effort of the NAFB by paying the value of ten one-minute spots in early morning time.

The job of sales marketing director had two major phases. In one, Kremer was a bird dog, covering the field, looking for quail, then pointing, so a salesman representing a station, or one hundred stations, could make the sale and sign a contract. In the other phase, he was a big brass band calling attention to 100 and more radio and television stations and networks, each one with a qualified, respected, and sales-minded farm director with many farm listeners. In the brass band phase, he bought space in the broadcasting and advertising trade publications such as *Agri-Marketing*, the NAMA yearbook, and *Television/Radio Age*. In addition, he persuaded *TR Age* to put out an annual issue featuring agriculture and carrying a good many ads by individual stations and by station representative firms whose client stations had farm directors.

Kremer made calls on advertising managers of agribusiness corporations and agency people who handled farm accounts. He also mailed an "Inside Report" to the subscriber stations, which provided much information to the benefit of stations and corporations and included who was advertising what and what the new product discoveries were. Several of the advertisers and their clients were Richardson, Myer, and Donofrio for American Cyanamid; MAP Advertising Agency for the Paul Mueller Company; and Foote, Cone, and Belding for International Harvester.

Ray Kremer, bird dog, pointed to the target—agency, manufacturer, product, person who did the planning, person who did the buying, what kinds of agriculture might be involved. Presumably each station's sales staff followed through on making the actual sales.

One of the things he found quickly in 1973 was that he needed evidence that farm people listened to NAFB stations. He proposed a survey of farm families. This would mean an additional fee, but more than seventy stations signed up. A survey was done of 9,300 Class I and II farm families (sales over $20,000 per year) in thirty states, representing about 90 percent of total farm production and dollars.

The survey produced about 450 pages of statistics, which showed that 93.5 percent of the farmers listened to radio each day, an average of two and one-quarter hours per day, with the largest proportion from 6:00 to 7:30 in the morning and at noon. More than 58 percent listened to one of the NAFB stations some time during the day; 39 percent listened to some of the 640 other stations carrying some kind of farm service; 45 percent listened to one or more of the 2,997 stations that carried no farm programs. The survey statisticians said their findings indicated that "to reach as many commercial farmers as are reached by the average NAFB radio station, an advertiser would be forced to use 10 average 'other farm' stations or 39 nonfarm stations, and the average farm program over NAFB stations has more than four times as many commercial-farm listeners as the average farm program broadcast over stations not members of the NAFB." More than 76 percent could name a farm broadcaster and a third said they knew one personally.

The farmers who listened to NAFB stations spent ten times as much for fertilizers, chemicals, machinery, and buildings as the farmers who listened to other farm stations.

The survey results brought more business to some of the stations and networks, but they also brought more questions! Corporations and agency people wanted to know, "What's the cost per thousand farm listeners? Per thousand acres of corn? Per thousand head of slaughter cattle? Per thousand broilers? What stations give us the best coverage and lowest cost for cotton herbicides? For hybrid sorghum seed? The farm magazines can answer these questions for us; the direct mail people can tell us; why can't the broadcasters?"

Kremer reported to the Sales Marketing Committee, "We need another survey, in more detail, to provide information about the audience of *each NAFB station and network.*" The committee authorized another survey and another assessment on participating stations.

The survey was announced in December 1975 and was taken in March and April 1976. A total of 100 firms put money on the barrelhead, including sixty-seven radio stations in twenty-eight states, ten radio networks, ten TV stations, and thirteen station representative firms.

Each station designated the counties that it wanted to have surveyed. Only the station received copies of the forty-eight–page report for its viewing area, and, at Kremer's insistence, each station produced a four-page summary of highlights. Each station or network chose the counties that would make it look good and, from the survey results, they chose wisely.

For example, Leland Glazebrook of the Illinois Corn-Soybean Network chose twenty counties to be surveyed, and was doubtless pleased that the statistics showed 29 percent of the farmers listened to stations in his network compared with 23 percent listening to Orion Samuelson and Bill Mason on WGN, with no other station scoring more than 5 percent. Wally Ausley, of WPTF, Raleigh, designated nineteen counties around Raleigh, and the survey showed 46.8 percent named WPTF as the station providing the best information on weather, markets, farm news and information.

KMA, Shenandoah, Iowa, designated twenty-five counties in Iowa and Nebraska as its survey area and learned 44.9 percent of the farmers thought it was most reliable, nearly four times the rating of its nearest competitor in those counties.

KMJ, Fresno, designated six California counties for the survey and found it had 90 percent of the farm listeners between 5:30 and 6:00 in the morning, about 69 percent in the first half hour after noon. The station noted that Fresno county alone produced over one billion dollars worth of farm products in 1975, the only county ever to hit the billion dollar mark.

By the time the NAFB annual convention was held in Kansas City in mid-November 1976, all station customers had been using their reports for many weeks, and the convention provided a forum for farm broadcasters to testify to the survey's successful results.

Charlie Rankin from the lower Rio Grande Valley of Texas reported, "I've got Cyanamid buying time on my programs for the first time; I've got International Harvester back after an absence of seven years. A lot of accounts had been buying on the basis of ARB ratings, and some of them bought time on a rock and roll station that had no farm service at all. Now I've got figures that show my program has more farmers listening than the total number of people credited to my station by ARB."

Larry Edwards, general manager of WNAX, Yankton, South Dakota, testified, "The 1974 survey proved that farm broadcasters are a good way to reach farmers; the 1976 survey lets a buyer know what station to use, when to use it, and how to use it."

Edwards didn't stop there because he had something up his sleeve: a second sales marketing representative had joined Kremer and it would require a

50 percent boost in assessments to support the increased effort. So he shouted—"Do you believe? If you believe, stand up!" Of course, virtually everyone stood up. Then he started talking in dollars. The budget for the sales marketing project in 1977 would be about $94,000, compared with $57,000 in 1976. "Just three more commercial spots a year to have two men doing what one man has been doing."

The new man, Charles Might, knew farm broadcasting thoroughly. He had been farm director of WMRN, Marion, Ohio, 1953–1959, and since that time had handled advertising for J. I. Case and other firms while he was employed by several different advertising agencies.

At the 1979 NAFB meeting, the Sales-Marketing Board announced that Kremer was reducing his activity but he and Might would be joined by Jim Mills, public affairs director of the National Agricultural Chemicals Association and a former farm broadcaster; so the NAFB sales marketing effort would have the equivalent of at least two and one-half workers in the field.

A total of 105 individual radio stations, seventeen television stations, twenty radio networks, one television network, and eight firms of sales representatives at the beginning of 1980 had agreed to financially support the sales marketing project. Implicit in their support was the belief that this was the most effective way to keep farm service programs going to farm people over commercial stations.

NAFB FOUNDATION. "Here is a stack of hundred dollar bills; take it and use it for some worthy cause." Simple enough? Not really. The Internal Revenue Service is watching; the IRS has been known to put people in jail or make them pay heavy fines for violating tax laws and IRS rules.

So when Charles Dana Bennett, upon receiving the NAFB Award for Meritorious Service in the fall of 1972, suggested that he and his wife, Edith, would like to help finance a foundation to be run by the NAFB, he sounded a warning: "Set it up so the damned IRS won't take any of it."

That meant creating a public foundation, supported by many people and organizations, rather than a private foundation, with only one principal source of money.

After more than three years of negotiations with the Internal Revenue Service, in 1976 the NAFB Foundation was born.

The executive committee of the NAFB chose a set of officers and directors for the NAFB Foundation: five former presidents, the current president, and the president-elect of the NAFB. To symbolize contributions from many sources, each member of the board put up one hundred dollars out of his own pocket, and forty other NAFB members contributed, in amounts ranging from $25 to $500, in the first year. Dana Bennett contributed $1,000, promising he would soon provide a nest egg that would produce an annual income so the Foundation could carry on a program to improve farm broadcasting, year after year.

Early in 1977 the foundation announced its first project: a one-year scholarship of $1,000 to a land grant college student interested in agricultural broadcasting.

Of the first three winners of scholarships in 1977, 1978, and 1979; two went into farm broadcasting and the third went into public relations work for an agricultural trade association.

In the coming years, the Foundation officers see an expansion into perhaps three areas: first, more scholarships established each year to help produce more young farm broadcasters; second, a series of workshops conducted for NAFB members, to improve their understanding of such things as cash and futures markets, economics, international trade, or government regulation of pesticides; third, a helping hand overseas—one experienced farm broadcaster, or a small team might spend one year in a developing country to help establish farm broadcasts on local radio stations. This would be in addition to, and probably independent of, anything the U.S. AID program was doing.

Chapter Fifty-seven

Sponsors

BACK in 1950, John Crosby, radio-TV columnist of the now defunct *New York Herald Tribune,* wrote: "Radio sold its beautiful white body to the advertisers before it was old enough to know what it was doing." You can picture Crosby clucking and shaking his head in sadness.

But, in my opinion, without advertisers' dollars, farm broadcasts over the last thirty years would have been limited to about twenty-four agricultural college stations. Without advertisers' products and farm broadcasters to tell about them, American farmers would have produced much less food and fiber than they have for several decades. Without such high production per farm worker, per acre, per animal, Americans would not eat as well or have as many conveniences and luxuries as they do.

Advertisers, sometimes referred to in the broadcasting business as "sponsors," have been useful to agriculture and to farm broadcasting.

It seems appropriate to review a bit of history and some examples of the advertisers who have made use of radio and television to sell their goods and services to agricultural producers.

Westinghouse might be considered the earliest sponsor of a farm program, merely by establishing a farm service on KDKA, the first Westinghouse radio station in 1921. Henry Field on KFNF and Earl May on KMA used their stations, beginning in 1924 and 1925, to sell their seeds, nursery stock, and other merchandise. Sears Roebuck hid behind its Agricultural Foundation to start WLS and farm programs on WFAA, WSB, and WMC, but merely identifying the programs with the name Sears Roebuck must have called to mind the company's catalog and its stores.

Montgomery Ward, which sponsored three quarters of the "National Farm and Home Hour" on the NBC network during its first year, 1928–1929, was the first sponsor of a network farm program, and the first to decide it didn't pay off.

The Ralston Purina Company began using radio to sell its livestock and poultry feeds about 1922, before farm directors had been invented. In the early days Purina went heavily for entertainment with several programs called "Checkerboard Time," using local entertainers. On WLS "Checkerboard Time" presented Ralph Waldo Emerson, organist and comic; Hal O'Halloran, announcer and comic; the Maple City Four, singers and comics; and one straight character, a white rooster.

It was not until 1951 that Purina began to make extensive use of farm broadcasters. Gordon M. Philpott, advertising vice-president, and Maury Malin worked with Bill and Charlie Brown, who had their own radio production firm, in a series of promotions built around "Mike and Ike," a pair of littermate pigs, in each market area. Mike was fed on Purina feeds while Ike was given nothing but corn. A farm broadcaster in each area reported regularly on the pigs' weights, and of course Mike gained faster. The broadcaster who was most energetic in working with local dealers won a Plymouth station wagon, and the wagon in 1951 went to Bob Nance of WIOU, Kokomo. The next year Nance moved to WMT, Cedar Rapids, and with the help of another Mike and Ike and a different group of dealers, he won a trip to the Rose Bowl for himself, a Purina dealer, and both their wives. Dick Woods, for many years Purina's radio-TV manager, recalled that on behalf of Purina he played host to forty-six people—farm broadcasters, Purina dealers and their wives—at the Rose Bowl on January 1, 1953. Besides Nance the group included Henry Schacht, KNBC, San Francisco; Paul Nelson, KFRE, Fresno; Harold Schmitz, KFEQ, Saint Joseph; and Harry Martin, WFBM, Indianapolis. Other winners earned trips to other bowl games that year.

Gordon Philpott was quoted in *Sponsor* magazine of February 15, 1952, saying that about half Purina's agricultural advertising budget of $1.5 million was spent on about 500 radio stations.

About this time, Purina sponsored a series of platters featuring Eddie Arnold, country singer; later it sponsored a daily network program of five minutes of farm news from Washington, by Richard Harkness.

In 1976 Dick Wood wrote, "Radio-TV supplements print media today and, in total, our print media budget exceeds radio-TV about five times. Keep in mind that our dealers spend about three times as much money on radio-TV as they do on newspapers, and we share 50% of this cost. I would estimate over 1000 dealers use some kind of radio."

One of the big spenders among agricultural advertisers was International Harvester, but its radio-TV advertising was not always spent on farm programs. In 1945, with World War II just ended, the company sponsored a network musical program, "Harvest of Stars," spending $150,000 the first year, building up to $561,000 in 1949. In 1947 the company celebrated its 100th birthday with a big exposition on Chicago's lakefront and sponsored a half hour broadcast over WBBM, with farm director George Menard presiding from the exposition grounds each noon for sixteen days. The half-million visitors included about 100,000 farm people. That same year the company took heed of falling farm prices and cut the prices of its tractors and other farm equipment by 5 percent across the board.

Beginning in the fifties, IH began sponsoring farm broadcasters, usually buying entire farm programs, as opposed to spots, and generally buying them fifty-two weeks per year. In most years, about 30 percent of the advertising budget was spent on radio and TV. The account executive of the advertising agency reported, "We pay talent fees to radio farm directors where needed. Of course, in return, we expect our fair share of his off-the-air activities and his exclusive voice on the air."

When Jim Hill was half of a two-man farm team on WCCO, he started a feature for IH and its dealers. Maynard Speece, his boss, associate, and friend, could sell another brand of farm equipment, but Hill was the exclusive property of IH. Dealers in his area would give him the name of a farmer who had bought a tractor or some other piece of equipment, and Hill would name the farmer, tell about his farming operations, and ring a handbell in his honor. One dealer reported that a farmer who had bought a tractor came back a few days later and said, "After all the nice things Jim Hill said about me, I think I'd better buy that bale thrower I was looking at."

For several years IH had a crew of repair men called the "IH Combine Patrol" on the road in the Great Plains during wheat harvest. IH's advertising agency arranged for someone from each Patrol team to report at least once each day to several farm directors on the progress of wheat harvest as they saw it. This was news, and IH had its name mentioned without having to pay for it.

Another effective IH and advertising agency gimmick was that each year at the National 4-H Club Congress, the agency set up a makeshift radio recording studio where farm broadcasters could interview award winning youngsters; IH then shipped the tapes to stations in the youngsters' home areas.

A sponsor's claim to a farm broadcaster's off-the-air time can be a delicate issue. A situation occurred in 1958 that became a small storm among the farm broadcasters. A firm that made a feed ingredient offered a flashlight to any farmer who sent in a sales slip proving he'd bought a ton of feed. The company sent out thousands of flashlights, but in one area a couple of farmers didn't qualify. The company asked a farm broadcaster to call in person on these farmers and explain why they were not eligible to receive a free flashlight. The broadcaster told some of his fellow broadcasters about this unreasonable request. Layne Beaty, USDA radio-TV chief, became involved and called on at least one leading advertiser and its advertising agency people to try to set some guidelines. Beaty told his boss in the USDA that he feared such abuses might increase, with more advertisers trying to wring extra services out of the broadcasters and this could "interfere with the free flow of useful information to farmers."

But in some instances the contract between an advertiser and station specified that the farm broadcaster would do certain things off the air on behalf of the advertiser, and many broadcasters took pride in reporting the extra things they had done.

The American Cyanamid Company spent about $450,000 each year on farm programs to sell its products in the early sixties, according to estimates in "U.S. Radio."

In its 1975 report to stockholders, American Cyanamid printed a color photo of a 100-acre cornfield in Iowa where a press conference was held to introduce a new weed killer called "Prowl." Farm broadcasters and other farm reporters were flown in by helicopter, each one dressed in a yellow jump suit with black paratrooper boots to spend a day learning the wonders of "Prowl" and some evening hours enjoying Cyanamid food and drink.

When the American Pork Congress was held in Kansas City, a great many farm broadcasters showed up to cover the event, and Elanco officials called them into a meeting to talk about advertising "Treflan." Many gatherings like this are held, satellites to larger affairs. Sometimes an advertiser will pick up the tab for a meal at the NAFB convention, and if he does that, he's likely to make a sales pitch. At one convention an advertiser who paid for a dinner put a tie clip with a manure spreader at each place; and in the main speech of the evening the company sales manager urged everybody to "get behind the manure spreader," even though he was buying time on probably only one-fourth of the stations represented.

Sponsor magazine of December 3, 1951 reported on the success of a small advertiser, Pilot Brand Oyster Shell, spending about half its total advertising budget, $80,000 per year, on farm radio programs in egg producing areas since 1936. On most stations, only one announcement per week was broadcast each week of the year.

In the same issue Frank Baker of Reinke, Meyer, and Finn advertising agency said D-Con rat killer had been putting 70 percent of its advertising dollars into radio, mostly farm programs, and in 1952 had increased the share to 72 percent.

In the January 14, 1952 issue of *Sponsor,* the following success stories were reported.

Indiana Farmers Mutual Insurance Company sponsored a five-minute commentary by Dix Harper on WIBC, Indianapolis, to announce a new farmers' theft insurance policy. In three weeks the company sold more than a half million dollars worth of policies, at an advertising cost of $155.70.

Myzon, a hog and poultry feed supplement, started buying time on WGN in 1950. The company's sales were about $36,000 per year. After six months on WGN, the firm began to buy time in six other markets. After two years of advertising on seven farm programs the company sales had climbed to a million dollars per year.

Armour Creameries was a longtime sponsor on WHAS. Farm director Barney Arnold ran a contest in 1951 to "Name the Calf," with a purebred Jersey calf as first prize and dairy farm equipment as other prizes. Entrants had to go to an Armour cream buying station to get an entry blank. The contest ran for six weeks and drew 29,735 entries.

Standard Oil of California, using farm radio since 1946, sponsored three daily farm programs in California in 1958: Henry Schacht's "Farmers' Digest" on KNBC, San Francisco; Wally Erickson's "Standard Farm News" on KFRE, Fresno; and Jim Todd's "Standard Farm Highlights" on KFI, Los Angeles.

Swift and Company used twenty-five radio stations to advertise five brands of plant food and pesticides; Swift's hatchery divisions used twenty stations in the Midwest.

In the fifties, the Campbell Soup Company sponsored Amos Kirby's "Rural Digest," on WCAU, Philadelphia, aimed at the growers who were under contract to produce tomatoes and carrots for the company. In two years, growers increased their yields by about 30 percent.

In the Dakotas, Armour bought a considerable amount of time on farm radio programs aimed at persuading livestock farmers that they were given a better deal when they sold their animals to Armour—or at least that they were given honest weight and a fair price. One company official was quoted, "Maybe they don't like us any better, but at least they don't cuss us out as much as they used to."

Bob Kunkel of the Leo Burnett advertising agency bought advertising for Purina, DuPont, USI Agricultural Chemicals, and Pfizer for over thirty years. He recalled that Pfizer began using farm radio in 1952 to introduce a synthetic sows milk called Terralac, on a half-dozen stations: WHO, WMT, WOW, WLS, WIBC, and WCCO. Soon afterward Pfizer bought time on most radio stations with farm directors, as far west as Colorado, as far east as New York, and as far south as southern Texas. As some of the larger stations cut out their farm programming in the sixties, Pfizer began to use the state radio networks.

Pfizer's first venture in television, according to Kunkel, came in 1955, in three TV test markets, Cedar Rapids, Green Bay, and Binghamton, to introduce Terramycin for mastitis. The commercial featured a "county agent type" announcer throwing a bucket of milk right into the camera and then asking, "You wouldn't throw out good milk, would you?" A survey showed twice as many dairymen recognized the name Terramycin in the three TV markets as in three non-TV areas, and Pfizer used TV for another ten years, until the number of dairymen decreased and TV costs went up so it didn't pay.

In 1962, Kunkel talked to his fellow advertisers about "how to use radio to advertise to farmers." In the Corn Belt, he said, Pfizer advertised several products on farm shows for hens, hogs, beef, and dairy cattle. "Our rule of thumb is to get 3 spots a week for each product on each station and go down the list of stations as far as the budget will go. We have computed the number of dairy cows, hogs, beef animals and laying hens in the listening area of all the likely stations from coast to coast. By making a composite of costs, we arrive at a list of markets and stations we will consider. Under our measurement, Cedar Rapids is our best hog area; Omaha is our best beef area; Yankton is our best egg area— not because of covering the most animals but because of covering the most animals per dollar."

In broiler areas, Pfizer and the Leo Burnett agency in the fifties sponsored live broadcasts of the local broiler auctions in Selbyville, Delaware; Gainesville, Georgia; Cullman, Alabama; Springdale, Arkansas; and Center, Texas. As soon as each auction was completed, officials of the auction teletyped a summary of the day's trading to an office in Washington, set up by the Burnett advertising agency. The auction reports were summarized and promptly teletyped to fourteen local radio stations in broiler areas making up what they called the Pfizer National Broiler Price Network. The government's report on broiler prices was a day later.

Sponsor magazine of November 2, 1957 listed the firms and products most widely advertised in that year on radio and TV: Allied Feeds, Allis Chalmers, D-Con, DeKalb, Salsbury Laboratories, DX petroleum, Eveready batteries, Ford tractors, Goodrich, Hercules, Hubbard Hall chemicals,

Keystone fencing, Olin-Mathieson, Merck, Murphy, Myason, Northrup King, Nutrena Mills, Oyster Shell products, Pfister hybrids, Charles Pfizer, Purina, Sears, Sisalkraft, Staley Milling Company, U.S. Steel, and Wayne feeds.

About ten years later, March 6, 1967, *Sponsor* listed Allied Chemical, Alcoa, Cyanamid, Coca-Cola, Pepsi Cola, Gulf, Mobil Oil, Reader's Digest, Sears, Dow Chemical, Union Carbide, DuPont, International Harvester, Republic Steel, Pfizer, Squibb. "These blue chip giants are pace setters in 1967 in the use of radio and TV, mostly the former, aimed at the three million plus farm families."

Butler Manufacturing Company used its first farm radio advertising in 1967 to introduce a new grain bin late in the season. A dealer's name was mentioned in the commercials only after he had erected a display bin; so many bins went up quickly. The schedule involved umbrella coverage from the power stations like WHO, WCCO, WMT, and KMA; and at least two dozen local or regional stations were added in Iowa and Minnesota for closer, more frequent mention of dealers. The schedule on these stations consisted of ten to twenty spots each week on farm programs, or weather or news programs.

In the hybrid seed category, Pfister Associated Growers was a longtime user of radio. They employed umbrella coverage year-round, using farm programs on WHO, KMA, KDHL, and WGN, supplemented with participation on the WGN "Barn Dance" each Saturday night. During the peak selling seasons of early spring, and fall in some areas, short-term flights of spot announcements were scheduled on a larger number of other stations in the major corn and sorghum growing areas. Each PAG program or spot contained what the agency called a "trademark in sound" (a rhythmic clink of seeds going through a corn planter).

The advertising director of DeKalb Agricultural Research said his firm had used radio since 1937, and in 1969 was using radio fifty-two weeks on forty-eight stations, 3 spots per week, plus 5 spots per week on thirty additional stations for five weeks in the spring at seed corn buying time; a total of 18,200 spots per year.

Television/Radio Age reported Ciba-Geigy Chemical in 1970 was spending about $1.5 million per year, equally divided between radio and TV—45 radio stations yearly and 150 on a seasonal basis, and 47 TV stations. The company advertised thirty-five different products for farmers.

Massey-Ferguson in 1975 started a program feature of its own, "Farm Profit," taking a look at the future in agriculture. It was a daily three-minute program on tape, used by about 100 stations, principally in the Midwest plus Georgia and the Carolinas, and sponsored jointly by Massey-Ferguson and its dealers.

Carleton Loucks, of Susquehanna Productions and producer of the program, said, "Every day we present an interview with an agricultural expert on what can be expected in the future in his particular field of expertise. We regularly call on brokers to predict whether prices for wheat, corn, beef cattle or other commodities will go up or down in the next two weeks to a month; we recently had a man from one of the big chemical firms talking about fertilizing crops through the leaves; the head of DeKalb talked about types of corn we may see in the future.

"Lanny Walters in Akron handles the interviews. From our recording and duplicating facilities in Akron we prepare a reel of programs for two weeks. We record and ship on Friday, with programs to start the following Tuesday. We use special delivery mail to get tapes to the stations."

How do you advertise hog breeding on TV without making it offensive? Monsanto Chemicals had a subsidiary called Boar Power that sold breeding hogs, and in the seventies it wanted to use TV to spread the message that "our boars are lovers." Its advertising agency, Creswell, Munsell, Schubert and Zirbel of Cedar Rapids, noted that other companies had sold cigarettes, perfume and many other products showing a girl and a boy racing through a meadow toward each other. "Let's do it with a boar and a gilt across a green pasture, under a clear blue sky. They'll just touch noses." As reported in *Agri-Marketing*, the camera crew spent all morning filming the boar; the early afternoon filming the gilt; and the late afternoon filming the two as they came together. On the first take, the lovers touched noses, but the cameraman wanted another take. This time the boar didn't stop with touching noses! It took producer, director, script writer, grips, and herdsman to separate the lovers, but the edited film showed them trotting toward each other and discreetly rubbing noses, while the audience heard, "Our boars are lovers—our gilts are, too."

Farmers and advertisers and broadcasters often have to look over their shoulders to see if someone in government is about to lower the boom. In 1974 Russell Train, administrator of the Environmental Protection Agency, announced that he intended to put a ban on insecticides containing heptachlor and chlordane because evidence showed that they might cause cancer in humans. About 38 million pounds of these two chemicals were sold each year. The Velsicol company came out fighting, with page after page of documents, sent to news editors and farm broadcasters, taking issue with the chemistry, physiology, and medical evidence, and with the timing of the government news release.

The company's viewpoint was reported in general news and farm news programs. But the government views prevailed, and use of the products was banned on all food products almost immediately, and use for nonfood purposes, such as termite control, was phased out over a period of the next few years.

Dix Harper recalled a time in the sixties when he was with an agency and handling some of Monsanto's advertising, when the company came up with a weed killer they called "Lasso." The agency planned a million dollar advertising campaign, about 20 percent of it going to radio and TV, while the herbicide was awaiting approval by the government. Indications were given that the answer would be "OK," but it was slow in coming and the season was advancing. Then one day Harper stuck his neck out and started the advertising campaign, in print and on the air, before the final approval had been granted.

TABLE 57.1—Radio/TV Expenditures by Agricultural and Horticultural Advertisers 1965–1975.

| | Radio* | | Television† | | | |
| | Agriculture & horticulture | | Agriculture | | Horticulture | |
	Local	Network	Local	Network	Local	Network
1965	...	...	$ 889,000	$ 579,500	...	...
1966	$4,000,000	...	1,050,000	...	...	...
1967	5,000,000	...	5,291,100	1,221,100	...	...
1968	4,800,000	...	5,257,000	1,130,700	...	...
1969	6,698,000	...	4,620,300	1,031,000	$3,117,600	$2,840,800
1970	7,369,000	$ 40,000	4,198,300	217,300	4,430,500	2,470,900
1971	6,687,000	449,000	4,285,300	...	4,326,500	3,543,900
1972	5,808,000	350,000	5,435,200	48,000	6,383,900	4,022,900
1973	7,591,000	295,000	7,610,400	1,039,000	6,516,200	6,151,000
1974	7,873,000	142,000	6,969,300	597,100	8,053,900	7,385,500
1975	8,236,000	670,000	7,738,500	81,300	10,823,700	6,531,700

* Figures from Radio Advertising Bureau.
† Figures from Television Bureau of Advertising.

One of the office jokesters suggested the name should be changed from "Lasso" to "Noose" because "Harper may be hanging himself." Happily, the government OK came through before anyone had serious trouble.

According to the FCC total revenue of all radio stations and networks climbed from $118 million in 1937 to $1.7 billion in 1975; revenue of TV stations and networks climbed from under $9 million in 1948 to more than $4 billion in 1975.

And according to the Radio and Television Advertising Bureaus, national advertisers in the categories labeled "agriculture" and "horticulture" in 1975 totaled about $28 million, or less than half of one percent of the grand total spent in broadcast media. Those figures included money spent on nonfarm programs, but they omitted money spent on farm programs by local advertisers and money spent by national advertisers on such things as cars, refrigerators, and other nonagricultural products. Table 57.1 shows expenditures of national advertisers to reach farmers and home gardeners.

It was in the fifties that a group of agricultural advertising people in Chicago began to meet once each month for lunch; and before long, they found themselves with officers, dues, and a name, the Chicago Agricultural Advertising Club.

Around 1964 a group of people in New York with similar interests organized themselves, and it wasn't long until the two groups merged and formed the National Agricultural Advertising and Marketing Association. Other groups formed on the west coast and in Minneapolis, Des Moines, and Raleigh. Meanwhile a national headquarters was established in Kansas City, and the name was squeezed down to the National Agri-Marketing Association (NAMA). Membership climbed past 2,000, and most of them met at the annual national convention, economic outlook meetings, and other events which helped to keep the organization going.

In the mid-seventies, NAMA sponsored American Agriculture Day, a spiritual successor to National Farm City Week. NAMA members used their talent and clout with television, radio, and the press to get publicity for the event. In 1975, for example, there was a fifteen-minute spot on NBC's "Today" show with farm people and agribusiness people talking about the plight of the farmer (farm prices were down and agribusiness was slack). In Fresno the Rotary Club had an Agriculture Day luncheon attended by 500; Ronald Reagan devoted much of his daily commentary on 200 radio stations to Ag Day and farmers. In New York, NAMA members took reporters, TV people, and consumer activists out to a dairy farm. In Chicago, Ag Day was the wind up of an exchange in which some city couples lived on a farm and farm couples tried living in the city. In Madison, Wisconsin, university agricultural journalism students arranged special sales by Madison retailers and a total of 132 speeches by members of the Wisconsin legislature.

So far as farm broadcasters and their sales representatives were concerned, NAMA meetings made it easier to reach many advertisers at one time, and it became a custom for NAFB to play host at a hospitality suite at the national NAMA convention.

Chapter Fifty-eight

Preparing for a Career in Farm Broadcasting

WHAT do young persons need in the way of knowledge, experience, and ability to be farm broadcasters? I believe they need:

- ability to learn
- ability to get along with people
- ability to talk understandably and easily
- ability to gather information and organize it
- knowledge and understanding of agriculture
- skill in handling radio and TV equipment

You may be born with some of these skills; some you may acquire just by growing up on a farm or ranch; some you can learn, or add to, in school; some you can learn on the job.

Some farm broadcasters start out lacking one or more of them but few last very long if they are short on the first two: ability to learn and ability to get along with people.

Ability to learn does not necessarily mean good grades in school. One farm broadcaster claimed he was at the bottom of his class in high school and college; but he was a successful farm broadcaster, very capable farm organization worker, and a good farmer. He learned from life.

Getting along with people certainly is not an exact science, but this much is sure: if you don't like to meet people, listen to them, and talk to them face-to-face, you're going to be unhappy as a farm broadcaster. When farm broadcasters complete their jobs in front of a microphone or camera, they go out to interview a farm organization official, report a farm meeting, participate in a committee session, or perhaps make a speech to a chamber of commerce. If they don't get in tune with people they may not make it as a farm broadcaster.

Speaking ought to be divided into reading from script and ad-libbing. If you have trouble reading a script and making it sound as though you are talking, don't worry; you can learn. Ask an experienced announcer or a speech teacher to help. Your first efforts at ad-lib broadcasting may be full of "uh"; and "ah," but as you get more confidence in yourself they will disappear. If you have the habit of saying "y'know" three or four times in each sentence I

323

recommend special treatment: the old-fashioned ducking stool—and very cold water.

"Do I have a good voice?" Probably you do; so forget about it. The important thing is to use whatever voice you have so people can understand you, and to have something interesting and worthwhile to say.

Gathering and organizing information are the skills of a journalist, and a farm broadcaster is a journalist. As a farm broadcaster there will be hundreds of facts and thousands of words coming to your attention every day, on paper, tape, and film. What's important? Who is important? Are the statements true? Do you need to find out what's behind them? And who's behind them? What will be the effect on farmers—of different kinds? What will be the effect on consumers? How much do your listeners already know about the subject? What is your opinion? Do you know enough about the subject to have an opinion? Where do you turn for more information? What questions do you ask? These are questions that a good farm broadcaster needs to ask himself many times each day.

You will have a *knowledge and understanding of agriculture* if you grew up on a farm or ranch and especially if your parents let you share in the decisions—what and how much to produce, what equipment to buy, whether to borrow money, when and where to sell—you have a good start. You probably know things you don't realize you know. No matter how well you know your own place and what worked for you, though, you'll need to remember that one hundred miles away things may be different. Some of the new information that comes out of the experiment station may not work everywhere, in all circumstances.

Skill in handling radio and TV equipment is a must. A good many farm broadcasters have to "run the board" while they are on the air, and often before they go on the air, they have to rerun tapes they may have recorded and cut and splice them to include the important statements and eliminate the unnecessary. On TV, the farm broadcasters use a sound-on-film or video camera and then cut and splice the film or tape they have shot to fit the time allowed. In a way, they are like carpenters: farm broadcasters must know how to handle their tools.

Where do you learn the things you need to know, understand, and be able to do as a farm broadcaster? At a four year agricultural college that offers a degree in agricultural broadcasting. The universities that offer degrees in agricultural broadcasting have different names for "broadcasting," names like "electronic journalism," "communications," or "telecommunicative arts." Whatever it is called, combine it with courses in a wide range of agricultural subjects, and some generous shots of English, speech, history, economics, chemistry, and physics, and the day may come when you can wave your diploma and announce: "Farm broadcaster; have degree; will travel."

The universities that offer degrees in agricultural communications turned out many of these graduates each year in the seventies, and most of them found jobs as farm broadcasters, men and women alike.

Most of them have done things outside the classroom that have given them some added know-how and maybe more savvy. They have spent many hours at the university radio or TV station writing scripts, handling controls, wrestling TV cables, operating cameras, broadcasting, and occasionally sweeping out. At some schools, in some jobs, they were paid, but not always.

Some of the future farm broadcasters have found part-time paying jobs with the extension editor or university publicity director. Some have sneaked downtown or even out of town and found part-time jobs with a commercial broadcasting station. By the time they earned their diplomas there was no mystery to a control panel or editing tape, and no microphone fright.

Some have been on a judging team, a debating team, the student newspaper or magazine, or in a chorus or choir. Those things are right in line with what farm broadcasters are likely to do in their jobs. Students who find themselves busy sixteen hours each day are prepared for the schedule they may find as a farm broadcaster.

Almost all agricultural colleges offer good training in agriculture, but only about one in four awards a degree in agricultural broadcasting or agricultural communications. Beyond the degree, some of the universities with agricultural schools and communications training have their own broadcasting stations. If other things are equal, why not go to a school with a radio and TV station?

Below is a partial list of the universities that offer a degree in agricultural communications and have their own radio (R) and TV (T) stations. This information was acquired in a 1977 survey.

University	R	T
University of Arizona, Tucson	R	T
Colorado State University, Fort Collins	—	—
University of Illinois, Urbana	R	T
Purdue University, West Lafayette, IN	R	—
Iowa State University, Ames	R	T
Kansas State University, Manhattan	R	—
University of Kentucky, Lexington	—	T
University of Minnesota, Minneapolis	R	T
University of Missouri, Columbia	R	T
Cornell University, Ithaca, NY	R	T
Ohio State University, Columbus	R	T
South Dakota State University, Brookings	R	T
Texas Technical University, Lubbock	R	T
Texas A&M University, College Station	R	T
Washington State University, Pullman	R	T
University of Wisconsin, Madison	R	T

There are some schools that have radio and TV stations and offer courses in communications, but did not indicate they offered degrees in ag communications. They include the universities of Florida, Nebraska, Vermont, Michigan State, and North Dakota State.

If you can't afford four years of college, but still you want to be a farm broadcaster, there are other ways.

Several of the better-known farm broadcasters went to a broadcasting school, learned to handle the equipment, and how to be an announcer. Generally that took about one year in school, and usually it led to a job as operator, disc jockey, or news reporter; then came a day when the boss said, "You're our farm man." Or, in some instances the disc jockey said, "Boss, why don't we start a farm program?" Those things have happened in the past, and will happen in the future, especially if the disc jockey has a farm background.

One farm broadcaster, a farm boy who started as a disc jockey when he was in high school, became a full-time announcer and an assistant farm director. He did this while he was working toward a degree from an agricultural college. When he received his degree after seven years, he was ready to move to another location and did.

Several farm broadcasters began in a business related to agriculture and with no college broadcast training, or experience. They happened to be in the right place and available when a station wanted a farm broadcaster. They also proved to have the ability to do a good job.

MONEY AND OTHER BENEFITS. The money farm broadcasters earn comes from one or more of these sources: salary, commissions on sales, bonuses, talent fees, endorsements paid by sponsors, fees for talks and other personal appearances, reimbursements for travel, reimbursements for professional improvement, and outside enterprises. Some stations provide other benefits such as life insurance; retirement plans; health insurance; broadcasting, engineering, sales, and secretarial help; and houses. Because all these things can influence the attractiveness of a farm broadcasting job they are worth considering one at a time.

Salary. In general farm broadcasters earned larger salaries than county agricultural agents or vocational agriculture teachers, but they were not as large as executives in advertising, trade associations, finance, or agribusiness. Some broadcasters reported they were paid an annual salary; others were paid so much per month or week. One man was paid an hourly wage. One broadcaster formed a one-man corporation and the station contracted with the corporation. Another formed a corporation with himself and two radio stations as partners. Several farm broadcasters created their own networks and sold time to advertisers. One broadcaster worked free, six days per week, for many years.

Commissions on Sales. A few farm broadcasters reported they were salesmen as well as broadcasters and their entire income was from commissions on sales. Others assisted salesmen and were paid a portion of the sales commission in addition to salary.

Bonuses. A few farm broadcasters said they received a bonus at the end of each year based on the total revenues of their farm programs. At least one received a bonus only if this year's revenue was greater than that of the year before.

Talent Fees. A few farm broadcasters were paid a talent fee if they delivered the advertising message for a sponsor on their own programs. Others collected a talent fee only if they recorded an advertiser's message to be used on other stations.

Endorsements. Some advertisers paid a farm broadcaster for the right to use his name and possibly his photograph as part of their advertising in magazines, newspapers, direct mail, or billboards. Some stations do not permit their farm broadcasters to endorse products.

Fees for Personal Appearances. Almost every farm broadcaster was invited to attend many farm organization meetings or other events as a speaker, a master of ceremonies, or perhaps as an entertainer. Some broadcasters charged a fee plus travel expenses for such appearances; some charged no fee and the station paid travel expenses; others charged a fee for appearing at a money-making event, such as a fair or livestock show, but no fee for appearing at a typical farmers' meeting. One widely-known farm broadcaster explained, "I have to charge a fee to reduce the number of invitations so I can have some time with my family."

Travel. Most farm broadcasters travel several days per week, usually driving their own cars and collecting mileage fees. In the late seventies several complained that the station's mileage fees had not kept pace with the cost of owning and operating a car. One two-man farm broadcaster team drove rented cars paid for by the station. Some broadcasters were provided with a company car, pickup truck, or four-wheel-drive vehicle, usually labeled with the call letters, sometimes with the broadcaster's name. A few broadcasters did much of their traveling by light plane; either owned by the broadcaster, by the station, or rented. Some stations put restrictions on travel and expenses; others permitted or even encouraged their farm broadcasters to attend important events or to call on advertisers outside the range of their stations.

Entertainment. Most farm broadcasters say they are encouraged by management to entertain people who have been program participants at lunch or dinner, and the station will reimburse the broadcaster. Some stations also pay the cost of meetings of farmer advisory boards.

Professional Improvement. Most full-time farm broadcasters belonged to the NAFB, to the association of agricultural college editors, the National Agri-Marketing Association, or to farmer organizations. In some instances, but not all, stations paid membership dues, registration fees, meals, hotels, and travel expenses, sometimes for the broadcaster alone, sometimes for his wife. One organization that owned several stations told its farm broadcasters, "You may join and attend meetings, but don't let yourself get elected to office."

Outside Enterprises. A fairly large number of farm broadcasters operated their own farms or had a part interest in a farm or ranch. A few were in businesses related to agriculture, including retailing, farm management, seed production, and publishing. Several were hired not only to broadcast but also to write for newspapers or farm publications; others wrote for a publication as a sideline.

Fringe Benefits. Benefits such as a retirement plan, life insurance, and health insurance were more likely to be available in a large and prosperous station or a station that was part of a larger organization rather than one that was small and independent.

Promotion Help. Advertising, tours for listeners, remote broadcasts, contests for listeners, farm-city events, conservation days, plowing or corn picking contests, prizes at fairs, souvenirs, publicity releases to newspapers and magazines, and broadcast reminders about the farm program at other times of day are all examples of promotion efforts used to attract more listeners or more advertisers. In some instances the farm broadcaster himself has done most of the promoting; in others, the station's promotion department and top management have played important roles.

Staff Help. A station with wide coverage and good income was likely to allow its farm broadcaster to hire an assistant. A few stations assigned one salesman to specialize in selling time on farm programs to advertisers. Some farm broadcasters were provided with a full-time secretary; some had secretarial help available from a secretarial pool; other farm broadcasters did their own typing. Most farm broadcasters operated tape recorders and film or video cameras as part of their job, but in some instances the broadcaster was aided by a cameraman and sound engineer.

Housing. In the forties and fifties several stations owned farms and the farm broadcaster managed the farm as part of his job. Often he lived in the farmhouse and had someone else to do the work on the farm. Only a few such arrangements were in existence at the beginning of 1980.

Several farm broadcasters were farmers before they became broadcasters. Their activities in farm organizations got them acquainted with broadcasters and that led to their being hired by a station. One man started as a part-time broadcaster, making three or four broadcasts each month on an established farm program. When the regular broadcaster left, the part timer took over the programs but continued to operate his farm.

Several radio and TV stations offer scholarships to agricultural college students, often involving a summer working at the station and continuing as campus correspondent during the following year. In many instances the scholarship winner has become a member of the station's staff.

Even if you can't afford four years in an agricultural college, if you are determined to be a farm broadcaster you'll find a way to become one. You won't be satisfied until you do.

NARFD Code (1946)

Members of the National Association of Radio Farm Directors shall strive to gain a broad and thorough understanding of farm conditions and problems and thus, through radio, promote better agriculture and better farm family living.

In this effort, they shall have a two-fold responsibility: To management which supports their work; and to the farm people whom they serve.

Radio Farm Directors shall consider themselves as representatives of both radio and agriculture in their dealings and associations with groups and individuals. . . . in connection with their work and otherwise. . . . and shall constantly conduct themselves with this thought foremost in mind.

They shall clearly indicate their interest in the welfare of farm people in these associations; offer full cooperation to others having the same interest; and firmly resist any subordination of this interest to the selfish purposes of others.

Radio Farm Directors shall recognize radio's job of informing the people it serves. In dealing with subjects open to debate, they shall present all the information available in the clearest way possible. They shall bear in mind that the NAB Code admits no discussion of controversial issues on purchased radio time except in accepted forum fashion.

Commercial sponsorship of farm programs does not detract from the service they offer to farm people. However, Radio Farm Directors shall have a major voice in the approval of sponsors and shall have a free hand in directing commercial farm programs. Desirability of sponsors shall be determined by the usual standards of good taste and business ethics. It is recommended that sponsors be refused air time that:

Make statements known to be false, deceptive or exaggerated.

Use offensive terms to describe animal functions or ailments.

Make unfair attacks upon competition.

CHUCK WORCESTER
Code Committee

Recipients of the NARFD
Award for Meritorious Service

1957   Charlie Karr, advertising manager, Allis Chalmers tractors
1958   Louis H. Wilson, National Plant Food Institute
1959   Dix Harper, Aubrey, Finlay, Marley and Hodgson advertising agency
1960   Frank Mullen, founder and producer, and Bill Drips, producer, of the "National Farm and Home Hour"
1961   Roy Battles, Clear Channel Broadcasters
1962   Milt Bliss, ex-producer, "National Farm and Home Hour"
1963   Phil Alampi, New Jersey Secretary of Agriculture
1964   Wallace Kadderly, ex-chief, USDA Radio Service
1965   George Biggar, owner, WLBK, DeKalb, Ill.
1966   Stan Torgerson, manager, WMC, Memphis
1967   Jack Timmons, manager, KWKH
1968   Emmett Barker, vice-president, Agricultural Services, Inc.
1969   Larry Haeg, founder of the NARFD
1970   Ward Quaal, manager, WGN
1971   Jack Towers, USDA Radio Service
1972   Charles Dana Bennett, Foundation for American Agriculture
1973   Ben Ludy, president, KWFT
1974   Bill Alford, Agricultural Sales Manager, WMT
1975   Jim Mills, Agricultural Chemicals Association
1976   Lee Bullis, Allen and Dorward advertising agency
1977   Leo B. Olson, DeKalb Ag Research, Inc.
1978   Ray Senate, WIBW-TV
1979   Dr. Forrest L. Whan, KWFT

Appendix C

Attendance, Organization Meeting
of NARFD, May 5, 1944

Name	*Affiliation*	*Address*
*Bill Drips	NBC	Chicago
*Mert Emmert	WEAF	New York
Phil Evans	KMBC	Kansas City, Mo.
*Edward H. Faulkner	WTAM	Cleveland
*Stanley A. Flower	WBZ	Boston
*George B. German	WNAX	Yankton, S.D.
*Cliff Gray	WSPA	Spartanburg, S.C.
*Larry Haeg	WCCO	Minneapolis, Minn.
Ralph Harding	KSL	Salt Lake City
Hamilton Hintz	McClatchy Broadcasting Company	Sacramento, Calif.
C. W. "Jack" Jackson	Texas A & M	College Station, Tex.
*Wallace Kadderly	USDA	Washington, D.C.
*Emerson Markham	WGY	Schenectady, N.Y.
*Homer Martz	KDKA	Pittsburgh
*Ed Mason	WLW	Cincinnati, Ohio
John Merrifield	WHAS	Louisville, Ky.
*Jim Miles	WBAA	Lafayette, Ind.
Everett Mitchell	NBC	Chicago
*Bill Moshier	KJR-KOMO	Seattle, Wash.
Arthur C. Page	WLS	Chicago
*Jennings Pierce	NBC	Hollywood
*Herb Plambeck	WHO	Des Moines, Iowa
*George S. Round	Univ. of Nebraska	Lincoln, Nebr.
*Joe Ryan	KRNT-KSO	Des Moines, Iowa
Sam B. Schneider	KVOO	Tulsa, Okla.
*Jerry Seaman	Extension Service	Fargo, N. Dak.
*Charles P. Shoffner	WCAU	Philadelphia
*Charley Stookey	KMOX	St. Louis
Arthur Stringer	NAB	Washington, D.C.
Duncan Wall	Farm Reports	Washington, D.C.
*Chuck Worcester	CBS	Washington, D.C.
W. Judd Wyatt	War Food Adm.	Atlanta
Kenneth Yeend	KIRO	Seattle, Wash.
*Bill Zipf	Ohio State Univ.	Columbus, Ohio
Robert White	ABC	Chicago
Burnis Arnold	KVOO	Tulsa, Okla.
Roy Battles	WLW	Cincinnati, Ohio

* Denotes members of the NARFD at the end of 1944. Other persons who joined in 1944 are included below.

331

Name	*Affiliation*	*Address*
Layne Beaty	WBAP	Fort Worth, Tex.
Emil Bill	WMBD	Peoria, Ill.
Charles Bond	USDA Radio Service	Washington, D.C.
John Furman	WOC	Davenport, Iowa
Ray Hollingsworth	KGNC	Amarillo, Tex.
William MacDonald	KFAB	Lincoln, Nebr.
Ted Mangner	KMOX	St. Louis, Mo.
Nelson McIninch	KFI	Los Angeles
C. C. Moore	KOA	Denver
Hugh Muncy	KXEL	Waterloo, Iowa
Lennox Murdock	KSL	Salt Lake City
J. C. Rapp	KMA	Shenandoah, Iowa
Raymond Rogers	KMJ	San Francisco
Henry Schacht	KPO	San Francisco
Luke Roberts	KOIN	Portland, Oregon
Gene Shipley	WIBW	Topeka, Kans.
Gary Weigand	KSTP	St. Paul, Minn.
Henry Wood	WFBM	Indianapolis, Ind.

Appendix D

Presidents, National Association of Farm Broadcasters, 1944–1980

Year	President	Station	Present Position
1944–1945	Larry Haeg, *Minneapolis, Minn.*	WCCO	Consultant, WCCO
1946	Herb Plambeck, *Des Moines, Iowa*	WHO	Consultant, Des Moines, Iowa
1947	Layne Beaty, *Fort Worth, Tex.*	WBAP	Chief, Radio-TV, USDA, Washington, D.C.
1948	Chuck Worcester, *Cedar Rapids, Iowa*	WMT	Deceased
1949	Wallace Kadderly, *Portland, Oreg.*	KGW	Retired, La Jolla, Calif.
1950	Roy Battles, *Cincinnati, Ohio*	WLW	Farmers Home Adm., USDA, Washington, D.C.
1951	Phillip Alampi, *New York, N.Y.*	WNBC	Secretary of Agriculture, State of New Jersey
1952	Sam Schneider, *Tulsa, Okla.*	KVOO	St. Agnes School, Parkill, N.Y.
1953	Mal Hansen, *Omaha, Nebr.*	WOW	Vice-President, Travel & Transport, Inc., Omaha, Nebr.
1954	Jack Jackson, *Kansas City, Mo.*	KCMO	Deceased
1955	Frank Atwood, *Hartford, Conn.*	WTIC	Retired, Hartford, Conn.
1956	John McDonald, *Nashville, Tenn.*	WSM	Farm Director, WSM
1957	Jack Timmons, *Shreveport, La.*	KWKH	Deceased
1958	Bob Miller, *Cincinnati, Ohio*	WLW	Farm Director, WLW
1959	Maynard Speece, *Minneapolis, Minn.*	WCCO	Retired, Minneapolis, Minn.
1960	Wally Erickson, *Fresno, Calif.*	KFRE	President, Total Communications, Fresno, Calif.
1961	George Roesner, *Houston, Tex.*	KPRC	Deceased
1962	Carl Meyerdirk, *Tulsa, Okla.*	KVOO	Youth Director, American Oil Co., Chicago, Ill.
1963	Bruce Davies, *Omaha, Nebr.*	KFAB	Deceased
1964	George Menard, *Chicago, Ill.*	WBBM	Retired, Wilmette, Ill.
1965	Orion Samuelson, *Chicago, Ill.*	WGN	Farm Director, WGN
1966	George Stephens, *Kansas City, Mo.*	KCMO	Bruce B. Brewer, Advertising, Inc., Kansas, City, Mo.
1967	Bob Nance, *Cedar Rapids, Iowa*	WMT	Vigortone Products Company, Cedar Rapids, Iowa
1968	Keith Kirkpatrick, *Des Moines, Iowa*	WHO	Farm Director, WHO
1969	Wayne Liles, *Oklahoma City, Okla.*	KWTV	Farm Director, KWTV

Appendix D (*Continued*)

Year	President	Station	Present Position
1970	Jack Crowner, *Louisville, Ky.*	WAVE	Director, Kentucky Livestock Association
1971	Dean Curtiss, *Faribault, Minn.*	KDHL	Farm Director, KDHL
1972	George Logan, *Topeka, Kans.*	WIBW	General Manager, WIBW-TV
1973	Russell Pierson, *Oklahoma City, Okla.*	WKY	Retired
1974	Lynn Adair, *Salt Lake City*	KSL	State Director, ASCS
1975	Bill Mason, *Chicago*	WGN	Farm Director, WCFL
1976	Royce Bodiford, *Amarillo, Tex.*	KGNC	General Manager, KGNC
1977	Marvin Vines, *Little Rock, Ark.*	KAAY	Deceased
1978	Rich Hull, *Topeka, Kans.*	WIBW	General Manager, KGBX, Springfield, Mo.
1979	Gene Williams, *Yankton, S.D.*	WNAX	Farm Director, KFEQ
1980	Earl Sargent, *Wichita Falls, Tex.*	KWFT	Farm Director, KWFT

INDEX

Acree, Chuck, 104
"Across the Fence," 40, 68, 273
Adair, Lynn, 272
Adams, B. A. "Andy," 255
Adams, Cliff, 126, 132
Advertising expenditures, 321
Agri-Broadcasting Network, 222
"Agriculture USA," 38, 57
Agrinet, 277
"Agritape," 38
Alabama Extension Service, 12, 64
Alabama Farm Bureau, 65
Alabama Farm Network, 65
Alabama News Network, 66
Alampi, Phillip, 200
Alampi, Ruth, 200, 305
Alford, Bill, 130, 156
Allen, Phillip, 62
Allis Chalmers Co., 35
Allison, Bill, 78
Almburg, John, 106
Alstad, George, 67
American Broadcasting Co. (ABC), 36, 53
American Cyanamid Co., 40, 316
American Farm Bureau Federation, 59
"American Farmer," 36, 53
Anderson, Clinton P., 35
Anderson, Jim, 43
Anderson, Shirley, 146
Andrews, Harry (Leckrone), 114, 117, 217
Angell, Jack, 59
Arbour, Marjorie, 148
Arizona Extension Service, 67
Arizona Farmer, 67
Arizona Farm Network, 68
Arkansas Extension Service, 69
Arkansas Radio Network, 69
Armstrong, Edwin H., 5
Armstrong, Max, 111
Army Signal Corps, 41

Arnold, Burnis "Barney," 145, 224
Arnold, Dick, 158
Aroe, Alden, 276
Arthur, Ned, 116
Aspleaf, Harry, 166
Associated Press, 55
Association of Agricultural College Editors, 11
Atwood, Frank, 85
Auburn University, 64
"Aunt Sammy," 33
Ausley, Wally, 205
Austin, Robert, 241
Azleton, Bob, 176

Bailey, Fred, Sr., 54
Baird, Jack, 193
Baker, John C., 156
Balvanz, Rich, 184
Banister, Claire, 255
Barber, Solon, 26
Barrett, Lola, 300
Barron, Tex, 59
Bateman, Dave, 210
Battles, Roy, 214
Batts, Patrick, 59
Baukhage, H. R., 50
Baxter, Dean, 88
Bazyn, Wallace, 188
Beale, Clyde, 87
Beaty, Layne, 29, 37, 40, 256
Beavers, Tom, 127
Beeler, Bob, 111
Beers, Marvin, 42
Behrens, Ken, 102
Behymer, Bruce, 142, 143
Bell, Alexander Graham, 4
Bennett, Bill, 235
Bennett, Charles Dana, 146, 312
Bentley, R. C. "Cap," 124
Bernstein, Jim, 161, 163
Berry, Bill, 88
"Better Way," 41
Beyschlag, Frank, 73
Bier, Joe, 191
Biggar, George, 15, 16, 90, 100, 174, 215
Bill, Chuck, 36

Bill, Edgar, 98, 107
Bill, Emil, 107
Bishe, Al, 118
Bjornsen, Val, 166
Blair, Art, 134
Blaser, Ed, 96
Blauveldt, Leslie, 186
Bliss, Milton, 37, 51, 238, 286
Blue Network, 32
Bodiford, Royce, 266
Boicourt, Alfred, 156
Boler, John, 63
Bond, C. A., 43, 279, 280
Borg, Lyle, 135
Bowser, Perry, 260
Boyd, J. K., 8, 232
Boynton, Joly, 76, 79
Bradley, Dan (Modlin), 116
Brazzle, Ernest, 250
Breeders' Gazette, 102
Breeze, Marshall, 88
Brenner, Bernard, 55
Brewer, Lawrence, 144
Briggs, C. R., 29, 33, 230
Brofee, Linwood "Jake," 151
Brooks, Roland, 90
Brower, Stephen, 271
Brown, Joe, 156, 262
Brown, Rex, 81
Brown, Roger, 158
Brownfield, Derry, 179
Brownfield Network, 179
Bryan, A. B., 241
Bryson, Harold, 43
Buck, Douglas, 88
Buehler, Don, 169
Buffum, Jesse, 48, 157
Buice, Bob, 70
Buis, Bob, 118
Buker, Terry, 179
Burke, Billie, 32
Burlingham, Lloyd, 102, 104
Burnham, John, 67
Burns, Conrad, 181
Burroughs, Arthur, 158
Burrus, Dick, 209
Burtenshaw, Bob, 97
Bush, James L., 8, 98

335